GREAT MYTHS
OF THE BRAIN

Praise for *Great Myths of the Brain*

"The more we are interested in the brain and how it explains our behavior, the more important it is that we rid ourselves of untruths and half-truths. Myth-buster extraordinaire, Christian Jarrett is an engaging and knowledgeable guide who spring-cleans the cobwebs of misinformation that have accumulated over recent years. You will be surprised at some favorite beliefs that turn out to be scare stories or wishful thinking. Yet Jarrett conveys a strong optimism about fresh approaches that will result in new knowledge. All claims are well substantiated with references. It will be fun to learn from this book."

Professor Uta Frith DBE, UCL Institute of Cognitive Neuroscience

"Christian Jarrett is the ideal guide to the fascinating, bewildering, and often overhyped world of the brain. He writes about the latest discoveries in neuroscience with wonderful clarity, while cleanly puncturing myths and misinformation."

Ed Yong, award-winning science writer, blogger, and journalist

"*Great Myths of the Brain* provides an incredibly thorough and engaging dismantling of neurological myths and misconceptions that abound today. For anyone overwhelmed by copious bogus neuroscience, Christian Jarrett has generously used his own mighty brain to clear this cloud of misinformation, like a lighthouse cutting through the fog."

Dr Dean Burnett, Guardian *blogger, Cardiff University*

"Lots of people cling to misconceptions about the brain that are just plain wrong, and sometimes even dangerous. In this persuasive and forceful book, Christian Jarrett exposes many of these popular and enduring brain myths. Readers who want to embrace proper neuroscience and arm themselves against neurononsense will enjoy this splendid book, and profit greatly from doing so."

Elizabeth F. Loftus, Distinguished Professor,
University of California, Irvine

"Christian Jarrett, one of the world's great communicators of psychological science, takes us on a neuroscience journey, from ancient times to the present. He exposes things we have believed that just aren't so. And he explores discoveries that surprise and delight us. Thanks to this tour de force of critical thinking, we can become wiser – by being smartly skeptical but not cynical, open but not gullible."

Professor David G. Myers, Hope College, author,
Psychology, *11th edition*

"A masterful catalog of neurobollocks."

Dr Ben Goldacre, author of Bad Science *and* Bad Pharma

"In this era of commercialized neurohype, Christian Jarrett's engaging book equips us with the skills for spotting the authentic facts lost in a sea of brain myths. With compelling arguments and compassion for the human condition, Jarrett teaches us that the truth about the brain is more complicated, but ultimately more fascinating, than fiction."

The Neurocritic, neuroscientist and blogger

"Christian Jarrett has written a wonderful book that is as entertaining as it is enlightening. When it comes to brain science, a little knowledge is a dangerous thing. Jarrett has done us all a great service by peeling back the layers of hype to reveal what we really do know – and don't know – about how the brain functions."

Professor Christopher C. French, Goldsmiths,
University of London

"*Great Myths of the Brain* is essential reading for anyone who wants to navigate the maze of modern neuroscience, separating fact from fiction and reality from hype. Jarrett is an insightful, engaging guide to the mysteries of the human mind, providing an always smart, often humorous account that will equip you with the tools you need to understand both the power and the limitations of your own mind."

Maria Konnikova, author of Mastermind: How to Think Like
Sherlock Holmes

Great Myths of Psychology

Series Editors
Scott O. Lilienfeld
Steven Jay Lynn

This superb series of books tackles a host of fascinating myths and misconceptions regarding specific domains of psychology, including child development, aging, marriage, brain science, and mental illness, among many others. Each book not only dispels multiple erroneous but widespread psychological beliefs, but provides readers with accurate and up-to-date scientific information to counter them. Written in engaging, upbeat, and user-friendly language, the books in the myths series are replete with scores of intriguing examples drawn from everyday psychology. As a result, readers will emerge from each book entertained and enlightened. These unique volumes will be invaluable additions to the bookshelves of educated laypersons interested in human nature, as well as of students, instructors, researchers, journalists, and mental health professionals of all stripes.

www.wiley.com/go/psychmyths

Published

50 Great Myths of Popular Psychology
Scott O. Lilienfeld, Steven Jay Lynn, John Ruscio, and Barry L. Beyerstein

Great Myths of Aging
Joan T. Erber and Lenore T. Szuchman

Great Myths of the Brain
Christian Jarrett

Forthcoming

Great Myths of Child Development
Steven Hupp and Jeremy Jewell

Great Myths of Intimate Relations
Matthew D. Johnson

Great Myths of Personality
M. Brent Donnellan and Richard E. Lucas

Great Myths of Autism
James D. Herbert

Great Myths of Education and Learning
Jeffrey D. Holmes and Aaron S. Richmond

50 Great Myths of Popular Psychology, Second Edition
Scott O. Lilienfeld, Steven Jay Lynn, John Ruscio, and Barry L. Beyerstein

GREAT MYTHS OF THE BRAIN

Christian Jarrett

WILEY Blackwell

This edition first published 2015
© 2015 Christian Jarrett

Registered Office
John Wiley & Sons Ltd, The Atrium, Southern Gate, Chichester, West Sussex,
PO19 8SQ, UK

Editorial Offices
350 Main Street, Malden, MA 02148-5020, USA
9600 Garsington Road, Oxford, OX4 2DQ, UK
The Atrium, Southern Gate, Chichester, West Sussex, PO19 8SQ, UK

For details of our global editorial offices, for customer services, and for information about
how to apply for permission to reuse the copyright material in this book please see our
website at www.wiley.com/wiley-blackwell.

The right of Christian Jarrett to be identified as the author of this work has been asserted
in accordance with the UK Copyright, Designs and Patents Act 1988.

Library of Congress Cataloging-in-Publication Data
Jarrett, Christian.
  Great myths of the brain / Christian Jarrett.
      pages   cm
  Includes bibliographical references and index.
  ISBN 978-1-118-62450-0 (cloth) – ISBN 978-1-118-31271-1 (pbk.)
1. Brain–Popular works.   2. Brain–Physiology–Popular works.   I. Title.
  QP376.J345 2015
  612.8′6–dc23

                                        2014018392
A catalogue record for this book is available from the British Library.

Cover image: Male anatomy of human brain in x-ray view © CLIPAREA l Custom media /
Shutterstock; Cerebrum – female brain anatomy lateral view © CLIPAREA l Custom
media / Shutterstock
Cover design by Design Deluxe

Set in 10/12.5pt Sabon by SPi Publisher Services, Pondicherry, India
Printed and bound in Malaysia by Vivar Printing Sdn Bhd

1   2015

*For my dear mother,
Linda, my inspiration*

CONTENTS

ACKNOWLEDGMENTS

The invitation to write this book came to me courtesy of Andy Peart at Wiley Blackwell in 2011. Thanks Andy for reaching out then, and for all your support and encouragement since. I'm also grateful to the diligent editors who helped bring the book to fruition: Karen Shield, Leah Morin, and Alta Bridges.

I'm extremely fortunate to have benefited from the experience and knowledge of the series editors for this book: Professors Scott Lilienfeld and Steve Lynn. Their *50 Great Myths of Popular Psychology* (co-written with John Ruscio and Barry Beyerstein) set the standard for books in this genre, and they've been a trusted source of authority and encouragement through the writing process.

A small group of wise friends and colleagues read specific chapters for me and I'm indebted to them for their time and expert guidance: Tom Stafford, Karen Hux, Uta Frith, Jon Simons, and Charles Fernyhough. Many other researchers, too numerous to mention, helped me out by sending me their journal articles, or answering my queries. Any mistakes that remain are all mine.

I would like to draw attention to the various talented, expert bloggers who debunk brain myths on an almost daily basis, and some of whom I quote in the book: Neuroskeptic, Neurocritic, Neurobonkers, Vaughan Bell at Mind Hacks, Matt Wall at Neurobollocks, Dean Burnett and Mo Costandi at *The Guardian*, plus many more. Kudos to them all. Also special thanks to the historians Charles Gross and Stanley Finger, whose works I turned to many times while researching the defunct brain myths.

I should note that several passages in this book, or variants of them, have appeared as blog posts either on my Brain Myths blog at Psychology Today (http://www.psychologytoday.com/blog/brain-myths), or more recently on my Brain Watch blog at WIRED (http://www.wired.com/category/brainwatch/). Also, some of the quotes from experts in this book were originally provided to me for articles I wrote while working as staff journalist on *The Psychologist* magazine.

I might never have been a writer at all, if my mother Linda hadn't encouraged me down that path when I was still completing my doctoral research. She also turned her eagle eyes to the Brain Myths manuscript, and gave me supportive feedback throughout. Thanks Mum for believing in me!

Finally, to my beautiful family – my wife Jude, and our baby twins Charlie and Rose, who were born this year – thank you for everything. I love you more!

Christian Jarrett, June 2014

INTRODUCTION

"As humans, we can identify galaxies light years away, we can study particles smaller than an atom. But we still haven't unlocked the mystery of the three pounds of matter that sits between our ears." That was US President Barack Obama speaking in April 2013 at the launch of the multimillion dollar BRAIN Initiative. It stands for "Brain Research through Advancing Innovative Neurotechnologies" and the idea is to develop new ways to visualize the brain in action. The same year the EU announced its own €1 billion Human Brain Project to create a computer model of the brain (see p. 105).

This focus on neuroscience isn't new – back in 1990, US President George W. Bush designated the 1990s the "Decade of the Brain" with a series of public awareness publications and events. Since then interest and investment in neuroscience has only grown more intense; some have even spoken of the twenty-first century as the "Century of the Brain."

Despite our passion for all things neuro, Obama's assessment of our current knowledge was accurate. We've made great strides in our understanding of the brain, yet huge mysteries remain. They say a little knowledge can be a dangerous thing and it is in the context of this excitement and ignorance that brain myths have thrived. By brain myths I mean stories and misconceptions about the brain and brain-related illness, some so entrenched in everyday talk that large sections of the population see them as taken-for-granted facts.

With so many misconceptions swirling around, it's increasingly difficult to tell proper neuroscience from brain mythology or what one science blogger calls neurobollocks (see neurobollocks.wordpress.com), otherwise known as

Great Myths of the Brain, First Edition. Christian Jarrett.
© 2015 Christian Jarrett. Published 2015 by John Wiley & Sons, Ltd.

neurohype, neurobunk, neurotrash, or neurononsense. Daily newspaper headlines tell us the "brain spot" for this or that emotion has been identified (see p. 80). Salesmen are capitalizing on the fashion for brain science by placing the neuro prefix in front of any activity you can think of, from neuroleadership to neuromarketing (see p. 188). Fringe therapists and self-help gurus borrow freely from neuroscience jargon, spreading a confusing mix of brain myths and self-improvement propaganda.

In 2014, a journalist and over-enthusiastic neuroscientist even attempted to explain the Iranian nuclear negotiations (occurring at that time) in terms of basic brain science.[1] Writing in *The Atlantic*, the authors actually made some excellent points, especially in terms of historical events and people's perceptions of fairness. But they undermined their own credibility by labeling these psychological and historical insights as neuroscience, or by gratuitously referencing the brain. It's as if the authors drank brain soup before writing their article, and just as they were making an interesting historical or political point, they hiccuped out another nonsense neuro reference.

This book takes you on a tour of the most popular, enduring and dangerous of brain myths and misconceptions, from the widely accepted notion that we use just 10 percent of our brains (see p. 51), to more specific and harmful misunderstandings about brain illnesses, such as the mistaken idea that you should place an object in the mouth of a person having an epileptic fit to stop them from swallowing their tongue (see p. 284). I'll show you examples of writers, filmmakers, and charlatans spreading brain myths in newspaper headlines and the latest movies. I'll investigate the myths' origins and do my best to use the latest scientific consensus to explain the truth about how the brain really works.

The Urgent Need for Neuro Myth-Busting

When Sanne Dekker at the Vrije Universiteit in Amsterdam and her colleagues surveyed hundreds of British and Dutch teachers recently about common brain myths pertaining to education, their results were alarming. The teachers endorsed around half of 15 neuromyths embedded among 32 statements about the brain.[2] What's more, these weren't just any teachers. They were teachers recruited to the survey because they had a particular interest in using neuroscience to improve teaching.

Among the myths the teachers endorsed were the idea that there are left-brain and right-brain learners (see p. 55) and that physical coordination exercises can improve the integration of function between the brain hemispheres. Worryingly, myths related to quack brain-based teaching programs (see p. 207) were especially likely to be endorsed by the teachers. Most disconcerting of all, greater general knowledge about the brain was associated with stronger belief in educational neuromyths – another indication that a little brain knowledge can be a dangerous thing.

If the people educating the next generation are seduced by brain myths, it's a sure sign that we need to do more to improve the public's understanding of the difference between neurobunk and real neuroscience. Still further reason to tackle brain myths head on comes from research showing that presenting people, including psychology students, with correct brain information is not enough – many still endorse the 10 percent myth and others. Instead what's needed is a "refutational approach" that first details brain myths and then debunks them, which is the format I'll follow through much of this book.

Patricia Kowalski and Annette Taylor at the University of San Diego compared the two teaching approaches in a 2009 study with 65 undergraduate psychology students.[3] They found that directly refuting brain and psychology myths, compared with simply presenting accurate facts, significantly improved the students' performance on a test of psychology facts and fiction at the end of the semester. Post-semester performance for all students had improved by 34.3 percent, compared with 53.7 for those taught by the refutational approach.

Yet another reason it's important we get myth-busting is the media's treatment of neuroscience. When Cliodhna O'Connor at UCL's Division of Psychology and Language Sciences, and her colleagues analyzed UK press coverage of brain research from 2000 to 2010, they found that newspapers frequently misappropriated new neuroscience findings to bolster their own agenda, often perpetuating brain myths in the process (we'll see through examples later in this book that the US press is guilty of spreading neuromyths too).[4]

From analyzing thousands of news articles about the brain, O'Connor found a frequent habit was for journalists to use a fresh neuroscience finding as the basis for generating new brain myths – dubious self-improvement or parenting advice, say, or an alarmist health warning. Another theme was using neuroscience to bolster group differences, for example, by referring to "*the* female brain" or "*the* gay brain," as if all people fitting that identity all have the same kind of brain (see p. 65 for the truth about gender brain differences). "[Neuroscience] research was being applied out of context to create dramatic headlines, push thinly disguised ideological arguments, or support particular policy agendas," O'Connor and her colleagues concluded.

About This Book

This introductory section ends with a primer on basic brain anatomy, techniques, and terminology. Chapter 1 then kicks off the myth-busting by providing some historical context, including showing how our understanding of the brain has evolved since Ancient times, and detailing outdated myths that are no longer widely believed, but which linger in our proverbs and sayings. This includes the centuries' long belief that the mind and emotions are located in the heart – an idea betrayed through contemporary phrases like "heart break" and "learn by heart." Chapter 2 continues the historical theme, looking at brain techniques that have entered psychiatric or neurological folklore, such as the brutal frontal lobotomy. Chapter 3 examines the lives and brains of some of neurosciences mythical figures – including the nineteenth century rail worker Phineas Gage, who survived an iron rod passing straight through his brain, and Henry Molaison, the amnesiac who was examined by an estimated 100 psychologists and neuroscientists.

Chapter 4 moves on to the classic brain myths that refuse to die away. Many of these will likely be familiar to you – in fact, maybe you thought they were true. This includes the idea that right-brained people are more creative; that we use just 10 percent of our brains; that women lose their minds when they are pregnant; and that neuroscience is changing human self-understanding. We'll see that there is a grain of truth to many of these myths, but that the reality is more nuanced, and often more fascinating, than the myths suggest.

Chapter 5 deals with myths about the physical structure of the brain, including the idea that bigger means better. And we'll look at mythology surrounding certain types of brain cells – the suggestion that mirror neurons are what makes us human and that you have in your brain a cell that responds only to the thought of your grandmother.

Next we turn to technology-related myths about the brain. These relate to the kind of topical claims that make frequent appearances in the press, including the ubiquitous suggestion that brain scans can now read your mind, that the Internet is making us stupid, and that computerized brain training games are making you smart.

The penultimate chapter deals with the way the brain relates to the world and the body. We'll debunk the popular misconception that there are only five senses, and we'll also challenge the idea that we really see the world exactly how it is.

The book concludes in Chapter 8 by dealing with the many misconceptions that exist about brain injury and neurological illness. We'll see how conditions like epilepsy and amnesia are presented in Hollywood films and tackle the widespread belief that mood disorders somehow arise from a chemical imbalance in the brain.

The Need for Humility

To debunk misconceptions about the brain and present the truth about how the brain really works, I've pored over hundreds of journal articles, consulted the latest reference books and in some cases made direct contact with the world's leading experts. I have strived to be as objective as possible, to review the evidence without a pre-existing agenda.

However, anyone who spends time researching brain myths soon discovers that many of today's myths were yesterday's facts. I am presenting you with an account based on the latest contemporary evidence, but I do so with humility, aware that the facts may change and that people make mistakes. While the scientific consensus may evolve, what is timeless is to have a skeptical, open-minded approach, to judge claims on the balance of evidence, and to seek out the truth for its own sake, not in the service of some other agenda. I've written the book in this spirit and in the accompanying box on p. 7 I present you with six tips for applying this skeptical, empirical approach, to help you spot brain myths for yourself.

Before finishing this Introduction with a primer on basic brain anatomy, I'd like to share with you a contemporary example of the need for caution and humility in the field of brain mythology. Often myths arise because a single claim or research finding has particular intuitive appeal. The claim makes sense, it supports a popular argument, and soon it is cemented as taken-for-granted fact even though its evidence base is weak. This is exactly what happened in recent years with the popular idea, accepted and spread by many leading neuroscientists, that colorful images from brain scans are unusually persuasive and beguiling. Yet new evidence suggests this is a modern brain myth. Two researchers in this area, Martha Farah and Cayce Hook, call this irony the "seductive allure of 'seductive allure.'"[5]

Brain scan images have been described as seductive since at least the 1990s and today virtually every cultural commentary on neuroscience mentions the idea that they paralyze our usual powers of rational scrutiny. Consider an otherwise brilliant essay that psychologist Gary Marcus wrote for the *New Yorker* late in 2012 about the rise of neuroimaging: "Fancy color pictures of brains in action became a fixture in media accounts of the human mind and *lulled people* into a false sense of comprehension," he said (emphasis added).[6] Earlier in the year, Steven Poole writing for the *New Statesman* put it this way: "the [fMRI] pictures, like religious icons, inspire uncritical devotion."[7]

What's the evidence for the seductive power of brain images? It mostly hinges on two key studies. In 2008, David McCabe and Alan Castel showed that undergraduate participants found the conclusions of a study (watching TV boosts maths ability) more convincing when accompanied by an fMRI brain scan image than by a bar chart or an EEG scan.[8] The same year, Deena Weisberg and her colleagues published evidence that naïve adults and neuroscience students found bad psychological explanations more satisfying when they contained gratuitous neuroscience information (their paper was titled "The Seductive Allure of Neuroscience Explanations").[9]

What's the evidence against the seductive power of brain images? First off, Farah and Hook criticize the 2008 McCabe study. McCabe's group claimed that the different image types were "informationally equivalent," but Farah and Hook point out this isn't true – the fMRI brain scan images are unique in providing the specific shape and location of activation in the temporal lobe, which was relevant information for judging the study. Next came a study published in 2012 by David Gruber and Jacob Dickerson, who found that the presence of brain images did not affect students' ratings of the credibility of science news stories.[10]

Was this failure to replicate the seductive allure of brain scans an anomaly? Far from it. Through 2013 no fewer than three further investigations found the same or a similar null result. This included a paper by Hook and Farah themselves,[11] involving 988 participants across three experiments; and another led by Robert Michael involving 10 separate replication attempts and nearly 2000 participants. Overall, Michael's team found that the presence of a brain scan had only a tiny effect on people's belief in an accompanying story.[12] The result shows "the 'amazingly persistent meme of the overly influential image' has been wildly overstated," they concluded.

So why have so many of us been seduced by the idea that brain scan images are powerfully seductive? Farah and Hook say the idea supports non-scanning psychologists' anxieties about brain scan research stealing all the funding. Perhaps above all, it just seems so plausible. Brain scan images really are rather pretty, and the story that they have a powerful persuasive effect is very believable. Believable, but quite possibly wrong. Brain scans may be beautiful but the latest evidence suggests they aren't as beguiling as we once assumed. It's a reminder that in being skeptical about neuroscience we must be careful not to create new brain myths of our own.

Arm Yourself against Neurobunk

This book will guide you through many of the most popular and pervasive neuromyths but more are appearing every day. To help you tell fact from fiction when encountering brain stories in the news or on TV, here are six simple tips to follow:

1   Look out for gratuitous neuro references. Just because someone mentions the brain it doesn't necessarily make their argument more valid. Writing in *The Observer* in 2013, clinical neuropsychologist Vaughan Bell called out a politician who claimed recently that unemployment is a problem because it has "physical effects on the brain," as if it isn't an important enough issue already for social and practical reasons.[13] This is an example of the mistaken idea that a neurological reference somehow lends greater authority to an argument, or makes a societal or behavioral problem somehow more real. You're also likely to encounter newspaper stories that claim a particular product or activity really is enjoyable or addictive or harmful because of a brain scan study showing the activation of reward pathways or some other brain change. Anytime someone is trying to convince you of something, ask yourself – does the brain reference add anything to what we already knew? Does it really make the argument more truthful?

2   Look for conflicts of interest. Many of the most outrageous and farfetched brain stories are spread by people with an agenda. Perhaps they have a book to sell or they're marketing a new form of training or therapy. A common tactic used by these people is to invoke the brain to shore up their claims. Popular themes include the idea that technology or other aspects of modern life are changing the brain in a harmful way, or the opposite – that some new form of training or therapy leads to real, permanent beneficial brain changes (see p. 217 and p. 201). Often these kinds of brain claims are mere conjecture, sometimes even from the mouths of neuroscientists or psychologists speaking outside their own area of specialism. Look for independent opinion from experts who don't have a vested interest. And check whether brain claims are backed by quality peer-reviewed evidence (see point 5). Most science journals require authors to declare conflicts of interest so check for this at the end of relevant published papers.

3   Watch out for grandiose claims. No Lie MRI is a US company that offers brain scan-based lie detection services. Its home page states,

"The technology used by No Lie MRI represents the first and only direct measure of truth verification and lie detection in human history!" Sound too good to be true? If it does, it probably is (see p. 184). Words like "revolutionary," "permanent," "first ever," "unlock," "hidden," "within seconds," should all set alarm bells ringing when uttered in relation to the brain. One check you can perform is to look at the career of the person making the claims. If they say they've developed a revolutionary new brain technique that will for the first time unlock your hidden potential within seconds, ask yourself why they haven't applied it to themselves and become a best-selling artist, Nobel winning scientist, or Olympic athlete.

4   Beware of seductive metaphors. We'd all like to have balance and calm in our lives but this abstract sense of balance has nothing to do with the literal balance of activity across the two brain hemispheres (see also p. 196) or other levels of neural function. This doesn't stop some self-help gurus invoking concepts like "hemispheric balance" so as to lend a scientific sheen to their lifestyle tips – as if the route to balanced work schedules is having a balanced brain. Any time that someone attempts to link a metaphorical concept (e.g. deep thinking) with actual brain activity (e.g. in deep brain areas), it's highly likely they're talking rubbish. Also, beware references to completely made up brain areas. In February 2013, for instance, the *Daily Mail* reported on research by a German neurologist who they said had discovered a tell-tale "dark patch" in the "central lobe" of the brains of killers and rapists.[14] The thing is, there is no such thing as a central lobe (see also p. 69)!

5   Learn to recognize quality research. Ignore spin and take first-hand testimonials with a pinch of salt. When it comes to testing the efficacy of brain-based interventions, the gold standard is the randomized, double-blind, placebo-controlled trial. This means the recipients of the intervention don't know whether they've received the target intervention or a placebo (a form of inert treatment such as a sugar pill), and the researchers also don't know who's been allocated to which condition. This helps stop motivation, expectation, and bias from creeping into the results. Related to this, it's important for the control group to do something that appears like a real intervention, even though it isn't. Many trials fail to ensure this is the case. The most robust evidence to look for in relation to brain claims is the meta-analysis, so try to search for these if you can. They weigh up all the evidence from existing trials in a given area and help provide an

accurate picture of whether a treatment really works or whether a stated difference really exists.

6   Recognize the difference between causation and correlation (a point I'll come back to in relation to mirror neurons in Chapter 5). Many newspaper stories about brain findings actually refer to correlational studies that only show a single snapshot in time. "People who do more of activity X have a larger brain area Y," the story might say. But if the study was correlational we don't know that the activity caused the larger brain area. The causal direction could run the other way (people with a larger Y like to do activity X), or some other factor might influence both X and Y. Trustworthy scientific articles or news stories should draw attention to this limitation and any others. Indeed, authors who only focus on the evidence that supports their initial hypotheses or beliefs are falling prey to what's known as "confirmation bias." This is a very human tendency, but it's one that scrupulous scientists and journalists should deliberately work against in the pursuit of the truth.

Arming yourself with these six tips will help you tell the difference between a genuine neuroscientist and a charlatan, and between a considered brain-based news story and hype. If you're still unsure about a recent development, you could always look to see if any of the following entertaining expert skeptical bloggers have shared their views: www.mindhacks.com; http://blogs.discovermagazine.com/neuroskeptic/; http://neurocritic.blogspot.co.uk; http://neurobollocks.wordpress.com; http://neurobonkers.com. And check out my own WIRED neuroscience blog www.wired.com/wiredscience/brainwatch/

A Primer on Basic Brain Anatomy, Techniques, and Terminology

Hold a human brain in your hands and the first thing you notice is its impressive heaviness. Weighing about three pounds, the brain feels dense. You also see immediately that there is a distinct groove – the **longitudinal fissure** – running front to back and dividing the brain into two halves known as **hemispheres** (see Plate 1). Deep within the brain, the two hemispheres are joined by the **corpus callosum**, a thick bundle of connective fibers (see Plate 2). The spongy, visible outer layer of the hemispheres – the cerebral **cortex** (meaning literally rind or bark) – has a crinkled appearance: a swathe of swirling hills and valleys, referred to anatomically as **gyri** and **sulci**, respectively.

The cortex is divided into five distinct **lobes**: the frontal lobe, the parietal lobe near the crown of the head, the two temporal lobes at each side near the ears, and the occipital lobe at the rear (see Plate 1). Each lobe is associated with particular domains of mental function. For instance, the frontal lobe is known to be important for self-control and movement; the parietal lobe for processing touch and controlling attention; and the occipital lobe is involved in early visual processing. The extent to which mental functions are localized to specific brain regions has been a matter of debate throughout neurological history and continues to this day (see pp. 40, 45, and 80).

Hanging off the back of the brain is the cauliflower-like **cerebellum**, which almost looks like another mini-brain (in fact cerebellum means "little brain"). It too is made up of two distinct hemispheres, and remarkably it contains around half of the neurons in the central nervous system despite constituting just 10 percent of the brain's volume. Traditionally the cerebellum was associated only with learning and motor control (i.e. control of the body's movements), but today it is known to be involved in many functions, including emotion, language, pain, and memory.

Holding the brain aloft to study its underside, you see the **brain stem** sprouting downwards, which would normally be connected to the **spinal cord**. The brain stem also projects upwards into the interior of the brain to a point approximately level with the eyes. Containing distinct regions such as the **medulla** and **pons**, the brain stem is associated with basic life support functions, including control of breathing and heart rate. Reflexes like sneezing and vomiting are also controlled here. Some commentators refer to the brain stem as "the **lizard brain**" but this is a misnomer (see p. 137).

Slice the brain into two to study the inner anatomy and you discover that there are a series of fluid-filled hollows, known as **ventricles** (see p. 22 and Plate 7), which act as a shock-absorption system. You can also see the **midbrain** that sits atop the brainstem and plays a part in functions such as eye movements. Above and anterior to the midbrain is the **thalamus** – a vital relay station that receives connections from, and connects to, many other brain areas. Underneath the thalamus is the **hypothalamus** and **pituitary gland**, which are involved in the release of hormones and the regulation of basic needs such as hunger and sexual desire.

Also buried deep in the brain and connected to the thalamus are the horn-like **basal ganglia**, which are involved in learning, emotions, and the control of movement. Nearby we also find, one on each side of the brain, the **hippocampi** (singular hippocampus) – the Greek name for "sea-horse" for that is what early anatomists believed it resembled. Here too are the almond-shaped **amygdala**, again one on each side. The hippocampus plays a vital role in memory (see p. 46) and the amygdala is important for memory and learning, especially when emotions are involved. The collective name for the hippocampus, amygdala, and related parts of the cortex is the **limbic system**, which is an important functional network for the emotions (see Plate 3).

The brain's awesome complexity is largely invisible to the naked eye. Within its spongy bulk are approximately 85 billion **neurons** forming a staggering 100 trillion plus connections (see Plate 4). There are also a similar number of **glial cells** (see Plate 5), which recent research suggests are more than housekeepers, as used to be believed, but also involved in information processing (see p. 149). However, we should be careful not to get too reverential about the brain's construction – it's not a perfect design by any means (more about this on p. 135).

In the cortex, neurons are arranged into layers, each containing different types and density of neuron. The popular term for brains – "**gray matter**" – comes from the anatomical name for tissue that is mostly made up of neuronal cell bodies. The cerebral cortex is entirely made up of gray matter, although it looks more pinkish than gray, at least when fresh. This is in contrast to "**white matter**" – found in abundance beneath the cortex – which is tissue made up mostly of fat-covered neuronal **axons** (axons are a tendril-like part of the neuron that is important for communicating with other neurons, see Plate 6). It is the fat-covered axons that give rise to the whitish appearance of white matter.

Neurons communicate with each other across small gaps called **synapses**. This is where a chemical messenger (a "**neurotransmitter**") is released at the end of the axon of one neuron, and then absorbed into the **dendrite** (a branch-like structure) of a receiving neuron (see Plate 6). Neurons release neurotransmitters in this way when they are sufficiently excited by other neurons. Enough excitation causes an "**action potential**," which is when a spike of electrical activity passes the length of the neuron, eventually leading it to release neurotransmitters. In turn these neurotransmitters can excite or inhibit receiving neurons. They can also cause slower, longer-lasting changes, for example by altering gene function in the receiving neuron.

Traditionally, insight into the function of different neural areas was derived from research on **brain-damaged patients**. Significant advances were made in this way in the nineteenth century, such as the observation that, in most people, language function is dominated by the left hemisphere (see p. 41). Some patients, such as the railway worker Phineas Gage, have had a particularly influential effect on the field (see p. 37). The study of particular associations of impairment and brain damage also remains an important line of brain research to this day. A major difference between modern and historic research of this kind is that today we can use medical scanning to identify where the brain has been damaged. Before such technology was available, researchers had to wait until a person had died to perform an autopsy.

Modern brain imaging methods are used not only to examine the structure of the brain, but also to watch how it functions. It is in our understanding of brain function that the most exciting findings and controversies are emerging in modern neuroscience (see p. 177). Today the method used most widely in research of this kind, involving patients and healthy people, is called **functional magnetic resonance imaging** (fMRI; see Plate 8). The technique exploits the fact that blood is more oxygenated in highly active parts of the brain. By comparing changes to the oxygenation of the blood throughout the brain, fMRI can be used to visualize which brain areas are working harder than others. Furthermore, by carefully monitoring such changes while participants perform controlled tasks in the brain scanner, fMRI can help build a map of what parts of the brain are involved in different mental functions. Other forms of brain scanning include **Positron Emission Tomography** (PET) and **Single-Photon Computed Tomography**, both of which involve injecting the patient or research participant with a radioactive isotope. Yet another form of imaging called **Diffusion Tensor Imaging** (DTI) is based on the passage of water molecules through neural tissue and is used to map the brain's connective pathways. DTI produces beautifully complex, colorful wiring diagrams (see Plate 13). The **Human Connectome Project**, launched in 2009, aims to map all 600 trillion wires in the human brain.

An older brain imaging technique, first used with humans in the 1920s, is **electroencephalography** (EEG), which involves monitoring waves of electrical activity via electrodes placed on the scalp (see Plate 23). The technique is still used widely in hospitals and research labs today. The spatial resolution is poor compared with more modern methods such as fMRI, but an advantage is that fluctuations in activity can be detected at the level of milliseconds (versus seconds for fMRI). A more recently developed technique that shares the high temporal resolution of EEG is known as **magnetoencephalography,** but it too suffers from a lack of spatial resolution.

Brain imaging is not the only way that contemporary researchers investigate the human brain. Another approach that's increased hugely in popularity in recent years is known as **transcranial magnetic stimulation** (TMS). It involves placing a magnetic coil over a region of the head, which has the effect of temporarily disrupting neural activity in brain areas beneath that spot. This method can be used to create what's called a "virtual lesion" in the brain. This way, researchers can temporarily knock out functioning in a specific brain area and then look to see what effect this has on mental functioning. Whereas fMRI shows where brain activity correlates with mental function, TMS has the advantage of being able to show whether activity in a particular area is necessary for that mental functioning to occur.

The techniques I've mentioned so far can all be used in humans and animals. There is also a great deal of brain research that is only (or most often) conducted in animals. This research involves techniques that are usually deemed too invasive for humans. For example, a significant amount of research with monkeys and other nonhuman primates involves inserting electrodes into the brain and recording the activity directly from specific neurons (called **single-cell recording**). Only rarely is this approach used with humans, for example, during neurosurgery for severe epilepsy. The direct insertion of electrodes and cannulas into animal brains can also be used to monitor and alter levels of brain chemicals at highly localized sites. Another ground-breaking technique that's currently used in animal research is known as **optogenetics**. Named 2010 "method of the year" by the journal *Nature Methods*, optogenetics involves inserting light-sensitive genes into neurons. These individual neurons can then be switched on and off by exposing them to different colors of light.

New methods for investigating the brain are being developed all the time, and innovations in the field will accelerate in the next few years thanks to the launch of the US BRAIN Initiative and the EU Human Brain Project. As I was putting the finishing touches to this book, the White House announced a proposal to double its investment in the BRAIN Initiative "from about $100 million in FY [financial year] 2014 to approximately $200 million in FY 2015."

Notes

1 http://www.wired.com/wiredscience/2014/02/can-neuroscience-really-help-us-understand-nuclear-negotiations-iran/ (accessed May 7, 2014).
2 Dekker, S., Lee, N. C., Howard-Jones, P., & Jolles, J. (2012). Neuromyths in education: Prevalence and predictors of misconceptions among teachers. *Frontiers in Psychology*, 3.
3 Kowalski, P., & Taylor, A. K. (2009). The effect of refuting misconceptions in the introductory psychology class. *Teaching of Psychology*, 36(3), 153–159.

4   O'Connor, C., Rees, G., & Joffe, H. (2012). Neuroscience in the public sphere. *Neuron*, 74(2), 220–226.

5   Farah, M. J., & Hook, C. J. (2013). The seductive allure of "seductive allure." *Perspectives on Psychological Science*, 8(1), 88–90.

6   http://www.newyorker.com/online/blogs/newsdesk/2012/12/what-neuroscience-really-teaches-us-and-what-it-doesnt.html (accessed May 7, 2014).

7   http://www.newstatesman.com/culture/books/2012/09/your-brain-pseudoscience (accessed May 7, 2014).

8   McCabe, D. P., & Castel, A. D. (2008). Seeing is believing: The effect of brain images on judgments of scientific reasoning. *Cognition*, 107(1), 343–352.

9   Weisberg, D. S., Keil, F. C., Goodstein, J., Rawson, E., & Gray, J. R. (2008). The seductive allure of neuroscience explanations. *Journal of Cognitive Neuroscience*, 20(3), 470–477.

10 Gruber, D., & Dickerson, J. A. (2012). Persuasive images in popular science: Testing judgments of scientific reasoning and credibility. *Public Understanding of Science*, 21(8), 938–948.

11 Hook, C. J., & Farah, M. J. (2013). Look again: Effects of brain images and mind–brain dualism on lay evaluations of research. *Journal of Cognitive Neuroscience*, 25(9), 1397–1405.

12 Michael, R. B., Newman, E. J., Vuorre, M., Cumming, G., & Garry, M. (2013). On the (non) persuasive power of a brain image. *Psychonomic Bulletin & Review*, 20(4), 720–725.

13 http://www.theguardian.com/science/2013/mar/03/brain-not-simple-folk-neuroscience (accessed May 7, 2014).

14 http://www.dailymail.co.uk/sciencetech/article-2273857/Neurologist-discovers-dark-patch-inside-brains-killers-rapists.html (accessed May 7, 2014).

1 DEFUNCT MYTHS

The consensus used to be that the earth is flat. Combustible materials, eminent scientists once proposed, all contain the nonexistent substance phlogiston. Mars, they told us, is crisscrossed with canals. All these once-influential ideas have been consigned to the scrap heap of obsolete theories. Brain science too has its share of defunct notions. This chapter is about those brain myths that no one (or very few people) believes any more. We'll start with the ancient idea that the mind is located, not in the brain, but in the heart. As the importance of the brain was eventually accepted, other myths to emerge or persist were that the nerves are filled with animal spirits and the main mental functions are located in the fluid-filled hollows of the brain: the ventricles.

Myth #1 Thought Resides in the Heart

It seems obvious to us today that thoughts and reason are located in the brain. That's because we've grown up knowing this universally accepted fact. But from a subjective point of view, there's little, other than the position of our eyes, to tell us that our mental life is housed in our heads. So perhaps we shouldn't be too surprised that many ancient civilizations from the Greeks to the Egyptians believed that the seat of mental function was located not in the brain but in the heart.

It is not that these cultures were necessarily unaware of the functional significance of the brain. Extracts from the Edwin Smith Surgical Papyrus (bought by the American archaeologist Edwin Smith in Luxor in 1862

Great Myths of the Brain, First Edition. Christian Jarrett.
© 2015 Christian Jarrett. Published 2015 by John Wiley & Sons, Ltd.

and dated to approximately the age of the Pyramids) show us that the Ancient Egyptians recognized the potential effects of brain injury, including paralysis. But despite this knowledge, the cardiocentric view persisted, and the brain was seen as little more than a kind of bone marrow (today, the word for brain in many languages, including Russian "мозг," Maori "roro," Indonesian "benak," Persian "مغز," and Swahili "ubongo" means literally "marrow"). Ancient Egyptian practices regarding the burial of the dead are revealing. Although the heart and other organs were venerated after death, left in the body for burial or preserved in canopic jars, the brain was scooped out via the nostrils, or a hole drilled in the base of the skull, and simply discarded.

In Ancient Greece, the Homeric poems from the eighth century BC reveal a belief in there being three types of soul – the psyche (a life-soul that animates the body), the thymos (associated with emotions), and the noos (associated with reason and intellect). The noos and thymos were both located in the chest, although not specifically in the heart. Among the first scholars to identify the heart specifically as involved in thought was Empedocles of Acragas (circa 495–435 BC) who believed that blood around the heart produced thoughts.

Perhaps the best-known cardiocentric advocate was Aristotle (384–322 BC). Like many others he was swayed by the fact that life ended when the heart stopped beating. Aristotle also noted how the brain was cold, senseless and peripheral whereas the heart was warm and central; that the heart develops in embryos before the brain; and that it is connected to all the sense organs whereas the brain is not (or so he mistakenly thought). Aristotle further reasoned that the brain couldn't be the control center for movement and sensation because invertebrates don't have brains.[1]

Although he didn't see the brain as the seat of thought, Aristotle saw it as an important organ – he believed it was a bloodless, cooling radiator for the heart and that it was also involved in sleep. Another notable cardiocentrist was the physician Diocles of Carystus (circa fourth century BC) who made great breakthroughs in heart anatomy. Unfortunately, he interpreted his discoveries in line with his belief in the heart as a cognitive center, and so he saw the ear-like auricles of the heart as sense organs. Madness, he believed, is caused by the blood boiling in the heart (echoes of this idea remain today, as in "you make my blood boil"), and melancholy by the thickening of black bile, also in the heart.[2]

The cardiocentric view had actually been challenged decades before Aristotle by the philosopher-physician Alcmaeon of Croton (circa 450 BC), and later by Hippocrates, the "Father of medicine" (born circa 460 BC), and his followers. Alcmaeon was among the first scientists to perform animal dissections. Although his writings have been lost, quotations by others tell us that he wrote: "The seat of sensations is in the brain ... it [is] also the seat of thought." In a paper published in 2007, the neurobiologist Robert Doty at the University of Rochester argued that Alcmaeon's revelation was so profound as to be comparable in historical significance to the discoveries of Copernicus and Darwin.[3]

Also long before Aristotle, the Hippocratic treatise *On The Sacred Disease* (circa 425 BC) states: "Men ought to know that from the brain and the brain only, arise our pleasures, joys, laughter and jests, as well as our sorrows, pains, griefs and tears" and it goes on to attribute thinking and perceiving to the brain too. Another prescient Hippocratric treatise, On Injuries of the Head, states correctly that damage to one side of the brain causes impairments to the opposite side of the body.

After Hippocrates, further important breakthroughs were achieved by the Alexandrian anatomists, who were the first to perform systematic human dissections. Active around 300 BC, Herophilus of Chalcedon, often considered the founder of human anatomy, studied some of the cranial nerves and the ventricles (the fluid-filled hollows in the brain), while Erasistratus of Ceos compared the human cerebellum (the cauliflower-shaped "little brain" that hangs off the back of the brain) with the equivalent structure found in animals, deducing correctly that it must have something to do with movement. Both Herophilus and Erasistratus identified correctly the existence of separate sensory and motor (involved in movement) nerves in the human brain and spine.[4]

But as we've seen, long after the case for the brain (the encephalocentric view) was put forward, belief in cardiocentrism refused to go away. In the third century BC, all Stoic philosophers continued to believe that the intellect and soul reside in the heart. A particularly influential advocate at this time was the Stoic Chrysippus of Soli (277–204 BC). Among his arguments was that the mind must reside in the heart because the heart is the source of the voice, which is controlled by thought. Indeed, one of the reasons the cardiocentric view was so difficult to overturn was that many of its advocates were convinced by this kind of specious logic. They also believed the cardiocentric view must be true because it had been adhered to for so long and by so many great thinkers and poets. Incidentally, claiming that a fact must be true because it is endorsed by one or more authority figures is a hallmark of poor argument that is still used to today by those advocating pseudoscientific positions.

In the second century AD, frustrated by the continuing influence of Chrysippus and contemporary members of the cardiocentric camp, Galen "the Prince of physicians" famed for his treatment of gladiators at Pergamon, decided to perform a dramatic public demonstration in which he severed the recurrent laryngeal nerve of a pig.[5] Cutting this nerve, which travels from the brain to the larynx (voice box), had the effect of stopping the animal from squealing as it continued to thrash about. Following the logic espoused by the cardiocentric advocates, severing nerves that originated in the brain should not have stopped the pig from squealing, unless the cardio view was wrong and speech and thought were controlled by the brain, as Galen argued. Galen's demonstration undermined their claims in what the historian Charles Gross describes as the first experimental demonstration of the brain's control of behavior.

Unsurprisingly perhaps, not everyone was convinced. Galen was heckled by, among others, the philosopher Alexander Damascenus, who said the demonstration only applied to animals. In fact, belief in the mental function of the heart persisted in many quarters all the way through to the Renaissance. Consider the writings of William Harvey, the English physician celebrated for his description of the circulation of the blood round the body. His classic work, *De motu cordis et sanguinis in animalibus* (published in 1628), describes the heart as the highest authority, ruling over the rest of the body. There are still hangovers from this myth to this day, in the way we allude to the psychological function of the heart in expressions like "to learn by heart," and when we imply the heart is the seat of love.

It is important to add a note here that while cognitive function is based principally in the brain, there is growing evidence that the function of the heart certainly affects our thoughts and emotions (see pp. 163 and 166) so we ought not to be too dismissive of the cardiocentric views held by the Ancients.

Myth #2
The Brain Pumps Animal Spirits Round the Body

Some of the discoveries made by Galen and the Alexandrian anatomists seem remarkably modern. But their prescience can be misleading. The world at that time in fact knew virtually nothing about the biological brain processes that support mental function, and this remained the case for centuries to come.

For instance, despite his ground-breaking anatomical work, Galen, like most others of his time and beyond, was a strong believer that the body contains two different kinds of spirits. He thought inhaled air was transformed into "vital spirits" in the heart, and that these were converted into "animal spirits" or "pneumata psychikon" when they reached the brain. This conversion process he thought took place in the brain's hollow cavities (the ventricles) and in the *rete mirabile* (meaning "wonderful net") – an intricate network of blood vessels he'd discovered in the base of the brain of several animals. In fact this network isn't found in the human brain but Galen didn't know this because he only dissected animals. Movement and sensation, Galen further theorized, are made possible by animal spirits traveling up and down the hollow nerves of the body, pumped by the brain.

The idea that animal spirits pulse through body sounds ridiculous to us today, but it was another idea, like the cardiocentric view of mental function, that showed remarkable longevity, only being debunked in the seventeenth century. One reason for its persistence was its vagueness. No one ever spelled out exactly what animal spirits are supposed to be, other than that you can't see them or feel them because they're weightless and invisible. This meant the theory could not be falsified using the technologies of the time. Today scientists recognize that any respectable theory should be logically falsifiable. That is, it ought to be possible to imagine the kinds of evidence that would indicate the theory is wrong, even if such evidence does not exist.

Another reason for the staying power of animal spirits was the centuries-long reverence shown by generations of scientists and medics to Galen's writings. To challenge the great man was seen as sacrilege, partly because he'd managed to get so much correct, and partly because his mono-theistic religious beliefs were acceptable to Christianity and Islam, including his faith in the creative genius and power of God.[6] A long-running ban by the church on human dissection through the Middle Ages also slowed down advances in neuroanatomy.

Even if we fast forward to the "father of modern philosophy," René Descartes, who lived in the seventeenth century, we find that he still endorsed the idea of animal spirits – "a very fine wind," he called them, "or rather a very pure and lively flame." In fact these elusive entities were central to his influential ideas about the human soul and how it interacts with the physical body. Descartes located the soul in the brain's pineal gland (a small structure at the base of the brain) partly because he thought the structure was perfectly placed to purify the spirits and keep track of their movements. We know today that the pineal gland is located above the ventricles and is a hormone-releasing structure involved in regulating daily and seasonal cycles. Descartes thought it was located in the ventricles and that its ability to rock and tilt allowed it to direct the flow of spirits through the brain. When we sleep,

Descartes reasoned, the brain goes slack because of the lack of spirits in the nerves; by contrast when we're awake, the spirit-filled brain is taut and responsive.

Even as Descartes continued to beat the drum for animal spirits, some of his contemporaries were at last beginning to challenge the idea. The specific mystery they were trying to solve, and for which spirits had for so long been seen as the answer, was "How does the brain interact with the body?" "How are signals sent down the nerves?" The evidence had been mounting against spirits. One scientist noticed that flexing his arm in a tub of water failed to displace the water, as he thought it should if spirits had flowed into his arm. Rival theories to emerge in the seventeenth century suggested that the nerves are filled instead with fluids or that they operate via the vibration of ether within them. The former idea, espoused by the English physician and neuroanatomist Thomas Willis, was soon defeated by basic observations – for example, no fluid comes out when you cut a nerve. The vibrations idea put forward by Newton also failed to gain much momentum – to begin with, the nerves aren't pulled taut as you'd expect if they worked in the way that he suggested.[7]

The discoveries that finally killed off belief in animal spirits had to do with electricity. Scientists had known about electric fish since at least Galen's time (when they'd been used as a headache treatment), but it was only in the eighteenth century that "electrotherapy" really took off, with numerous claims that electricity could be used to cure paralysis. This led scientists to ponder whether electricity could be the mysterious means by which the nerves communicate with each other and the muscles of the body. Among the pioneers who developed this idea was the Italian anatomist Luigi Galvani, who conducted a series of important experiments with frogs.[8]

A key revelatory finding came about by chance when an assistant was using a scalpel on a frog. The assistant was standing near one of Galvani's electrical machines that generated static electricity from friction. At just the moment that the machine threw out a spark, the assistant happened to be touching his scalpel against a nerve that innervated the muscle of the frog's leg. The leg suddenly twitched. This observation was crucial because it suggested to Galvani that the spark must have somehow acted on electricity that was already present in the frog nerve.

Galvani's nephew Giovanni Aldini went further. In grisly work he reportedly collected severed heads from the guillotine and showed how applying electricity to the brain caused the faces to twitch.

He performed his most theatrical demonstration of this effect in London in 1803, on the corpse of George Forster, shortly after Forster had been hanged for the murder of his wife and child.

Galvani later showed that nerves contain fat, which supported his correct belief that they often have a fatty coating of insulation that speeds up the transmission of electricity along their length. Incidentally, in 1850, the speed of human nerve conduction was established by the German medic and physicist Hermann von Helmholtz to be 35 meters per second. The serious neurological condition multiple sclerosis, first described by French neurologists in the nineteenth century, is caused by a degeneration of this fatty insulation around the nerves, leading their signals to become scrambled.

Myth #3 Brain Cells Join Together Forming a Huge Nerve Net

As any neuroscience student will tell you, electricity isn't the complete answer as to how nerves communicate. Yes, a current is passed along a nerve (today nerve cells are called neurons, a term first coined by Wilhelm Waldeyer in 1891), but this ultimately triggers the release of chemicals – neurotransmitters – stored at the end of that neuron. These chemicals then make contact with the receiving neuron, which is located on the other side of a tiny gap known as the "synapse" (a term proposed by Charles Sherrington in 1897 before there was definitive evidence that such gaps existed). When these neurotransmitters act on the receiving neuron, they make it more or less likely that it too will experience a burst of electricity along its length.

However, it wasn't until the end of the nineteenth century and into the twentieth that we reached this level of understanding about how the messenger cells of the nervous system communicate. To reach that stage of knowledge required advances in microscope technology and in staining techniques that made it possible for the first time to see the structure of neurons in detail. A key character in this field was the Italian anatomist Camillo Golgi (known as the "savant of Pavia"), who developed a new silver stain technique in 1873. However, even his methods remained crude by modern standards. Golgi and his contemporaries couldn't see the gaps between neurons and they proposed that the cells of the nervous system are fused together, forming an elaborate nerve net – an erroneous idea known as the "reticular theory."

Among the first scientists to propose tentatively but correctly that there might be gaps between neurons were Wilhelm His and August Forel in the late 1880s. However, it was the Spanish neuroscientist Santiago Ramón y Cajal who really killed off the nerve net idea thanks to significant improvements he made to Golgi's staining technique. Although his technology still wasn't advanced enough to show the gaps (the synapses) between neurons, Cajal's superior images also provided no evidence that neurons are fused together. Based on his findings, Cajal argued convincingly that neurons are distinct elements, separate from each other – what became known as the "neurone doctrine." Cajal also proposed correctly that information flows in one direction along neurons.

Cajal and Golgi were jointly awarded the Nobel Prize in Physiology or Medicine in 1906 for their contributions to our understanding of brain anatomy. Here we find more evidence of the stubbornness of some old, incorrect ideas. Golgi used his winner's speech to espouse his original, outmoded ideas about nerve nets and, and in rather unsporting fashion, he described Cajal's neurone doctrine as little more than a fad.

Myth #4

Mental Function Resides in the Brain's Hollows

Before moving on to mythical neuroscience practices in the next chapter, let's rewind once more to deal with another long-defunct theory that was closely related to the idea of animal spirits. We know today that the ventricles are filled with cerebrospinal fluid, acting as a shock absorption system for the brain. However, for centuries it was thought that the ventricles were filled with animal spirits and that each one subserved a different kind of mental function (see Plate 7).

The ventricular theory has its roots in ancient writings in the West and East but was only forged into a comprehensive theory in medieval times. This theory stated that perception is located in the anterior ventricles, cognition in the middle ventricle, and memory in the posterior ventricle, near the cerebellum. Perhaps the first full account of this theory was put forward around the end of the fourth century AD by the physician Nemesius, the Bishop of Emesa in Syria. However, many versions of the theory were proposed through history and around the world, each varying in the exact way that functions were allocated to the different ventricles.

The historian Christopher Green in his 2003 paper "Where Did the Ventricular Location of Mental Faculties Come From?"[9] says that Nemesius was virtually unknown in his time and that his account was unlikely to have influenced later scholars. Green reckons instead that St Augustine was more influential, at least in the West, in spreading the theory, via his work "The Literal Meaning of Genesis" written in AD 401. In this text he describes three ventricles:

> One of these, which is in the front near the face, is the one from which all sensation comes; the second, which is in the back of the brain near the neck, is the one from which all motion comes; the third, which is between the first two, is where the medical writers place the seat of memory.

Centuries later, Leonardo da Vinci, whose anatomical discoveries were so astounding, was another advocate. Early in the sixteenth century, he injected hot wax into the brain of an ox to create a cast of the ventricular hollows, thus allowing him to depict the structures in greater detail than ever before. He labeled their functions according to Nemesius's ancient scheme.

The "ventricular localization of functions" idea remained influential until Victorian times but was first challenged by a Renaissance anatomist from Belgium, Andreas Vesalius. In his landmark book *De humani corporis fabrica* (*On the Workings of the Human Body*), published in 1543, Vesalius showed from his dissections of human cadavers that people don't have any ventricular cavities that aren't shared by other mammals, thus undermining the idea that they are the source of distinctly human mental functions. However, he conceded that based on anatomy alone he couldn't explain how mental functions are supported by the brain.

The ventricular theory was rejected in more compelling fashion in the seventeenth century by Thomas Willis, the author of the magisterial *Anatomy of the Brain*, which features illustrations by Christopher Wren. Drawing on evidence from patients with acquired brain damage and others with congenital brain abnormalities, as well from his own dissections, Willis made a convincing (and correct) case that many functions like memory and volition are located in the outer layers of convoluted brain tissue – the cerebral cortex – that are so much more developed in humans than in other animals. He roundly dismissed the possibility that such functions could reside in the brain's "vacuities," as he called them. Willis also discerned accurately that the stripy, kidney-shaped corpus striatum (located under the hemispheres) was involved in motor control (control over movements).

Despite Willis's arguments and his eminence, the scientific dogma right through into the eighteenth century continued to see the cerebral cortex as no more than a rind (the literal meaning of the Latin word cortex), packed full of blood vessels but little else. It wasn't until the rise of phrenology under Franz Joseph Gall in the nineteenth century that the functional importance of the cortex was more fully appreciated (see p. 28).

Notes

1   Finger, S. (2005). *Minds Behind the Brain: A History of the Pioneers and their Discoveries*. Oxford University Press.
2   Crivellato, E., & Ribatti, D. (2007). Soul, mind, brain: Greek philosophy and the birth of neuroscience. *Brain Research Bulletin*, 71(4), 327–336.
3   Doty, R. W. (2007). Alkmaion's discovery that brain creates mind: A revolution in human knowledge comparable to that of Copernicus and of Darwin. *Neuroscience*, 147(3), 561–568.
4   Finger, S. (2005). *Minds Behind the Brain: A History of the Pioneers and their Discoveries*. Oxford University Press.
5   Gross, C. G. (2009). *A Hole in the Head: More Tales in the History of Neuroscience*. The MIT Press.
6   Finger, S. (2005). *Minds Behind the Brain: A History of the Pioneers and their Discoveries*. Oxford University Press.
7   Finger, S. (2005). *Minds Behind the Brain: A History of the Pioneers and their Discoveries*. Oxford University Press.
8   Glynn, I. (1999). *An Anatomy of Thought: The Origin and Machinery of the Mind*. Oxford University Press.
9   Green, C. D. (2003). Where did the ventricular localization of mental faculties come from? *Journal of the History of the Behavioral Sciences*, 39(2), 131–142.

2 MYTH-BASED BRAIN PRACTICES

Since the dawn of history, mythical ideas about the brain have informed various neurosurgical and psychological practices. This chapter documents three that have entered psychiatric and neurological folklore: trepanation, phrenology, and lobotomy. True to their mythical status, these practices refuse to die away. Trepanning appears in contemporary films and is advocated by Internet eccentrics; phrenology busts stare out from bric-a-brac shops around the world; and lobotomy has evolved into more advanced forms of psychosurgery, such as deep brain stimulation and the implantation of stem cells.

Myth #5 Drilling a Hole in the Skull Releases Evil Spirits

Trepanning or trephining – a practice that began in prehistoric times – is the deliberate creation of holes in the skull (see Plate 9). The procedure is still performed by surgeons today for exploratory purposes, to relieve intracranial pressure, or to remove blood clots on the surface of the brain. However, its historic use without anesthesia has often been based around mythical beliefs about the brain, including the release of evil spirits or demons. Even today, some people – including remote tribes peoples and misguided eccentrics – continue to perform trepanation for scientifically unfounded reasons.

Archaeological evidence suggests trepanning was used in preliterate cultures all over the world from the Americas to Arabia.[1] The earliest

Great Myths of the Brain, First Edition. Christian Jarrett.
© 2015 Christian Jarrett. Published 2015 by John Wiley & Sons, Ltd.

confirmed trepanned skull was found in France and is estimated to be over 7000 years old. Possibly trepanned skulls found in Iraq are even older, dated to 11 000 years ago. The earliest forms of trepanning were performed using scraping and cutting techniques with crude stone, obsidian, flint, and metal tools. In Ancient Greece and through to the Middle Ages, increasingly sophisticated drilling devices and sawing instruments were introduced.[2]

One of the most famous trepanned skulls originates from fifteenth century Peru. It was obtained there by an Indiana Jones-like character, Ephraim George Squier, who was working as US Commissioner to the country in the nineteenth century. The skull, now housed in the American Museum of Natural History in New York, features a square hole over the frontal lobe, above the right eye socket.

Squier took it to Europe where it was inspected by Paul Broca, the anthropologist and neurologist better known today for his work on the neural correlates of language (see p. 40). Because of racist beliefs at the time linking brain size, intelligence, and ethnicity (and because of the high death rate from neurosurgery in contemporary hospitals), Broca's peers found it difficult to believe that Peruvian Indians could have been capable of head surgery. Broca shared these prejudices but was nonetheless convinced that the hole had been created after a closed-head injury, but before the patient had died, probably as a means of relieving intracranial pressure. In other words, he inferred, the Peruvians must have been capable of neurosurgery. Broca was right. Many Peruvian skulls have since been found with multiple trepanned holes, suggesting that some patients in fact survived numerous surgeries. The procedure was probably fairly common in their culture. One burial site south of Lima contained 10 000 bodies, six percent showing signs of trepanation.[3]

From the various Hippocratic texts we know that the Ancient Greeks prescribed trepanning specifically for the treatment of closed-head injuries (i.e. when a person suffers a blow to his or her head but the skull remains intact). Their rationale was that the hole would prevent the build-up of excess humors, in line with humoral theory, which stated that good health was associated with a balance of the four humors in the body and brain: yellow bile, black bile, phlegm, and blood. The relative strength of the humors was also thought to influence a person's character: yellow bile was associated with a bad temper; black bile with melancholy; phlegm with calmness (the word phlegmatic still has this meaning today); and blood with courage.

In the absence of treatment, the Greek physicians thought blood trapped beneath the skull would coagulate into a harmful dark pus. It's hard to believe, but some historians today claim the practice may actually have been beneficial for some patients. In some respects these early trepanning methods were impressive: for example, there's evidence that during Galen's time care was taken not to damage the meninges – the protective layers that cover the surface of the brain – and that consideration was given to the likely thickness of the skull based on the patient's age. The Ancient Greeks also used trepanning to treat epilepsy – the idea being that the hole would allow the release of evil vapors – a practice that continued into nineteenth century Europe, although its rationale by then was less mystical.

There's also evidence in early Renaissance Europe of a form of trepanning being used to treat mental illness through the removal of "stones," as conveyed in various texts (including Robert Burton's *Anatomy of Melancholy*, 1652) and depicted in Flemish Renaissance paintings like The Cure for Madness (or Folly) by Hieronymus Bosch (1450–1515; see Plate 10). Trepanning was effectively being used as a form of psychosurgery, in a way anticipating the arrival of lobotomies in the late nineteenth and early twentieth centuries. In his contribution to the book *Trepanation: History, Discovery, Theory* (published in 2003) the neuroscience historian Charles Gross explains how numerous art historians have interpreted Bosch's painting as allegorical, as if there's no way surgeons of the time would really have performed such operations. But Gross says this is a folly: "apparently, unknown to many of these historians Bosch's painting and derivatives by Bruegel and others, were based on a very real medical practice of their time."[4] Skeptics remain unconvinced. Writing on her Bioephemera blog in 2008, biologist and artist Jessica Palmer notes[5] that "these operations, if they were actually performed, clearly *had* to be shams – playacting in which the surgeon pretended to remove a pebble from the skull, in deference to the 'stone of madness' superstition."

According to Gross there are hundreds of accounts of trepanation continuing to be practiced in the twentieth century, including by doctors of traditional medicine in Africa. For example, in the second half of the last century, the Kisii of South Nyanza in Kenya were still using trepanning as a treatment for headaches arising from head injuries, although I couldn't find confirmation that they continue this practice today. Worldwide, outside of mainstream medicine, trepanning continues to attract a scientifically dubious following, aided by Internet propaganda.

The International Trepanation Advocacy Group (ITAG) (www.trepan.com/) website states:

> The hypothesis here at ITAG has been that making a [*sic*] opening in the skull favorably alters movement of blood through the brain and improves brain functions which are more important than ever before in history to adapt to an ever more rapidly changing world. (accessed May 12, 2014)

Recent decades have seen the emergence of some prominent self-trepanners, including Bart Hughes, who wrote the book *Trepanation: A Cure for Psychosis* and Joey Mellen, author of *Bore Hole*. Claims by self-trepanners that a hole in the skull can help one achieve a state of higher consciousness were also explored through the 1998 documentary film *A Hole in the Head*. In an interview with science writer Mo Costandi in 2008, another self-trepanner, Heather Perry, explained how she'd used an electric drill to create the hole, and that her motivation was to gain "more mental energy and clarity."[6]

Trepanation received even more publicity in an episode of ER broadcast in 1998; in the black and white film *Pi* that was broadcast the same year and depicts a self-trepanner; and in the 2003 blockbuster movie *Master and Commander*. Rather worryingly, today do-it-yourself trepanning instructional films can be found with a quick search online. The *British Medical Journal* reported in 2000 that doctors were concerned about the trepanation movement and keen to warn against the practice.[7] Let me end this section by making it clear – there is no evidence of any psychological or mystical benefits arising from trepanation!

Myth #6 Personality Can Be Read in the Bumps on the Skull

The popularity of another practice founded on misguided ideas about the brain peaked in the 1830s. Phrenology, developed by the German medic and skull collector Franz Joseph Gall and his disciple Johann Spurzheim, claimed psychological aptitudes and personality traits could be discerned from the bumps and lumps on the skull (see Plate 11). Gall's system proposed 27 faculties tied to discrete brain areas (he called them "cerebral organs"), 8 of which he considered unique to humans, including wisdom and poetic talent.

Gall called his approach "craniology" and later "organology." It was Spurzheim who popularized the term phrenology. He also extended Gall's list of faculties to 35, and he started applying the technique to social reform and self-help. Spurzheim toured the UK where phrenology became popular both in science and the parlors of the middle classes, boasting 29 societies devoted to its practice by 1832. The novelist George Eliot had a cast made of her head by the phrenologist James De Ville so that her skull could be more easily read.[8] The Brontë sisters Anne and Charlotte were also fans. Another leading phrenologist in the UK, George Combe, even counted the royal family among his clients.[9] Phrenology was also highly influential in the United States of America where prominent medical advocates included the physicians John Warren, John Bell, and Charles Caldwell.[10] Celebrity devotees included Walt Whitman and Edgar Allen Poe.

Gall's system was founded on a mix of evidence, including personal observations of people he knew. For instance, he recalled a classmate with superior verbal memory who'd had bulging eyes, indicative Gall thought, of a link between the frontal lobe and language. (He was broadly correct on this point, although he localized language too far forwards, right behind the eye sockets.)

Gall also studied the head shapes of people with particular talents or extreme personality types, such as math geniuses and criminals. For example, he observed that people (and animals) with unusually powerful sexual cravings tended to have thicker necks – a sign, he deduced, that the cerebellum in the brain, located above the nape of the neck, is the locus of sexual appetite.[11] He collected and compared various human and animal skulls to support his various theories.

A fatal flaw in Gall's approach was that he only went looking for evidence that supported his ideas – an example of confirmation bias (see p. 9). He largely ignored the behavioral study of people with brain damage, unless, that is, a case arose that backed up his system. The result was that the phrenological maps of function were largely inaccurate (color perception, for example, was located at the front of the brain, rather than in the visual cortex at the back of the brain), as was the central claim that a person's cortical idiosyncrasies and character are betrayed by the pattern of bumps on their skull.

A main challenger to phrenology was Gall's contemporary, the Frenchman Jean Pierre Flourens.[12] He performed experiments on animals and could find no evidence to back up Gall's map of the faculties. In fact, he found no evidence for cortical localization of function, probably in part due to the fact that he relied on crude animal experimentation, rather than studying humans or nonhuman primates. Although interest was sustained in phrenology as a form of pop psychology, by 1840 it was starting to lose its reputation as a serious field of science and was increasingly mocked by cartoonists and satirists.

Phrenology's dire reputation is unfortunate in some ways because it overshadows the important contributions to brain anatomy made by Gall, who was a skilled dissector of brains. Before Gall, despite the efforts of a minority, including Thomas Willis and Leonardo Da Vinci, the functional significance of the cortex had been completely underestimated. Since Ancient Greek times it had always been depicted as a uniform mass of intestine-like coiled tissue and it was considered by most to have no functionally distinct areas. The Swedish mystic Emmanuel Swedenborg had in the eighteenth century written extensively on the functional organization of the cortex, but having no academic affiliation, his ideas were completely ignored. Gall's broad claim that the cortex was made up of functionally distinct areas was not only correct, but it helped kick-start scientific interest in the business of finding out more about which parts of the cortex do what. Paul Broca, who localized language function to the left frontal lobe ("Broca's area," see p. 40), described Gall's work as "the starting point for every discovery in cerebral physiology in our century."

Today phrenology remains in the public consciousness mainly because of the popularity of those kitsch phrenology busts that depict a map of the faculties across the skull. Many still sport the Fowler trademark – a nod to the Fowler brothers, Orson and Lorezo, who spawned an entire phrenological industry in the United States in the nineteenth century. Phrenology is also used as a term of derision today by those seeking to challenge the claims of modern brain imaging studies that certain mental functions are subserved by discrete brain regions (see p. 80). There's no doubt that function is to some extent localized in the brain, including within the cortex, but increasingly neuroscientists are realizing that huge swathes of the brain are activated at any one time, and that it's more accurate to think of functional networks rather than discrete functional units.

Myth #7 Mental Illness Can Be Cured by Disconnecting the Frontal Lobes

Not to be confused with frontal lobectomy (removing some or all of the brain's frontal lobe), the frontal lobotomy – literally "the incision of a lobe" – involves destroying and/or severing tracts and tissue that link the prefrontal lobes with deeper structures in the brain. The first published report of the procedure was by the Portuguese neurologist Egas Moniz in 1936. He called it leucotomy, meaning "white cut" – a reference to the white matter tracts in the brain. His rationale was that destroying the healthy tissue would disrupt a patient's unhealthy and disordered mental fixations. He'd gotten the idea for the procedure the preceding year at the Second World Congress of Neurology held in London. There he heard about the work of John Fulton and Carlyle Jacobsen of Yale University, in which aggressive chimps and monkeys were becalmed by a procedure that severed links between the prefrontal cortex and the rest of the brain.

Together with his colleague Almeida Lima, Moniz initially injected ethanol into patients' brains to create the desired lesions. Later they honed their technique, using a rod (a "leucotome") with a retractable wire loop to inflict the damage. Moniz and Lima reported promising results with severely mentally ill patients – people for whom there was no other effective treatment at the time. Their apparent success culminated in a Nobel Prize for Medicine for Moniz in 1949. But not everything went well for Moniz – 10 years earlier he was left wheelchair bound after being shot multiple times by an embittered patient, though reportedly not one of the people he'd lobotomized.[13]

Across the Atlantic in the United States, lobotomy was practiced with evangelical zeal by the neurosurgeon Walter Freeman and his colleague James Watts. They adapted the technique, entering the brain through the eye socket, using a tool that looked like an ice pick (see Plate 12). They often performed the procedure without anesthetic, and their choice of patients became increasingly indiscriminate. Freeman would go on to perform thousands of these lobotomies around the country. Famous patients included US president John F. Kennedy's sister Rosemary and the Hollywood actress Frances Farmer.[14] Like Moniz, Freeman claimed favorable results. Also like Moniz, Freeman failed to follow his patients up over the long-term and he was apparently undaunted by patient deaths and adverse outcomes, including seizures and incapacitation. Outcomes were unpredictable partly because Freeman and Moniz and other loboto-mizers had no way of seeing the parts of the brain with which they were interfering. Critics claimed that even lobotomized patients who'd undergone successful operations weren't cured, they were merely quiet-ened or dulled.

The lobotomy was also performed with great fervor in the UK. There, its leading advocate was Wylie McKissock, another bombastic neurosur-geon who went on to perform the procedure on thousands of patients around the country.[15] McKissock was knighted in 1971. However, the lobotomy wasn't embraced everywhere – for example, it was banned in the USSR in 1950.

Although Moniz is usually regarded as the founding father of psycho-surgery – a term he coined – the idea of deliberately damaging healthy brain tissue for mental relief actually has its earliest roots in the trepan-ning practices of early Renaissance Europe, and later, in the nineteenth century, in the work of the Swiss psychiatrist Gottlieb Burckhardt.[16] His "topectomy" procedure introduced in the 1880s involved making several incisions in the frontal, parietal, and temporal cortices, but the idea never took off, probably in part because two of the six mentally ill patients in his trial died soon after he'd operated on them. Maybe Burckhardt also lacked the charisma and zeal that would help Moniz and Freeman, in the next century, sell their procedure to a world that was desperately seeking a way to treat mental illness more effectively.

It seems amazing today that the practice of this seemingly brutal and crude procedure was allowed to continue for so long. However, it's important to remember the lack of alternative options for many of the seriously disturbed patients who underwent the surgery. Many of them would have languished in asylums without the operation, and the media latched onto some remarkable stories of patients whose lives were appar-ently transformed for the better. "That troubled brain is at peace," was the simple verdict of the BBC radio coverage in 1950 when lobotomy was at the peak of its popularity. One could also argue that there are parallels today with chemotherapy, in which healthy tissue is destroyed deliber-ately to combat cancer. Or with cosmetic surgery, in which a healthy body or face is cut open to make physical changes that will, it's hoped, provide psychological benefit to the patient.

The prefrontal lobotomy fell out of favor with the discovery of phar-maceutical treatments for psychosis, starting with chlorpromazine (Thorazine) in the 1950s. There was also a gathering opposition to the gusto with which Freeman wielded his ice pick, and mounting awareness of the frequent negative outcomes associated with the procedure. The dire reputation of the frontal lobotomy in neurological folklore was sealed for good by the 1975 hit film *One Flew Over the Cuckoo's Nest*, which ends with the feisty patient Randle McMurphy (played by Jack Nicholson) undergoing the procedure against his will, leaving him as a mindless zombie.

It would be a mistake to think that psychosurgery has disappeared. It hasn't. It has simply evolved. Today some patients with severe depression or severe obsessive compulsive disorder, for whom no other treatment has worked, still undergo brain surgery as a last resort.

The procedures used are more precise than the frontal lobotomy, thanks to new scanning technologies and stereotactic equipment that pinpoints the target of surgery using coordinates in three dimensions. Modern procedures include the anterior cingulotomy, subcaudate tractomy, and limbic leucotomy, all of which target brain areas involved in emotional processing. Advocates of psychosurgery point to a hugely improved safety record compared with the dark days of lobotomy and they argue that their interventions are more precise than drug treatments that wash indiscriminately through the entire brain.[17] Protection today also comes from institutional review boards in the USA that weigh the pros and cons of experimental interventions before giving the go-ahead for trials to begin. Similar ethics committees operate in the UK and other countries.

Other modern forms of psychosurgery aren't based on the principle of destroying healthy brain tissue. There's deep brain stimulation, in which a device is implanted that deactivates a localized neural area through constant stimulation. This approach has been used for treating Parkinson's Disease and anxiety and depression. There's also transcranial magnetic stimulation in which a magnetic pulse is placed close to the scalp, temporarily deactivating key brain regions. And there are also experimental procedures in which stem cells are implanted into regions of brain damage or disease, in the hope that they will develop into healthy new cells appropriate for that brain location. Research is still ongoing to establish the effectiveness of these techniques and to rule out the part played by powerful placebo effects.

This is a fast moving area of medicine and no doubt many of today's experimental techniques will shock tomorrow's generation of neuroscientists. Having said that, it's hard to imagine a modern society ever again tolerating the gung-ho insouciance shown by Freeman and Watts.

What Is Electroconvulsive Therapy?

Another brain treatment that occupies a dark place in the public consciousness is electroconvulsive therapy (ECT), in which an electric shock is applied to the brain with the aim of triggering a seizure. The procedure was developed in the 1930s after psychiatrists noticed improvements in depressed patients who'd recently experienced an epileptic seizure.

Unlike lobotomy, ECT is still used widely today, usually as a last-resort treatment for patients with extremely severe depression. A meta-analysis published by Daniel Pagnin and colleagues in 2008 found ECT to be a superior treatment for depression compared with simulated ECT (a placebo) or antidepressant drugs.[18] Scott Lilienfeld and his colleagues wrote in 2010[19] that "few if any psychological treatments are the subject of as many misunderstandings as ECT." Surveys show that the public and some medics view the treatment as barbaric, and they believe it leaves patients as zombies.

Although ECT can lead to memory difficulties, the sinister caricature of the treatment in popular culture is largely inaccurate. Many patients in fact credit the treatment with having saved their lives, and often say they'd undergo the treatment again if their depression returned.[20]

The dire reputation of ECT stems in part from its history. The treatment was abused in its early years, including being used as a form of punishment for troublesome patients. Before the widespread use of anesthesia and muscle relaxants, the provoked seizures also led to violent convulsions in patients, occasionally resulting in broken bones or other serious injuries. Popular portrayals of ECT in movies have also sullied its image. This includes the infamous scene from One Flew Over the Cuckoo's Nest when Randle McMurphy is given shock treatment as a punishment for leading a patient rebellion.

Another reason for the fear and distrust of ECT is that psychiatrists still don't fully understand why it works. New clues appeared in 2012[21] when a team led by Jennifer Perrin at Aberdeen University claimed, based on functional brain scan results of nine patients before and after ECT, that the treatment helps reduce excess connectivity in the brain. Another recent study, published in 2013, found localized increases in gray matter volume in patients with bipolar and unipolar depression, who'd been treated with ECT. These brain changes were correlated with the magnitude of the therapeutic effect.[22] Nonetheless, ECT continues to be opposed by many. "I'm convinced that in 10 or 15 years we will have put ECT in the same rubbish bin of historical treatments as lobotomies and surprise baths that have been discarded over time," psychologist John Read told BBC news in 2013.[23]

Notes

1 Gross, C. G. (2009). *A Hole in the Head: More Tales in the History of Neuroscience.* The MIT Press.

2 http://neurophilosophy.wordpress.com/2007/06/13/an-illustrated-history-of-trepanation/ (accessed May 12, 2014).

3 Gross, C. G. (2009). *A Hole in the Head: More Tales in the History of Neuroscience.* The MIT Press.

4 Gross, C. C. (2003). Trepanation from the Palaeolithic to the Internet. In R. Arnott, S. Finger, C. U. M. Smith (eds), *Trepanation: History, Discovery, Theory.* Swets & Zeitlinger Publications, pp. 307–322.

5 http://scienceblogs.com/bioephemera/2008/08/25/the-stone-of-madness/ (accessed May 12, 2014).

6 http://neurophilosophy.wordpress.com/2008/08/04/lunch_with_heather_perry/ (accessed May 12, 2014).

7 Dobson, R. (2000). Doctors warn of the dangers of trepanning. *BMJ,* 320(7235), 602.

8 http://www.brainpickings.org/index.php/2013/10/29/george-eliot-phrenology/ (accessed May 12, 2014).

9 Summerscale, K. (2012). *Mrs Robinson's Disgrace, The Private Diary of A Victorian Lady.* Bloomsbury Publishing.

10 Finger, S. (2005). *Minds Behind the Brain: A History of the Pioneers and their Discoveries.* Oxford University Press.

11 Summerscale, K. (2012). *Mrs Robinson's Disgrace, The Private Diary of A Victorian Lady.* Bloomsbury Publishing.

12 Finger, S. (2005). *Minds Behind the Brain: A History of the Pioneers and their Discoveries.* Oxford University Press.

13 http://neurophilosophy.wordpress.com/2007/07/24/inventing_the_lobotomy/ (accessed May 12, 2014).

14 Geller, J. L. (2005). The lobotomist: A maverick medical genius and his tragic quest to rid the world of mental illness • The pest maiden: A story of lobotomy. *Psychiatric Services,* 56(10), 1318–1319.

15 http://www.bbc.co.uk/programmes/b016wx0w (accessed May 12, 2014).

16 Mashour, G. A., Walker, E. E., & Martuza, R. L. (2005). Psychosurgery: Past, present, and future. *Brain Research Reviews,* 48(3), 409–419.

17 Mashour, G. A., Walker, E. E., & Martuza, R. L. (2005). Psychosurgery: Past, present, and future. *Brain Research Reviews,* 48(3), 409–419.

18 Pagnin, D., De Queiroz, V., Pini, S., & Cassano, G. B. (2008). Efficacy of ECT in depression: a meta-analytic review. *FOCUS: The Journal of Lifelong Learning in Psychiatry,* 6(1), 155–162.

19 Lilienfeld, S. O., Lynn, S. J., Ruscio, J., & Beyerstein, B. L. (2009). *50 Great Myths of Popular Psychology: Shattering Widespread Misconceptions about Human Behavior.* Wiley Blackwell.

20   Pettinati, H. M., Tamburello, T. A., Ruetsch, C. R., & Kaplan, F. N. (1994). Patient attitudes toward electroconvulsive therapy. *Psychopharmacology Bulletin*, 30, 471–475.

21   Perrin, J. S., Merz, S., Bennett, D. M., Currie, J., Steele, D. J., Reid, I. C., & Schwarzbauer, C. (2012). Electroconvulsive therapy reduces frontal cortical connectivity in severe depressive disorder. *Proceedings of the National Academy of Sciences*, 109(14), 5464–5468.

22   Dukart, J., Regen, F., Kherif, F., Colla, M., Bajbouj, M., Heuser, I., ... & Draganski, B. (2014). Electroconvulsive therapy-induced brain plasticity determines therapeutic outcome in mood disorders. *Proceedings of the National Academy of Sciences*, 111(3), 1156–1161.

23   http://www.bbc.co.uk/news/health-23414888 (accessed May 12, 2014).

3 MYTHICAL CASE STUDIES

The history of neuroscience is populated by a handful of characters whose misfortunes have led to groundbreaking revelations in our understanding of the brain, cementing their place in folklore. This chapter documents three of these individuals, two born in the nineteenth century and one in the twentieth – Phineas Gage, Tan, and Henry Molaison.

Their stories have acquired a mythical status, appearing in hundreds of psychology and neuroscience textbooks and inspiring poems and films. We'll see that the study of these patients has contributed to the overturning of brain myths; yet in other respects myths and misinformation have developed around the stories themselves. Indeed, contemporary researchers remain fascinated by Gage and the others, and they continue to study their diseased and damaged remains, employing the latest technological tools to uncover fresh insights about the brain.

Myth #8 Brain Injury Turned Neuroscience's Most Famous Case into an Impulsive Brute

Surely the best known case in neuroscience folklore is Phineas Gage, the railway foreman whose personality changed after an iron rod passed through his brain. Gage suffered his accident in 1848 while tamping explosives into rock to make way for the Rutland and Barlington railroad in central Vermont. The detonation went off prematurely and his six kilogram, three and a half foot-long, one and a quarter inch diameter tamping iron was rammed straight into his face, under his left

Great Myths of the Brain, First Edition. Christian Jarrett.
© 2015 Christian Jarrett. Published 2015 by John Wiley & Sons, Ltd.

eye, and clean out through the top of his head, landing 20 meters behind him. After being taken on an ox-cart to nearby doctors, it's remarkable that he helped himself down from the cart unaided. But he wasn't the same man.

In the immortal words of John Harlow, one of the first doctors to attend the scene and treat him thereafter, Gage's "mind was radically changed, so decidedly that his friends and acquaintances said he was 'no longer Gage.'"[1] The reason, Harlow explained in an 1868 report, is that "The equilibrium or balance, so to speak, between his intellectual faculties and his animal propensities, seems to have been destroyed." Harlow contrasted this situation with Gage's character prior to the accident: "he possessed a well-balanced mind, and was looked upon by those who knew him as a shrewd, smart business man, very energetic and persistent in executing all his plans of operation." The new, aggressive Gage, rod in hand, became a circus freak and wanderer until his death eleven years later. Or so the myth, found in hundreds of psychology and neuroscience textbooks, plays, films, poems and YouTube skits, would have us believe. Personality is located in the frontal lobes, the myth says, and once these are damaged, a person is changed forever.

In fact, over the last two decades there has been a dramatic re-evaluation of the Gage story, thanks largely to the painstaking investigative work of Malcolm Macmillan at the University of Melbourne and Matthew Lena, based in Massachusetts[2] (also supported by new photographic evidence, see tinyurl.com/a42wram). Their research shows that Gage's stint as an exhibition piece at Barnum's Museum and elsewhere was short-lived. In 1851 he began work for a coach-line service in Hanover, New Hampshire for 18 months. Then in 1852 or 1854 he emigrated to Chile where he worked as a driver of six-horse coaches on the Valparaiso-Santiago road – a hugely demanding job, which would have required him to pick up new vocabulary, deal politely with passengers, control the horses, and navigate a treacherous route of over hundred miles. By Macmillan and Lena's account, all this suggests that Gage made an impressive psychosocial recovery; that the picture painted by Harlow of a brutish drifter was only accurate in the short term. Macmillan and Lena think Gage's post-accident employment may have provided him with just the kind of structured environment needed for rehabilitation, consistent with contemporary accounts of brain-damaged patients who have recovered well (although see p. 260). In the end, Gage fell seriously ill in 1859 and left Chile to be with his family in San Francisco where he died in 1860 after suffering several seizures. Gage's skull and iron rod are now housed in the Warren Anatomical Museum in Boston.

Part of the reason there is so much ambiguity about Gage's injury and recovery has to do with the lack of knowledge about brain function at the time of his accident. As we learned in Chapter 1, neuroscience was only just coming around to the idea that the cerebral cortex, including the frontal lobes, had functional significance and was made up of functionally distinct areas. Much of the information that was available was based on the erroneous claims of phrenology. It didn't help either that no autopsy was performed on Gage.

Gage's skull was exhumed in 1868 and sent to Harlow. Based on his inspections, he concluded that the left frontal and middle lobes must have been destroyed and that the partial recovery made by Gage was likely due to compensation by the intact right hemisphere. Gage's skull was then left untouched for nearly a hundred years. However, beginning in the 1980s, each new generation of scientists has used the technology of the day to make another attempt to recreate Gage's injury. The most technically advanced effort was published in 2004 using computational anatomy techniques. Peter Ratiu, based at Brigham and Women's Hospital and Harvard Medical School, and his colleagues created a multilayered, 3-D CT scan of Gage's skull and overlaid it on a 3-D model of a normal brain. They then reconstructed the passage of the iron rod through the skull. Consistent with the revised account of Gage's recovery by Macmillan and Lena, Ratiu's team established that Gage most likely suffered damage to the left frontal lobe only, specifically affecting the orbito-frontal and dorso-lateral regions, with the ventricles spared from damage. This contradicts some previous accounts that supposed Gage's brain damage was bilateral (on both sides of the brain), and it could help explain why he was able to recover as well as he apparently did.

Most recently, in 2012, a team led by John van Horn, based at the University of California and Harvard Medical School, used sophisticated diffusion tensor imaging data, together with anatomical MRI, to try to find out how Gage's injury affected the connective tissues of his brain – an issue they said previous investigators had neglected[3] (see Plate 13). By superimposing the estimated trajectory of the rod through Gage's skull against the averaged connective brain pathways of 110 similarly aged healthy men scanned in the twenty-first century, they concluded that 4 percent of Gage's cortical gray matter was probably damaged in the left hemisphere and 11 percent of his cortical white matter, including several important major nerve bundles. They said this would have had profound consequences, affecting not only left hemisphere function but, indirectly, right hemisphere function too. Unfortunately, this doesn't really tell us anything about how much Gage's damaged connective pathways may or may not have adapted to his injuries.

Although it is Gage's story that has gained a mythical status within neuroscience, he is in fact far from the only man of his era who survived a serious brain injury.[4] The archives of the *British Medical Journal* are littered with numerous remarkable cases of people living relatively normal lives after losing significant amounts of their brains. One example is the 1853 paper "Case of recovery after compound fracture of the frontal bone and loss of cerebral substance," which documents the story of a 60-year-old man, Mr Booth, who lost "no less than one to two tablespoons" of "cerebral matter" in an accident involving the handle of a rapidly rotating windlass. Three months later Booth's doctor reported that his patient's intellect was unimpaired and his muscular power, "not at all paralysed."

Myth #9 The Faculty of Language Production Is Distributed Through the Brain

Through the latter half of the nineteenth century, as the functional importance of the cerebral cortex became more widely accepted, medics and scientists increasingly turned to brain-damaged patients as a way to find out which parts of the brain do what. Such "accidents of nature" could be incredibly informative. If a lesion to a specific part of the brain led to a specific deficit, yet damage to another region did not, this would suggest a functional independence between the two areas. Even more revealing would be a so-called "double-dissociation" – if one patient had damage to one area, another patient had damage somewhere else, and each exhibited a distinct pattern of impairment. Case studies of this kind are still incredibly useful today.

One landmark neurological case from history was Monsieur Leborgne, the 51-year-old long-term patient who was transferred to the surgical ward of the Bicêtre hospital in Paris on 11 April 1861 to see the French neurologist and anthropologist Paul Broca. His fate helped overturn the myth, still endorsed by many at that time, that the faculty of language production is distributed throughout the brain.

Leborgne was nicknamed "Tan" because, besides uttering the expletive phrase "sacré nom de Dieu" when frustrated[5] (literally "the sacred name of God," which was then considered a serious profanity), the only speech he could manage was to repeat the nonsense syllable "Tan." Although his comprehension was intact, Tan had lost his powers of language production at age 31, probably as a complication of the epilepsy he'd suffered since his youth. First hospitalized in 1833 with serious headaches possibly caused by exposure at work to toxic metal fumes,[6] over the years he also progressively lost the use of the right side of his body. His referral in 1861 to the Bicêtre surgical ward was for the recently developed gangrene of his right leg. Tan wasn't long for this world; he died a week after Broca first examined him.

The timing of Tan's demise was fortuitous for Broca, coinciding with a debate that had been raging in academic circles about whether or not the front of the brain supports the ability to produce language. Still wary of the recently discredited claims of phrenology, many experts endorsed the idea that language production and other mental faculties are distributed throughout the brain.

Jean-Baptiste Bouillaud, Marc Dax, and others had already amassed dozens of cases of patients with frontal damage who'd lost their ability to speak. But still the academic community remained unconvinced (see box below). Tan changed all that. Broca examined Tan's brain after he died and presented the findings to the Société d'Anthropologie (which he'd founded) and the Société Anatomique. Broca described Tan's speech problems, his apparently intact comprehension, and the lesion he'd found on the third convolution of Tan's left frontal lobe – a portion of brain tissue that came to be named Broca's area (see Plate 14).

Broca's reputation, together with the quality and detail of the case he presented, made all the difference, and finally there was an acceptance among neuroscience scholars of the day that the language production faculty appeared to be tied to the frontal lobes. The historian Stanley Finger describes this moment as a "key turning point in the history of the brain sciences."[7] Broca soon noticed from further cases that it was predominantly left-sided frontal brain damage that led to speech deficits (the French neurologist Marc Dax actually made this observation decades earlier but he died before he could publish his findings)[8]. Broca termed these language problems *aphémie* (meaning "without speech"), but it was the Greek term *"aphasia"* (also meaning "speechlessness") coined soon after by Armand Trousseau that took hold. Today the syndrome of speech and language deficits associated with damage to Broca's area is called Broca's aphasia.

Tan is like the opposite of Gage, in the sense that we know a lot about his brain damage but very little about his life story. Tan is described in some accounts as mean and vindictive, but Broca included very few biographical details in his medical notes. Thankfully, the Polish historian Cezary Domanski improved the record in a pair of papers published in

2013. These outline the results of his archive searches, including analysis of Leborgne's medical files.[9]

We now know that "Tan's" full name was Louis Victor Leborgne and that he was born in Moret-sur-Loing – the picturesque town that inspired Monet and other impressionists. He was the son of Pierre Christophe Leborgne, a school teacher, and Margueritte Savard. Before his incapacitation through illness, Leborgne was a "*formier*" in Paris, a kind of skilled craftsman who made the wooden forms used by shoemakers in their work. When ill health forced him to stop work, he would have been severely impoverished, says Domanski. This provokes sympathy from the Polish historian. He's not surprised that reports suggest Leborgne was unlikable. An adult life spent in penury, almost permanently hospitalized, "it may be hard to imagine that [Leborgne's] character ... could have been shaped differently, living in such sad conditions, without hope of improvement," says Domanski.

The new information on Leborgne's family and early career also corrects a historical myth. The oft-told idea that Leborgne "was an uneducated illiterate from the lower social class should once and for all be deemed erroneous," writes Domanski. He also offers a further intriguing speculation – given that Leborgne's birthplace of Moret was home to several tanneries, Domanski wonders if his repeated utterance of Tan was somehow connected to childhood memories of the pretty town.

The reason we know so much about Tan's brain, is that, rather than dissect it, Broca chose to observe Tan's brain superficially only, so that it could be stored for posterity (today it's housed at the Dupuytren Museum in Paris). It's since been scanned three times with modern imaging technology, first using computerized tomography in 1980, using MRI in 1994 and then high-resolution MRI in 2007, contributing to its status as "perhaps the most famous brain in the history of brain sciences," in the words of Finger.

Like all cases that acquire a mythical status, the interpretation of Tan and his brain continues to evolve. Nina Dronkers and her team who performed the scan in 2007 found evidence that Tan's lesions were far more extensive than Broca realized, extending deeper into the interior of the left frontal lobe, including damage to the arcuate fasciculus, an important nerve bundle linking anterior and posterior regions.[10] In fact the most significant damage to Tan's brain is not in Broca's area and it could be this more buried damage that contributed in large part to his severe speech problems. Broca failed to pick up on much of this damage because of his decision not to dissect the brain.

Dronkers and her colleagues also point out that the specific area (the posterior third of the inferior frontal gyrus) that is considered to be Broca's area today is not, ironically, the same anatomical region as the larger area (the entire posterior half of the inferior frontal gyrus) first identified by Broca. This means we're faced with a bizarre situation in which Broca's area is smaller than Broca's original area, and Broca's aphasia may be caused by damage to areas other than the old or new Broca's area. According to Dronkers and her colleagues, all this "by no means detracts from Broca's phenomenal discovery." Indeed many historians believe that Broca and his study of Tan helped launched the discipline of cognitive neuropsychology.

So what's the verdict of modern neuroscience on what exactly Broca's area does? Although Broca was correct that damage to this area usually affects speech production, it's known today, on the one hand, that speech is possible without Broca's area, and on the other hand that the area is also involved in other mental functions, including aspects of language comprehension; listening and performing music; and performing and observing actions. Psychologists today generally consider Broca's area important for processing syntax, in both production *and* comprehension. A more posterior region (Wernicke's area), near the junction with the parietal lobe, by contrast, is considered important for processing meaning.

A last note on Broca's area – there is evidence that it's possible for speech production to recover after damage to this area. We know this thanks to another remarkable case study, this one contemporary. FV, a male patient, had had a large tumor removed from the front of his brain, a region encompassing Broca's area. Despite this, his speech was largely unaffected. Monique Plaza and her colleagues who documented his case in 2009 believe FV recovered so well because the tumor had grown slowly and other brain regions (including premotor cortex and the head of the caudate nucleus) had taken on the functions usually served by Broca's area.[11] However, FV was left with one strange deficit – he was unable to talk about other people's speech.

Another relevant and extraordinary case study worth mentioning was published in 2013 and involved a 17-year-old boy who, at age two, had lost not just his Broca's area but almost his entire left hemisphere (to remove a huge benign tumor)! The case report documents how he slowly reacquired his nascent language abilities via his right hemisphere and to most casual observers his speech and reading eventually appeared normal.[12] Intriguingly, the new language network that developed in his right hemisphere appeared to follow the same functional organization as a typical healthy left hemisphere, as if following a kind of neural "blue print."

Returning briefly to Tan, there's no doubt his story is central to the history of psychology and neuroscience. But new insights into the specific damage he incurred, especially considered alongside modern case studies like FV, show that things are rarely straightforward when it comes to brain injury and recovery. Although functional localization is a recognized feature of the brain, specific faculties rarely map neatly onto specific neural areas. Any account of the brain has to take into account the organ's amazing capability of adjusting to damage.

"The Bet!"

Although it is Paul Broca who is usually celebrated for having located speech function specifically to the left frontal lobe, it was the French physician Jean-Baptiste Bouillaud who was the first to make the vaguer argument about the importance of the frontal lobes to speech production. He published a book and journal article in 1825 documenting brain-damaged patients who had lesions in their frontal lobes and who'd lost the ability to speak, often with no other obvious impairment.

The problem for Bouillaud was that his claims sounded too much like phrenology, which in 1848 was derided in scholarly circles (see p. 28). Twenty-three years later, after recording hundreds of similar cases, he was so convinced that the ability to speak was somehow dependent on having intact frontal lobes that he made a dramatic gesture – if anyone could present him with a patient who had frontal brain damage, but preserved speech, he'd give them a reward of 500 French Francs, a huge sum at the time. Historian Stanley Finger calls it possibly "the most famous bet in the history of the brain sciences."

Many years passed before Bouillaud's prize was claimed. It was in discussions at the Académie de Médecine in 1865, at which all the neuro-luminaries of the day were arguing about laterality of function, that a surgeon called Velpeau brought up the topic of Bouillaud's earlier challenge and said a case he'd seen in 1843 meant he was entitled to the winnings. Imagine Bouillaud's look of incredulity after so much time had passed!

You can read about Velpeau's case in the book *On Aphasia, or Loss of Speech in Cerebral Disease* by Sir Frederic Bateman, published in 1868, and now available on Google Books.[13] According to Bateman, Velpeau said his case – a 60-year-old wigmaker – had a tumor that had "taken the place of the two anterior lobes" and yet ... this is the best bit ... one remarkable symptom of the patient before he'd died, was his "intolerable loquacity." In fact, Bateman tells us, "A greater chatterer never existed; and on more than one occasion complaints were made by the other patients of their talkative neighbor, who allowed them to rest neither night nor day."

We'll probably never know now if Velpeau presented his case accurately, and if he did, how the patient managed to speak without any frontal lobes (it's probably likely that a good deal of frontal brain matter was left intact). What we do know is that Bouillaud lost out. According to Broca's biographer, Francis Shiller, "After a long and heated discussion, Bouillaud had to pay."[14]

Myth #10 Memory Is Distributed Throughout the Entire Cortex

When Henry Gustav Molaison died at 5.05 p.m. on December 2, 2008 at the age of 82, the worlds of neuroscience and psychology mourned the passing of one of the most influential cases in the history of the disciplines. Known in the literature since the 1950s as H.M. to protect his identity, Henry's life changed forever at the age of 27 after he underwent neurosurgery in a last-ditch attempt to cure his severe epilepsy. His seizures had started at age 9 after he was struck by a cyclist and hit his head, and they'd deteriorated ever since. By age 16 he was having more than ten tonic-clonic seizures a day (affecting both his brain hemispheres; see p. 280 for more on epilepsy). After the strongest anti-convulsant drugs failed to help him, Henry was ready to try anything.

William Beecher Scoville, a student of the celebrated Canadian neurosurgeon Wilder Penfield, had considerable experience removing small chunks of brain from psychiatric patients. He operated on Henry using a radical procedure called fractional lobotomy that was intended to be more precise and therapeutically beneficial than classic lobotomies. Scoville knew it would be risky (and certainly this procedure would never be used today), but he was hopeful that removing slices from Henry's temporal lobes had a good chance of eradicating his terrible seizures.

At the time the operation was performed at Hartford Hospital, Connecticut, most experts believed that memory was distributed throughout the cortex. As we heard earlier, Broca in the last century had overturned the distributed perspective on speech production, but belief in the distributed nature of memory persisted. This was in large part because of the results of rat experiments performed by the US psychologist Karl Lashley and his colleague Shepherd Franz in 1917.[15] No matter which parts of the animals' cortex Lashley and Shepherd removed, they still seemed to be able to remember their way around a maze. Based on this finding and others, Lashley proposed the concept of equipotentiality – the idea that memory impairment depends not on the location of brain damage, but on its extent.

So it was to everyone's shock when Henry woke up that not only were his seizures gone, his memory had too. Well, not all aspects of his memory. Brenda Milner, a British-born psychologist based at McGill University, began conducting comprehensive neuropsychological tests with Henry and soon discovered that he was specifically unable to store any new information in long-term memory. His short-term memory, over a few seconds, was fine, and he could also recall episodes from his past. But each day Milner met him, Henry would greet her like a stranger. Half an hour after eating a meal, if offered another, he would sit down and eat again. It became clear that Henry had one of the purest forms of amnesia ever documented (see also p. 265), caused by Scoville removing large parts of the hippocampus and the amygdala on both sides of his brain – specific regions of tissue that we know now are essential for memory function.

During his lifetime and beyond, Henry has been mentioned in over 12 000 journal articles and the focus of investigation by over 100 psychologists and neuroscientists. The first paper published on his memory performance by Milner and Scoville in 1957 has been cited over 4000 times.[16] Alan Baddeley at the University of York in England, one of the foremost authorities on memory alive today, told me that: "H.M. is arguably the most important single patient in terms of his influence on neuroscience."

Later studies, many of them by Suzanne Corkin at MIT (a student of Brenda Milner's), provided new insights about which aspects of Henry's memory were preserved. For example, he was able to learn the tricky skill of mirror drawing, even though on each attempt he had no recollection of ever having done it before. This awkward task involves drawing a shape while looking at the view of your hand in the mirror. Henry's improvement at the challenge suggests his "procedural" memory – the kind that we rely on for skills like riding a bike – was intact. He was also able to draw a detailed plan of his house. A few new pieces of general knowledge also lodged in his mind – for example, after 1963 he was aware that a US President had been assassinated in Dallas. He could rate the intensity of smells, but couldn't identify them. Researchers also discovered that Henry had high pain tolerance. Pain perception has a strong psychological component based in part on the memory of past experiences. Henry's pain tolerance may therefore have been related to his missing amygdalae, which are known to be involved in remembering past painful experiences.

Henry lived for decades at Bickford Health Care Center, Connecticut, where he was undisturbed by the media, his location known only to the select few researchers who worked with him. When he died, a procedure had been planned in advance for his brain to be preserved. He was taken to the Brain Observatory at the University of California, San Diego, where his brain was removed, scanned, and cut into 2401 paper-thin slices by Jacapo Annese and his colleagues (see Plate 15). These have been used to create a highly detailed digital map down to the level of individual neurons, and made available to researchers the world over in 2014. The project has been likened to creating a Google Earth of the brain. The painstaking 53-hour slicing procedure was itself streamed live on the Internet, watched by over 400 000 people.[17]

In 2013, Suzanne Corkin published a book about Henry Molaison titled Permanent Present Tense, The Man With No Memory and What He Taught The World. "We continue to study him," Corkin told The Guardian. "He has gone but is still very present for us every day." Film rights to the book have been obtained by Columbia Pictures and the producer Scott Rudin. Henry was apparently a genial man, always willing to help. His insight into his situation was limited, but when Corkin asked him one day if he was happy, he reportedly said: "The way I figure it is, what they find out about me helps them to help other people."[18]

H.M. was right. His impact on the science of memory has been immense. But not everyone believes this is a good thing. Writing in 2013,[19] the British psychologist John Aggleton at Cardiff University expressed his fears that the dominant influence of H.M. on memory research has had a biasing effect. H.M.'s brain damage extended beyond his hippocampi, Aggleton writes, and included damage to white-matter tracts with possible consequences for far-reaching brain regions.

In fact the precise extent of Henry's brain injuries has been subject to some debate. However in 2014, Annese's team at the Brain Observatory in San Diego published their first detailed 3-D reconstruction of Henry's injuries. They confirmed that the anterior portion of his hippocampus was removed by suction on both sides, but the posterior portion was left behind and the tissue was healthy.[20] Annese's team also discovered that the entorhinal cortex was almost entirely missing – this is the "gateway" to the hippocampus from the cerebral cortex and subcortical sites. The removal of Henry's amygdala by scalpel was confirmed to be almost total. A surprising discovery was a scar in the left prefrontal cortex, which the researchers speculated was likely unintentional damage caused by Scoville. There were also signs of brain damage caused by strokes later in life. Aggleton told me that these new findings actually add to the mystery of Henry's precise brain damage, without solving it. For example, the results leave open the possibility that Henry's posterior hippocampus was connected with the rest of the brain.

Whatever the true extent of Henry's injuries, modern neuroscience has tended to fixate on the importance of the hippocampus for memory, in large part because it's always been known that the most famous amnesiac of all lost most of this structure bilaterally. Far less attention has been given to the fact that damage to other structures, including the nearby mammillary bodies, can also cause severe amnesia. "It feels almost sacrilegious to criticize the impact of H.M., especially given the quality of the associated research," writes Aggleton, "nevertheless, the resultant narrow focus on the hippocampus for memory and memory disorders could well have excessively biased our thinking, with far-reaching, unwitting consequences."

Karl Lashley was wrong about all areas of the cortex being equally important for memory. Clearly some structures play a far more important role than others, and the hippocampus and amygdalae are vital. But Aggleton is also correct – we must guard against oversimplifying the story and assuming that these are the only structures that matter. Later in the book we'll revisit this question of just how far mental functions can be localized to specific brain structures (see p. 80).

Notes

1 Harlow, J. M. (1869). *Recovery from the Passage of an Iron Bar through the Head*. Clapp.

2 Macmillan, M. (2008). Phineas Gage – unravelling the myth. *The Psychologist*, 21, 828–831.

3 Van Horn, J. D., Irimia, A., Torgerson, C. M., Chambers, M. C., Kikinis, R., & Toga, A. W. (2012). Mapping connectivity damage in the case of Phineas Gage. *PloS One*, 7(5), e37454.

4 Horne, J. (2011). Looking back: Blasts from the past. *The Psychologist*, 21, 622–623.

5 Code, C. (2013). Did Leborgne have one or two speech automatisms? *Journal of the History of the Neurosciences*, 22(3), 319–320.

6 Domanski, C. W. (2014). Post scriptum to the biography of *Monsieur Leborgne. Journal of the History of the Neurosciences*, 23(1), 75–77.

7 Finger, S. (2005). *Minds Behind the Brain: A History of the Pioneers and their Discoveries*. Oxford University Press.

8 Manning, L., & Thomas-Antérion, C. (2011). Marc Dax and the discovery of the lateralisation of language in the left cerebral hemisphere. *Revue neurologique*, 167(12), 868–872.

9 Domanski, C. W. (2013). Mysterious "Monsieur Leborgne": The mystery of the famous patient in the history of neuropsychology is explained. *Journal of the History of the Neurosciences*, 22(1), 47–52; Domanski, C. W. (2014). Post scriptum to the biography of *Monsieur Leborgne. Journal of the History of the Neurosciences*, 23(1), 75–77.

10 Dronkers, N. F., Plaisant, O., Iba-Zizen, M. T., & Cabanis, E. A. (2007). Paul Broca's historic cases: high resolution MR imaging of the brains of Leborgne and Lelong. *Brain*, 130(5), 1432–1441.

11 Plaza, M., Gatignol, P., Leroy, M., & Duffau, H. (2009). Speaking without Broca's area after tumor resection. *Neurocase*, 15(4), 294–310.

12 Danelli, L., Cossu, G., Berlingeri, M., Bottini, G., Sberna, M., & Paulesu, E. (2013). Is a lone right hemisphere enough? Neurolinguistic architecture in a case with a very early left hemispherectomy. *Neurocase*, 19(3), 209–231.

13 Bateman, F. (1868). *On Aphasia, or Loss of Speech in Cerebral Disease*. GP Bacon.

14 Schiller, F. (1992). *Paul Broca: Founder of French Anthropology: Explorer of the Brain*. Oxford University Press.

15 Lashley, K. S., & Franz, S. I. (1917). The effects of cerebral destruction upon habit-formation and retention in the albino rat. *Psychobiology*, 1(2), 71.

16 Scoville, W. B., & Milner, B. (1957). Loss of recent memory after bilateral hippocampal lesions. *Journal of Neurology, Neurosurgery, and Psychiatry*, 20(1), 11.

17 http://thebrainobservatory.ucsd.edu/hm (accessed May 13, 2014).
18 Watts, G. (2009). Henry Gustav Molaison, "HM." *The Lancet*, 373(9662), 456.
19 Aggleton, J. (2013). Understanding amnesia – Is it time to forget HM? *The Psychologist*, 26, 612–615.
20 Annese, J., Schenker-Ahmed, N. M., Bartsch, H., Maechler, P., Sheh, C., Thomas, N., ... & Corkin, S. (2014). Postmortem examination of patient H.M.'s brain based on histological sectioning and digital 3D reconstruction. *Nature Communications*, 5(3122). doi: 10.1038/ncomms4122.

4 THE IMMORTAL MYTHS

Some myths run out of steam, go out of fashion, or exist only on the fringes of popular belief. But others show remarkable zombie-like endurance, managing to march on through mounting contradictory evidence. It's these stubborn and popular beliefs that are often picked up by self-appointed gurus or evangelists looking to bolster their quack courses or misguided campaigns. The staying power of some of these classic myths is also helped along by their seductive appeal – they extol facts that would be great news if only they were true. This chapter is about 10 Teflon brain myths (or themes), from the old chestnut that we only use 10 percent of our brains, to the fallacy that pregnant women's brains go haywire just when they need to be at their most prepared.

Myth #11

We Only Use Ten Percent of Our Brains

This is the immortal idea that most of us get by using just a small fraction of our brains, leaving the bulk of our cerebral potential massively untapped. The supposed amount of our gray matter that we squander has gone up and down over the decades, but 90 percent is the most popular claim.

It's easy to see the appeal. Who wouldn't want to believe that they have vast reserves of latent brain power just waiting to be unlocked? "You know how they say that we can only access twenty percent of our brains," says a character in the 2011 hit movie *Limitless* "this [pill] lets you access all of it." With the help of the magic drug, the film's protagonist played by Bradley Cooper writes his overdue novel in days, picks up foreign languages overnight and makes millions on the stock market.

Similarly, in 2014, came *Lucy*, starring Scarlett Johansson as a woman injected with a powerful drug. "The average person uses 10% of their brain capacity," says the movie poster, "imagine what she could do with 100%." A lot apparently, including mastering all knowledge and hurling cars with her mind. "I'm not sure that mankind is ready for it," says the film's fictional neuroscientist – an impressively straight-faced Morgan Freeman.

Advertisers have also played their part in spreading the myth. On his Neuroscience for Kids website,[1] Eric Chudler has gathered together several examples of the myth being invoked to flatter and entice potential customers, including an airline that boasted: "It's been said that we use a mere 10% of our brain capacity. If, however, you're flying **** from **** Airlines, you're using considerably more."

According to Christopher Wanjek, author of a book about misconceptions in medicine,[2] the use of the myth in advertising dates back as far as 1944 with claims by the Pelman Institute, the London-based purveyors of self-improvement correspondence courses. "What's holding you back?" their newspaper advert said, "Just one fact – one scientific fact ... Because as Science says, you are only using one-tenth of your real brain-power!"

Modern surveys show the continuing prevalence of people's belief in the 10 percent myth, including among those meant to be imparting their wisdom to the next generation. For a survey published in 2012, Sanne Dekker and her colleagues quizzed 137 primary and secondary school teachers in England and 105 from the Netherlands.[3] Forty-eight percent of the English sample believed wrongly that we use just 10 percent of our brains (26 percent said they didn't know) and 46 percent of the Dutch sample believed the myth, with 12 percent saying they didn't know.

Belief in the myth can be found right across the world. In 2002, Suzana Herculano-Houzel of the Museum of Life in Rio de Janeiro conducted a survey of over 2000 members of the public and, focusing on just those with a college-education, found that 59 percent believed that we use only 10 percent of our brains.[4] Somewhat worryingly, a comparison sample of 35 international neuroscientists showed that 6 percent of them also thought the 10 percent myth was true!

Background to the Myth

So where does it come from, this idea that we have vast swathes of gray matter lying dormant? When the late psychologist and myth-buster Barry

Beyerstein attempted to hunt down the source of the myth he found multiple culpable candidates rather than a single smoking gun. He also discovered many of these leads were based on misinformation and misquotes.[5]

Early in the twentieth century, the pioneering psychologist William James wrote and spoke about the idea that people have "latent mental energy," although he didn't put a precise figure on it.[6] Note that James's point was about energy and potential, not how much of our brains we use. This confusion likely helps explain the longevity of the 10 percent myth – it can mean different things to different people, and the claim that we have untapped potential is far less contentious than the specific idea that we only use a small fraction of our brains.

Unfortunately, the first claim easily morphs into the second. The journalist Lowell Thomas aided this process in his preface to Dale Carnegie's classic mega-selling 1936 self-help book *How to Win Friends and Influence People*, where he attached the precise 10 percent figure to James's point about potential, writing: "Professor William James of Harvard used to say that the average person develops only 10 percent of his latent mental ability." In doing this Thomas exposed millions of readers to an early version of this brain myth.

Another possible source is a quote attributed to Albert Einstein. He supposedly explained to a reporter that the secret to his genius was that he used the full capacity of his brain, rather than the mere 10 percent that the rest of us use. However, when Beyerstein called on the experts at the Albert Einstein Archives to find this quote, they were unable to locate it, so this is probably yet another apocryphal story.

Also fueling the 10 percent myth are misinterpretations of neuroscience research. For example, in the 1930s the Canadian neurosurgeon Wilder Penfield found that he could provoke various sensations in epilepsy patients by directly stimulating the surface of their brains (the opportunity to do this arose during surgery to help alleviate their seizures). Crucially, Penfield also found that zapping some areas had no effect, leading to the notion that there are large areas of "silent cortex." Today these regions of tissue are known as "association cortex" and they are in fact involved in our most sophisticated mental functions. Ill-founded medical claims in the last century that lobotomy patients were cured without ill effects further indulged this idea that large chunks of the brain are functionally useless. There's also the common-place but mistaken estimate that neurons are outnumbered by glial cells by ten to one, which could be misinterpreted as meaning that just 10 percent of all our brain cells are involved in mental functions (glial cells are a kind of brain cell involved in various functions including clearing debris and controlling blood flow; see p. 149 for more information).

Finally, there are case reports, such as of patients with hydrocephalus (excess fluid in their brains), who have smaller than normal brains, but appear to function without any difficulty. And there are numerous accounts of people surviving bullet wounds to the head, or other cerebral injuries, sometimes with little obvious impairment (in fact, serious brain injury always has long-lasting consequences, see p. 260). The apparent implication of such cases was stated most provocatively in a 1980 paper in *Science* "Is your brain really necessary?"[7] in which the late British neurologist John Lorber is quoted describing a young student at his university with hydrocephalus "who has an IQ of 126, has gained a first-class honors degree in mathematics, and is socially completely normal. And yet the boy has virtually no brain."

A UK television documentary with the same title aired in 1991 and featured Lorber making the same claims based on several of his patients. According to Beyerstein, Lorber was known at the time for making controversial pronouncements, and it's likely the cases were exaggerated for dramatic effect. The scans used in the documentary don't allow one to distinguish between compression of cortex and actual loss of brain cells. Beyerstein's view was that it's untrue that the documented cases had "virtually no brain" above the brainstem, although their cortex was clearly deformed.

The Reality

How much of our brains do we really use? The truth is that we use all of them: there is no spare neural matter lying around waiting to be given a job to do. This has been confirmed by thousands of brain scans, in which waves of activity can be seen coursing through the entire brain, even when participants are asked to think of nothing. In fact, there's an entire network of areas – dubbed the "default mode network" – that becomes more active when people do their best to disengage from the outside world.

Other evidence that refutes the 10 percent myth comes from studies of brain-damaged patients for whom even the smallest lesion can have devastating consequences (see p. 258). Over time, it's true the brain does have a remarkable capacity to adapt to damage. In fact it's this plasticity that explains the hydrocephalus cases reported by Lorber in his documentary and in the journal *Science*. Slowly developing conditions like hydrocephalus allow the brain to find new ways to function. But just because the brain can find ways to work around lost neurons doesn't mean that those neurons weren't doing something in the first place.

In fact, if any neurons do end up out of work – for example, say the limb that they received sensory signals from is lost – what happens is that hungry neighboring brain systems will invade and hijack that redundant brain matter. This can give rise to the strange situation where touching an amputee on their face triggers sensations in their missing "phantom" limb – precisely because the face neurons have hijacked the gray matter that used to represent the limb.

The idea that we use only a small fraction of our brains also makes no sense from an evolutionary point of view. The brain is a notorious gas guzzler, accounting for 20 percent of our energy consumption even though it only makes up two percent of our body mass. Evolution by natural selection tends to weed out the inefficient so it's implausible that we would have such a costly organ that's mostly redundant. Imagine a company in which most of the staff sat around doing nothing – they'd be fired. It's the same with our brain cells. Do we have huge potential to learn new skills and recover from injury? Definitely. Do we only use 10 percent of our brains? No way.

Myth #12

Right-Brained People Are More Creative

"Are you a righty or a lefty?" asks the promotional blurb for the "Left Brain Right Brain" game, marketed by entertainment giant Nintendo. "What if you could be both?" it adds, before claiming that it will help you train, not one, but both your brain hemispheres!

With this game, Nintendo, rather shrewdly, was targeting several popular ideas that have melded together to form the left brain, right brain myth. These are: the notion that the two sides of the human brain have different strengths (the left rational, the right creative); that some people are dominated by one side more than the other; that the two sides don't communicate well; and that it can be tricky (without special brain training) to develop the strengths of both hemispheres. There is certainly a grain of truth to these ideas, but it's one that's often buried in a mound of hype and oversimplification.

The myth offers up numerous opportunities for exploitation by self-enhancement gurus. They promise to help you access talents locked up in your non-dominant hemisphere (usually presumed to be the supposedly more creative right brain), or they say they'll get your two brain halves communicating better. Other "experts" have diagnosed problems in the business world in terms of the two brain hemispheres. In *War in the Boardroom: Why Left-Brain Management and Right-Brain Marketing Don't See Eye-to-Eye*,[8] typical of the genre, the authors explain that the secret to business success is helping a company's right-brainers and left-brainers to speak the same language.

The myth has also been linked with gender differences. "Men are typically very left brained," the Christian Working Woman website states,[9] adding with confidence: "Women tend to be more right brained, but we have a bridge between the right and left brain that men do not have." The topic of supposed brain-based gender differences is a myth of its own that we'll examine in more detail on p. 65, but suffice to say that the picture painted by the Christian Working Women is an inaccurate oversimplification.

Part of the explanation for this myth's stubborn appeal is that the idea of a focused, rational left brain and broad-minded, creative right brain has taken on an incredible metaphorical power. The thinking style of one hemisphere is sometimes attributed, not only to particular types of company personnel, but to entire languages and religions. Take the example of Britain's Chief Rabbi Jonathan Sacks talking on Radio 4 in the spring of 2012. "What made Europe happen and made it so creative," he explained, "is that Christianity was a right-brain religion ... translated into a left-brain language, because all the early Christian texts are in Greek."

The myth found its most effective champion to date in psychiatrist Iain McGilchrist, author of the exhaustively detailed and scholarly book *The Master and His Emissary*, first published to critical acclaim in 2009.[10] Through 534 pages of meticulous but ultimately misguided argument, McGilchrist takes the myth to the extreme, personifying the two brain hemispheres and claiming that it is the West's shift to the atomistic, decontextualized thinking style of the left hemisphere (the "emissary") and away from big-picture holistic right-hemisphere thinking that has led to numerous societal problems in the Western world, from the financial crash to environmental catastrophe. "East Asian cultures use both hemispheres more evenly," writes McGilcrist, "while Western strategies are steeply skewed toward the left hemisphere."

Background to the Myth

It's true the cortex of the human brain does look like two mirror-image halves fitted together. And a deeper inspection with a surgeon's scalpel reveals that the main structural features of each half are repeated on the other. It's also true that in humans and many other animals the two hemispheres of the brain don't function in identical fashion.

This became increasingly obvious in the nineteenth century, starting with the French neurologist Marc Dax's observation that all his patients who'd lost their powers of speech had damage to the left-hand side of their brain. This idea that language is left-lateralized (i.e. controlled mostly by the left brain hemisphere) was groundbreaking but it went largely unnoticed until Dax's son published his father's paper in 1865.[11] Dax junior was moved to do so after witnessing Broca's seminal presentation about his brain-damaged patient Leborgne (see also pp. 40–45).

There was intense interest in the lateralization of other functions after the discoveries of Dax, Broca, and their contemporaries. With language seemingly dominated by the left hemisphere, experts began to speculate about the functional specialization of the right. The English neurologist John Hughlings Jackson proposed that the right side is for perception, whereas the French neurologist Jules Bernard Luys made the case for the emotions being localized to the primitive right, with the intellect being the preserve of the civilized left. Around the same time, and pre-empting the self-help gurus of the late twentieth and early twenty-first centuries, individuals richer in enterprise than scientific integrity began to offer brain-based therapies, such as the placing of metal discs and magnets onto the surface of the body ("metallotherapy"). Such techniques purported to target one or other hemisphere, thus bringing supposed benefits to personality or mental function.[12]

With the dawn of the twentieth century, the whole left-brain right-brain obsession went relatively quiet until the 1960s, when researchers began conducting dramatic psychological experiments with split-brain patients. These were people who'd had the chunky bundle of fibers between their hemispheres (the corpus callosum) cut as a last-resort treatment for epilepsy. The findings were a revelation and earned a Nobel Prize for the lead scientist involved in the early research, the US neuropsychologist Roger Sperry.

By asking the patients to stare straight ahead, and then presenting an image on just one side of this midpoint, the researchers were able to show that the two halves of the separated brain act independently and in accordance with their respective functional strengths. For example, presented with a picture of an apple on the left-hand side of space (processed by the right hemisphere because the optic nerve crosses to the opposite side of the brain), a split-brain patient wouldn't be able to say what the picture depicted. That's because, in most people, the power of speech lies in the left hemisphere. However, if a bag of objects were placed within reach of the patient's left hand (controlled by the right hemisphere), he'd reach in and pick out the apple, indicating that he'd seen the earlier picture, but just couldn't name it. So long as the apple were kept out of sight of the left hemisphere, the patient could be holding the apple, but at the same time unable to tell you what he was holding!

Using studies like these, presenting information to just one brain hemisphere or the other, the researchers were able to document the respective strengths and weaknesses of the two sides of the brain. For example, as well as being dominant for language processing, the left hemisphere is also usually more proficient at problem solving. It's also more prone to false memories and to "filling in" missing information. The right hemisphere, by contrast, seems to be more involved in processing morality, emotions, and representing other people's mental states (what psychologists call "theory of mind").

Correcting the Myth

The two brain hemispheres clearly are different. However, neuroscience has moved on from ascribing particular functions to one hemisphere or the other. The emphasis has shifted instead to styles of processing and figuring out how the hemispheres work together. This latter point is important to emphasize because, unlike the hemispheres of split-brain patients, our two brain halves are well connected by a massive bundle of fibers, the corpus callosum, which the fictional doctor Gregory House called aptly "the George Washington Bridge of the brain" (there are also other, less significant connections). This means information and cognitive duties are shared between the hemispheres working in a cooperative style.

We probably evolved these functional asymmetries in our brain processing because it makes multitasking easier. Supporting this hypothesis, a study with chicks showed that preventing hemispheric specialization in their brains (by raising them in the dark) meant they, unlike their healthy siblings, were unable to search for food and look out for a predator at the same time.[13]

Regarding the distinctive processing styles of the human brain hemispheres, a particularly pertinent imaging paper was published in 2003 by Klaas Stephan and his colleagues at the Institute of Medicine in Germany and the Institute of Neurology in London.[14] They used the same stimuli throughout but varied the task instructions. The stimuli were 4-letter German nouns, with three letters in black and one in red. When the task was to say whether each word contained an "A," it was mainly the left hemisphere that was activated. Conversely, when the task was to say whether the single red letter was located to the left or right of the center of each word, it was mainly the right hemisphere that was activated. This study was important because it showed that the engagement of the two hemispheres varies strategically according to what we're doing, not according to the stimuli placed in front of us.

Nevertheless, exactly how to describe and categorize the processing styles of the two hemispheres isn't always clear cut, and that's important to note because it means their relative strengths don't necessarily map onto the simple constructs – such as "creative vs. logical" – bandied around by pop psychologists. Consider research by Gereon Fink, now at the Ruhr-Universität, the late psychologist John Marshall, and others.[15] In one study they presented participants with a large letter made up of little letters. Asking them to focus on the large letter led to extra activation in the right hemisphere, whereas asking them to focus on the little letters led to greater activation in the left hemisphere. It sounded like a neat dissociation between focusing on the big picture versus focusing on the details, but then they repeated the task using tiny images of an object – for example, cups – formed into the shape of a larger object, such as an anchor. Now the results were reversed – focusing on the bigger object activated the left hemisphere!

Taken together, it seems the kinds of task that activate one hemisphere more than the other is far from being straightforward. It's a similar story of complexity even for language, which as we've seen is nearly always dominated by the left hemisphere. Although speech is largely the preserve of the left hemisphere, we now know that the right usually has some language capabilities of its own, for example, in relation to perceiving intonation and emphasis in speech.

Let's turn now to look at the left brain, right brain myth in relation to creativity, since one of the most popular ideas seems to be that the right brain is the hub of the imagination and that "right-brained" people are more creative. Supporting the myth, one study found that activity was greater in the right hemisphere when participants solved a task via insight, rather than piecemeal. Another showed that brief exposure to a puzzle clue was more useful to the right hemisphere, than the left, as if the right hemisphere were nearer the answer.[16]

But insight is just one type of creativity. Telling stories is another. One of the most fascinating insights from the split-brain studies was the way the left hemisphere made up stories to explain what the right hemisphere was up to – what's known as the "interpreter phenomenon" (see Plate 16). In a typical study, Michael Gazzaniga, a student of Sperry's who would go on to study these patients for decades, began by presenting each half of a patient's brain with a different picture – say a snow storm to the right hemisphere and a bird's foot to the left. Next, four further picture cards were made available to each hand and the patient had to choose with each hand which one card from each set matched the original pictures.

The patient's left hand (controlled by the right hemisphere) chose a shovel, which correctly matched a snow storm; their right hand chose a chicken, which matched the bird foot. So far so good. But then Gazzaniga asked the patient why their left hand had chosen a shovel. Remember, only the left hemisphere had the capacity for speech and it had no access to the right hemisphere's decision making, nor could it see the snow storm picture. What Gazzaniga found was that the left hemisphere, rather than claiming ignorance, would make up stories to account for the behavior of the right hemisphere-controlled left hand. In our particular example, the patient said he'd chosen the shovel to clear out the chicken shed.

The interpreter effect shows us that it's simplistic to characterize the left hemisphere as incapable of creativity. In fact, when he reviewed decades of split-brain research in a 2002 article for *Scientific American*, Gazzaniga characterized the left hemisphere as "inventive and interpreting," compared with the "truthful, literal right brain."[17] This seems at odds with the myth invoked by Rabbi Sacks and many others.

What about the popular claim that some of us are right-brained and some of us are left-brained? This notion is so vague as to be virtually meaningless. We all use our left or right brain hemispheres to different degrees depending on what mental activities we're currently engaged in. I might be more right hemisphere dependent than you on one kind of task, but the opposite could be true for another. Of course, it's true that most of us differ consistently in which hand we prefer to use, and this in turn is related to the likelihood that our language faculty is largely supported by our left or right hemisphere. But if we take handedness as the most obvious measure of a person's hemispheric dominance then the left-brain, right-brain myth would suggest that left-handers (with a dominant right hemisphere) ought to be more creative. In fact, many have claimed a link between left-handedness and creativity. But alas, this is yet another myth (see box on p. 62).

A particularly pertinent paper was published in 2013, from a team led by Jared Nielsen at the University of Utah.[18] They examined functional brain scans taken of over a thousand people as they rested in the scanner. The researchers were interested in the connections between hubs of brain activity and whether they were localized to one brain hemisphere or the other. They indeed found distinct functional hubs that tended in most participants to be lateralized to just one brain hemisphere – for example (and not surprisingly), language functions were often localized to the left, attentional functions to the right. But crucially for our purposes, they found no evidence that some people have better connected left-sided or right-sided hubs than others. "[W]e just do not see patterns where the whole left-brain network is more connected or the whole right-brain network is more connected in some people," Nielsen explained to the press at the time.[19]

Finally, we should examine the extreme claims of Iain McGilchrist, including his suggestion that the left hemisphere "does not understand things," "jumps to conclusions," "is narcissistic," and that its purpose is to "use the world." In fact, he writes, it "sees everything – education, art, morality, the natural world – in terms of a utilitarian calculus only." Furthermore, because we in the Western world rely too much on left-hemisphere thinking, McGilchrist warns that we are "the least perceptive, most dangerous people that have ever lived."[20]

Needless to say, the neuroscience evidence does not support this far-fetched personification of the left hemisphere. Nor is there any evidence that changes in the brain have *caused* any of the Western world's travails. Though he denies it, McGilchrist's central thesis is really no more than an extended metaphor that links different philosophical approaches to the West and East and then to the functions of the two brain hemispheres. Unfortunately, not only does he overreach the neuroscience, he's also been criticized for spreading the "dubious notion" that there is a fundamental distinction and opposition in Eastern and Western ways of thinking. "McGilchrist has taken a long-standing dubious argument about cultural differences and modernized it by locating it in the brain," writes Kenan Malik. "Doing so has not made a dubious argument any less dubious."[21]

The myth of the creative right brain is likely to live on for a while yet. In fact the latest version of The Faces iMake – Right Brain Creativity app for the iPad – "an extraordinary tool for developing right brain creative capabilities" – is available for download right now! The logical left-brain, creative right-brain myth has a seductive simplicity about it. People can ask – which kind of brain have I got? They can buy an app to target their weaker half. They can categorize languages and people as right-brained or left. It's tricky to combat that belief system by saying the truth is really more complicated. But it's worth trying, because it would be a shame if the simplistic myth drowned out the more fascinating story of how our brains really work.

Myths and Facts about Lefties

It is a curious quirk of human nature that most of us prefer using our right hand, while a minority of around 10 percent prefer using their left – a ratio that has remained relatively stable throughout human history. Experts remain unsure of how handedness emerges in a developing child, and they struggle to explain the persistence of the ratio of right- to left-handers. Against this backdrop, a number of cultural myths have grown up around the differences between left- and right-handers. Let me debunk an immediate misnomer. There really is no such thing as strict left- or right-handedness. Most people can do something with their weaker hand. A more important distinction might be the strength of preference we have for one hand, be it left or right (researchers use the term "mixed-handedness" for a lack of preference).

Myth: Left-handers Are More Introverted, Intelligent, and Creative

There are anecdotal accounts of artists and musicians tending to be left-handed, an observation given wings by the overly simplistic notion that the right hemisphere (which controls the left hand) is the seat of creativity. Advocates point to Leonardo de Vinci, a leftie, Paul McCartney, another leftie, and many more. But as psychologist Chris McManus explains in his award-winning book *Right Hand Left Hand*, "although there are recurrent claims of increased creativity in left-handers, there is very little to support the idea in the scientific literature."[22] Regarding lefties having an introverted personality, a paper published in 2013[23] surveyed 662 New Zealand undergraduates about their handedness and personality. "Left- and right-handers did not differ on any personality factor," the researchers reported. However, there was a tendency for people with a weaker preference for either hand (i.e. the mixed-handed) to be more introverted. What about IQ? One massive study found no link with handedness; another found a slight IQ advantage for right-handers (put both studies together and any intelligence/handedness link is negligible).

Fact: Left-Handers Are Less Likely to Be Left-Hemisphere Dominant for Language

In the vast majority of the population, language function is nearly always localized to the left hemisphere. This is why a stroke or other brain injury suffered to the left side of the brain tends to lead to language problems. Among right-handers, left-sided dominance for language approaches upwards of 95 percent prevalence. However, among left-handed people this drops to 70 percent, with the others either having language localized to the right hemisphere, or spread evenly across both hemispheres.

Myth: Left-Handed People Die Earlier and Suffer More Immune Diseases

The early death myth originates with a 1988 *Nature* paper by Diane Halpern and Stanley Coren, "Do Right-Handers Live Longer?"[24] The psychologists analyzed death records for baseball players and found that those who were left-handed had died younger. But as Chris McManus explains, this is a statistical artifact borne by the fact that left-handedness increased through the twentieth century, meaning that left-handers, on average, were born later in that century. As an analogy, McManus points to Harry Potter fans who tend to be younger than nonfans. "Ask the relatives of a group of recently deceased people whether their loved one had read Harry Potter and inevitably one will find a younger age at death in Harry Potter enthusiasts," he writes, "but that is only because HP readers are younger overall." If this statistical argument makes your head spin, let me offer you the straightforward conclusion from a 1994 study of longevity in cricketers: "Left handedness is not, in general, associated with an increase in mortality," the researchers said.[25] A related myth, propagated by Norman Geschwind, is that left-handers are more vulnerable to immune disorders.[26] McManus and Phil Bryden analyzed data from 89 studies involving over 21 000 patients and an even greater number of controls:[27] "Left-handers showed no systematic tendency to suffer from disorders of the immune system," McManus writes in his book.

Fact: We Get More Mixed-Handed As We Get Older

For a 2007 study Tobias Kalisch and his colleagues recruited 60 participants who were all strongly right-handed and tested them on a range of awkward manual tasks, including: line tracing, aiming, and tapping.[28] Whereas the younger participants (average age 25 years) performed far better with their right hand on all tests, the middle-aged (average age 50) right-handers performed just as well with either hand on the aiming task. And two older groups (average age 70 and 80 years) performed just as well with either hand on all tasks bar one. Unfortunately, the main reason for the older participants' greater ambidexterity was the fact they'd lost their superior performance with their right hand.

Myth: Left-Handers Are Persecuted

Reviewing a recent book on left-handers (Rik Smits's *The Puzzle of Left Handedness*), a *The Guardian* critic observed:[29] "Sadly, prejudice against left-handedness is deep-rooted and universal." Is it? There's no doubt that left-handers have had a rough time in the past. Many were forced to use their right hand, and across many cultures there's a deep bias toward right being good and left bad. Consider expressions like "right-hand man," "two left feet"; that the word "sinister" comes from the Latin for "left"; and the fact that Muslims use their right hand for eating and their left hand for ablutions. However, in Western cultures at least, the persecution of lefties appears to be over. Look at the fact that five out of the last seven US presidents have been left-handed. If life is so tough for lefties, you'd hardly expect them to reach the most powerful position in the world so frequently. Okay, that's largely conjecture, but what about the 2013 study I mentioned earlier,[30] which also involved over a hundred New Zealand students rating the personality of a typical left- or right-hander. Their belief was that left-handers tend to be more introverted and open to experience. As the authors wrote, this "artistic" stereotype "can hardly be considered negative." They added: "We found no evidence that left-handers are a stigmatized minority in our young Western population."

Fact: Lefties Have an Advantage In Many Sports

Left-handers are disadvantaged in some sports because of the safety rules – for example, in polo, the mallet must be held on the right-hand side of the horse. However, in sports where opponents compete against each other directly, face-to-face, such as boxing or tennis, the left-hander has a distinct advantage. Stated simply, they are more used to facing right-handed opponents (which the majority of their rivals will be) than right-handers are used to facing left-handers. Indeed, one evolutionary account for why left-handedness has survived is that it confers a fighting advantage – the so-called "fighting hypothesis."[31] There are many studies in the literature that have demonstrated left-handers tend to win more often on average than do right-handers in sports like boxing[32] and fencing.[33] Oh, in case you were wondering, one last thing: left-handers tend to perform better at various tasks with their right hand than right-handers do with their left.

Myth #13 The Female Brain Is More Balanced (and Other Gender-Based Brain Myths)

There are some structural differences in the brains of men and women – let's get that clear right away (see Plate 17). However, many self-appointed experts in this area mix up true brain differences with entirely fictitious ones, or they continue to endorse sex differences that used to be recognized by neuroscience, but which have since been shown to be spurious. Worse still, these mythmakers often link purported brain differences between the sexes with behavioral differences in ways that are entirely unsupported by evidence. And in some cases they use this specious logic to advocate particular policies or politics.

Myth: Women's Brain Functioning Is More Balanced and Global

Take the example of John Gray, author of the mega-selling book *Men Are From Mars, Women Are From Venus*. In his later 2008 effort *Why Mars and Venus Collide*, he explains how men's brains use "a specific part of a single hemisphere to accomplish a task." Women, by contrast, he says use "both hemispheres for many tasks." Gray then extrapolates from this purported brain difference to explain the supposed fact that men tend to think about one thing at a time: "he may be focusing on how to get that promotion, so he forgets to bring home the milk."

The myth invoked by Gray, that activity in men's brains is more localized and one-sided, is widespread, quoted by countless writers online and in print. After a ten-second search on Google, here's an article I found on gender differences from the popular Canadian website Suite 101: "It is true," the author says with misplaced confidence, "that men use one side of their brain to listen while women use both sides."[34]

One source of this myth is a theory proposed by the late US neurologist Norman Geschwind and his collaborators in the 1980s[35] that higher testosterone levels in the womb mean the left hemisphere of male babies develops more slowly than in females, and that it ends up more cramped. But the Geschwind claim is not true: John Gilmore and his team at the University of North Carolina scanned the brains of 74 newborns and found no evidence for smaller left hemispheres in male babies compared with females.[36] Also debunking the idea of greater lateralization in male brains, a meta-analysis by Iris Sommer and her colleagues at the University Medical Center, Utrecht, of 14 studies, involving 377 men and 442 women, found no evidence of differences in language lateralization (its allocation to one hemisphere or the other) between the sexes.[37]

A related idea is that women have a thicker corpus callosum than men – that's the bridge that connects the two brain hemispheres. Were it true, presumably having a thicker callosum would help women use both sides of their brain more efficiently than men. On this issue, Mikkel Wallentin at the University of Aarhus reviewed the evidence in a 2009 paper, drawing on both postmortem and brain-imaging studies. His conclusion? "The alleged sex-related corpus callosum size difference is a myth," he wrote.[38] A 2012 diffusion tensor paper actually found "stronger inter-hemispheric connectivity between the frontal lobes in males than females."[39]

Myth: Women Have Hyperactive Mirror Neurons

There is modest evidence that women are better at processing emotions than men – for example, a 2010 study by researchers in Canada and Belgium found that women were better than men at categorizing facial expressions of fear and disgust, whether presented visually or aurally.[40] However, many pop-psychology authors embellish the situation and speculate wildly about the brain-basis for the female emotional advantage. Chief culprit in this regard is Louann Brizendine, author of *The Female Brain* published in 2006. Brizendine claims that women are especially good at emotional mirroring, that they have heightened sensitivity to other people's pain, and she speculates that this may be because women have more mirror neurons, or more active mirror neurons (see also p. 154). These are the brain cells, first discovered in nonhuman primates, that are activated both when an animal performs an action and when it observes someone else performing that same action.

Cordelia Fine, the author of *Delusions of Gender, The Real Science Behind Sex Differences*,[41] devotes several pages of her book to debunking Brizendine's claims. One of the brain-imaging studies that Brizendine cited to show women's heightened empathy in fact only involved women – there was no comparison with men![42] Another[43] showed that men only showed empathy-related brain activity to a person's pain if they thought that person had played fairly in a game. Women were less discerning in their empathy, showing feeling for people regardless of whether they'd played fairly. But Brizendine went further, interpreting this study as showing that empathy responses were entirely lacking in the men.

When it comes to the claim about mirror neurons, Fine reviews the literature and finds there is no evidence showing that mirror neurons are more plentiful or more active in the brains of women compared with men. On this point Brizendine cited as evidence a personal communication with a Harvard-based psychologist – Lindsay Oberman. But Fine contacted Oberman and she denied ever having any communication with Brizendine and, moreover, said she knew of no evidence for better mirror neuron functioning in women!

Myth: Men's and Women's Brains Are Wired Up Differently

Many sections of the media, and some scientists, seem desperate to find new neuroscientific evidence to back up old stereotypes about the sexes. This appears to cloud their judgment, so that when new evidence comes in, it's interpreted in a superficial and biased way, so as to reinforce old ideas about gender.

This is what happened late in 2013 when a brain wiring study was published in the respected journal *PNAS*.[44] The researchers led by Ragini Verma at the University of Pennsylvania used diffusion tensor imaging to plot the brain wiring maps of 949 people aged 8 to 22, and they claimed to have found that men's and women's brains really are wired differently. They said their results revealed "fundamentally different connectivity patterns in males and females."

Specifically, they reported that men's brains had more connectivity within each brain hemisphere, whereas women's brains had more connectivity across the two hemispheres. Moreover, they stated or implied, in their paper and in statements to the press, that these findings help explain behavioral differences between the sexes, such as that women are intuitive thinkers and good at multitasking whereas men are good at sports and map reading. I bet John Gray couldn't contain his excitement.

The world's media lapped up this new research. "The connections that mean girls are made for multi-tasking," said the *Daily Mail*. "… hard-wired difference between male and female brains could explain why men are 'better at map reading,'" announced *The Independent*.

The technical wizardry involved in this research was certainly impressive. But unfortunately, the researchers and the subsequent press coverage got a lot of things in a tangle. First, the differences in brain wiring between the sexes were not as noteworthy as the researchers implied. They said they were "fundamental," but other experts crunched the numbers[45] and they stated that although the differences were statistically significant, they were actually not substantive. Remember too, these are average differences with a lot of overlap. It's possible that my male brain is wired more like an average female brain than yours, even if you're a woman.

Second, despite the impression given by the misleading media coverage, this paper did not in fact look at behavioral differences between the sexes – things like intuitive thinking and multitasking. The researchers were only guessing about this. In earlier research they had tested the same sample on various tasks, but as Cordelia Fine has pointed out, the sex differences they found were "trivially small" and they didn't look at the kind of activities being cited in the media for this study, such as map reading.

The way Verma and her colleagues arrived at the idea that their results support gender stereotypes about map reading, and so on, is via a logical mistake known as "reverse inference" (more on this error on p. 181). They looked at where in the brain they found wiring differences and then made assumptions about the functional meaning of those differences based on what other studies have suggested those brain regions are for. For example, they dredged up the left brain/right brain myth (see p. 55) by implying that the left-brain hemisphere is for analytical thought and the right hemisphere for intuition. The one brain region where they claimed men had more cross-hemisphere interconnectivity than women – the cerebellum – the researchers linked purely with motor function, which they said supports the idea that men are wired for action. Yet modern research has shown that the cerebellum is involved in lots of other functions too. Writing an authoritative review in 2009, Peter Strick and his colleagues explained: "The range of tasks associated with cerebellar activation is remarkable and includes tasks designed to assess attention, executive control, language, working memory, learning, pain, emotion, and addiction."[46]

Of course, it's also important to interpret any new research in the context of previous findings. Verma and her team admitted that a previous paper looking at the brain wiring of 439 participants failed to find significant differences between the sexes. And we know that there are those prior studies on the corpus callosum (see p. 66). This is the main communication channel between the hemispheres, so if women have more connectivity between their hemispheres as claimed by Verma and colleagues, we'd expect consistent evidence for them having a thicker corpus callosum – yet some studies have found the opposite. Reporting on this brain wiring study for my WIRED blog, this was my summary: "Wow, those are some pretty wiring diagrams! Oh … shame about the way [the researchers] interpreted them."

Myth: Girls Have a Larger Crockus Than Boys

Nevermind hyped studies and biased interpretations, the claims of some charlatans in this area have no scientific basis at all. One American educational speaker has reportedly[47] been touring the country telling audiences that the ability of girls to "see the details of experiences" (quoted from one of his slides) is linked to their having a "crockus" that's four times larger than in boys – an astonishing claim given that the crockus is an entirely imaginary brain area!

Mark Liberman, a linguistics professor at the University of Pennsylvania, detailed the crockus incident on his Language Log blog in 2007, including investigating the real evidence for gender differences in the approximate region that the speaker seemed to be talking about – the left frontal lobe. Liberman cites a 2004 study[48] by Rebecca Blanton and colleagues at the UCLA School of Medicine, in which they performed structural brain scans of 25 girls and 21 boys. Contrary to the crockus individual's claims, this comparison turned up the finding that the left inferior frontal gyrus (an area that looked similar to the "crockus" as depicted on the speaker's slides) was actually significantly larger in boys, although there was a lot of overlap between the sexes.

This is an opportune moment to emphasize again an important point about gender brain differences. Even though there are often average differences between the sexes, there is no straightforward way to extrapolate from these brain differences to behavioral differences. We should therefore treat with extreme skepticism those evangelists who argue for gendered educational practices based on their misinterpretation of, and unfounded extrapolation from, brain findings.

One such person is Leonard Sax, a psychologist who ran the organization that used to be known as the National Association for Single Sex Public Education. In his writings, Sax argues for girls and boys to be taught differently based on the differences in their brains. To take one example, he argues that in boys, the amygdala (a sub-cortical region involved in emotional processing) develops connections with the cerebral cortex much later than it does in girls. In turn, he claims this has an adverse effect on boys' ability to talk about their emotions.[49]

The brain-imaging paper[50] cited by Sax involved nine boys (aged 11 to 15) and ten girls (aged 9 to 17) staring passively at fearful faces. The researchers didn't actually look at connectivity between the amygdala and cortex – that would have required a different kind of brain scan than was used. What they did was compare the amount of activity in the amygdala versus the amount of activity in prefrontal cortex while participants looked at the fearful faces. Furthermore, they noted how the size of that difference varied with age. The finding that Sax latched onto was that older girls showed more cortex versus amygdala activation than younger girls, whereas no such age difference was found among the boys.

It's an interesting finding, but the sample was small, the girls had a wider age range, and the task was entirely passive. It's hard to know what this means about the way girls and boys process emotions, or what they have to say about how they're feeling. The authors themselves wrote, "conclusions based on these findings must be viewed as tentative." To extrapolate from this finding to say something about the ability of the sexes to talk about their feelings, as Sax does, is a huge leap. To go even further and use such data like this to argue for distinct educational practices for girls and boys is ridiculous and potentially harmful. Oh, and in case you're wondering, a massive meta-analysis published in 2014 of 184 studies found that the best quality research provides no evidence that single-sex education brings academic advantages for boys or girls.[51]

The Reality

As I said at the outset, there are differences in the average brain of a man and the average brain of a woman. I say "average brain" because there's a lot of overlap and many differences only appear reliably when averages are taken across many men and many women. One such difference is size – men usually have bigger brains than women, even taking into account their larger body size.

This has been documented time and again. To take just one example, Sandra Witelson and her colleagues weighed the brains of 58 women and 42 men postmortem and found the women's were 1248 grams on average, compared with 1378 grams for the men.[52] Remember, because of the overlap between the sexes, some women will have larger brains than some men. A Danish study of 94 brains published in 1998 estimated that the larger male brain volume translated into an average 16 percent greater amount of neurons in the neocortex of men versus women.[53]

There are also sex differences in the size of individual brain structures. For instance, the hippocampus, a structure involved in memory, is usually larger in women; the amygdala is larger in men.[54] Sometimes localized brain areas are activated differently in the two sexes – for instance, emotional memories tend to activate the left amygdala more in women, but the right amygdala more in men. It's also true that the cortical mantle (made up of gray matter) is thicker in women, and that women tend to have a higher ratio of gray to white matter (white matter being the kind of brain cells that are insulated).[55] However, it's important to note that these differences may have more to do with brain size than with sex – in other words it could be that smaller brains tend to have a higher ratio of gray matter, and it just happens that women tend to have smaller brains.

It's tempting to see these kinds of brain differences between the sexes and think that they explain behavioral differences, such as 'men's usual superiority on mental rotation tasks[56] and women's advantage with emotional processing. In fact, in many cases we simply don't know the implications of the sex-related brain differences. It's even possible that brain differences are responsible for behavioral similarities between the sexes. This is known as the "compensation theory" and it could explain why men and women's performance on various tasks is similar even while they show different patterns of brain activity. Relevant here is a new brain-imaging study of girls and boys watching funny videos. The girls' brains showed a more heightened response to humor, but their subjective appreciation of the videos was no different from the boys.[57] Another common mistake is to extrapolate too literally from the physical to behavioral – for example, to see localized brain activity as a sign of a focused mind.

It's also important to remember that behavioral differences between the sexes are rarely as fixed as is often made out in the mass media. Cultural expectations and pressures play a big part. For instance, telling women that their sex is inferior at mental rotation or math tends to provoke poor performance (an effect known as "stereotype threat"). By contrast, giving them empowering information, or allowing them to perform under an alias,[58] tends to nullify any sex differences. Related to this, in countries that subscribe less strongly to gender-stereotyped beliefs about ability, women tend to perform better at science[59] (although bear in mind that any causal relationship between these two facts could run both ways).

Findings like these remind us that over-simplifying and over-generalizing findings about gender differences risks setting up vicious self-fulfilling prophesies, so that men and women come to resemble unfounded stereotypes. In fact there's specific evidence that spreading myths on this topic could harm social progress. A 2009 study by researchers at the University of Exeter found that exposing people to arguments that gender differences in behavior and biology are fixed had the effect of increasing the likelihood that they'd agree that society treats women fairly.[60]

As a final thought – it's important to remember that sex differences in the brain do matter. Yes, we should be cautious about how we interpret these differences (Fine reminds us that "the male brain is like nothing in the world so much as a female brain"). But it's also important not to take political correctness too far and deny that differences do exist. The neuroscientist Larry Cahill makes this point in his 2006 paper "Why sex matters for neuroscience," in which he reviews many of the sex-related brain differences. Apart from increasing our understanding of the brain for its own sake, a better understanding of sex-related brain differences could also help cast much needed light on conditions like autism and depression that tend to be found much more often in men and women, respectively. A team of scholars, led by Margaret McCarthy at the University of Maryland School of Medicine, made a similar point in 2012 in their paper "Sex Differences in the Brain: The Not So Inconvenient Truth."[61]

Sex is relevant with neurodegenerative disorders too. In Alzheimer's, for example, the presence of pathological tangles in the brain is a much more significant risk factor for women than it is for men, and there's evidence that women with Alzheimer's are more adversely affected in terms of mental decline than are men[62] (see also p. 259 on brain injury). From a practical point of view, it's also important to consider the potential confounding effects of sex differences when conducting any kind of brain research. McCarthy's team point out that "the number of published studies limited to males remains stunningly and stubbornly high."

Do Girls Really Prefer Pink?

An issue that has become a microcosm for the larger debate about the origins of gender differences is whether or not girls prefer pink, and if they do, whether this is an innate or a cultural phenomenon. In 2007,[63] researchers at Newcastle University asked men and women to choose between colored rectangles. Both genders preferred shades of blue, but women showed a greater preference than men for reddish shades. This was true in Britain and in China. The researchers speculated that through history women were more specialized for gathering fruit rather than hunting and that this "underpin[s] the female preference for objects 'redder' than the background." Uncritical news headlines followed, such as "Why Girls Really Do Prefer Pink"[64] from BBC Online.

Nevertheless, other research argues against any innate gender differences in color preference. For a 2011 paper[65] Vanessa LoBue and Judy DeLoache presented 192 boys and girls aged between seven months and five years with pairs of differently colored small objects (e.g. coasters and plastic clips). Beyond the age of two, but not before, the children showed gender typical preferences – the girls started favoring pink objects and the boys began shunning them. This is just the age when young children start to become aware of their gender so the finding suggests the girls' pink preference is learned rather than innate.

The debate has taken a curious twist over the last few years with the claim that the typical "pink for girl," "blue for boy" association is a relatively recent phenomenon, and was actually reversed prior to the 1920s. For instance, here's the *Ladies Home Journal* in 1890: "Pure white is used for all babies. Blue is for girls and pink is for boys, when a color is wished." Over the last decade this supposed gender-color reversal has been cited by many authors and journalists as a *coup de grâce* against the idea that gender–color preferences are innate.

But the plot thickened in 2012[66] when Marco Del Giudice at the University of Turin turned detective and exposed the supposed reversal in pink/blue gender associations as a modern urban myth. He described how the argument was based on just four short magazine quotations discovered by Jo B. Paoletti, with typos or other errors a possible explanation. Then he conducted a Google Ngram text search on the entire corpus of British and American English books published between 1800 to 2000. He failed to uncover a single mention of the phrase "blue for girls," "blue for a girl," "pink for a boy" or "pink for boys." On the other hand, "blue for boys," "pink for girls," and so on, first appeared around 1890 and intensified after the Second World War.

Of course, this is still consistent with the idea that gender–color associations are a cultural phenomenon, but Giudice's paper appears to refute the idea of a reversal in these associations in the early part of the last century. All in all, the saga appears to be another example of how myths are born and spread. The reversal story aside, further evidence against the innateness argument for gendered color preferences was published in 2013 by Chloe Taylor and colleagues.[67] Among the Himba in rural Namibia, an ethnic group cut off from Western consumer culture, they found no sign of women preferring reddish or pink shades.

Myth #14

Adults Can't Grow New Brain Cells

Adult brains can rewire and form new connections, but they're completely incapable of forming new neurons. Like a spender with savings but no income, we have no choice but to witness our balance of brain cells dwindle through life. This was the erroneous idea once endorsed by the entire neuroscience establishment. In fact, many eminent scientists clung to the idea stubbornly, right through the last century, even in the face of mounting contradictory evidence.

The roots of what became known as the "no new adult brain cells" dogma are found in the writings of the great Spanish neuroscientist Santiago Ramón y Cajal (see also p. 22). He conducted groundbreaking work on the mechanisms that underlie the way the brain responds to experience and injury. In agreement with other experts of the early twentieth century, Cajal proposed what he called a "harsh decree" – that no new brain cells are created in the adult mammalian central nervous system (the brain and spinal cord), thus limiting the potential for regeneration there compared with the peripheral nervous system (the nerves extending out into the body and limbs) and other organs of the body like the liver and heart. Cut your skin and it grows back; knock your head and you lose a bunch of brain cells forever. Or so it was thought.

"Once the development was ended, the founts of growth and regeneration of the axons and dendrites dried up irrevocably," Cajal wrote in his 1913 masterpiece *Degeneration and Regeneration of the Nervous System*.[68] "In the adult centers, the nerve paths are something fixed, ended, and immutable. Everything may die, nothing may be regenerated." Cajal's verdict was supported through much of the last century. And his account made sense in the light of clinical observations. People who suffer brain damage from strokes usually experience ensuing difficulties with language, movement, or memory. Rehabilitation, to the extent that's possible, is long and difficult.

Battling the Dogma

The first evidence that the Cajal decree could be wrong emerged in the 1960s when Joseph Altman and his colleague Gopal Das at MIT used a new technique for labeling dividing cells.[69] In rats, cats and guinea pigs, they reported evidence for the existence of new neurons in the hippocampus (a curled structure involved in memory that's found deep in the brain), in the olfactory bulb (involved in the sense of smell) and in the cerebral cortex. But even though Altman's findings were published in prestigious journals, they were largely ignored. His research funding dried up and he moved to a different university to pursue less contentious work.[70]

This cool reception was due in part to the limitations of the labeling techniques used, with some experts arguing that the new cells were probably the support cells known as glia, rather than neurons. At that time there was also no concept of neural stem cells – these are immature cells with the capacity to divide *and* to become any kind of specialist brain cell. Ignorant that such cells exist, scientists at the time assumed new neurons could only originate from mature neurons dividing, which they knew to be impossible.

Nevertheless, the historian Charles Gross believes there was also an agenda: that elements of the old guard deliberately ignored the new findings in an attempt to maintain the decades-long "no new neurons" dogma. In his collection of essays, *Hole In The Head*,[71] Gross quotes Altman's reflections on the affair, published in 2009: "[T]here appears to have been a clandestine effort by a group of influential neuroscientists to suppress the evidence we have presented," Altman wrote, "and, later on, to silence us altogether by closing down our laboratory." Gross goes on to describe how, 15 years after Altman's seminal findings, a young researcher called Michael Kaplan used refined techniques that appeared to confirm Altman's work. Kaplan too published in prestigious journals, yet still his findings weren't taken seriously by the neuroscience community.

Writing about the experience first-hand in the review journal *Trends in Neurosciences* in 2001,[72] Kaplan himself put it like this: "In the midst of a revolution one must choose allegiance, and during the 1960s and 1970s, those who chose to support the notion of neurogenesis [the creation of new neurons] in the adult brain were ignored or silenced." Eventually Kaplan said he became so frustrated at the resistance to his work that he left his research post for a career in medicine.

After the papers of Altman and Kaplan, further evidence for adult neurogenesis emerged from studies in the 1980s conducted by Fernando Nottebohm and his colleagues, who showed that the size of song-related brain regions in adult male canaries fluctuated with the seasons.[73] When song-learning demands increased, so too did the number of new neurons in that part of the brain. Similarly, with adult chickadees – in the winter months when a scarcity of food placed more demands on their memories, new neurons were created in the hippocampus.[74]

Nevertheless, the dogma continued to survive because the skeptics of adult neurogenesis argued that all these positive findings were specific to rats and birds and didn't apply to primates, including humans. Among the leading defenders of the "no new neurons" dogma was Pasko Rakic of Yale, an eminent scholar and former president of the Society for Neuroscience. His team published a study in the mid-1980s that found no evidence of adult neurogenesis in Rhesus monkeys.[75] "They think I'm the guy who always says 'Read my lips – no new neurons," Rakic told the *New Yorker* in an article published in 2001.[76] "But that was never really my position. I did not object to Fernando's birds. I only objected when he said that what he saw in canaries could be applied to human beings."

Rakic's belief was that the creation of new neurons made sense for canaries because they learned new songs from one season to the next. He thought the loss of this flexibility was the price we paid as a species for having such sophisticated, enduring memories – essential for our complex social interactions. Rakic's view was consistent with the broader picture in which neurogenesis was found to be more prevalent in species with simpler brains.

Neurogenesis in Humans

Despite opposition from Rakic and others, further refinements through the 1980s and 1990s in the techniques used for labeling dividing cells led to ever more convincing evidence of adult neurogenesis – not just in rats and birds, but primates too. Much of this work came from the lab of

Elizabeth Gould at Princeton. She reported finding new neurons in the adult brains of tree shrews, marmosets, and then macaques,[77] each species more closely related in evolutionary terms to humans than the last. At first Rakic's lab criticized these findings, but since then his lab too has documented the existence of new neurons in adult primates.[78]

Arguably, however, the finding that really smashed the "no new neurons" dogma for good was the first observation that neurogenesis occurs in the brains of adult humans. This was no easy task. Research with animals usually followed the same pattern. The animal was injected with a dye that marked any cells before they divided, and over time the dye would be passed on to any daughter cells. A wait of minutes, months or years, depending on the study, and then the animal was killed, the brain sliced. Other staining was then used to identify cells as neurons or glia. Any neurons that came up dyed must have been newly created.

Obviously the need to slice the brain and study it under a microscope precluded these kinds of studies with humans. In the late 1990s, however, Peter Eriksson discovered that cancer patients were being injected with the crucial dye used in neurogenesis studies (bromodeoxyuridine) as a way to monitor the growth of their tumors. Together with another pioneer in the field, Fred Gage (who happens to be a descendant of Phineas Gage;[79] see p. 37), he obtained permission to study the hippocampi of five such patients after they died. Although it's what they predicted, you can imagine the researchers' excitement when they found dyed neurons in the hippocampus slices from all five patients, thus confirming that neurogenesis must have occurred after the time they'd been injected with the dye.[80] "These patients donated their brains to this cause, and we owe this proof of adult neurogenesis to their generosity," Gage wrote in 2002.[81]

Further direct evidence for adult neurogenesis came from an ingenious study published in 2013.[82] Kirsty Spalding at the Karolinska Institutet in Sweden and her colleagues exploited the fact that surface cold war nuclear bomb tests conducted between 1955 and 1963 increased levels of carbon-14 in the atmosphere. Diffusion and absorption by plants means these levels have gradually reduced over the ensuing decades, a fact that's reflected in human cells. This is because we take in carbon-14 through the plants we eat and its concentration is recorded in the DNA of our cells every time they divide.

Inspecting dozens of brains donated at postmortem, the researchers used levels of carbon-14 in cellular DNA to judge the age of the neurons and non-neuronal cells in the dentate gyrus (so-called because its appearance reminded early scholars of a row of teeth) of the hippocampus. Neurons in the brains of individuals who'd been born before 1955 had higher levels of carbon-14 than were present in the atmosphere at the time of their birth and youth, thus confirming they must have grown new neurons in adulthood. Further analysis indicated that the adult hippocampus grows about 700 new neurons every day, a process that slows only slightly with age.

Today it is widely accepted that new neurons are created in two areas of the mammalian (including human) adult brain where stem cells reside: the dentate gyrus of the hippocampus, as we learned, and the lateral ventricles, which are part of the system of brain cavities that contain cerebrospinal fluid (see Plate 18). Neurons created in the lateral ventricles migrate to the olfactory bulb (a relay center, located on the underside of the forebrain, that's involved in processing smells) along a route that's known as the rostral migratory stream, and there, over time, they come to resemble the mature neurons already resident. "Neurogenesis is a process, not an event," Gage wrote in another article in 2003.[83]

Mysteries Remain

Although we now know that adult neurogenesis is possible, many mysteries and controversies remain. A hot issue is whether new neurons are found in the frontal cortex. Elizabeth Gould's lab at Princeton claims to have found evidence of this,[84] but the arch-skeptic Rakic turned up a negative result.[85] Research also shows that stem cells can be harvested from many brain areas, but for some reason it's only in the ventricles and hippocampus that they give rise to new neurons.

An urgent ongoing question is whether adult neurogenesis is functionally meaningful. A stroke or a seizure can trigger a frenzy of neurogenesis but paradoxically in a way that seems to be harmful to the brain. To hijack these mechanisms for rehabilitative medicine will require many years of painstaking research. We need to know more about the molecular factors that control stem cell division, differentiation, and migration. And we need to learn more about the factors that affect whether new neurons become embedded in existing neural networks.

Answers have started to appear. Research by Gould, Tracey Shors, and Fred Gage and others has uncovered dramatic evidence in rats that the rate at which new neurons are created varies according to environmental factors. For example, a study published in 1999 showed that a rat running on a wheel grew double the number of new neurons in a day (up to 10 000 in the hippocampus) compared with a sedentary companion.[86] Enriched environments with more opportunity for spatial and associative learning, socializing, and play also increase neurogenesis.[87] Most recently, in 2013, a team led by Shors found that the opportunity to learn new physical skills (balancing on a rotating tube) also increased the number of newly created neurons that survived in the dentate gyrus of adult rats.

A consistent finding across these studies is that it is only challenging learning tasks that protect the survival of new neurons, ensuring that they become functionally integrated into the brain, even in older rats. For example, in the 2013 study that involved rats learning to balance, those who trained in an easier version did not show increased survival of new neurons, neither did rats who failed to learn the harder version of the task. In another line of research, preventing neurogenesis in rats has been shown to impair their performance on long-term memory tests.[88] Taken together, these results suggest there's a meaningful link between the process of learning and the creation and fate of new neurons. However, we still don't really know what these new cells are doing to aid learning.

One speculative theory is that they help date-stamp new memories. Another idea is that new neurons play a role in what's known as "pattern separation" – that is, our ability to tell similar contexts apart. Without pattern separation you get over-generalization: for example, mistaking the harmless pop of a firework for the sound of bombs. This actually fits in with other research suggesting that antidepressant and anti-anxiety drugs exert their therapeutic effect via increased neurogenesis, which may help patients avoid seeing danger in safe situations that resemble past threats. On the negative side, Gould has found that stress and threats diminish neurogenesis.

In a related line of work, a 2007 study reported that long-term use of antidepressant drugs was beneficial to patients with Alzheimer's disease, perhaps due to effects on neurogenesis.[89] However, other findings are less promising – a team led by Arturo Alvarez-Buylla published a report in 2011 that confirmed the existence of a stream of neural stem cells migrating from the lateral ventricles to the olfactory bulb in infants aged under 18 months (plus another unexpected stream to the cortex), but the researchers also reported that both these streams had slowed dramatically in older children and were virtually nonexistent in adults.[90] This result puts a dampener on hopes of inducing neurogenesis artificially in damaged regions of the brain.

Taken all together, we can say for sure now that the century-long dogma of "no new neurons" is wrong – but many more mysteries remain, above all the question of whether we can exploit adult neurogenesis effectively to combat brain injury and illness, or even to enhance the performance of healthy brains. Some experts are optimistic. "I imagine a time when selective drugs will be available to stimulate the appropriate steps of neurogenesis to ameliorate specific disorders," Gage wrote in 2003. But in his review of the field in 2012 neurobiologist turned writer Mo Constandi was more pessimistic:[91] "Maybe the old dogma was right and the brain does favor stability over plasticity," he said. "Maybe the neural stem cells that persist into adulthood are an evolutionary relic, like the appendix."

Myth #15 There's a God Spot in the Brain (and Other Lesser-Spotted Myths)

The possibility that religious experience originates from a single "God spot" in the brain seems to hold an eternal fascination. The obsession is fed by the work of researchers looking for the neural correlates of religiosity. But for some reason, authors and headline writers go beyond the science and continually recycle the idea that there's one spiritual sweet spot, spawning book titles like *Your God Spot: How the Brain Makes and the Mind Shapes All Forms of Faith* (by Gerald Schmeling) and articles like "Belief and the Brain's 'God Spot'" (from *The Independent* newspaper in 2009).[92]

An odd thing about this myth is that the notion of a God spot or module is often touted by writers who don't actually believe in it. For example, Matthew Alper's 2001 book *The God Part of the Brain*, doesn't actually locate religious faith to a specific part of the brain. Similarly, newspaper headlines mention the God spot even while their very own accompanying reports debunk it. "Research into Brain's 'God Spot' Reveals *Areas* of Brain Involved in Religious Belief," (emphasis added) the UK's *Daily Mail* trumpeted in contradictory fashion in 2009.[93]

This *Daily Mail* report went on to describe a study published in 2009[94] – the same one covered by *The Independent* – that found thinking about God activated the very same brain networks (note the plural) that are at work when we think about a person's emotions or intentions. "Religion doesn't have a 'God spot' as such," the study co-author Jordan Grafman told the *Daily Mail*. "[Religion] is embedded in a whole range of other belief systems in the brain that we use every day," he told *The Independent*.

Origins

The sources of religious piety have fascinated scholars for centuries, but the modern idea of a neural God spot seems to have its roots in the observations of Canadian neurosurgeon Wilder Penfield in the 1950s. When directly stimulating parts of the exposed cortex of his patients (undergoing surgery for intractable epilepsy), he noticed that zapping the temporal lobe sometimes led to his patients having odd bodily sensations and powerful emotions.

Later in the 1960s, two London clinicians, Eliot Slater and A. W. Beard, reported on 69 patients with epilepsy at the Maudsley psychiatric hospital and the National Hospital for Neurology.[95] Three quarters of these patients had temporal lobe epilepsy and 38 percent reported having religious or mystical experiences, such as "seeing Christ come down from the sky." Of those patients reporting the mystical experiences, three quarters had temporal lobe epilepsy (but bear in mind this was the same proportion with temporal lobe epilepsy in the sample as a whole).

These early observations planted the seed of the idea that the temporal lobes are somehow linked with religious experience, thus fueling the myth of a single God spot or module in that part of the brain. In the 1970s, Norman Geschwind together with Stephen Waxman also noted how some patients with temporal lobe epilepsy experience intense feelings of religiosity, alongside a raft of other distinctive characteristics (including an insatiable desire to write) – leading to the notion of Geschwind Syndrome or a Temporal Lobe Personality.[96] Historians and psychiatrists have since speculated that many ultra-religious characters from the past are likely to have had temporal lobe epilepsy, including: Joan of Arc, St Paul, Emmanuel Swedenborg and even Muhammad.

More recently, the idea of a temporal lobe link with religious experience has been spread by the influential neuroscientist and science communicator V. S. Ramachandran. For example, in his popular book *Phantoms in the Brain*[97] co-authored with Sandra Blakeslee, he cited as evidence two temporal lobe patients who showed a particularly heightened emotional response (as measured by hand-sweatiness) to the sight of religious words.

Ramachandran has since taken great pains to try to correct the idea that this has anything to do with a God spot. "A few years ago the popular press inaccurately quoted me as having claimed there's a God Centre or G-spot in the temporal lobes," he said in the BBC Horizon program "God on the Brain" broadcast in 2003. "This is complete nonsense. There is no specific area in the temporal lobes concerned with God, but it's possible there are parts of the temporal lobes whose activity is somehow conducive to religious belief."

Then there's the "God Helmet." Nothing has probably done as much as neuroscientist Michael Persinger's strange piece of apparatus to give legs to the God spot myth. Based at Laurentian University in Ontario, Canada, Persinger first reported on the effects of his God helmet back in the 1980s (he calls it the Koren helmet, after its inventor). Persinger claims that the helmet delivers weak magnetic fields (1 to 5 microtesla) to the temporal lobe and that this triggers odd feelings in most people, sometimes the sensation of a sensed presence or even a confrontation with God. In a paper published in 2006,[98] Persinger and his colleagues analyzed all the data they'd collected over the previous decades, amounting to 407 participants tested in 19 experiments. Their conclusion? "The sensed presence, a feeling of a Sentient Being, can be experimentally produced within the laboratory."

It's easy to see how writers and journalists have been seduced by all this talk of devout epilepsy patients and powerful God helmets. In fact, for many, the temporal lobe God spot has become a given. Today one of the most prominent advocates is the medic and self-proclaimed near-death expert Melvin Morse, who's appeared as a guest on Oprah Winfrey and Larry King, among other popular TV shows. "It's … well known that the right temporal lobe is the source of spiritual visions," he claimed[99] while promoting his 2001 book on the brain and religiosity. "We all have a God Spot," he wrote on the website of The Institute for the Scientific Study of Consciousness,[100] "an area in the brain that permits communication with a source of knowledge and wisdom outside our physical bodies."

The Reality

Despite this myth's high-profile advocates, the truth is, the purported special link between the temporal lobes and intense religious feelings is decidedly shaky. First off, the prevalence of religious experiences in patients with temporal lobe epilepsy has likely been hugely exaggerated. Writing in *The Psychologist* magazine in 2012,[101] Craig Aaen-Stockdale highlights a comprehensive study published in the late 1990s[102] that documented 137 patients with temporal lobe epilepsy, finding that just three of them had had religious experiences – a lower proportion than you'd expect to find in the general population.

Experts have also challenged the retrospective diagnosis of religious figures from history. Take the example of Joan of Arc. In a 2005 paper "Did all those famous people really have epilepsy?"[103] John Hughes points out that odd perceptual experiences in epilepsy are nearly always brief and simple – "like light flashes" – in stark contrast to the hours-long elaborate visions experienced by Joan of Arc. Hughes cites the neurologist Peter Fenwick, another expert on epilepsy, who says: "It is likely that the earlier accounts of temporal lobe epilepsy and temporal lobe pathology and the relationship to mystic and religious states owe more to the enthusiasm of their authors than to the true scientific understanding of the nature of temporal lobe functioning."

Persinger's God Helmet has also come in for criticism. A team of Swedish researchers led by Pehr Granqvist at Uppsala University hired an engineer to replicate the magic helmet and they performed a double-blind trial (so neither they nor the participants knew whether the gadget was switched on) with 89 volunteers.[104] In 2005 they reported they'd found no evidence whatsoever for the stimulation eliciting religious-like effects or any feeling of a sensed presence. There was a hint that more suggestible participants were more likely to report odd feelings, which provides a clue as to why Persinger's lab may have found such striking effects. The lack of an effect was no surprise to Granqvist's team given the weakness of the magnetic fields produced by the God helmet. As Aaen-Stockdale puts it in his *Psychologist* magazine article – the fields produced by the helmet are around 1 millitesla, "that's 5000 times *weaker* than a typical fridge magnet." Persinger disagrees with Granqvist's interpretation and says the Swedish team's magnetic fields obviously weren't working properly.

Putting aside the specific claims about the temporal lobe, the idea that there is a specific God spot in any part of the brain has also been exposed as nonsense by results from the parade of nuns and monks who've had their brains scanned. The overwhelming message from this often-contradictory research is that religious beliefs and experiences are associated with varied activity patterns all over the brain. For instance, research involving meditating Buddhist monks, conducted by Andrew Newberg, his late collaborator Eugene d'Aquili and others, revealed increased activation in the monks' right prefrontal cortex (a sign of concentration) and reduced activation in the parietal lobe (possibly associated with feelings of transcending the physical body).[105] By contrast, the same lab scanned the brains of five women "speaking in tongues" (including "singing, vocal utterances, and ecstatic bodily experiences," also known as glossolalia, considered by some as a spiritual miracle), and found their brains had reduced activity in the frontal lobes, which is a sign of reduced control and concentration.[106]

Another lab at the University of Montreal, headed up by Mario Beauregard, scanned the brains of 15 nuns in three conditions – resting with their eyes closed, recalling an intense social experience, and recalling a time they achieved union with God.[107] The religious condition was associated with particularly lively activity in six brain regions, including the caudate, insula, inferior parietal lobe, parts of the frontal cortex and the temporal lobe. Speaking to *Scientific American Mind* magazine, Beauregard summed up the findings from this and several similar studies conducted at his university: "There is no single God spot localized uniquely in the temporal lobe of the human brain."[108]

Other Lesser-Spotted Myths

The world's obsession with the possible existence of a God spot is part of a wider pattern of spotty fixation. The media doles out headlines on everything from neural love spots to cerebral humor spots, and we lap them up. As I was writing an initial draft of this chapter in the summer of 2012, *The Atlantic* published a story entitled "Scientists Find Brain's Irony-Detection Center!"[109] The reporter goes on to say, "Using magnetic resonance imaging, scientists seem to have located the part of the brain centrally involved in grasping irony." Here's another spotty headline, from *The New York Times*, that I "spotted" in 2014: "Afraid of Snakes? Your Pulvinar May Be to Blame."[110] (The pulvinar is part of the thalamus – see p. 10.)

There's a clue right there in that 2012 *Atlantic* report. Our cultural obsession with specific spots or structures in the brain has been fueled by the explosion, since the 1990s, of brain-imaging experiments in psychology and neuroscience. By comparing patterns of blood flow when a person performs one particular task compared with another condition when they're resting or doing some other task, researchers identify "hot" areas of the brain that seem to play an important role in whatever activity is under investigation (see also pp. 177–192).

These scanning studies have been complemented by the arrival of Transcranial Magnetic Stimulation – a technology I mentioned earlier, that allows researchers to temporarily disrupt activity in specific parts of the brain (often referred to as "virtual lesions") and watch the consequences. This approach has the advantage of being able to show that activity in a particular area is necessary for the successful performance of a particular mental faculty.

Let's be clear – there is functional specialization in the brain. The organ in our heads isn't one homogenous pulsating mass. We've known this since the nineteenth century when the neurologists of the day observed the effects of localized brain damage on patients' behavior (see pp. 40–50). However, the picture is far more complicated than the newspaper headlines would have us believe. Just because a particular brain area is involved in a mental function doesn't mean it's the only area, doesn't mean it's the most important area, doesn't mean it's the only thing that area does, or even that it's always involved.

Some of this is about common sense. Who's to say how precisely to define various functions? We could ask what's the neural correlate of thinking about other people. Or thinking about another person in pain. Or about a close relative in pain. Or about a sister who's in emotional pain. And so on. And what are we looking for in the brain – a specific lobe that's involved? One of the particular bulges (the gyri) on the surface of the cortex? A particular network of neurons? A particular neuron (see p. 11)?

Consider the processing of irony for a moment – it's clear that this is going to be related to other fundamental processes, such as language comprehension and representing other people's intentions and perspectives (known as "theory of mind"; ToM). Indeed, if we go back to the *Atlantic* report, we see the study authors are quoted as saying "We demonstrate that the ToM network [not a single spot!] becomes active while a participant is understanding verbal irony." Later on, the reporter Robert Wright admits to the hyperbole in his own headline: "Of course," he writes, "there may be parts of the brain outside of the ToM network that are involved in grasping irony." But he couldn't resist that headline, could he? Maybe his whole article was deliberately ironic.

This conundrum of how far to "zoom in" when considering cognitive functions and anatomical brain areas can be illustrated by a brief visit to the prefrontal cortex – the front-most part of the brain. As Charles Wilson at INSERM in France and his colleagues discuss in their 2010 opinion paper,[111] countless studies have documented functional subregions of this part of the brain. But this is a complex literature in which there's great variation in the precise demarcation of subareas between studies. The different subregions are also hugely interconnected, and there are many different reported ways to carve this region up functionally. Some evidence suggests different areas are activated depending on the level of abstraction of the task, while other studies show that the specific recruitment of areas depends on the demands placed on memory.

Wilson's team point out that the gold standard in this kind of research is to look for "double-dissociations," which is when two specific locations are compared and damage to each one leads to a distinct cognitive impairment that's not associated with damage to the other (see also p. 40). But despite all the studies on prefrontal cortex, such double-dissociations are thin on the ground, probably in part due to the fact that patients rarely have such localized damage, and when they do, it often only affects one side of the brain, thus allowing for compensation from the other side.

To complicate things further, Wilson and company argue that the prefrontal cortex as a whole has a distinct cognitive function ("the processing of temporally complex events") that can't be explained based on the function of the region's subareas. "Our argument," they write, "is that it is important to see the entire forest, no matter how visible the individual trees might be."

Finally, consider the idea of "neural reuse" proposed by, among others, Michael Anderson at the Franklin and Marshall College. This is the suggestion that recently evolved brain functions often depend on evolutionarily "old" brain circuits, so that most subdivisions in the brain end up being involved in many different mental functions. In a position paper published in 2010,[112] Anderson points out that even Broca's area, which is associated strongly with language function (see p. 43), is also involved in non-language processing, including preparing bodily movements and recognizing other people's actions. Similarly, the so-called "fusiform face area" of the brain, found in the temporal lobes, which has been seen by many as a dedicated face-processing module, is also involved in processing cars and birds. The debate goes on regarding just how specialized the area is.

In a particularly revealing analysis, Anderson reviewed the findings from 1469 brain-imaging studies that between them reported on 10701 significant activations in 968 different subdivisions of the brain. On average, each little brain area was activated by functions in over four different domains of mental function. Of course, divide the brain into larger areas, of the kind often examined in brain-scan studies, and the amount of functional overlap increases still further. Slicing up the cortex into 66 larger areas, Anderson found that each one was activated by an average of nine different domains of mental function. Suddenly the notion of a God spot or any other kind of neat functional subdivision of the brain looks like a gross oversimplification! "Regional selectivity had long been one of the central guiding idealizations of neuroscience," Anderson wrote on his *Psychology Today* blog in 2011. "But recent findings had led many of us to give that up, and to replace it with the notion of stable, identifiable functional networks of regions that brains seem to have in common."[113]

Myth #16

Pregnant Women Lose Their Minds

"When I was pregnant," *The Guardian* columnist and feminist Zoe Williams recalled in 2010, "I managed to lose the dog's lead, between the common and the house. So I took my jumper off and tied him to that, only I forgot that I wasn't wearing a proper top underneath – I was wearing something in the region of a string vest. How could I not notice? Why was I even wearing a string vest?"[114]

Williams believes she was suffering from a kind of mental impairment brought on by the biological changes associated with pregnancy – an idea that's been called variously preghead, pregnesia, momnesia and baby brain. Anecdotal evidence for the condition is everywhere and frequently shared by writers and broadcasters.

"Oh my gosh, I think my brain is permanently shrunk after having three kids," said CBS Early Show presenter Hannah Storm in 2007. In a diary for *New Statesman*, a pregnant Sarah Montague, who co-presents the BBC's flagship Today news program, said: "My biggest worry has been what you might call 'preg-head.'"[115] The idea has even been endorsed by respected health authorities. An NHS pamphlet published in 2005 on "50 things would-be fathers should know," put it this way: "Pregnant women are a bit vague … it's their hormones."

The "condition" is also cited frequently by social commentators. Reflecting on British presenter Natasha Kaplinsky's announcement of her pregnancy after she'd signed a new lucrative contract, *The Sunday Times* columnist Minette Marrin warned Kaplinsky what was to come: "at some point her brain will be affected by the amnesia of pregnancy. This is a phenomenon that is now widely admitted, even by feminists."

Surveys suggest that belief in pregnesia is widespread among the public. In 2008 Ros Crawley at the University of Sunderland quizzed dozens of pregnant and nonpregnant women and their partners and found that they all agreed that pregnancy is typically associated with cognitive decline.[116]

Given these views, perhaps it's no wonder that researchers have uncovered disconcerting evidence about the prejudice shown toward pregnant women, especially in work contexts. Although such prejudice is driven by multiple factors, widespread public belief in "pregnesia" or "preghead" likely plays an important part. Consider a study published in 1990, in which Sara Corse at the University of Pennsylvania, invited male and female MBA students to interact with a female manager they'd never met before, and then rate her afterwards. In fact the "manager" was a research assistant acting the part, and the key finding was that students given the additional information that the woman was pregnant reported finding their interaction with her less satisfying than students not fed this lie.[117]

More recently, a 2007 field study led by Michelle Hebl involved female researchers posing as customers at a store, either with or without a pregnancy prosthesis. The women were treated differently if they appeared pregnant – on the one hand they were victim to more rudeness, but at the same time they were more likely to be the target of touching and over-friendliness.[118] The same study also revealed hostility toward pregnant women applying for store jobs, especially for roles considered tradition-ally to be for men. Similarly, in a study published the same year, Jennifer Cunningham and Therese Macan found that undergraduate participants playing the role of employer chose to hire a pregnant woman less often than a competing nonpregnant candidate with the exact same qualifica-tions and interview performance.[119]

The Reality

The myth of pregnesia hasn't come out of thin air. Countless surveys of pregnant women, using questionnaires and diary reports, have found that many of them – usually about two thirds – *feel* that being pregnant has affected their mental faculties, especially their memories. Of course, that doesn't mean that it has. Neither does it prove that the cause is some biological consequence of the state of pregnancy as opposed to lifestyle factors like fatigue and stress.

The most dramatic claim about the biological effect of pregnancy on the brain is that it causes shrinkage (as mentioned by the CBS host Hannah Storm). Given how drastic this sounds, you'd think it would be backed up by plenty of evidence. In fact, the idea is based almost entirely on a small study published in 2002 by researchers at Imperial College School of Medicine in London.[120] Angela Oatridge and her colleagues scanned the brains of nine healthy pregnant women and five pregnant women with preeclampsia (a condition associated with high blood pres-sure), finding evidence of brain shrinkage of between 2 to 6.6 percent volume during pregnancy that was reversed 6 months after giving birth. There was also evidence of an increase in the size of the ventricles and the pituitary gland. Nevertheless, without replication and a larger sample it's difficult to take this single study too seriously.

Returning to the issue of cognitive impairment, whereas subjective reports of this from pregnant women are widespread, objective laboratory studies are far less consistent. For many years, for every study that turned up an apparent impairment in memory, another was published that drew a blank. Some experts believed this was a sign that the effect is unreliable and small; others said it was simply due to different labs using different methods.

An attempt to weigh all the evidence and get to the truth was published in 2007 by Julie Henry of the University of New South Wales in Sydney and Peter Rendell at the Australian Catholic University in Melbourne. They conducted a meta-analysis that gathered together all the evidence from 14 studies published over 17 years. Their conclusion? There is a real effect of pregnancy on women's cognition, but it's a "relatively subtle" one, "relatively small in magnitude," and it manifests most noticeably during tasks that require executive functioning – that is, juggling lots of information at once.[121]

Unfortunately, Henry and Rendell's abstract (the summary) of their paper was worded in a way that proved ripe for misinterpretation. They wrote "The results indicate that pregnant women are significantly impaired on some, but not all, measures of memory." By "significant" they meant statistically significant: that is, unlikely to be due to chance. But as Nicole Hurt details in her critique of the coverage,[122] journalists worldwide misunderstood the research summary and the public message became sensationalized: "many [pregnant] women ... suffer *considerable* memory loss" (*The Observer*; emphasis added) and "pregnant women were *considerably* impaired" (*Hindustan Times*; emphasis added) are just two examples of many.

Since that meta-analysis by Henry and Rendell, the literature has taken a number of further twists and turns. An Australian study published in 2010 was superior to many of its predecessors in following a large group of women over time and testing their cognitive abilities, including working memory and processing speed, prior to pregnancy, during, and after. Helen Christensen and her colleagues found no evidence of pregnancy being associated with cognitive decline.[123] In turn this spawned a whole new set of headlines around the world – "Pregnant women's brains are not mush" the *The Daily Telegraph* announced; "Forgetful mums can no longer 'blame it on the bump'" said *The Times*.

And yet the evidence supporting the idea of pregnancy-related cognitive impairments just keeps coming. Here's a flavor of some recent findings: In 2011, Carrie Cuttler and her colleagues studied 61 pregnant women and found evidence of memory problems in real-life "field tests" of their prospective memory (remembering to do things in the future), but no evidence of memory problems in the lab.[124] The following year, Jessica Henry and Barbara Sherwin found that 55 pregnant women performed worse than 21 nonpregnant controls on verbal recall and processing speed, and these differences were related to hormonal changes in the pregnant women.[125] Also in 2013, Danielle Wilson and her team published a study that found evidence of memory impairment in pregnant women compared with nonpregnant controls.[126] Crucially, this study involved sleep monitoring and the verbal memory impairment in the pregnant women wasn't attributable to sleep disturbance.

Taken altogether, it looks as though pregnancy really is associated with cognitive changes in some women, including memory problems. The inconsistent results could be a consequence of different methods used and how relevant the tests are to real life. This prompts an obvious question – if pregnesia is a genuine phenomenon, why should female humans have evolved to be mentally impaired just when you'd think they need to be at their most alert?

Animal Research and the Maternal Upgrade

The cognitive problems associated with human pregnancy are all the more mysterious in light of research with rats and other mammals that suggests pregnant females undergo cognitive enhancements, not impairments, that stay with them into motherhood. A pioneer in this field is Craig Kinsley at the University of Richmond. He told me in 2010: "Our [maternal] rats get better at virtually everything they need to, to successfully care for their expensive genetic and metabolic investments. Foraging, predation, spatial memory all improve; stress and anxiety responsiveness decreases."[127]

Research by Kinsley and Kelly Lambert at Randolph-Macon College shows that these maternal upgrades appear to be mediated by changes to a region of the brain called the medial preoptic area of the hypothalamus (mPOA), known to be involved in nurturing behaviors; and changes to the hippocampus, which is involved in memory. Specifically, pregnancy is associated with increased cell density and volume in the mPOA, and more dendritic spines in the hippocampus – these are thorn-like protrusions on neurons that improve signaling efficiency, which could help explain maternal improvements in foraging and other spatial skills.[128]

When I asked Craig Kinsley in 2010 why the human literature was full of findings about cognitive impairments while the animal research points to improvements, he said the disparity may have to do with the kinds of tasks and behaviors that were being studied in humans. "Much of the data from human mothers has been derived from asking females to demonstrate cognitive enhancements to skills, behaviors, occupations that are largely irrelevant to the care and protection of young," he said. Another suggestion is that the "pregnesia" in humans is a side effect of the dramatic changes underway in mothers' brains that are gearing them up for the demands that lie ahead. Framed this way, pregnesia is the price that's paid for what ultimately is a maternal neuro-upgrade.

Recently a spate of human studies has been published that may be hinting at these maternal advantages. For instance, James Swain's lab at the University of Michigan has shown how several areas in the brains of new mothers are especially responsive to the sound of their own baby crying, compared with the sound of other babies' cries.[129] Regarding physical brain changes, a team led by Pilyoung Kim at Cornell University and Yale University School of Medicine scanned the brains of 19 new mothers in the weeks immediately after giving birth and then again several months later. The later scan showed up increased volume in a raft of brain areas that are likely to be involved in mothering activities – the prefrontal cortex, parietal lobes, hypothalamus, substantia nigra, and amygdala.[130]

And in 2009[131] and 2012,[132] labs at the University of Bristol and Stellenbosch University, respectively, reported evidence that pregnant women have a superior ability to determine whether a face is angry or fearful, and they show heightened attention to fearful faces. The Stellenbosch team wrote: "Heightened sensitivity to danger cues during pregnancy is consistent with a perspective that emphasizes the importance of parental precaution and the adaptive significance of responding to potentially hazardous stimuli during this period."

More findings like these are bound to appear as researchers begin to test pregnant and recently pregnant women on behaviors and mental activities that are directly relevant to raising a child. That pregnancy has a profound effect on the brain and mental function of women seems increasingly certain. But the idea that it's a purely negative effect is a myth that's in the process of being debunked. Any pregnancy-related impairments are likely a side effect of what ultimately is a maternal neuro-upgrade that boosts women's ability to care for their vulnerable offspring. Many will welcome the demise of the pregnesia myth, because it's a simplistic, one-sided concept that almost certainly encourages prejudice against women.

Myth #17

We All Need Eight Hours of Continuous Sleep (and Other Dozy Sleep Myths)

Considering how much of our lives we spend sleeping – years and years, if you added up all our time in slumber – it's remarkable how much mystery still surrounds this most fundamental of behaviors. Mystery, of course, is the perfect breeding ground for myths and it follows that there isn't just one sleep-related brain myth for us to examine here, but several.

Even the basic idea that we all need about eight hours solid sleep a night has been challenged recently. Hundreds of historical records[133] show that until the late seventeenth century, the norm used to be for two separate sessions of sleep interspersed with a period of one to two hours of nocturnal activity. Some experts believe this is our more "natural" inclination, and the frustrations of insomniacs who wake in the middle of the night could be related to these old instincts for having two periods of sleep.

Myth: Sleep Is a Chance for the Brain to Switch Off

Since scientists started studying sleep seriously in the 1950s, we've learned a lot about the relevant basic physiology. We know that the brain is remarkably busy while we sleep, contrary to the folk idea that it's a chance for our minds to switch off. Sleep is associated with four distinct phases, which are repeated in 90-minute cycles. Each cycle consists of three phases of non-rapid eye-movement sleep, also known as "slow wave sleep" or "orthodox sleep" (which takes up about 80 percent of a typical night), and there's a phase of REM (rapid eye movement) sleep, which is particularly associated with dreaming and lively neural activity. We've also learned much about the various hormones, such as melatonin, that are involved in regulating the sleep/wake cycle. Yet despite these advances, exactly why we sleep remains an open question.

All mammals and birds sleep, and even more "basic" creatures like flies exhibit sleep-like periods of rest. One proposal is that sleep has evolved simply as a behavior for animals to indulge in when there's little to be gained from being active. Other experts think sleep must have a more pro-active function than this. Why else, they ask, is a lack of sleep so detrimental? We all know the painful costs of a lost night of sleep, and longitudinal research has revealed the serious health implications of long-term sleep disturbance incurred through shift work. Research with rats has even shown that extended sleep deprivation can lead to death.

A recent suggestion is that sleep is a chance for brain cells to reduce their overall levels of excitability.[134] As learning depends on strengthening connections among cells, it follows that the longer we're awake, acquiring new information and skills, excitability between neurons must be forever on the increase. Given that excess stimulation of brain cells can risk neurotoxicity, sleep could be a way for the brain to tone down activity levels, while still retaining the relative strengths of network connections.

As these investigations into the ultimate purpose of sleep remain ongoing, numerous myths continue to swirl around our nocturnal habit, some of which turn out to be true or to have a kernel of truth. Let's examine five of these in turn, starting with the popular idea that teenagers need more sleep than adults. Then we'll go on to explore whether Freud was right about dreams providing a unique window into the psyche; whether anyone really has been experimented on by aliens while they sleep; whether it's possible to control our dreams; and finally we'll take a look at whether you really can exploit your time asleep to learn from vocabulary tapes and other educational gizmos.

Myth: Teenagers Who Lie In Are Just Being Lazy

Most teenagers stay up late and then sleep through the morning, dead to the world. If you left them undisturbed, who's betting they wouldn't sleep right through to lunchtime and beyond? But do they really need all this extra sleep as they claim or is it merely a handy myth for the adolescent idler?

In fact, the evidence is mounting that the teenage body clock really is set differently from an adult's. A survey published in 2004 of over 25 000 Swiss and German people compared the time of day they slept to when they didn't have any social obligations. This time became progressively later through adolescence, peaking abruptly at the age of 20.[135]

Of course, this observation doesn't prove that the late sleeping is borne of need rather than laziness. However, another study published in 2010 found that adolescents, more than adults, suffered daytime sleepiness when they were forced to adhere to a strict 8-hour-a-night sleep schedule for several days. There's also evidence from Mary Carskadon's sleep and chronobiology lab at E. P. Bradley Hospital in Rhode Island that melatonin (a hormone involved in regulation of the sleep cycle) continues to be secreted at a higher level later into the day among older teens.

Regarding the teen preference for late bedtimes, Carskadon's lab also compared the effects of 36 hours sustained wakefulness on teens and children and found that the teens showed a slower buildup of "sleep pressure" based on recordings of their brain waves.[136] Carskadon told *New Scientist* this could explain why teens are able to stay up late into the night.[137]

There's also some persuasive anecdotal evidence from a British school to suggest that teens really do have different sleep needs from adults. A few years ago, Monkseaton High School in Tyneside changed their timetables for a trial period so that lessons didn't begin until 10 in the morning, instead of the previous 9 a.m. start. What happened? Absenteeism plummeted and grades in math and English soared, with the school enjoying its best overall results since 1972. The UCL Academy in London has also recently instituted 10 a.m. start times on the basis that teens really do benefit from a later wake-up time.

Myth: Dreams Are the Royal Road to the Unconscious

From a subjective point of view, dreams are probably the most mysterious aspect of sleep. It's a common experience to be dazzled by the creativity of our own brains as we wake up with memories of surreal plots and outlandish characters. A question that remains controversial is whether these nocturnal stories we tell ourselves have any meaning. Sigmund Freud famously believed that dreams were the "royal road to the unconscious." He argued that nightmares and other dreams are filled with symbolism, which if decoded, could reveal our deepest desires and fears. Pertinent to Freud's claim that many dreams act as a form of wish-fulfilment is a survey of 15 paraplegics that found, although they often walked in their dreams, they walked less frequently than able-bodied comparison participants did in their dreams. The researchers, led by Marie-Thérèse Saurat, concluded that these results were incompatible with Freudian theory. The paraplegics were quite open about their strong desires to walk again and if dreams act as an outlet for wish-fulfilment, you'd expect paraplegics' dreams to be far more dominated by walking than they were.[138]

Nonetheless, the idea that dreams are filled with symbolism is incredibly popular, with many people struggling to believe that the intricate events of their dreams could be entirely meaningless (surveys suggest around 50 percent of Americans believe their dreams have meaning or reveal hidden desires and many said they'd avoid flying if they dreamt of a crash). Books like *5 Steps to Decode Your Dreams: A Fast, Effective Way to Discover the Meaning of Your Dreams* (Sourcebooks, 2011) continue to sell well, and today there are even software programs for interpreting your dreams. There are also the self-proclaimed experts like Lauri Quinn Loewenberg, who describes herself as a "certified dream analyst" and the USA's "most trusted dream expert."[139]

When I posted a *Psychology Today* blog post about the myth of dream symbolism, Ms. Lowenberg commented online to say that I hadn't done my homework and that she'd been researching dreams since 1996, finding that they do have meaning. But I did a literature search and I told her I couldn't find a single study she'd published. "I have not subjected my research to peer review," she replied, "as I use it solely in my private practice." Of course, this makes it difficult to judge the veracity of her claims.[140]

The truth is, there's little published research showing that dreams have any useful meaning. What evidence there is tends to be of poor scientific quality. For instance, in 2013, a team led by Christopher Edwards at Cardiff University reported that participants who used the "Ullman Dream Appreciation technique" (this involves discussing the meanings of one's dreams in a group with other people) subsequently reported having gained insight into problems in their waking lives.[141] However, the researchers admitted that because there was no control condition, it's impossible to know if the benefits were really due to analyzing dreams, or merely to do with discussing problems with a group of people. Another study published in 2014[142] reported that student therapists gained insights into their clients after dreaming about them – but there was no independent verification of whether this was really true or merely an illusion of hindsight.

One influential neurobiological theory even contends that dreams originate from sporadic neural activity in the brain stem and the random activation of memories. By this account, dreams are partly the consequence of our higher brain areas attempting to translate this haphazard activity into some kind of coherent subjective experience.[143] Of course, this doesn't mean we can't look for meaning in our dreams (many people get great enjoyment from it), but the idea that they conceal hidden truths waiting to be decoded is a myth. Based on current evidence, there simply are no hard and fast rules to say what the events in dreams mean.

That's not to say that the content of our dreams is entirely random. There is evidence that our behavior during the day can affect our dream content (Freud called this day-residue). Anyone who's binged on a DVD box-set will be familiar with the experience of dreaming about the fictional worlds and characters from the just-watched drama. Another common experience is to incorporate outside sounds and sensations into our dreams. The car-alarm wailing outside becomes the sound of a police siren in our exciting chase through dreamland. Calvin Kai-Ching Yu at Hong Kong Shue Yan University has even provided tentative survey evidence that sleeping face down can induce dreams with more sexual content, possibly because of the pressure of the mattress on the genitals.[144] Another study from 2014 found that people who dreamt that their partner was unfaithful tended to have more relationship trouble the next day – most likely not because the dream foretold the future, but because the dream left the dreamer feeling irrationally jealous and suspicious.[145]

Myth: Aliens Visit People in the Night

If you've ever woken in the night, unable to move, and sensed a presence in the room, maybe also a weight on your chest, then you were probably experiencing an episode of what doctors call "sleep paralysis." The phenomenon, which many of us will experience at least once in our lives, is thought to occur when wakefulness interrupts a period of REM dream-sleep. The body is typically paralyzed during REM sleep to prevent us from acting out our dreams (for this reason sleep walking is more common during Stage 4 of non-REM sleep when the muscles are not paralyzed). During sleep paralysis, the body remains in this incapacitated state and elements of dreaming continue, despite the fact that we're partly awake. Sleep paralysis is particularly common when REM sleep occurs unusually early in the sleep cycle. Jet-lag, stress, over-tiredness – all these things can interrupt the typical sleep cycle, induce more instances of early REM sleep, and in turn make sleep paralysis more likely.

Sleep paralysis provides a fresh perspective on the mythical tales some people tell about their sleep experiences, including the many accounts that exist of alien abduction in the night (one high-profile "abductee" was Miyuki Hatoyama, the wife of former Japanese Prime Minister Yukio Hatoyama). It is highly likely that many of these contemporary nocturnal alien visitations are really a result of people interpreting bouts of sleep paralysis in the context of one of the dominant cultural themes of our time.

When Chris French, professor of anomalistic psychology at Goldsmiths in London, surveyed 19 alien abductees he found that they experienced significantly higher rates of sleep paralysis than a comparison group of age-matched participants.[146] It's also revealing that in previous eras and in other locations, episodes of sleep paralysis were, or are, often interpreted differently, in line with other relevant cultural beliefs. In Medieval Europe, for example, people who experienced sensations that sound a lot like sleep paralysis tended to interpret the episodes in terms of visits from seductive demons – the female succubus and the male incubus. For Inuits in Canada, people who experience sleep paralysis often believe they've been visited by malevolent spirits.[147]

Whether it's blamed on aliens, spirits, or described in terms of neurobiology, there's no doubt that sleep paralysis can be an upsetting experience. Writing in *The Psychologist* magazine in 2009, Professor French said that there was an urgent need for greater awareness of the condition among the public and health professionals, "in order to minimize the anxiety and distress that often result from such attacks."

Myth: You Can't Control Your Dreams

In Christopher Nolan's 2010 film *Inception*, Leonardo DiCaprio's character is one of several with the expertise and technical equipment to get inside other people's dreams and interfere with the way events unfold. This technology remains a fantasy, but the film was apparently inspired by the real phenomenon of lucid dreaming.

Where sleep paralysis describes the situation in which wakefulness occurs during dreaming and yet the dream remains out of control, lucid dreaming is the more enjoyable state of being partly awake while dreaming and having the ability to control the dream. Lucid dreaming occurs most often toward the end of a period of sleep, just when you're in that twilight zone between dreamland and waking up.

If you've never had a lucid dream, there are tips out there for how to make the experience more likely. In the e-book *Control Your Dreams* by University of Sheffield psychologist Tom Stafford and lucid dreamer Cathryn Bardsley,[148] it's recommended that you practice noticing whether you're awake or asleep. By day this sounds daft, but if you get into the habit when you're awake then it's more likely that you'll be able to make the distinction when you're sleeping.

Flicking a light switch is a good test of whether you're really awake, the authors say, since in your dreams the light levels won't change. By contrast, pinching yourself is actually a bad test, because it's all too easy to actually dream the act of pinching oneself. If you do become aware of being in a dream, then try to stay calm because if you get too excited you'll probably wake yourself up. Finally, set yourself goals to aim for the next time you do manage to achieve lucidity in a dream. "Flying. Always good," Stafford and Bardsley write. "Sex. Popular. And Consequence free."

Key to the plot of *Inception* is the idea that dream events can influence real life. Remarkably there is evidence that activities in lucid dreaming can have real consequences for our waking lives. In a paper published in 2010, University of Bern researcher Daniel Erlacher showed that time practicing tossing a coin into a cup during lucid dreaming led to superior coin-tossing performance in later real life.[149]

Myth: Learn-While-You-Sleep Tapes Can Improve Your Golf and French-Speaking Skills

The coin-tossing experiment would appear to be an impressive case of learning while sleeping. However, it pays to remember that the participants in that study were selected because of their unusually reliable ability to lucid dream; that many of them actually failed to have the coin-tossing dreams; and that the study was about the practice of a simple skill rather than the acquisition of new knowledge. There is no evidence that foreign language vocabulary tapes, "play better golf sleep hypnosis" CDs or similar night-time listening material has any benefit whatsoever. Current evidence suggests we can't absorb complex information while we sleep.

That said, there is emerging evidence that very basic forms of learning can take place while we're snoozing. A revolutionary study published in 2012 provided the first ever evidence of conditioning occurring as people slept.[150] Specifically, a research team led by Anat Arzi at the Weizmann Institute of Science in Israel exposed sleeping participants to auditory tones paired with pleasant (shampoo or deodorant) or unpleasant smells (rotten fish or carrion). The next day, the participants sniffed more deeply when they were played the tone that had previously been paired with a pleasant smell. That's despite the fact that they had no memory of the tone or the smells from the previous night.

There's also plenty of evidence of how important sleep is to the learning that we do in the daytime. Consider a study by Ysbrand van der Werf and colleagues that used carefully timed beeping noises to interrupt the slow wave sleep of their participants on certain nights.[151] The key finding was that participants' memory performance was substantially poorer for material learned during a day that followed a disturbed night of only shallow sleep, as compared with material learned after an undisturbed night.

In fact, so important is sleep for learning that it's not worth students staying up late to revise for longer, if doing so means they miss out on quality sleep. Researchers at the University of California tested this in a study published in 2012, for which hundreds of students kept sleep and study diaries for two weeks. The results showed that extra studying at the expense of sleep led to academic problems the next day, including trouble understanding lessons and poorer test performance.[152]

Other research has shown how important sleep is for the consolidation of material learned during the preceding day. A classic study[153] showed how neurons in the hippocampus of sleeping rats fired in the same pattern as they had done when those rats had been engaged in a foraging task during the day. It's as if while snoozing the rats were mentally rehearsing the routes they'd learned when awake.

On the back of results like this, attention has turned recently to the optimum time to learn before going to sleep. In 2012 Johannes Holz and his colleagues reported that teenage girls showed greater improvement on a finger tapping task (a form of procedural learning) when they practiced that task just before sleep as compared with practice in the afternoon.[154] By contrast, the research showed that performance on factual learning was superior when the material was studied in the afternoon, as compared with being studied just before sleep. "We propose that declarative memories, such as vocabulary words, should be studied in the afternoon and motor skills, like playing soccer or piano, should be trained in the late evening," the researchers concluded. Before adjusting your weekly timetable, bear in mind this small study needs to be replicated.

Sleep still harbors many mysteries, including why we bother with it at all. However, we've seen that there are many ideas about sleep that the current evidence suggests are myths. Watch for more research on this topic because neuroscientists are making rapid breakthroughs in understanding the importance of sleep for learning and memory, and it's possible new ways of exploiting these processes could be on the horizon.

What Is Hypnosis?

"And … sleep," says the stage hypnotist as his latest volunteer appears to nod off with the click of the fingers. Although the word hypnosis originates from the Greek *hupnos* meaning sleep, in fact hypnosis is not a form of sleep. We know this because of the brain's activity during hypnosis and thanks to subjective accounts that it is actually a focused, absorbed state of mind.

Various techniques are used to induce a hypnotic "trance," including guided imagery and attention to internal or external events, such as one's breathing or a clock's ticking. However, whether the induced state really reflects a unique form of consciousness is still open to debate. People who are hypnotized typically do show telltale patterns of brain activity, including reduced activity in what's known as the default mode network,[155] and increased activity in frontal attentional regions.[156] But it's not yet clear that this is truly unique to hypnosis.

What's more, hypnosis is often used to induce a state of suggestibility, and yet people who are prone to suggestion (e.g. told they feel tired, they start to feel tired) often appear to be just as suggestible whether they've been hypnotized or not. Take the demonstration that hypnotic suggestion can nullify the Stroop effect[157] – a phenomenon previously considered involuntary. This is when the meaning of color words (e.g. blue) interferes automatically (or so it was assumed) with people's ability to identify the ink color they are printed in. That hypnotic suggestion can remove this effect implies it is more than role-play. But another study replicated this finding using the power of suggestion alone, without prior hypnosis.[158] Such findings leave a question mark over the claim that hypnosis is more than the power of suggestion.

Notwithstanding these issues, and despite the popular depiction of hypnosis as a form of stage trickery, neuroscientists are increasingly using hypnotic suggestion as a useful way to model unexplained neurological symptoms. For example, provoking limb paralysis in people using hypnotic suggestion appears to have many parallels with the paralysis observed in people with "conversion disorder" – where their physical problem stems from emotional trauma rather than any organic disease or injury[159] (see also Plate 19). In their authoritative review of neuroscience and hypnosis published in 2013,[160] the psychologists David Oakley and Peter Halligan said that the psychological and neurological effects of suggestion remain "one of the most remarkable but under-researched human cognitive abilities."

Myth #18

The Brain Is a Computer

> We have in our head a remarkably powerful computer.
>
> Daniel Kahneman[161]

An alien landing on earth today might well come to the conclusion that we consider ourselves to be robots. The computer metaphors are everywhere, including in popular psychology books (see above); also in the self-help literature: "your mind is an operating system" says Dragos Roua, "Do you run the best version of it?"; and in novels too, like this example in *The Unsanctioned* by Michael Lamke: "It had become a habit of his when deeply troubled to clear his mind of everything in an effort to let his brain defragment the jumbled bits and pieces into a more organized format."

The popularity of the mind-as-computer metaphor has to do with the way psychology developed through the last century. Early on, the dominant "behaviorist" approach in psychology outlawed speculation about the inner workings of the mind. Psychologists like John Watson in 1913 and Albert Weiss during the following decade argued the nascent science of psychology should instead concern itself only with outwardly observable and measurable behavior.

But then in the 1950s, the so-called Cognitive Revolution began, inspired in large part by innovations in computing and artificial intelligence. Pioneers in the field rejected the constraints of behaviorism and turned their attention to our inner mental processes, often invoking computer metaphors along the way. In his 1967 book, *Cognitive Psychology*, which is credited by some with naming the field, Ulric Neisser wrote: "the task of trying to understand human cognition is analogous to that of ... trying to understand how a computer has been programmed." Writing in 1980, the American personality psychologist Gordon Allport was unequivocal. "The advent of Artificial Intelligence," he said, "is the single most important development in the history of psychology."[162]

Where past generations likened the brain to a steam engine or a telephone exchange, psychologists today, and often the general public too, frequently invoke computer-based terminology when describing mental processes. A particularly popular metaphor is to talk of the mind as software that runs on the hardware of the brain. Skills are said to be "hardwired." The senses are "inputs" and behaviors are the "outputs." When someone modifies an action or their speech on the fly, they are said to have performed the process "online." Researchers interested in the way we control our bodies talk about "feedback loops." Eye-movement experts say the jerky saccadic eye movements performed while we read are "ballistic," in the sense that their trajectory is "pre-programmed" in advance, like a rocket. Memory researchers use terms like "capacity," "processing speed" and "resource limitations" as if they were talking about a computer. There's even a popular book to which I contributed, called *Mind Hacks*, about using self-experimentation to understand your own brain.[163]

Is the Brain Really a Computer?

The answer to that question depends on how literal we're being, and what exactly we mean by a computer. Of course, the brain is not literally made up of transistors, plastic wires, and mother boards. But ultimately both the brain and the computer are processors of information. This is an old idea. Writing in the seventeenth century, the English philosopher Thomas Hobbes said "Reason ... is nothing but reckoning, that is adding and subtracting."[164] As Steven Pinker explains in his book *The Blank Slate* (2002), the computational theory of mind doesn't claim that the mind *is* a computer, "it says only that we can explain minds and human-made information processors using some of the same principles."[165]

Although some scholars find it useful to liken the mind to a computer, critics of the computational approach have argued that there's a deal-breaker of a difference between humans and computers. We think, computers don't. In his famous Chinese Room analogy published in 1980, the philosopher John Searle asked us to imagine a man in a sealed room receiving Chinese communications slipped through the door.[166] The man knows no Chinese but he has instructions on how to process the Chinese symbols and how to provide the appropriate responses to them, which he does. The Chinese people outside the room will have the impression they are interacting with a Chinese speaker, but in fact the man has no clue about the meaning of the communication he has just engaged in. Searle's point was that the man is like a computer – outwardly he and they give the appearance of understanding, but in fact they know nothing and have no sense of the meaning of what they are doing.

Another critic of computational approaches to the mind is the philosopher and medic Ray Tallis, author of *Why The Mind is Not a Computer* (2004). Echoing Searle, Tallis points out that although it's claimed that computers, like minds, are both essentially manipulators of symbols, these symbols only actually have meaning to a person who understands them. We anthropomorphize computers, Tallis says, by describing them as "doing calculations" or "detecting signals," and then we apply that same kind of language inappropriately to the neurobiological processes in the brain. "Computers are only prostheses; they no more do calculations than clocks tell the time," Tallis wrote in a 2008 paper. "Clocks help us to tell the time, but they don't do it by themselves."[167]

These criticisms of the computer metaphor are all arguably rather philosophical in nature. Other commentators have pointed out some important technical differences between computers and brains. On his popular Developing Intelligence blog[168] Chris Chatham outlines 10 key differences, including the fact that brains are analog whereas computers are binary. That is, whereas computer transistors are either on or off, the neurons of the brain can vary their rate of firing and their likelihood of firing based on the inputs they receive from other neurons.

Chatham also highlights the fact that brains have bodies, computers don't. This is particularly significant in light of the new field of embodied cognition, which is revealing the ways our bodies affect our thoughts. For example, washing our hands can alter our moral judgments; feeling warm can affect our take on a person's character; and the weight of a book can influence our judgment of its importance (see p. 164). The opportunity to make hand gestures even helps children learn new math strategies. In each case, it's tricky to imagine what the equivalent of these phenomena would be in a computer.

Memory provides another useful example of how, even on a point of similarity, brains do things differently from computers. Although we and they both store information and retrieve it, we humans do it in a different way from computers. Our digital friends use what psychologist Gary Marcus calls a "postal-code" system – every piece of stored information has its own unique address and can therefore be sought out with almost perfect reliability. By contrast, we have no idea of the precise location of our memories. Our mental vaults work more according to context and availability. Specific names and dates frequently elude us, but we often remember the gist – for example, what a person looked like and did for a living, even if we can't quite pin down his or her name.

Myth: The Computational Theory of the Mind Has Served No Benefit

So, there are important differences between computers and brains, and these differences help explain why artificial intelligence researchers frequently run into difficulties when trying to simulate abilities in robots that we humans find easy – such as recognizing faces or catching a Frisbee. But just because our brains are not the same as computers doesn't mean that the computer analogy and computational approaches to the mind aren't useful. Indeed, when a computer program fails to emulate a feat of human cognition, this suggests to us that the brain must be using some other method that's quite different from how the computer has been programmed.

Some of these insights are general – as we learned with memory, brains often take context into account a lot more than computer programs do, and the brain approach is often highly flexible, able to cope with missing or poor quality information. Increasingly, attempts to simulate human cognition try to factor in this adaptability using so-called "neural networks" (inspired by the connections between neurons in the brain), which can "learn" based on feedback regarding whether they got a previous challenge right or wrong.

In their article for *The Psychologist* magazine, "What computers have shown us about the mind," Padraic Monaghan and his colleagues provided examples of insights that have come from attempting to simulate human cognition in computer models.[169] In the case of reading, for example, computer models that are based on the statistical properties of a word being pronounced one way rather than another, are better able to simulate the reading of irregular words than are computer models based on fixed rules of pronunciation. Deliberately impairing computer models running these kinds of statistical strategies leads to dyslexia-like performance by the computer, which has led to novel clues into that condition in humans.

Other insights from attempts to model human cognition with computers, include: a greater understanding of the way we form abstract representations of faces, based on an averaging of a face from different angles and in different conditions; how, with age, children change the details they pay attention to when categorizing objects; and the way factual knowledge is stored in the brain in a distributed fashion throughout networks of neurons, thus explaining the emerging pattern of deficits seen in patients with semantic dementia – a neurodegenerative disease that leads to problems finding words and categorizing objects. Typically rare words are lost first (e.g. the names for rare birds). This is followed by an inability to distinguish between types of a given category (e.g. all birds are eventually labeled simply as bird rather than by their species), as if the patient's concepts are becoming progressively fuzzy.

There's no question that attempts to model human cognition using computers have been hugely informative for psychology and neuroscience. As Monaghan and his co-authors concluded: "computer models ... have provided enormous insight into the way the human mind processes information." But there is clearly debate among scholars about how useful the metaphor is and how far it stretches. The philosopher Daniel Dennett summed up the situation well. "The brain's a computer," he wrote recently,[170] "but it's so different from any computer that you're used to. It's not like your desktop or your laptop at all."

Will We Ever Build a Computer Simulation of the Brain?

"It is not impossible to build a human brain and we can do it in 10 years," said the South African-born neuroscientist Henry Markram during his TEDGlobal talk in 2009. Fast forward four years and Markram's ambitious ten-year Human Brain Project was the successful winner of over €1 billion in funding from the EU. The intention is to build a computer model of the human brain from the bottom up, beginning at the microscopic level of ion channels in individual neurons.

The project was borne out of Markram's Blue Brain Project, based at the Brain and Mind Institute of the École Polytechnique Fédérale de Lausanne, which in 2006 successfully modeled a part of the rat's cortex made up of around 10 000 neurons (see Plate 20). The Human Brain Project aims to accumulate masses of data from around the world and use the latest supercomputers to do the same thing, but for an entire human brain. One hoped-for practical outcome is that this will allow endless simulations of brain disorders, in turn leading to new preventative and treatment approaches. Entering the realms of sci-fi, Markram has also speculated that the final version of his simulation could achieve consciousness.

Experts are divided as to the credibility of the aims of the Human Brain Project. Among the doubters is neuroscientist Moshe Abeles at Bar-Ilan University in Israel. He told Wired magazine:[171] "Our ability to understand all the details of even one brain is practically zero. Therefore, the claim that accumulating more and more data will lead to understanding how the brain works is hopeless." However, other experts are more hopeful, even if rather skeptical about the ten-year time frame. Also quoted in Wired is British computer engineer Steve Furber. "There aren't any aspects of Henry's vision I find problematic," he said. "Except perhaps his ambition, which is at the same time both terrifying and necessary."

The Mind Can Exist Outside of the Brain

Philosophers have grappled with the question of how the mind is related to the brain for millennia (see Plate 21). The view of contemporary, mainstream neuroscience is that the mind is an emergent property of the brain. Without the brain (and body, see p. 160), there is no mind, and every mental experience has an underlying neurophysiological correlate.

But many thinkers remain unsatisfied with this account. They point out that a purely neurobiological description can never explain or capture what it feels like to see red, taste a Mars bar, or have any other phenomenological experience – what philosophers call qualia. They see this as an intractable problem – that it will never be possible to reconcile the objective and subjective perspectives. However, many neuroscientists are more sanguine and believe that as our understanding of the brain develops, the "hard problem" as it's known, will evaporate in the heat of our greater knowledge.

We're not going to be able to solve this ancient debate here. But what we can do is look at some specific claims about the mind apparently existing outside of the brain, or exerting an influence on its own, without need of a body. To overthrow such a fundamental tenet of neuroscience – that the mind emerges from and is dependent on the brain – the evidence must be robust and overwhelming. However, in each case we discuss, it will be shown that the evidence is often highly tenuous, and at best shaky and inconsistent. Therefore the idea that the mind can function without its brain remains for now a myth.

Before tackling some specific claims, let's remind ourselves of a few basic facts that suggest the mind *is* inextricably bound to the physical brain. First off, doing things to your brain has effects on your mind. Inebriate your brain with chemicals, like alcohol, and as we all know, you'll experience mental side effects. More radically, if you were to undergo neurosurgery, and the surgeon stimulated your cortex with an electrode, you'd likely experience mental sensations, such as reminiscences, the nature of which would vary with the brain location that was zapped.

On the other hand, do things with your mind, and it has corresponding effects on the brain. For example, London cab drivers, who have committed the tangled web of the city's streets to memory, have enlarged hippocampi – a structure known to be crucial to spatial memory. When Elizabeth Maguire, the lead researcher in this area, then followed trainee cab drivers over time, she found that their hippocampi were larger at the end of their years of training, compared with at the start, providing even more compelling evidence that it really was the mental act of remembering the routes that led to the brain changes (men who failed to get their license, or other men who weren't trainees, didn't show the hippocampi growth).[172]

Or consider research on the neural effects of psychotherapy. We tend to think of talking therapies as having a "psychological" effect, in contrast to drug treatments that exert a neurobiological effect on the brain. But if the mind *is* the brain, as modern neuroscience contends, then of course the psychotherapy should have effects on the brain too. That's exactly what the research has shown.[173] For example, brain imaging demonstrates that recovery from depression is associated with decreased metabolism in the ventrolateral prefrontal cortex, both in patients who have taken the drug Paxil, and in patients who have undergone successful cognitive behavioral therapy (CBT). Successful CBT was also associated with brain changes not seen with Paxil, including increased activity in the cingulate, frontal, and hippocampus regions, probably reflecting a cortical "top down" mechanism of action (i.e. driven by expectations and beliefs). Another brain-imaging study looked at patients with obsessive–compulsive disorder, finding that recovery was associated with changes to the metabolic rate of the right caudate (a basal ganglia structure involved in movement, memory, and emotion), regardless of whether the treatment was behavioral therapy or Prozac (fluoxetine), an antidepressant medication.

Myth: Near-Death Experiences Prove the Mind Can Leave the Brain and Body

The apparently inextricable, two-way relationship between mind and brain that I've described is challenged by dramatic accounts of near-death experiences (NDEs), in which a person's mind – their consciousness – appears to continue functioning, even while their brain is almost entirely incapacitated. Since at least the nineteenth century, stories have been told of heart-attack patients and other trauma victims floating above their bodies, seeing tunnels with a welcoming light at the end, reliving their life stories, and even meeting deceased relatives.

Most recently, the phenomenon attracted fresh attention with the publication by a neurosurgeon of his own first-hand account of a near-death experience, entitled *Proof of Heaven, A Neurosurgeon's Journey Into The Afterlife* (Simon & Schuster, 2012). The book was promoted with a front-page *Newsweek* article, "Heaven Is Real; A Doctor's Experience of the Afterlife." In the magazine Dr Eben Alexander describes how he contracted a serious brain infection in 2008, which left him in a coma, with his cortex "stunned to complete inactivity." While in that state, he says he traveled to a place with "big, puffy, pink-white" clouds, "flocks of transparent, shimmering beings" and that he rode on a butterfly wing with a beautiful woman with golden tresses, "high cheekbones and deep-blue eyes."

Freely admitting his identity as a "faithful Christian" prior to the trauma, Dr Alexander believes his experience proves the existence of the afterlife and – crucially for our purpose – that consciousness is not rooted in the brain. Alexander concludes with a promise: "I intend to spend the rest of my life investigating the true nature of consciousness and making the fact that we are more, much more, than our physical brains as clear as I can, both to my fellow scientists and to people at large."

Skeptics were quick to pour scorn on the doctor's interpretation. Writing for *The Telegraph*, the eminent neuroscientist Colin Blakemore thought it revealing that so many accounts of near-death experiences appear saccharine and reassuring.[174] "Is it not significant that the NDEs of Christians are full of Biblical metaphor?" he wrote. "Either this confirms the correctness of their particular faith or it says that NDEs, like normal perception and memory, are redolent of culture, personal prejudice and past experience."

On his blog, Sam Harris the neuroscientist and arch-atheist, expressed his bewilderment (as did Blakemore) at the neurosurgeon's apparent ignorance of basic brain science.[175] Dr Alexander cited a CT scan as evidence for the inactivity in his cortex, yet any introductory neuroscience course will tell you that CT scans only provide information on structure, not function. "Everything – absolutely everything – in Alexander's account rests on repeated assertions that his visions of heaven occurred while his cerebral cortex was 'shut down,' 'inactivated,' 'completely shut down,' 'totally offline,' and 'stunned to complete inactivity,'" Harris wrote. "The evidence he provides for this claim is not only inadequate – it suggests that he doesn't know anything about the relevant brain science."

What does the scientific literature say about NDEs? Well, they are surprisingly common – for instance, it's estimated that 12 to 18 percent of people who survive cardiac arrest report having had a near-death experience. Just like the butterfly-riding neurosurgeon, some researchers in the field think a purely materialist view of the mind is challenged by all these experiences of complex mental states occurring during periods of brain inactivity.

One such expert is Bruce Greyson at the University of Virginia. In his 2010 paper, "Implications of Near-Death Experiences for a Postmaterialist Psychology,"[176] Greyson draws attention to accounts from near-death experiencers that they could see and hear things during their spell of brain incapacitation, such as witnessing surgeons operating on them. There are even stories from some blind people that they were able to "see" while in the midst of their NDE. Greyson argues that the "conflict between a materialist model of brain–mind identity and the occurrence of NDEs under conditions of general anesthesia or cardiac arrest is profound and inescapable."

There's no doubt the reports of NDEs are fascinating. If nothing else, these people have clearly lived through a powerful, emotionally intense psychological event that warrants much more study. Many of them are changed forever by what they think they saw and felt. But should we at this point abandon the idea that the mind is rooted in the brain, given that to do so would shake our understanding of the natural laws of science to its very foundations? The onus surely is on those who seek a "supernatural" explanation to demonstrate beyond doubt that near-death experiences defy explanation in more conventional terms.

As things stand, there are good reasons to doubt that NDEs disprove the inextricable mind–brain connection. First off, many of the features of NDEs occur in other situations when we have no reason to believe anything particularly brain-defying is going on. For instance, out-of-body experiences are frequently reported during sleep paralysis (see p. 96), and they've been triggered by direct stimulation of the right tempero-parietal junction (during surgery for intractable epilepsy). Pilots exposed to high G-force often report a tunneling of their vision, caused by a lack of blood and oxygen supply to the eyes. The effects of hypoxia and many recreational drugs – for example, the trips experienced by users of ketamine and especially DMT – also resemble aspects of the NDE. These examples demonstrate that it's perfectly possible for changes in the brain to lead to unusual experiences akin to elements of the NDE. DMT (N, N-Dimethyltryptamine) is actually present in small amounts in the brain, making it a particularly likely candidate for playing a role in NDEs.

Perhaps the biggest problem with taking accounts of NDE too literally is that they are by necessity always retrospective, rendering them vulnerable to the tricks and biases of memory. Greyson and others, who think that NDEs challenge a materialist account of the mind, always emphasize how the NDE occurs during brain inactivity – that NDEs are a case of the mind–brain link being broken. But we can't know that that's really true. Often the precise amount of brain activity that's still ongoing is unknown. And it's possible the NDE itself occurred in the lead up to brain inactivity, or during the post-trauma recovery. It's well known that states of altered awareness often play havoc with people's sense of time, so it's plausible that an experience that feels to the patient as though it was long-lasting in fact took place in a fraction of a second, either before or after their brain went offline.

Most compelling would be evidence of NDE patients having access to information that could only have been available if they really were floating atop the room, "fully alert" while in surgery. But existing accounts of these claims are purely anecdotal, and it's possible patients heard what was going on while under anesthesia, or pieced together a sense of what was happening from snippets of information they heard from other people before or after the surgery.

During a study published in 2001, involving 63 cardiac arrest survivors, researchers hung boards close to the ceiling, with pictures on them that could only be seen from above.[177] The idea was to test whether patients reporting an out-of-body experience would be able to recall the pictures, but unfortunately, none of the near-death experiencers in this study had an out-of-body experience. Greyson also claims that some patients have encountered dead people during a NDE, whose deaths they had no prior knowledge of. However, these claims too are anecdotal.

As the psychologists Dean Mobbs and Caroline Watt concluded in a review published in 2011 for the respected journal *Trends in Cognitive Sciences*, there is at present no reason to believe that NDEs are paranormal.[178] "Instead," they wrote, "near-death experiences are the manifestation of normal brain function gone awry." Meanwhile, research on NDEs is ongoing. In 2012, the Templeton Foundation ear-marked $5 million for its multidisciplinary Immortality Project, part of which will involve cross-cultural research into near-death phenomena.

Myth: The Sense of Being Stared At Shows the Mind Extends Beyond the Brain and Body

Have you ever felt the urge to turn around, only to discover that someone was staring right at you? Surveys suggest that around 80 to 90 percent of people have had this experience, a statistic that some fringe scientists interpret as evidence that when we stare, our vision projects outwards and can be detected by others via a kind of "sixth sense," even if they are looking the other way. If true this would be another example of the mind exerting an effect beyond the brain.

Today the most prominent advocate of this interpretation is the British researcher Rupert Sheldrake, a biologist by training. Writing in 2005, Sheldrake argued that visual images don't just reside in our minds, they project out into the world. "My own hypothesis," he said, "is that [this] projection takes place through perceptual fields, extending out beyond the brain, connecting the seeing animal with that which is seen."[179] (See box on p. 115 for more on this.)

Research into the idea that we can feel when we are being stared at has been carried out since at least the end of the nineteenth century when one of the founding fathers of psychology Edward Titchener concluded that there was no evidence that the effect is real. He explained the phenomenon as a memory bias – if we get the feeling, turn around and no one is looking at us, then we tend to forget the experience. By contrast, if we turn around and catch someone boring holes in our back, well then it sticks in our memory. Another obvious possibility is that when we turn, it catches the attention of someone behind us, who then looks our way, giving us the misleading impression that they were staring all along.

In more modern times, Sheldrake has performed many investigations into the phenomenon, including a massive study conducted in collaboration with *New Scientist* magazine and The Discovery channel, in which thousands of volunteers performed tests of the effect at home and reported back their results. Such tests by Sheldrake and others usually come in two forms. So-called "direct looking" experiments involve a pair of people occupying the same room; one stares at the other's back on some trials, but not others, and the receiving person reports on each trial whether they believe they were stared at or not. The other "remote staring" approach involves one person staring at another via CCTV, so the two people aren't even in the same room. In this case, the bodily arousal is measured of the person who is sometimes stared at, to see if their skin is sweatier when they are in fact being stared at (remotely) compared with when they are not.

Reviewing the evidence in 2005, Sheldrake said that the results from many studies suggest that there is a small, but highly significant (in statistical terms) positive effect. He said that overall, people tend to guess correctly that they are being stared at about 55 percent of the time, whereas you'd expect them to be right only 50 percent of the time if there is really no way for us to detect that someone is staring at us. Similarly, in 2004, a team led by Stefan Schmidt conducted two meta-analyses, combining data from 36 studies using direct looking and 7 studies using the CCTV method.[180] For both experiment types, they concluded that: "there is a small, but significant effect." However, unlike Sheldrake, who interprets the subtle effect in line with his radical theory of vision, Schmidt's team wrote: "There is no specific theoretical conception we know of that can incorporate this phenomenon into the current body of scientific knowledge."

The research on the feeling of being stared at has been criticized on several levels by skeptics. They point out, for example, that it is poorer quality studies that tend to report significant results. Questions have also been raised about the order of stare/no stare trials, raising the possibility that participants are detecting a non-random order. This is a particular risk for those studies that provide participants with ongoing feedback on how they are faring. When in 2000, David Marks and John Colwell published a staring study that used proper randomization of trials, they found no evidence that people can detect staring.[181]

Another issue is how to score participants' success at detecting whether they are being stared at. Skeptics have highlighted the way many people show biased responding – being more likely to say they are being stared at than not. It's important, these experts warn, to take into account false alarm rates – all those occasions that a person says they think they are being stared at when in fact they are not. A study published in 2009 by Thomas Wehr of the University of Trier used a scoring system that accounted for biased responding and found no evidence for a sense of being stared at.[182]

Finally, there are concerns that experimenters are somehow affecting the results on staring that they are collecting. There's a clear pattern in the data that suggests "believers" tend to find significant results whereas skeptics nearly always draw a blank. The believer Marilyn Schlitz and the skeptic Richard Wiseman have worked together to try to get to the bottom of this. In one study they found that a staring effect was present whenever Schlitz did the greeting of participants and the staring, but no staring effect was found when Wiseman did the greeting and staring.[183] Later, in a paper published in 2006,[184] they mixed things up – so sometimes Schlitz did the greeting, while Wiseman did the staring and vice versa. The idea was to isolate the specific part of the experimental process where the researchers were having an effect. In fact this study, which followed the remote staring format, found no positive evidence, regardless of who was doing what.

Taken altogether, it is certainly intriguing that so many studies have found modest evidence that people can feel that they are being stared at. But there are so many methodological issues and inconsistencies that it simply isn't justified on the basis of this evidence to reject everything we know about how vision works. As Thomas Gilovich has written: "Adding together a set of similarly flawed investigations does not produce an accurate assessment of reality." Sheldrake aside, even many researchers who are open-minded about the staring literature are skeptical about the suggestion that the mind somehow projects vision outwards beyond the brain into the world.

As I was putting the finishing touches to this book, I learned that in 2013 *Skeptic Magazine* published yet another test of the sense of being stared at, conducted by Jeffrey Lohr and his colleagues.[185] They performed what they describe as "the most rigorously controlled empirical investigation" of the phenomenon ever conducted. Lohr's team divided 134 participants into several groups – some were stared at via a one-way mirror; others via CCTV. Some were exposed to Sheldrake's writings, others to conventional visual theory. The researchers also employed several dozen students to act as experimenters, thereby reducing any effects of experimenter bias on the results. The key finding was that reading Sheldrake boosted people's confidence in their ability to detect whether they were being stared at, but did not boost their actual ability. In fact, this research produced no evidence for the sense of being stared at. Lohr and his colleagues concluded that future research should focus, not on the validity of this phenomenon (they believe their study shows convincingly it has none), but on why people come to believe in the phenomenon in the first place.

Myth: Telekinesis Shows That the Mind Extends Beyond the Brain and Body

Another phenomenon, which if proven, would challenge the idea of an inextricable mind–brain connection is telekinesis (also known as psychokinesis) – the manipulation of physical objects, not with the body, but purely with the mind. It's a "skill" that made the self-proclaimed psychic Uri Geller a superstar in the 1970s, with his apparent dramatic bending of spoons and speeding up of watches. Audiences were wowed by the demonstrations, but skeptics were convinced that Geller was using simple conjuring tricks to achieve his supposed feats of mental power. When in 1973 the arch-skeptic James Randi was invited to help the Tonight Show in the US prepare for Geller's appearance, he advised them to use all their own props and to forbid Geller's team from getting near them prior to broadcast. That night, Geller was unable to perform any feats of telekinesis, blaming his failure on a temporary lack of strength.[186]

Scientists investigating telekinesis do so under highly controlled circumstances. A favored method is to see whether people can use mind power alone to bias the output of an electronic random number generator. If the pattern of numbers produced under the deliberate influence of a person's thoughts is different from the pattern produced without human interference, this is taken as evidence for telekinesis. There was excitement and much controversy in 2006 when Holger Bosch at the University Hospital Freiburg and his colleagues combined the results from over 300 such experiments and concluded that there was evidence for a tiny but statistically significant distorting effect of people's thoughts on random number output.[187]

Nevertheless, there were problems with the data. The anomaly of three exceptionally large studies, all of which reported an effect in the opposite direction to participants' intention, combined with a tendency for smaller studies to report more positive results (suggesting the possibility that studies with negative results went unpublished), led Bosch and colleagues to declare the existence of telekinesis "unproven." They did nonetheless argue that if the effect they'd uncovered were proven, it would be of "fundamental importance."

Skeptics disagreed, arguing that if you combine enough studies, meaningless differences can produce statistically significant results, and that it's the size of those effects that's most important. In the case of the new meta-analysis, they said the average effect size was so small as to be meaningless. Two skeptical commentators, David Wilson and William Shadish, used the analogy of a coin-tossing game to illustrate the infinitesimal size of the supposed telekinesis effects uncovered by Bosch's research. If a player won a dollar for every head and lost a dollar for every tail, Wilson and Shadish explained, then using telekinesis would leave the player just $48 up after hundreds of thousands of tosses during over two months of continuous play. "This is not of great fundamental importance," they wrote.[188]

Nevertheless, another commentator on the meta-analysis, Dr Dean Radin at the Institute of Noetic Sciences, told me that Wilson and Shadish were making a common mistake by confusing small effect size with immediate pragmatic importance. "The magnitude of the charge on the electron is extremely small, but after gaining an improved understanding of this miniscule charge we eventually powered the world," he said. "If there is indeed a mind–matter interaction," he added, "then its eventual pragmatic consequences are probably far greater than electricity or atomic power."

The phenomena I've covered here are intriguing and warrant more research. But none of them as yet poses a robust challenge to the conventional view that the brain gives rise to the mind. Effects like the feeling of being stared at, or telekinesis, are suspiciously small, and when a non-believer tries to replicate the results under the most stringent conditions, they nearly always draw a blank. Where positive effects are found, their tiny size invariably leads to debate about whether the result has any meaning or is merely a statistical artifact. We should keep an open mind, but for now it's a mind that remains firmly rooted in the brain.

Seeing Outwards

Rupert Sheldrake's belief that something comes out of the eyes when we see is a direct contradiction of our established understanding of the science of vision. It's been known since at least the writings of the Muslim scholar Alhazan (965–1040) that vision works via rays of light entering the eye and (more modern research has shown) stimulating cells in the retina, at the back of the eye. The opposite and erroneous idea, that vision involves rays issuing forth from the eye, can be traced back at least as far as the fifth century BC, with the writings of Alcmaeon of Croton (we also heard from him on p. 16). Plato was another advocate, and the idea appears throughout history and literature in the myth of the evil eye (the ability to issue curses merely via looking) and the myth of love arrows (e.g. from Shakespeare's *Love's Labour's Lost:* "A lover's eye will gaze an eagle blind.")

Nevertheless, simple experiments expose the absurdity of so-called extramission theories. Consider how the brightness of a bulb is experienced as glare – too bright and it's actually painful. Staring at the sun damages the eye! Perceiving a star, according to extramission theories, would require that the beams exit the eye at a speed faster than light.

But Sheldrake isn't alone in being sympathetic to the idea of vision issuing outwards from the eye. A series of investigations by Gerald Winer and Jane Cottrell in the 1990s and early 2000s revealed that nearly 60 percent of school children and around a third of college students endorse the idea that something exits the eyes when we use our sense of vision.[189] In a further survey of undergraduates, they even found that these views remained resistant to introductory classes on the science of vision.[190] Winer and Cottrell confessed they were somewhat baffled by the stubbornness of the myth, although they said it may have to do with the subjective sense of seeing – images look like they are "out there" in the world. The widespread belief in the sense of being stared at could also have a mutually reinforcing influence on the idea of sight issuing outwards.

Myth #20   Neuroscience Is Transforming Human Self-Understanding

Most of the emphasis in this book is on the mismatch between popular beliefs about the brain and scientific fact. But regardless of whether the public and media have an accurate understanding of neuroscience, a distinct question is whether or not the rise of neuroscience is changing how we see ourselves, including how we think about topics of human interest such as art, law, creativity, and leadership.

The ascent of brain science is undeniable. I mentioned in this book's introduction the mammoth investments in neuroscience that have just been announced on both sides of the Atlantic. A cursory look at the history of the discipline also shows its astonishing growth over the last few decades. The Society for Neuroscience (SFN) formed as recently as 1969 with a modest crowd of approximately 1300 people in attendance at its first annual meeting in 1979. Interest and funding intensified as George H. W. Bush designated the 1990s the "Decade of The Brain," triggering a series of high-profile public engagement neuroscience events and publications. By 2005, the SFN delegate count had exploded, reaching a peak of nearly 35 000. In terms of output, the rise has also been stellar – in 1958 approximately 650 papers were published in neuroscience worldwide; in 2008, this had risen to over 26 500 papers published in more than 400 journals.[191]

Many commentators believe this tsunami of neuroscience is already having a profound effect on everyday human life and self-understanding. Consider the claims of Zach Lynch in his 2009 book, *The Neuro Revolution: How Brain Science is Changing Our World*. He argues that neuroscience findings are: "propelling humanity toward a radical reshaping of our lives, families, societies, cultures, governments, economies, art, leisure, religion – absolutely everything that's pivotal to humankind's existence." Is this really true or yet another brain myth in the making?

The Case For

There are many examples in this book of the efforts being made by people to use neuroscience to understand or influence others, albeit that this is usually based on distortions or misunderstandings of the science. This includes attempts to explain the travails of the Western world in terms of the bi-hemispheric nature of the brain (see p. 56), and the linking of humankind's unique powers of empathy to the existence of mirror neurons, ironically enough first discovered in monkeys (see p. 154).

Commentators also point to "brain branding"[192] – the way that mention of the brain is increasingly invoked to help sell ideas, and to present self-improvement techniques and therapies as somehow more scientific and cutting edge, as seen in the spread of "neurolinguistic programming" (see box), neuromarketing (see p. 188) and the Brain Gym (see p. 207). Following a similar trend, 2007 saw the inauguration of The Neuroleadership

Institute[193] on a mission to "encourage, generate and share neuroscience research that transforms how people think, develop and perform."

Recent years have also brought us the world's first Institute of Neuroesthetics[194] based at UCL in London and Berkeley, California. According to the Institute's founder Semir Zeki:[195] "It is only by understanding the neural laws that dictate human activity in all spheres – in law, morality, religion and even economics and politics, no less than in art – that we can ever hope to achieve a more proper understanding of the nature of man." There's also the recently inaugurated MacArthur Foundation Research Network on Law and Neuroscience. Neurotheology, neurocriminology, and neuroethics too have emerged as burgeoning fields. In 2013, the RSA in London announced its latest project on "the brains behind spirituality."[196]

There's more. Writing in 2009,[197] Marco Roth announced the rise of the "neuro novel," including books by Ian McEwan, Jonathan Lethem, Mark Haddon, Richard Powers and many others, covering De Clérambault's syndrome, Tourette's syndrome, autism and Capgras syndrome, respectively, and all published since 1997. "the trend follows a cultural ... shift away from environmental and relational theories of personality back to the study of brains themselves, as the source of who we are," says Roth.

Others describe this phenomenon as "brain centrism" or "neurocentrism" – the contemporary tendency to trace all human emotion, creativity, and responsibility back to its source in the brain. "The individual is no longer defined so much by the self as by the brain, so that authors refer to neuronal man or the synaptic self, if not, indeed, to the self as an illusion created by the brain," wrote Marino Pérez Álvarez in 2011.[198]

There are also signs that the dominance of neuroscience is altering how we speak about ourselves. In late July 2013 I conducted a quick search for the word "brain" on Twitter and found the following tweets among hundreds of similar examples: "Heading for London and an exciting day ... Can feel brain whirring already"; "I want to study but my brain says 'No way fu*ker' ..." said another; "Scumbag brain: crams all the people I hate in one dream," wrote one more unfortunate Twitterer.

In 2006[199] Paul Rodriguez at the University of California conducted a systematic analysis of these ubiquitous brain references in everyday conversation and writing. He noted how people invoke the substance of the brain to represent the substance of ideas, as in "brainstorm," "brainwash," and "brain child"; how people refer to their brains routinely as separate from themselves, as in "this menu is confusing my brain," or paradoxically as an essential part of themselves – "I feel brain dead."

Clinical neuropsychologist Vaughan Bell picked up this theme in a column for the *Observer* newspaper in 2013.[200] "I never used to discuss neuroscience on the bus but it's happened twice in the last month," he wrote, recalling the occasion a fellow passenger told him their brain wasn't working that day, and another instance when an overseas student told him that learning abroad makes your brain more efficient. "it's the sheer penetration of neuroscience into everyday life that makes it remarkable," said Bell.

The Case Against

Few people would dispute the claim that the brain and its scientific study have entered the public consciousness as never before. Neuroscience has seeped into our conversation and into new areas of inquiry, many of them previously assumed to fall under the humanities. But has this advance really transformed the way that we see ourselves? Has neuroscience truly revolutionized the subject areas onto whose territory it has so recently trespassed? The evidence to date suggests not.

Look at the new field of neuroleadership. Management scholars such as Dirk Lindebaum and Mike Zundel have raised concerns with many aspects of the new field, including the idea that looking at the neural correlates of good leadership will allow the ingredients of an effective leader to somehow be reverse engineered.[201] Lindebaum and Zundel argue that this assumes the brain is the "ultimate cause" for human behavior, and yet it's clear that the brain can just as easily be influenced by bodily states, past experiences, and thoughts. "We suggest that a first step in the right direction is to abandon the expectation that organizational neuroscience can single-handedly 'revolutionize' our understanding of leadership," they wrote in 2013.

Management consultant and founder of TrustedAdvisor.com, Charles Green is another skeptic. Writing on his blog in 2013[202] he highlighted several examples of neuroscience being invoked by high-profile scholars and management gurus, including Daniel Goleman on the "neuroscience of habit change" and Srinivasan Pillay on ways that brain science can "enhance understanding within the executive environment."

In each case, Green says the experts mentioned neurochemicals and parts of the brain and then distilled the neuroscience into actionable pieces of advice. But, he says, their advice amounts to "non-sequiturs and blinding flashes of the obvious." For example, Goleman's advice to help others break bad habits boiled down to tips like "empathize before giving advice" and "offer a caring gesture." Pillay's arguments included the idea that reframing old ideas in neuroscience jargon makes them more acceptable. In each case, Green says that he finds their conclusions "either completely unrelated to the neuroscience itself," or "numbingly old hat."

What about the new discipline of neuroaesthetics? So far this has largely involved identifying patterns of brain activity associated with finding art beautiful. The findings are certainly proving useful for the scientific understanding of pleasure and revealing ways that artists exploit the mechanisms of human vision. But there's little sign yet that the field is altering our consumption of, or conversation about, art.

Writing in *Nature*,[203] the science writer and author Philip Ball says he fears that a reductionist approach to art could even lead to the unwelcome idea that there is a right or wrong way of creating it – a mistake given that aesthetics is about culture and circumstance, not merely a fundamental property of the brain. But above all, he just doesn't hold out much hope for what the field can achieve. "Indications so far are that it may be along these lines," he says: "'Listening to music activates reward and pleasure circuits in brain regions such as the nucleus accumbens, ventral tegmental area and amygdala.' Thanks, but no, thanks."

What about the effect of neuroscience on self-understanding among the general public? We've seen there are signs we're mentioning the brain more in our everyday speech, but is that amounting to a changing sense of self? In their review of this issue published in 2013, Cliodhna O'Connor and Helene Joffe at UCL argue that talk of a neurorevolution in self-understanding is overblown. They pointed to a survey and focus groups with female teenagers published in 2012.[204] This showed many were aware of the notion of the "adolescent brain" and thought it was an important topic, and yet, when it came to self-understanding, none thought it could offer insights and many said it was boring. "None of our participants appropriated 'neurotalk' or descriptions of cortical plasticity (to which they were exposed) into their own understanding of their own behavior," the researchers said.

Another study published in 2012[205] explored how adults with ADHD understood their condition. Far from being side-tracked by neuroscience, the participants made reference to a wide range of factors taking in biology, psychology, and social issues. "Neurobiology resonates among adults with ADHD," the researchers observed, "but does not dominate their thinking."

What about our belief in individual free will and interpretations of criminal culpability? Some commentators think the more we understand about the neural correlates of behavior, the harder it will be to maintain a belief in individual choice and responsibility. "Modern neuroscience is eroding the idea of free will" said an *Economist* headline,[206] typical of the genre, published in 2006.

In fact, the evidence is mixed. A 2008 paper[207] found that people held wrong-doers just as responsible for their actions whether the perpetrator had a condition described in psychological or neurological terms. However, a later study involving US State Trial judges[208] found that they were more lenient toward a convict diagnosed with psychopathy if presented with testimony describing a neurobiological cause for his condition.

In 2013 Laurence Steinberg assessed the influence of neuroscience in four landmark US Supreme Court decisions on whether adolescent criminals should be considered as culpable as adults. His analysis shows neuroscience has played a progressively larger role in the Court's decision making, in particular through showing that the adolescent brain is not yet fully developed, and that immature teens may yet develop into more responsible adults. However, it's not clear that this is the neurorevolution that Zach Lynch and others have heralded. Laurence concluded that "the neuroscientific evidence was probably persuasive to the Court not because it told us something new but precisely because it aligned with common sense and behavioral science."

It's possible that the influence of neuroscience findings on our moral behavior is more insidious. A line of research has claimed that exposure to neurobiological explanations for human behavior and decision making leads participants to behave more unethically. For instance, a 2008 study[209] found that students exposed to an account by Francis Crick suggesting that free will is an illusion went on to award themselves more money for correct answers in a quiz, as compared with students who didn't read the passage. It's unlikely these students really did get more answers right, so they were probably cheating. The authors Kathleen Vohs and Jonathan Schooler took their finding seriously. "If exposure to deterministic messages increases the likelihood of unethical actions," they concluded, "then identifying approaches for insulating the public against this danger becomes imperative." Nevertheless, we probably shouldn't be too concerned just yet. In 2013 Rolf Zwaan at the Erasmus University of Rotterdam reported his failure to replicate the effect of exposure to deterministic neurobiology on cheating.[210]

I said in the introduction that today's myths could become tomorrow's facts and the idea that we're in the midst of a neuroscience-inspired revolution in self-understanding is a prime candidate for such a transformation. The tide of brain science is lapping at the shores of many areas of human study and everyday life. It may yet cause a flood and overturn established doctrines and beliefs. But for now this vision remains a myth, an exaggeration.

"Claims that neuroscience will dramatically alter people's relations with their selves, others and the world are overstated," is how O'Connor and Joffe concluded their 2013 review. "In many cases," they added, "neuroscientific ideas have assimilated in ways that perpetuate rather than challenge existing modes of understanding."

"Despite all the grand promises and expectations generated by neuroentrepreneurs, we cannot know for certain whether any lasting new bodies of expertise will emerge," wrote Nikolas Rose and Joelle Abi-Rached in their 2013 book *Neuro: The New Brain Sciences and the Management of the Mind*, "nor can we foretell the role of neurobiology in the government of conduct across the next decades." Weighing up all the evidence, it seems clear that neuroscience hasn't yet transformed how we see ourselves, nor has it overhauled the arts and humanities – but watch this space!

Myth: Neurolinguistic Programming Is a Valid Psychological Technique

These days anyone wanting to cash in on the excitement and prestige of neuroscience simply has stick the "neuro-" prefix in front of their product or therapeutic technique. Certainly this strategy worked a dream for US self-help gurus Richard Bandler and John Grinder when they launched neurolinguistic programming (NLP) in the 1970s. Their system was based on the idea of observing the most effective psychotherapists in action and deducing the mechanisms behind their success. A key idea Bandler and Grinder developed was that each of us has a "preferred representational system" for thinking about the world, dominated by input from one of the supposed five human senses. A related claim they made is that mirroring a person's preferred system will help you build up rapport with them.

Based on teachings like these, NLP grew into a hugely successful international self-help and training movement and it remains incredibly popular in business and sport. With anyone able to become a NLP practitioner with just a short spell of training the movement continues to thrive, enjoying constant promotion through its new converts, each of whom gains from myth that it works. Promotional websites make impressive claims that NLP techniques can help anyone achieve almost anything.[211] Today many companies pay high fees to send their staff on NLP workshops. In return, staff receive glossy teaching materials, a belief that they've learned the secrets of human psychology and, if they're lucky, they may even gain the impressive-sounding "Master Practitioner" title.

And yet NLP today is largely outcast from mainstream psychology and neuroscience. This is because the computational and neurological references used by NLP are largely gratuitous and the central tenets don't stand up to scrutiny. It's a difficult system to interrogate because its methods and claims are so amorphous, inconsistent, and slippery. Nonetheless, over the years attempts have been made to validate key claims, especially around the idea of preferred representation systems. In 2009, Tomasz Witkowski performed a comprehensive analysis of all properly controlled empirical tests of NLP published to date. Out of 33 relevant studies, just 18.2 percent found results supportive of NLP, 54.5 percent were non-supportive, with 27.3 percent ambiguous. Writing in the *Polish Psychological Bulletin*,[212] Witkowski's verdict was clear: "My analysis leads undeniably to the statement that NLP represents pseudoscientific rubbish, which should be mothballed forever."

Some may argue that NLP must be doing something right and should be allowed to prosper from its popularity. In an open marketplace, no one is forced to attend its workshops. However, sending middle-managers away with dubious psychological techniques is one thing, using a form of NLP therapy to treat traumatized war veterans is quite another. Late in 2013, a Welsh NHS service for veterans called a local charity to task for using NLP therapy to treat traumatized soldiers and instructed them to stop. Dr Neil Kitchiner, principal clinician with the NHS All Wales Veterans Health and Wellbeing Service told the BBC:[213] "Some have been made very unwell as a result of going there [for NLP therapy] and have needed a lot of support from NHS and veterans' charities." For the record, NLP therapy for trauma is not currently recognized as a scientifically supported treatment.

Notes

1   http://faculty.washington.edu/chudler/neurok.html (accessed May 15, 2014).
2   Wanjek, C. (2003). *Bad Medicine: Misconceptions and Misuses Revealed, from Distance Healing to Vitamin O*. Wiley.
3   Dekker, S., Lee, N. C., Howard-Jones, P., & Jolles, J. (2012). Neuromyths in education: Prevalence and predictors of misconceptions among teachers. *Frontiers in Psychology*, 3, 1–8.
4   Herculano-Houzel, S. (2002). Do you know your brain? A survey on public neuroscience literacy at the closing of the decade of the brain. *The Neuroscientist*, 8(2), 98–110.

5 Beyerstein, B. L. (1999). Whence cometh the myth that we only use 10% of our brains. In Della Sala (ed.), *Mind Myths: Exploring Popular Assumptions about the Mind and Brain*. J. Wiley & Sons, pp. 314–335.

6 James, W. (1907). The energies of men. *The Philosophical Review*, 16(1), 1–20.

7 Lewin, R. (1980). Is your brain really necessary? *Science*, 210(4475), 1232–1234.

8 Ries, A., & Ries, L. (2009). *War in the Boardroom: Why Left-Brain Management and Right-Brain Marketing Don't See Eye-to-Eye – and What to Do About It*. Collins Business.

9 http://christianworkingwoman.org/broadcast/why%2baren%2527t%2b women%2blike%2bmen-or%2bvice%2bversa%253f%2b-1/ (accessed May 15, 2014).

10 McGilchrist, I. (2009). *The Master and His Emissary: The Divided Brain and the Making of the Western World*. Yale University Press.

11 Dax, M. (1865). Lésions de la moitié gauche de l'éncephale coincident avec l'oubli des signes de la pensée. *Gaz Hebdom Méd Chirurg*, 11, 259–260.

12 Corballis, M. C. (1999). Are we in our right minds? In Della Sala (ed.), *Mind Myths: Exploring Popular Assumptions about the Mind and Brain*. J. Wiley and Sons, pp. 25–41..

13 Rogers, L. J., Zucca, P., & Vallortigara, G. (2004). Advantages of having a lateralized brain. *Proceedings of the Royal Society of London. Series B: Biological Sciences*, 271(Suppl. 6), S420–S422.

14 Stephan, K. E., Marshall, J. C., Friston, K. J., Rowe, J. B., Ritzl, A., Zilles, K., & Fink, G. R. (2003). Lateralized cognitive processes and lateralized task control in the human brain. *Science*, 301(5631), 384–386.

15 Fink, G. R., Marshall, J. C., Halligan, P. W., Frith, C. D., Frackowiak, R. S. J., & Dolan, R. J. (1997). Hemispheric specialization for global and local processing: The effect of stimulus category. *Proceedings of the Royal Society of London. Series B: Biological Sciences*, 264(1381), 487–494.

16 Bowden, E. M., Jung-Beeman, M., Fleck, J., & Kounios, J. (2005). New approaches to demystifying insight. *Trends in Cognitive Sciences*, 9(7), 322–328.

17 Gazzaniga, M. (2002). The split brain revisited. *Scientific American*, 279(1), 50.

18 Nielsen, J. A., Zielinski, B. A., Ferguson, M. A., Lainhart, J. E., & Anderson, J. S. (2013). An evaluation of the left-brain vs. right-brain hypothesis with resting state functional connectivity magnetic resonance imaging. *PloS One*, 8(8), e71275.

19 http://www.medicalnewstoday.com/articles/264923.php (accessed May 15, 2014).

20 Rowson, J., & McGilchrist, I. (2013). Divided brain, divided world. http://www.thersa.org/action-research-centre/learning,-cognition-and-creativity/social-brain/reports/the-divided-brain (accessed May 15, 2014).

21 http://kenanmalik.wordpress.com/2013/02/21/divided-brain-divided-world/ (accessed May 15, 2014).

22 McManus, I. C. (2004). *Right Hand, Left Hand: The Origins of Asymmetry in Brains, Bodies, Atoms, and Cultures.* Harvard University Press.

23 Grimshaw, G. M., & Wilson, M. S. (2013). A sinister plot? Facts, beliefs, and stereotypes about the left-handed personality. *Laterality: Asymmetries of Body, Brain and Cognition,* 18(2), 135–151.

24 Halpern, D. F., & Coren, S. (1988). Do right-handers live longer? *Nature,* 333(6170): 213.

25 Aggleton, J. P., Bland, J. M., Kentridge, R. W., & Neave, N. J. (1994). Handedness and longevity: Archival study of cricketers. *BMJ,* 309(6970), 1681.

26 Geschwind, N., & Behan, P. (1982). Left-handedness: Association with immune disease, migraine, and developmental learning disorder. *Proceedings of the National Academy of Sciences,* 79(16), 5097–5100.

27 Bryden, M. P., McManus, I. C., & Bulmanfleming, M. B. (1994). Evaluating the empirical support for the Geschwind-Behan-Galaburda model of cerebral lateralization. *Brain and Cognition,* 26(2), 103–167.

28 Kalisch, T., Wilimzig, C., Kleibel, N., Tegenthoff, M., & Dinse, H. R. (2006). Age-related attenuation of dominant hand superiority. *PLoS One,* 1(1), e90.

29 http://www.guardian.co.uk/books/2012/sep/25/puzzle-of-left-handedness-rik-smits-review (accessed May 15, 2014).

30 Grimshaw, G. M., & Wilson, M. S. (2013). A sinister plot? Facts, beliefs, and stereotypes about the left-handed personality. *Laterality: Asymmetries of Body, Brain and Cognition,* 18(2), 135–151.

31 Raymond, M., Pontier, D., Dufour, A. B., & Moller, A. P. (1996). Frequency-dependent maintenance of left handedness in humans. *Proceedings of the Royal Society of London. Series B: Biological Sciences,* 263(1377), 1627–1633.

32 Gursoy, R. (2009). Effects of left-or right-hand preference on the success of boxers in Turkey. *British Journal of Sports Medicine,* 43(2), 142–144.

33 Harris, L. J. (2010). In fencing, what gives left-handers the edge? Views from the present and the distant past. *Laterality,* 15(1–2), 15–55.

34 http://suite101.com/article/do-men-and-women-speak-the-same-language-a347042 (accessed May 15, 2014).

35 Gerschwind, N., & Galaburda, A. (1987). Cerebral Lateralization. MIT Press.

36 Gilmore, J. H., Lin, W., Prastawa, M. W., Looney, C. B., Vetsa, Y. S. K., Knickmeyer, R. C., … & Gerig, G. (2007). Regional gray matter growth, sexual dimorphism, and cerebral asymmetry in the neonatal brain. *The Journal of Neuroscience,* 27(6), 1255–1260.

37 Sommer, I. E., Aleman, A., Bouma, A., & Kahn, R. S. (2004). Do women really have more bilateral language representation than men? A meta-analysis of functional imaging studies. *Brain,* 127(8), 1845–1852.

38 Wallentin, M. (2009). Putative sex differences in verbal abilities and language cortex: A critical review. *Brain and Language,* 108(3), 175–183.

39 Westerhausen, R., Kompus, K., Dramsdahl, M., Falkenberg, L. E., Grüner, R., Hjelmervik, H., … & Hugdahl, K. (2011). A critical re-examination of sexual dimorphism in the corpus callosum microstructure. *Neuroimage,* 56(3), 874–880.

40 Collignon, O., Girard, S., Gosselin, F., Saint-Amour, D., Lepore, F., & Lassonde, M. (2010). Women process multisensory emotion expressions more efficiently than men. *Neuropsychologia*, 48(1), 220–225.

41 Fine, C. (2010). Delusions of Gender: How Our Minds, Society, and Neurosexism Create Difference. W. W. Norton.

42 Singer, T., Seymour, B., O'Doherty, J., Kaube, H., Dolan, R. J., & Frith, C. D. (2004). Empathy for pain involves the affective but not sensory components of pain. *Science*, 303(5661), 1157–1162.

43 Singer, T., Seymour, B., O'Doherty, J. P., Stephan, K. E., Dolan, R. J., & Frith, C. D. (2006). Empathic neural responses are modulated by the perceived fairness of others. *Nature*, 439(7075), 466–469.

44 Ingalhalikar, M., Smith, A., Parker, D., Satterthwaite, T. D., Elliott, M. A., Ruparel, K., ... & Verma, R. (2014). Sex differences in the structural connectome of the human brain. *Proceedings of the National Academy of Sciences*, 111(2), 823–828.

45 http://figshare.com/articles/Illustrative_effect_sizes_for_sex_differences/866802 (accessed May 15, 2014).

46 Strick, P. L., Dum, R. P., & Fiez, J. A. (2009). Cerebellum and nonmotor function. *Annual Review of Neuroscience*, 32, 413–434.

47 http://tinyurl.com/cydgvbd (accessed May 15, 2014).

48 Blanton, R. E., Levitt, J. G., Peterson, J. R., Fadale, D., Sporty, M. L., Lee, M., ... & Toga, A. W. (2004). Gender differences in the left inferior frontal gyrus in normal children. *Neuroimage*, 22(2), 626–636.

49 Sax, L. (2007). *Why Gender Matters: What Parents and Teachers Need to Know about the Emerging Science of Sex Differences*. Random House Digital.

50 Killgore, W. D., Oki, M., & Yurgelun-Todd, D. A. (2001). Sex-specific developmental changes in amygdala responses to affective faces. *Neuroreport*, 12(2), 427–433.

51 Pahlke, E., Hyde, J. S., & Allison, C. M. (2014). The Effects of Single-Sex Compared With Coeducational Schooling on Students' Performance and Attitudes: A Meta-Analysis. *Psychological Bulletin*. doi: 10.1037/a0035740.

52 Witelson, S. F., Beresh, H., & Kigar, D. L. (2006). Intelligence and brain size in 100 postmortem brains: sex, lateralization and age factors. *Brain*, 129(2), 386–398.

53 Pakkenberg, B., & Gundersen, H. J. G. (1997). Neocortical neuron number in humans: Effect of sex and age. *Journal of Comparative Neurology*, 384(2), 312–320.

54 Cahill, L. (2006). Why sex matters for neuroscience. *Nature Reviews Neuroscience*, 7(6), 477–484.

55 Allen, J. S., Damasio, H., Grabowski, T. J., Bruss, J., & Zhang, W. (2003). Sexual dimorphism and asymmetries in the gray–white composition of the human cerebrum. *Neuroimage*, 18(4), 880–894.

56 Voyer, D., Voyer, S., & Bryden, M. P. (1995). Magnitude of sex differences in spatial abilities: A meta-analysis and consideration of critical variables. *Psychological Bulletin*, 117(2), 250.

57 Vrticka, P., Neely, M., Walter Shelly, E., Black, J. M., & Reiss, A. L. (2013). Sex differences during humor appreciation in child-sibling pairs. *Social Neuroscience* 8(4), 291–304.

58 Zhang, S., Schmader, T., & Hall, W. M. (2013). L'eggo my ego: Reducing the gender gap in math by unlinking the self from performance. *Self and Identity*, 12(4), 400–412.

59 Nosek, B. A., Smyth, F. L., Sriram, N., Lindner, N. M., Devos, T., Ayala, A., … & Greenwald, A. G. (2009). National differences in gender–science stereotypes predict national sex differences in science and math achievement. *Proceedings of the National Academy of Sciences*, 106(26), 10593–10597.

60 Morton, T. A., Postmes, T., Haslam, S. A., & Hornsey, M. J. (2009). Theorizing gender in the face of social change: Is there anything essential about essentialism? *Journal of Personality and Social Psychology*, 96(3), 653.

61 McCarthy, M. M., Arnold, A. P., Ball, G. F., Blaustein, J. D., & De Vries, G. J. (2012). Sex differences in the brain: The not so inconvenient truth. *The Journal of Neuroscience*, 32(7), 2241–2247.

62 Irvine, K., Laws, K. R., Gale, T. M., & Kondel, T. K. (2012). Greater cognitive deterioration in women than men with Alzheimer's disease: A meta analysis. *Journal of Clinical and Experimental Neuropsychology*, 34(9), 989–998.

63 Hurlbert, A. C., & Ling, Y. (2007). Biological components of sex differences in color preference. *Current Biology*, 17(16), R623–R625.

64 http://news.bbc.co.uk/1/hi/health/6956467.stm (accessed May 15, 2014).

65 LoBue, V., & DeLoache, J. S. (2011). Pretty in pink: The early development of gender-stereotyped colour preferences. *British Journal of Developmental Psychology*, 29(3), 656–667.

66 Del Giudice, M. (2012). The twentieth century reversal of pink–blue gender coding: A scientific urban legend? *Archives of Sexual Behavior*, 1–3.

67 Taylor, C., Clifford, A., & Franklin, A. (2013). Color preferences are not universal. *Journal of Experimental Psychology: General*. 142(4), 1015–1027.

68 Ramón y Cajal, S. R. (1913). *Estudios sobre la degeneración del sistema nervioso*. Moya.

69 Altman, J., & Das, G. D. (1965). Autoradiographic and histological evidence of postnatal hippocampal neurogenesis in rats. *Journal of Comparative Neurology*, 124(3), 319–335.

70 Gross, C. G. (2009). *A Hole in the Head: More Tales in the History of Neuroscience*. MIT Press.

71 Gross, C. G. (2009). *A Hole in the Head: More Tales in the History of Neuroscience*. MIT Press.

72 Kaplan, M. S. (2001). Environment complexity stimulates visual cortex neurogenesis: Death of a dogma and a research career. *Trends in Neurosciences*, 24(10), 617–620.

73 Nottebohm, F. (1981). A brain for all seasons: Cyclical anatomical changes in song control nuclei of the canary brain. *Science*, 214(4527), 1368–1370.

74 Barnea, A., & Nottebohm, F. (1994). Seasonal recruitment of hippocampal neurons in adult free-ranging black-capped chickadees. *Proceedings of the National Academy of Sciences*, 91(23), 11217–11221.

75 Rakic, P. (1985). Limits of neurogenesis in primates. *Science*, 227(4690), 1054–1056.

76 http://www.newyorker.com/archive/2001/07/23/010723fa_fact_specter (accessed May 15, 2014).

77 Gould, E., & Gross, C. G. (2002). Neurogenesis in adult mammals: Some progress and problems. *The Journal of Neuroscience*, 22(3), 619–623.

78 Kornack, D. R., & Rakic, P. (1999). Continuation of neurogenesis in the hippocampus of the adult macaque monkey. *Proceedings of the National Academy of Sciences*, 96(10), 5768–5773.

79 http://www.pnas.org/site/misc/gage_transcript.pdf (accessed May 15, 2014).

80 Eriksson, P. S., Perfilieva, E., Björk-Eriksson, T., Alborn, A. M., Nordborg, C., Peterson, D. A., & Gage, F. H. (1998). Neurogenesis in the adult human hippocampus. *Nature Medicine*, 4(11), 1313–1317.

81 Kempermann, G., & Gage, F. (2002). New nerve cells for the adult brain. *Scientific American*, 280(5), 48–53.

82 Spalding, K. L., Bergmann, O., Alkass, K., Bernard, S., Salehpour, M., Huttner, H. B., ... & Frisén, J. (2013). Dynamics of hippocampal neurogenesis in adult humans. *Cell*, 153(6), 1219–1227.

83 Fred, G. H. (2003). Brain, repair yourself. *Scientific American*, 298(3), 28–35.

84 Gould, E., Reeves, A. J., Graziano, M. S., & Gross, C. G. (1999). Neurogenesis in the neocortex of adult primates. *Science*, 286(5439), 548–552.

85 Kornack, D. R., & Rakic, P. (2001). Cell proliferation without neurogenesis in adult primate neocortex. *Science*, 294(5549), 2127–2130.

86 Van Praag, H., Kempermann, G., & Gage, F. H. (1999). Running increases cell proliferation and neurogenesis in the adult mouse dentate gyrus. *Nature Neuroscience*, 2(3), 266–270.

87 Shors, T. J. (2009). Saving new brain cells. *Scientific American*, 300(3), 46–54.

88 Shors, T. J. (2009). Saving new brain cells. *Scientific American*, 300(3), 46–54.

89 Mowla, A., Mosavinasab, M., Haghshenas, H., & Haghighi, A. B. (2007). Does serotonin augmentation have any effect on cognition and activities of daily living in Alzheimer's Dementia? A double-blind, placebo-controlled clinical trial. *Journal of Clinical Psychopharmacology*, 27(5), 484–487.

90 Sanai, N., Nguyen, T., Ihrie, R. A., Mirzadeh, Z., Tsai, H. H., Wong, M., ... & Alvarez-Buylla, A. (2011). Corridors of migrating neurons in the human brain and their decline during infancy. *Nature*, 478(7369), 382–386.

91 Constandi, M. (2012). Fantasy fix. *New Scientist*, 213(2852).

92 http://www.independent.co.uk/news/science/belief-and-the-brains-god-spot-1641022.html (accessed May 15, 2014).

93 http://www.dailymail.co.uk/sciencetech/article-1160904/Research-brains-God-spot-reveals-areas-brain-involved-religious-belief.html (accessed May 15, 2014).

94   Kapogiannis, D., Barbey, A. K., Su, M., Zamboni, G., Krueger, F., & Grafman, J. (2009). Cognitive and neural foundations of religious belief. *Proceedings of the National Academy of Sciences*, 106(12), 4876–4881.

95   Slater, E., & Beard, A. W. (1963a). The schizophrenia-like psychoses of epilepsy: i. Psychiatric aspects. *British Journal of Psychiatry*, 109, 95–112. Slater, E., & Beard, A. W. (1963b). The schizophrenia-like psychoses of epilepsy: v. Discussion and conclusions. *British Journal of Psychiatry*, 109, 143–150.

96   Geschwind, N. (1979). Behavioral changes in temporal lobe epilepsy. *Psychological Medicine*, 9, 217–219.

97   Ramachandran, V. S., & Blakeslee, S. (1999). *Phantoms in the Brain: Probing the Mysteries of the Human Mind*. HarperCollins.

98   Pierre, L. S., & Persinger, M. A. (2006). Experimental facilitation of the sensed presence is predicted by the specific patterns of the applied magnetic fields, not by suggestibility: Re-analyses of 19 experiments. *International Journal of Neuroscience*, 116(19), 1079–1096.

99   His comments were made to the online magazine New Sun while promoting his 2001 book, *Where God Lives: The Science of the Paranormal and How Our Brains are Linked to the Universe*.

100 http://spiritualscientific.com/spiritual_neuroscience/the_god_spot (accessed May 15, 2014).

101 Aaen-Stockdale, C. (2012). Neuroscience for the soul. *Psychologist*, 25(7), 520–523.

102 Ogata, A., & Miyakawa, T. (1998). Religious experiences in epileptic patients with a focus on ictus-related episodes. *Psychiatry and Clinical Neurosciences*, 52(3), 321–325.

103 Hughes, J. R. (2005). Did all those famous people really have epilepsy? *Epilepsy & Behavior*, 6(2), 115–139.

104 Granqvist, P., Fredrikson, M., Unge, P., Hagenfeldt, A., Valind, S., Larhammar, D., & Larsson, M. (2005). Sensed presence and mystical experiences are predicted by suggestibility, not by the application of transcranial weak complex magnetic fields. *Neuroscience Letters*, 379(1), 1–6.

105 Newberg, A., Alavi, A., Baime, M., Pourdehnad, M., Santanna, J., & d'Aquili, E. (2001). The measurement of regional cerebral blood flow during the complex cognitive task of meditation: A preliminary SPECT study. *Psychiatry Research: Neuroimaging*, 106(2), 113–122.

106 Newberg, A. B., Wintering, N. A., Morgan, D., & Waldman, M. R. (2006). The measurement of regional cerebral blood flow during glossolalia: A preliminary SPECT study. *Psychiatry Research: Neuroimaging*, 148(1), 67–71.

107 Beauregard, M., & Paquette, V. (2006). Neural correlates of a mystical experience in Carmelite nuns. *Neuroscience Letters*, 405(3), 186–190.

108 Biello, D. (2007). Searching for God in the brain. *Scientific American Mind*, 18(5), 38–45.

109 http://www.theatlantic.com/health/archive/2012/08/scientists-find-brains-irony-detection-center/260728/ (accessed May 15, 2014).

110 http://www.nytimes.com/2013/10/31/science/afraid-of-snakes-your-pulvinar-may-be-to-blame.html (accessed May 15, 2014).

111 Wilson, C. R., Gaffan, D., Browning, P. G., & Baxter, M. G. (2010). Functional localization within the prefrontal cortex: Missing the forest for the trees? *Trends in Neurosciences*, 33(12), 533–540.

112 Anderson, M. L. (2010). Neural reuse: A fundamental organizational principle of the brain. *Behavioral and Brain Sciences*, 33(4), 245.

113 http://www.psychologytoday.com/blog/after-phrenology/201109/mit-scientists-declare-there-is-no-science-brains (accessed May 15, 2014).

114 http://www.guardian.co.uk/lifeandstyle/2010/feb/04/pregnant-women-forgetful-science (accessed May 15, 2014).

115 http://www.newstatesman.com/node/143178 (accessed May 15, 2014).

116 Crawley, R., Grant, S., & Hinshaw, K. (2008). Cognitive changes in pregnancy: Mild decline or society stereotype? *Applied Cognitive Psychology*, 22, 1142–1162.

117 Corse, S. (1990). Pregnant managers and their subordinates: The effects of gender expectations on hierarchical relationships. *Journal of Applied Behavioural Science*, 26, 25–47.

118 Hebl, M. R., King, E. B., Glick, P., Singletary, S. L., & Kazama, S. (2007). Hostile and benevolent reactions toward pregnant women: Complementary interpersonal punishments and rewards that maintain traditional roles. *Journal of Applied Psychology*, 92(6), 1499.

119 Cunningham, J., & Macan, T. (2007). Effects of applicant pregnancy on hiring decisions and interview ratings. *Sex Roles*, 57(7–8), 497–508.

120 Oatridge, A., Holdcroft, A., Saeed, N., Hajnal, J. V., Puri, B. K., Fusi, L., & Bydder, G. M. (2002). Change in brain size during and after pregnancy: Study in healthy women and women with preeclampsia. *American Journal of Neuroradiology*, 23, 19–26.

121 Henry, J. D., & Rendell, P. G. (2007). A review of the impact of pregnancy on memory function. *Journal of Clinical and Experimental Neuropsychology*, 29, 793–803.

122 Hurt, N. E. (2011). Legitimizing "baby brain": Tracing a rhetoric of significance through science and the mass media. *Communication and Critical/ Cultural Studies*, 8(4), 376–398.

123 Christensen, H., Leach, L. S., & Mackinnon, A. (2010). Cognition in pregnancy and motherhood: Prospective cohort study. *British Journal of Psychiatry*, 196, 126–132.

124 Cuttler, C., Graf, P., Pawluski, J. L., & Galea, L. A. (2011). Everyday life memory deficits in pregnant women. *Canadian Journal of Experimental Psychology/Revue canadienne de psychologie expérimentale*, 65(1), 27.

125 Henry, J. F., & Sherwin, B. B. (2012). Hormones and cognitive functioning during late pregnancy and postpartum: A longitudinal study. *Behavioral Neuroscience*, 126(1), 73.

126 Wilson, D. L., Barnes, M., Ellett, L., Permezel, M., Jackson, M., & Crowe, S. F. (2013). Reduced verbal memory retention is unrelated to sleep disturbance during pregnancy. *Australian Psychologist*, 48(3), 196–208.

127 http://www.thepsychologist.org.uk/archive/archive_home.cfm?volumeID= 23&editionID=184&ArticleID=1641 (accessed May 15, 2014).

128 Kinsley, C. H., & Lambert, K. G. (2006). The maternal brain. *Scientific American*, 294(1), 72–79.

129 Swain, J. E., Kim, P., & Ho, S. S. (2011). Neuroendocrinology of parental response to baby-cry. *Journal of Neuroendocrinology*, 23(11), 1036–1041.

130 Kim, P., Leckman, J. F., Mayes, L. C., Feldman, R., Wang, X., & Swain, J. E. (2010). The plasticity of human maternal brain: Longitudinal changes in brain anatomy during the early postpartum period. *Behavioral Neuroscience*, 124(5), 695.

131 Pearson, R. M., Lightman, S. L., & Evans, J. (2009). Emotional sensitivity for motherhood: Late pregnancy is associated with enhanced accuracy to encode emotional faces. *Hormones and Behavior*, 56(5), 557–563.

132 Roos, A., Lochner, C., Kidd, M., Van Honk, J., Vythilingum, B., & Stein, D. J. (2012). Selective attention to fearful faces during pregnancy. *Progress in Neuro-Psychopharmacology and Biological Psychiatry*, 37(1), 76–80.

133 Ekirch, A. R. (2006). *At Day's Close: Night in Times Past*. W. W. Norton.

134 Huber, R., Mäki, H., Rosanova, M., Casarotto, S., Canali, P., Casali, A. G., … & Massimini, M. (2013). Human cortical excitability increases with time awake. *Cerebral Cortex*, 23(2), 1–7.

135 Roenneberg, T., Kuehnle, T., Pramstaller, P. P., Ricken, J., Havel, M., Guth, A., & Merrow, M. (2004). A marker for the end of adolescence. *Current Biology*, 14(24), R1038–R1039.

136 Jenni, O. G., Achermann, P., & Carskadon, M. A. (2005). Homeostatic sleep regulation in adolescents. *Sleep*, 28(11), 1446–1454.

137 Vince, G. (2006). It came from another time zone. *New Scientist*, 191(2567), 40–43.

138 Saurat, M. T., Agbakou, M., Attigui, P., Golmard, J. L., & Arnulf, I. (2011). Walking dreams in congenital and acquired paraplegia. *Consciousness and Cognition*, 20(4), 1425–1432.

139 Quotes taken from her website in 2013: www.lauriloewenberg.com (accessed May 15, 2014).

140 Online exchange took place during 2012 at http://www.psychologytoday. com/blog/brain-myths/201210/seize-control-your-dreams/comments and was still available in 2013 (accessed May 15, 2014).

141 Blagrove, M. (2013). Dreaming and insight. *Frontiers in Psychology*. doi: 10.3389/fpsyg.2013.00979.

142 Hill, C. E., Knox, S., Crook-Lyon, R. E., Hess, S. A., Miles, J., Spangler, P. T., & Pudasaini, S. (2014). Dreaming of you: Client and therapist dreams about each other during psychodynamic psychotherapy. *Psychotherapy Research* (Jan. 6, Epub), 1–15.

143 Hobson, J. A., & McCarley, R. M. (1977). The brain as a dream state generator: An activation-synthesis hypothesis of the dream process. *American Journal of Psychiatry*, 134, 1335–1348.

144 Yu, C. K. C. (2012). The effect of sleep position on dream experiences. *Dreaming*, 22(3), 212.

145 Selterman, D. F., Apetroaia, A. I., Riela, S., & Aron, A. (2014). Dreaming of you: Behavior and emotion in dreams of significant others predict subsequent relational behavior. *Social Psychological and Personality Science*, 5(1), 111–118.

146 French, C. C., Santomauro, J., Hamilton, V., Fox, R., & Thalbourne, M. A. (2008). Psychological aspects of the alien contact experience. *Cortex*, 44(10), 1387–1395.

147 Santomauro, J., & French, C. C. (2009). Terror in the night. *The Psychologist*, 22, 672–675.

148 http://www.smashwords.com/books/view/118271 (accessed May 15, 2014).

149 Erlacher, D., & Schredl, M. (2010). Practicing a motor task in a lucid dream enhances subsequent performance: A pilot study. *Sport Psychologist*, 24(2), 157–167.

150 Arzi, A., Shedlesky, L., Ben-Shaul, M., Nasser, K., Oksenberg, A., Hairston, I. S., & Sobel, N. (2012). Humans can learn new information during sleep. *Nature Neuroscience*, 15, 1460–1465.

151 Van der Werf, Y. D., Altena, E., Schoonheim, M. M., Sanz-Arigita, E. J., Vis, J. C., De Rijke, W., & Van Someren, E. J. (2009). Sleep benefits subsequent hippocampal functioning. *Nature Neuroscience*, 12(2), 122–123.

152 Gillen-O'Neel, C., Huynh, V. W., & Fuligni, A. J. (2012). To study or to sleep? The academic costs of extra studying at the expense of sleep. *Child Development*, 84(1), 133–142.

153 Louie, K., & Wilson, M. A. (2001). Temporally structured replay of awake hippocampal ensemble activity during rapid eye movement sleep. *Neuron*, 29(1), 145–156.

154 Holz, J., Piosczyk, H., Landmann, N., Feige, B., Spiegelhalder, K., Riemann, D., … & Voderholzer, U. (2012). The timing of learning before night-time sleep differentially affects declarative and procedural long-term memory consolidation in adolescents. *PloS One*, 7(7), e40963.

155 McGeown, W. J., Mazzoni, G., Venneri, A., & Kirsch, I. (2009). Hypnotic induction decreases anterior default mode activity. *Consciousness and Cognition*, 18(4), 848–855.

156 Deeley, Q., Oakley, D. A., Toone, B., Giampietro, V., Brammer, M. J., Williams, S. C., & Halligan, P. W. (2012). Modulating the default mode network using hypnosis. *International Journal of Clinical and Experimental Hypnosis*, 60(2), 206–228.

157 Raz, A., Shapiro, T., Fan, J., & Posner, M. I. (2002). Hypnotic suggestion and the modulation of Stroop interference. *Archives of General Psychiatry*, 59(12), 1155.

158 Raz, A., Kirsch, I., Pollard, J., & Nitkin-Kaner, Y. (2006). Suggestion reduces the Stroop effect. *Psychological Science*, 17(2), 91–95.

159 Pyka, M., Burgmer, M., Lenzen, T., Pioch, R., Dannlowski, U., Pfleiderer, B., ... & Konrad, C. (2011). Brain correlates of hypnotic paralysis – A resting-state fMRI study. *Neuroimage*, 56(4), 2173–2182.

160 Oakley, D. A., & Halligan, P. W. (2013). Hypnotic suggestion: Opportunities for cognitive neuroscience. *Nature Reviews Neuroscience*, 14(8), 565–76.

161 Kahneman, D. (2011). *Thinking, Fast and Slow*. Macmillan.

162 Allport, D. A. (1980). Patterns and actions: Cognitive mechanisms are content-specific. In G. Claxton (ed.), *Cognitive Psychology: New Directions*. Routledge and Kegan Paul, pp. 26–64.

163 Stafford, T., & Webb, M. (2005). *Mind Hacks*. O'Reilly Media, p. 218.

164 Hobbes, T. (1969). *Leviathan*, 1651. Scolar Press.

165 Pinker, S. (2002). *The Blank Slate: The Modern Denial of Human Nature*. New American Library.

166 Searle, J. R. (1980). Minds, brains, and programs. *Behavioral and Brain Sciences*, 3(3), 417–457.

167 Tallis, R., & Aleksander, I. (2008). Computer models of the mind are invalid. *Journal of Information Technology*, 23(1), 55–62.

168 http://scienceblogs.com/developingintelligence/2007/03/27/why-the-brain-is-not-like-a-co/ (accessed May 15, 2014).

169 Monaghan, P., Keidel, J., Burton, M., & Westermann, G. (2010). What computers have shown us about the mind. *Psychologist*, 23(8), 642–645.

170 http://www.edge.org/conversation/the-normal-well-tempered-mind (accessed May 15, 2014).

171 http://www.wired.com/wiredscience/2013/05/neurologist-markam-human-brain/all/ (accessed May 15, 2014).

172 Woollett, K., & Maguire, E. A. (2011). Acquiring "the knowledge" of London's layout drives structural brain changes. *Current Biology*, 21(24), 2109–2114.

173 Kumari, V. (2006). Do psychotherapies produce neurobiological effects? *Acta Neuropsychiatrica*, 18(2), 61–70.

174 http://www.telegraph.co.uk/comment/9598971/Is-the-afterlife-full-of-fluffy-clouds-and-angels.html (accessed May 15, 2014).

175 http://www.samharris.org/blog/item/this-must-be-heaven (accessed May 15, 2014).

176 Greyson, B. (2010). Implications of near-death experiences for a postmaterialist psychology. *Psychology of Religion and Spirituality*, 2(1), 37.

177 Parnia, S., Waller, D. G., Yeates, R., & Fenwick, P. (2001). A qualitative and quantitative study of the incidence, features and aetiology of near death experiences in cardiac arrest survivors. *Resuscitation*, 48(2), 149–156.

178 Mobbs, D., & Watt, C. (2011). There is nothing paranormal about near-death experiences: How neuroscience can explain seeing bright lights,

meeting the dead, or being convinced you are one of them. *Trends in Cognitive Sciences*, 15(10), 447–449.

179 Sheldrake, R. (2005). The sense of being stared at – Part 2: Its implications for theories of vision. *Journal of Consciousness Studies*, 12(6), 32–49.

180 Schmidt, S., Schneider, R., Utts, J., & Walach, H. (2004). Distant intentionality and the feeling of being stared at: Two meta-analyses. *British Journal of Psychology*, 95(2), 235–247.

181 Marks, D., & Coiwell, J. (2000). The psychic staring effect: An artifact of pseudo-randomization. *Skeptical Inquirer*, 41, 49.

182 Wehr, T. (2009). Staring nowhere? Unseen gazes remain undetected under consideration of three statistical methods. *European Journal of Parapsychology*, 24, 32–52.

183 Wiseman, R., & Schlitz, M. (1997). Experimenter effects and the remote detection of staring. *Journal of Parapsychology*, 61, 197–207.

184 Schlitz, M., Wiseman, R., Watt, C., & Radin, D. (2006). Of two minds: Sceptic-proponent collaboration within parapsychology. *British Journal of Psychology*, 97(3), 313–322.

185 Lohr, J. M., Adams, T. G., Schwarz, M., & Brady, R. E. (2013). The sense of being stared at. An empirical test of a popular paranormal belief. *Skeptic Magazine*, 18, 51–55.

186 http://www.youtube.com/watch?v=M9w7jHYriFo (accessed May 15, 2014).

187 Bösch, H., Steinkamp, F., & Boller, E. (2006). Examining psychokinesis: The interaction of human intention with random number generators – A meta-analysis. *Psychological Bulletin*, 132(4), 497.

188 Wilson, D. B., & Shadish, W. R. (2006). On blowing trumpets to the tulips: To prove or not to prove the null hypothesis – Comment on Bösch, Steinkamp, and Boller (2006), *Psychological Bulletin*, 132(4), 524–528.

189 Winer, G. A., & Cottrell, J. E. (1996). Does anything leave the eye when we see? Extramission beliefs of children and adults. *Current Directions in Psychological Science*, 5(5), 137–142.

190 Winer, G. A., Cottrell, J. E., Gregg, V., Fournier, J. S., & Bica, L. A. (2002). Fundamentally misunderstanding visual perception: Adults' belief in visual emissions. *American Psychologist*, 57(6–7), 417.

191 Rose, N., & Abi-Rached, J. M. (2013). *Neuro: The New Brain Sciences and the Management of the Mind*. Princeton University Press.

192 Chancellor, B., & Chatterjee, A. (2011). Brain branding: When neuroscience and commerce collide. *AJOB Neuroscience*, 2(4), 18–27.

193 http://www.neuroleadership.org/institute/index.shtml (accessed May 15, 2014).

194 http://neuroesthetics.org/institute.php (accessed May 15, 2014).

195 http://www.neuroesthetics.org/statement-on-neuroesthetics.php (accessed May 15, 2014).

196 http://www.rsablogs.org.uk/2013/socialbrain/brains-spirituality/ (accessed May 15, 2014).

197 http://nplusonemag.com/rise-neuronovel (accessed May 15, 2014).

198   Álvarez, M. P. (2011). The magnetism of neuroimaging: Fashion, myth and ideology of the brain. *Papeles del Psicólogo*, 32(2), 98–112.

199   Rodriguez, P. (2006). Talking brains: A cognitive semantic analysis of an emerging folk neuropsychology. *Public Understanding of Science*, 15(3), 301–330.

200   http://www.theguardian.com/science/2013/mar/03/brain-not-simple-folk-neuroscience (accessed May 15, 2014).

201   Lindebaum, D., & Zundel, M. (2013). Not quite a revolution: Scrutinizing organizational neuroscience in leadership studies. *Human Relations*, 66(6), 857–877.

202   http://trustedadvisor.com/trustmatters/how-neuroscience-over-reaches-in-business (accessed May 15, 2014).

203   http://www.nature.com/news/neuroaesthetics-is-killing-your-soul-1.12640 (accessed May 15, 2014).

204   Choudhury, S., McKinney, K. A., & Merten, M. (2012). Rebelling against the brain: Public engagement with the "neurological adolescent." *Social Science & Medicine*, 74(4), 565–573.

205   Bröer, C., & Heerings, M. (2012). Neurobiology in public and private discourse: The case of adults with ADHD. *Sociology of Health & Illness*, 35(1), 49–65.

206   http://www.economist.com/node/8453850 (accessed May 15, 2014).

207   De Brigard, F., Mandelbaum, E., & Ripley, D. (2009). Responsibility and the brain sciences. *Ethical Theory and Moral Practice*, 12(5), 511–524.

208   Aspinwall, L. G., Brown, T. R., & Tabery, J. (2012). The double-edged sword: Does biomechanism increase or decrease judges' sentencing of psychopaths? *Science*, 337(6096), 846–849.

209   Vohs, K. D., & Schooler, J. W. (2008). The value of believing in free will: Encouraging a belief in determinism increases cheating. *Psychological Science*, 19(1), 49–54.

210   http://rolfzwaan.blogspot.nl/2013/03/the-value-of-believing-in-free-will.html (accessed May 15, 2014).

211   http://skepdic.com/neurolin.html (accessed May 15, 2014).

212   Witkowski, T. (2010). Thirty-five years of research on neuro-linguistic programming. NLP research data base. State of the art or pseudoscientific decoration? *Polish Psychological Bulletin*, 41(2), 58–66.

213   http://www.bbc.co.uk/news/uk-wales-24617644 (accessed May 15, 2014).

5 MYTHS ABOUT THE PHYSICAL STRUCTURE OF THE BRAIN

Broadcasters, writers and a lot of scientists too, tend to work themselves into a fit of excitement about the human brain. They marvel at its complexity. They boast about our big brains, our billions of neurons, and all those gazillions of connections between them. At the microscopic level, there's frequent far-fetched speculation that particular brain cell types can explain all that makes us human. This chapter takes an objective look at all these myths and more concerning the physical structure of the brain. It ends with a reminder about the importance of the bony bag of tissue to which the brain is attached – the body! We'll see that it's more than just a leggy vehicle for transporting the mighty brain. It too affects how we think and feel.

Myth
#21

The Brain Is Well Designed

"The human brain is nature's most finely tuned and exacting creation" – according to a breathless brain special issue of *The Times* newspaper's Eureka science magazine published in 2010. This reverence for our three pounds of meaty head sponge is almost universal. "Within each of our skulls resides an organ more powerful than the fastest supercomputer," gasps the back-cover blurb for *The Rough Guide to the Brain*.

Sometimes it can seem as if writers are competing to outdo each other in extolling the organ's awesomeness. "Of all the objects in the universe, the human brain is the most complex," declared neuroscientist David Eagleman in *Discover* magazine, "There are as many neurons in the brain

Great Myths of the Brain, First Edition. Christian Jarrett.
© 2015 Christian Jarrett. Published 2015 by John Wiley & Sons, Ltd.

as there are stars in the Milky Way galaxy." Another favored comparison is with the Internet. Apparently, with an estimated 100 trillion connections linking our neurons, a single human brain comfortably surpasses the 1 trillion links connecting the webpages of the global Internet.

Wow! The brain sure does sound amazing. Not particularly modest, but spectacularly complex, fast, and finely tuned. However, over the last decade or so, some psychologists and neuroscientists have grown concerned that all this reverence is cultivating a new myth: the idea that the brain represents the peak of biological perfection.

Among the perturbed is neuroscientist David Linden. On the jacket to his book *The Accidental Mind*,[1] he writes: "You've probably seen it before: A human brain lit from the side, the camera circling it like a helicopter shot of Stonehenge and a modulated baritone voice exalting the brain's elegant design in reverent tones ... To which this book says Pure Nonsense." Another detractor is Gary Marcus, the author of *Kluge, The Haphazard Construction of the Human Mind*.[2] "Kluge" is an engineering term to describe an inelegant, makeshift design that somehow manages to do a good job. Both Linden and Marcus believe that it is more accurate to see the brain as a kluge, rather than to marvel at it as some kind of exemplary feat of biological engineering.

Redressing the Balance

Hoping to redress the balance and spread a more realistic perception of the brain, Linden, Marcus and others highlight the organ's flaws. Generally speaking, their observations fall into three main categories – the overall construction of the brain and how it came to be the way it is; the physiological limitations of the brain; and, related to that, examples of ways that our thinking is flawed or unreliable. Let's take a brief look at these in turn.

The brain is a product of evolution by natural selection. So rather than being built for purpose from scratch, any modifications or additions were applied to what came before. Linden likens this building process to an ice cream cone – "through evolutionary time, as higher functions were added, a new scoop was placed on top, but the lower scoops were left largely unchanged." Crudely put, he says this means the lower parts of the brain – including the brain stem and parts of the midbrain – are not so different from the equivalent regions in the brains of animals we usually consider to be less advanced than us, like lizards and frogs. The huge, expanded cerebral cortex of humans is the top scoop.

This certainly takes the gloss off the design of the brain. But it's important to point out that the ice cream model has come in for criticism.[3] Animals like lizards don't only have one scoop. They too have forebrains, they just aren't anywhere near as large and developed as ours. Some experts also point out that the human brain's stem and midbrain have continued evolving. We don't literally have a "lizard brain" in our heads, as implied by many people, such as celebrity weight loss coach Alejandra Ruani ("When you're shopping for food, or watching TV … your lizard brain lights up like a Christmas tree,")[4] and US author Seth Godin ("The lizard brain is not merely a concept. It's real, and it's living on the top of your spine").[5] Notwithstanding this point, Linden's basic assertion remains true: evolution works by progression from what came before, constraining and compromising the way the human brain functions.

So, what are some of the specific physiological brain flaws or weaknesses? One of the brain's most serious limitations is its sluggishness. This is related to the woefully inefficient way it transmits electricity along its neurons. This is hugely consequential because it's a fundamental part of the way information flows through the brain. In short, when a neuron is stimulated beyond a certain threshold, an "action potential" is triggered and an electrical current travels down its length triggering it to release chemicals (neurotransmitters), which pass across a tiny gap to a neighboring neuron or neurons. This is how neurons communicate with each other.

The maximum speed of conduction through neurons in this way is around 400 miles per hour (for the slowest neurons it's just 1 mph) compared with the 669 million mph achieved by simple copper wire. This has a lot to do with the fact that the charge traveling down a neuronal axon (the long fiber that branches away from the cell body) is achieved via the opening and closing of channels in the axon wall, allowing charged atoms to enter or leave. Linden likens this process to transmitting water through a narrow garden hose with holes dotted along its length. Brain cells are also limited in how quickly they can fire an action potential repeatedly – around 400 spikes per second is the upper limit – and they need a rest after a busy spell.

Combined with the widespread noise in the brain's information processing pathways ("noise" used here in the engineering sense of a meaningless signal), this sluggishness has important implications for how we detect what's going on, and how we move through the world – something I'll look at in more detail in Chapter 7.

There are all sorts of other inefficiencies and inconsistencies in the business of neuronal communication. Many of these were outlined in a review paper "Noise in the Nervous System" published by Aldo Faisal and his colleagues in 2008.[6] For instance, the channels in the cell wall that allow an action potential to propagate down an axon sometimes open randomly, potentially interfering with the signal. Once the action potential reaches the end of the axon, prompting the release of neurotransmitters, more variability awaits: the bag-like vesicles, which transport the neurotransmitters, vary in how many molecules they contain; their dispersion across the gap (the synapse) is somewhat unpredictable; and on the other side, there's great variability in the number of receptors that await (see Plate 6).

The brain attempts to compensate for these delays and noise issues by averaging signals and by anticipating what the world is probably like at any given time. It then compares its predictions against the incoming signals, providing another opportunity for noise cancellation. "All of this complex math serves a paradoxical purpose: to make up for the mistakes built into our very biology," said Carl Zimmer, writing about these processes for *Wired* magazine.[7]

Other obvious biological flaws in the brain relate to its vulnerability to injury and neurological illness, from the loss of neuronal insulation in multiple sclerosis (see also p. 21) to the cascade of collateral damage that follows the occurrence of a stroke (see p. 264), which results from a loss of oxygen to the brain. We'll be discussing illnesses in the final chapter of the book; for now let's consider one specific vulnerability for which we could have our brains to thank.

A recent theory put forward by John McDonald at the Georgia Institute of Technology is that cancer is a heightened risk for humans because of the very evolutionary changes that allowed us to develop such big brains relative to our body size. Specifically, he's found evidence that the process of apoptosis – the technical term for programmed cell-death – is reduced in humans relative to other primates, which makes the risk of cancer greater. "Natural selection for reduced apoptotic function only makes sense with respect to an increase in brain size," McDonald told *New Scientist* magazine.[8] If he's right, this would be an example of the messy reality of brain evolution – we may have ended up with an astonishingly powerful intellect, but it's come at a price.

The idea of the brain as some kind of peerless supercomputer also clashes with the numerous flaws in our thinking and perception that have been documented by psychologists. There are enough of these to fill an entire book, and in fact many books have been so filled – from *Brain Bugs* by Dean Buonomano to *Predictably Irrational* by Dan Ariely and *You Are Not So Smart* by David McRaney. Let's focus here on the proposed flaws in two of the most fundamental aspects of our thinking – memory and language.

Unlike computers, our memories tend to operate via association – recalling one item automatically activates related items in an ever-expanding network. There are myriad vulnerabilities to this system, including – confusing when things happened, trouble recalling names, absentmindedness (i.e. failing to remember to do things in the future), and our tendency to form false memories. In his seminal paper "The Seven Sins of Memory,"[9] psychologist Daniel Schacter summarizes all these glitches under seven headings – transience, absentmindedness, blocking, misattribution, suggestibility, bias, and persistence. It's because of these flaws that psychologists advocate treating eye-witness testimony with far more suspicion than is usually the case in most court rooms around the world.

In his book, Gary Marcus weighs up the pros and cons of human memory and confesses that he would prefer to have a more computer-like memory, in which every item of stored information is given a unique look-up code (see p. 103). "Given the liabilities of our contextual memory, it's natural to ask whether its benefits (speed, for example) outweigh its costs," Marcus writes. "I think not."

Marcus also finds fault in the way we use language, which he says is "filled with foibles, imperfections, and idiosyncrasies." He points to the ambiguities in language, caused by among other things the fact that we have so many words that have multiple meanings, rather than simply allocating one word for each concept. The rules of grammar can also permit ambiguities, so that it's not always clear who is doing what to whom. Taken altogether, Marcus says the languages of the world are suboptimal – a consequence of their haphazard evolution fueled in part by the nature of the human mind. Were we to design a language from scratch, he says it would operate very differently, more like Esperanto – created by Ludovic Zamenhof in the late nineteenth century and intended to be quickly and easily learned, with simple rules and fewer than usual ambiguities.

Marcus himself holds up computer languages like Pascal and C as superior to our own in many ways, free as they are of any irregularities or ambiguities – "no computer ever wavers about what it should do next," he says. Unfortunately (for those sharing Marcus's admiration for computer code), neither computer languages nor Esperanto have ever taken off as a means of human-to-human communication. Presumably this is because they are an ill-fit for the human brain, which favors a system with more variety and ambiguity.

Human language is imperfect, Marcus proposes, because it runs on a system – the human mind – which is itself profoundly flawed and imprecise. The constraints of our speech system (the way the tongue and lips shape the sounds made by the vocal cords) also plays a part. "This is not to say that language is terrible," Marcus says, "only that it could, with forethought, have been even better." Whether it's the foibles of memory or the ambiguity of language, Marcus's message is that the brain is compromised – it does some things well, but it's far from being a perfect thinking machine.

We do need to guard against seeing the brain with too much reverence and we shouldn't be fooled into thinking it has an elegant design. Hopefully this short overview has provided something of a reality check. That said, we also need to be careful not to go too far in correcting the hype.

Writing in the journal *Evolutionary Psychology*, James Liddle and Todd Shackelford criticized Marcus's presentation of evolutionary theory, including the idea that there is even such a thing as an optimal solution to various biological problems, or that evolution is capable of achieving them.[10] Psychologist Tom Stafford aired similar concerns in *BBC Focus* magazine: "I'm pretty happy with my biological-style memory that gets things wrong but never needs to be rebooted," he wrote.[11] Others[12] have responded to Linden's claims about the poor design of the brain by asking why, if it's so poor, so many Artificial Intelligence labs around the world are trying so hard to design computers that work like brain.

Balance seems to be the order of the day here. Let's acknowledge the cracks and seams where they lie. But also let's not lose sight of the fact the brain is pretty darn awesome.

Myth #22 The Bigger the Brain, the Better

The evil Marvel comics character "Leader" was exposed to Gamma radiation in an accident, just like the Incredible Hulk. But rather than it giving him superhuman strength, Leader (formerly known as Samuel Sterns) became an ultra-intelligent genius. You'd realize this as soon as you saw him because he sports a towering bulbous cranium housing an absolutely massive brain. And we all know that bigger means better when it comes to brains, right?

In fact, the truth is far more complicated. First off, we need to make clear whether we are talking about brains in general, across the animal kingdom, or human brains specifically. Let's deal with human brains first and the simple question – are people with bigger brains really more intelligent?

Human Brains

Within the human species, overall brain volume does correlate with intelligence, with a value of 0.3 to 0.4 (where 1 would be a perfect match) – a relationship that experts describe as "moderate" in size. Crucially, making sense of this relationship between brain volume and intelligence is far from straightforward and many questions remain.[13]

It could be the case that it's only extra volume in certain areas of the brain, or only extra brain matter of certain types, that is linked with more intelligence. Researchers have looked at correlations between the size of the various brain lobes (including the frontal and temporal lobes) and people's intelligence, and the values usually come out at around 0.25. They've also focused on either the amount of gray matter (made up of cell bodies) or white matter (which forms the connections between cells), with gray matter having a slightly stronger correlation with intelligence, but still only around 0.3.[14]

Another factor that could be as, or more, important for intelligence than gross brain size is the efficiency of the connectivity among neurons. Consider a study led by Paul Thompson of the University of California, in which 92 identical and nonidentical twins underwent diffusion tensor imaging of their brains.[15] This technique charts the connective, white matter pathways of the brain and Thompson's team found that participants who scored higher on intelligence tests tended to have quicker, more efficient neural pathways. "When you say someone is quick-thinking, it's generally true," Thompson at the time, "the impulses are going faster and they're just much more efficient at processing information and then making a decision based on it."

In perhaps the most ambitious attempt to document the brain basis of intelligence, Rex Jung and Richard Haier analyzed the combined results from 37 brain-imaging papers, and writing in 2007 they concluded intelligence is linked with 14 specific regions extending across the front and rear of the brain and the connections between them – what they called the P-FIT network (which stands for parieto-frontal integration theory).[16] One of the world's leading authorities on human intelligence, Ian Deary, and his colleagues, stated in a review published in 2010[17] that "P-FIT can be considered the best available answer to the question of where in the brain intelligence resides."

So, rather than bigger meaning better when it comes to human brain power, the correct but less eloquent rule is more like, "bigger sometimes equals better in some areas of the brain, and having fast and efficient connections helps a lot too." Before we move on, a final characteristic of the brain that's been linked with greater intelligence is the precise ratio of neuronal brain cells to glial brain cells (see also pp. 153). However, we should treat this claim with a healthy dose of skepticism since the evidence is sketchy, based mostly on an examination of Albert Einstein's brain (which incidentally is smaller than average).

Comparing the great physicist's brain with the brains of 11 "normal people," Marian Diamond and her colleagues found that in one particular brain area, in the parietal lobe, he had more glial cells than usual for every neuron.[18] Reporting their results in 1985, the group concluded: "these data suggest that neuronal/glial ratios in selected regions of Einstein's brain might reflect the enhanced use of this tissue in the expression of his unusual conceptual powers in comparison with control brains." It sounds very simplistic, but this study – and the fact that Einstein had a small brain – reinforces the main point that intelligence is likely related to localized features of the brain as much or more than its overall size. Consistent with this, in 2013 yet another analysis of the physicist's brain, based on newly discovered photos[19] found that he had enlarged association areas in his prefrontal cortex, larger than normal regions in the somatosensory and motor cortices of his left hemisphere, an unusually thick corpus callosum, and unusual anatomy in his parietal lobes – all in the context of his overall brain size being unexceptional.

Animal Brains

The case for bigger meaning smarter becomes even harder to support when we turn our attention to brains across the entire animal kingdom. We usually think of ourselves as the smartest creature on the planet and yet many animals have bigger brains than we do. Elephants and whales beat us by a long way, boasting brains that are up to six times the size of ours (see Plate 22)! They also have more neurons. A 20 pound (9 kg) whale brain will have over 200 billion neurons compared with around 85 billion neurons in a typical 3 pound (1.3 kg) human brain.

One reason that brain size often has more to do with body size than with intelligence is because of simple anatomical and computational logistics. Bigger animals tend to have bigger sensory organs, which means more data coming in and the need for more brain matter to process it. More skin, for instance, means more skin receptors and a larger somatosensory cortex (the area of the brain given over to processing touch signals from the body) for processing that information. Similarly, bigger muscles require more motor neurons, which goes hand in hand with a larger motor cortex. The key thing is that this extra neural capacity associated with animal size is about "more of the same" kind of processing, rather than extra brain power being diverted into more sophisticated forms of thinking.

Increasingly it's recognized that more revealing of intelligence than absolute brain size is the relative size of the brain to the body for an animal of that type – known as the encephalization quotient (EQ). Such a measure is more comforting for our human egos, as we emerge with a leading quotient of 7.6 (versus 5.3 for dolphin, 2.4 for chimp and 1 for a cat). Indeed, our brain is three times the size of the chimp's, our nearest relative. Moreover, a brain-imaging study published in 1999[20] compared 11 species of primate and found that, for our body size, the human brain has an unusually large neocortex (located at the front of the brain and responsible for many complex mental functions), more convolutions than you'd expect (these are the folds in the surface of the cortex – more folds equals more surface area and more processing power), and more extensive white matter connections.

Nevertheless, even the encephalization quotient has its critics. Suzana Herculano-Houzel, a neuroscientist at Universidade Federal do Rio de Janeiro, has pointed out[21] that the quotient you come up with depends on which animals you choose to lump together as being of the same type. She also points out anomalies – for example, small-bodied capuchin monkeys found in Central and Southern America, score a higher EQ than the much bigger gorilla, and yet gorillas are considered the more intelligent based on their behavior and problem-solving skills.

Herculano-Houzel further points out that the brains of different animal types scale up differently. That is to say, the association between brain size and number of brain cells varies across different groups of animals. For example, as rodent brains get bigger, so too do the neurons, meaning that a big rodent brain contains relatively fewer neurons than you'd expect for its size. In contrast, brain cells are the same size in bigger primate brains as compared with smaller primate brains, meaning that a large primate brain, like ours, contains lots of neurons for its size, relatively speaking, compared with large brains in other animal groups.

What does this mean for gauging intelligence? Herculano-Houzel says it shows again why brain size is a poor proxy for intelligence when comparing across the animal kingdom. For some animal groups a bigger brain doesn't necessarily mean a proportionate increase in neurons.

She says it's therefore more valid to focus on absolute number of neurons as a marker of intelligence rather than brain size.

A final important challenge to the "bigger equals better" myth is the astonishing feats of intelligence achieved by creatures with miniature brains. Consider the bumblebee, with a brain volume that's one millionth the volume of a human brain. Despite its tiny brain, the bee's behavior is highly complex. In a review published in 2009, Lars Chittka and Jeremy Niven identified 59 discrete behaviors, including different types of dancing (communicating different messages to other bees), foraging for nectar (including memorizing the location of flowers over several square kilometers or miles), grooming, guarding, and collecting water.[22]

Carefully controlled tests of the bee's learning powers are particularly impressive. For example, they can pick up "sameness-difference rules" – realizing that a visual pattern which is the same as the last, rather than one that's different, will bring reward ... and then realizing the rule has changed, so now it's always the pattern that's different from the last that will bring reward.

This is also an opportune moment to correct a related myth about animal intelligence. A common playground taunt is "Bird brain!" as if having the brain of a bird were something of which to be ashamed. In fact, many species of bird, despite having much smaller brains than us, are extraordinarily intelligent. This is particularly true for members of the crow family (corvids), who engage in behavior that betrays sophisticated social intelligence (it's notable that they have a high EQ and a relatively enlarged frontal part of the brain).

One example relates to food hiding by scrub-jays.[23] If, and only if, potential thieves are around when they first hide their bounty, a scrub-jay will go to the trouble of re-hiding it. They'll also use shadows to conceal their movements when others are around, but not when they're on their own. Would-be thieves also show great cunning. A thieving raven, for example, will peck in the wrong place to trick a bird that's burying food into thinking they don't know where their stash is, even though they do really.

Clearly many mysteries remain about the links between brain matter and intelligence, both when we compare between humans, and when we look across the animal kingdom. What's for sure is that not all brain matter contributes in the same way toward complex mental abilities, and the health and efficiency of connections is probably just as important as raw size. Meanwhile, the mental feats of insects serve as a useful demonstration of just how much cognitive power can be achieved with relatively little neural hardware.

Myth: Extinct Boskop Man Was Smarter and Bigger Brained Than Us

We think of ourselves – smart, big-brained humans – as representing the pinnacle of evolution. But what if we had an ancestor that was smarter than we are, with an even bigger brain? Let me introduce you to "Boskop man," the owner of a huge skull discovered in Boskop, South Africa in 1913.

According to the neuroscientists Gary Lynch and Richard Granger, authors of *Big Brain, the Origins and Future of Human Intelligence*, the owner of this skull had a brain likely 25 percent bigger than our own. They claim that other similarly large skulls were discovered in the region soon after, and that members of this race all shared another strange feature – a child-like face.

"We're drawn to the idea that we are the end point, the pinnacle not only of the hominids but of all animal life," wrote Lynch and Granger in *Discover magazine* in 2009.[24] "Boskops argue otherwise. They say that humans with big brains, and perhaps great intelligence, occupied a substantial piece of southern Africa in the not very distant past." The pair then go on to speculate about the extraordinary intellectual powers of this brainy, long-lost ancestor: "they would have seen farther than we can: more potential outcomes, more possible downstream costs and benefits."

This raises an obvious question – if the Boskops were so smart, how come they died out and we're still here? Well, it looks like the answer is because they never existed in the first place. John Hawks may not be a neuroscientist, but he is Professor of Anthropology at the University of Wisconsin–Madison and an expert on fossilized human remains. Writing on his blog in 2010, he criticized Lynch and Granger for ignoring the last forty years of anthropology. "I am unaware of any credible biological anthropologist or archaeologist who would confirm [Lynch and Granger's] description of the 'Boskopoids,'" he writes, "except as an obsolete category from the history of anthropology." In fact, the idea of a lost Boskop race was apparently debunked back in the 1950s by Ronald Singer of the University of Cape Town. Comparing huge numbers of locally collected skulls, he concluded that the supposed Boskop skulls were well within the normal range. "It is now obvious that what was justifiable speculation (because of paucity of data) in 1923, and was apparent as speculation in 1947, is inexcusable to maintain in 1958," wrote Singer.[25]

You Have a Grandmother Cell

This is the idea that you have in your brain one or more cells devoted exclusively to representing the concept of your grandmother, and only your grandmother. Thinking about her, looking at her and hearing her mentioned will stir this specific kind of cell into activity, but no others. In fact, the grandmother cell theory goes further and says that the same principle applies to all concepts, with each having its own dedicated cell or cells in the brain. You don't just have a grandmother cell, the idea goes, you have a putative mother cell that responds specifically to the concept of your mother, a wife cell for your wife (if you have one), a Michael Jackson cell (assuming you know who he was), an Empire State Building cell – and on the list goes.

The popular press love this idea, especially when the concept in question happens to be an attractive female celebrity. In response to new findings published in 2008, the UK's *Daily Mail* announced the discovery of "The Jennifer Aniston brain cell," explaining the results showed how: "single neurons spring into action when we see pictures of our favorite celebrities."[26] Earlier in 2005, *The New York Times* ran a similar story[27] headlined: "A Neuron with Halle Berry's Name on It." *Scientific American* wrote about the same research under the more sober headline: "One Face, One Neuron."[28]

Origins of the Grandmother Cell

The specific term grandmother cell has a strange history. It originates from a fictional story told around 1969 by the late cognitive scientist Jerry Lettvin to his students at MIT, to help them understand the problem of how the brain might represent concepts. Lettvin's story was about a fictional character, from Philip Roth's novel *Portnoy's Complaint*, who was obsessed by his mother and sought help from a neurosurgeon. This neurosurgeon believed in the idea that specific cells represent specific concepts and he went about destroying all the "mother cells" in Portnoy's brain. After the surgery, Portnoy understood the generic concept of mothers, but not the concept of his specific mother. The neurosurgeon in the story subsequently went on to look for "grandmother cells" and for some reason it was this label that took hold in the imagination of psychologists and neuroscientists as they debated the issue of how the brain represents concepts.

According to the vision scientist and historian Charles Gross,[29] although the specific term grandmother cell can be traced to Lettvin's

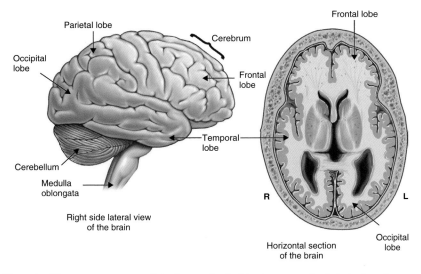

Right side lateral view
of the brain

Horizontal section
of the brain

Plate I The gross anatomy of the human brain. The image on the left depicts the brain as seen from the side (if the eyes were present, they would be located on the right-hand side of this image); in the image on the right, the brain is viewed from above, as it would look if the top part of the skull and brain had been sliced off.
Source: Nucleus Medical Art/Visuals Unlimited/Science Photo Library.

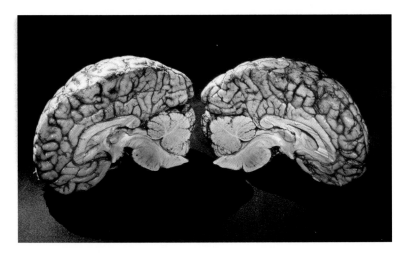

Plate 2 Photograph of a healthy human brain cut into two halves. This brain has been sliced down the sagittal plane, into its left and right halves (imagine a straight line running from the nose to the back of the head, and slicing along this line). The cut reveals some of the brain's inner anatomy, including the corpus callosum and the third ventricle.
Source: Geoff Tompkinson/Science Photo Library.

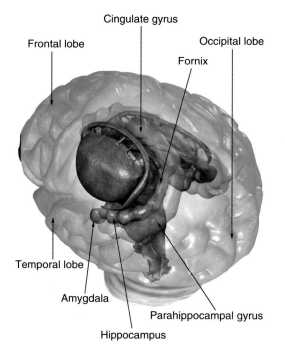

Plate 3 The limbic system. An artist's depiction of the limbic system, a network of brain regions that is particularly important for emotional functioning.
Source: 3D4Medical.com/Science Photo Library.

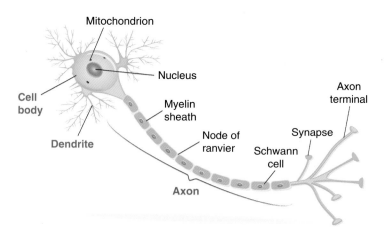

Plate 4 A human neuron. An artist's depiction of a typical human neuron with the main anatomical structures labeled.
Source: © Designua/Shutterstock.

Plate 5   Glial cells, as viewed with an electron microscope. Seen at approximately 2000 × magnification, these are ependymal cells – a kind of glial cell that lines the ventricles and produces cerebrospinal fluid. The fluid-filled ventricles act as a shock-absorption system for the brain.
Source: Steve Gschmeissner/Science Photo Library.

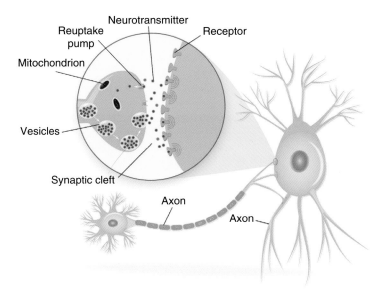

Plate 6   A chemical synapse. A graphical representation of a typical chemical synapse in the human brain. Synapses are small gaps between neurons. Most neurons communicate with each other by releasing chemicals that cross this gap. There is also a minority of purely electrical synapses in the human brain.
Source: © Designua/Shutterstock.

Plate 7 A historical drawing of the brain's ventricles. The ventricles are fluid-filled hollows in the brain. A theory influential into the Victorian era stated (incorrectly) that mental function resides in these hollows. This drawing, by an unknown artist, appears in a sixteenth-century edition of *Philosophia naturalis* by the German saint and scientist Albertus Magnus, who died in 1280.
Source: from Albertus Magnus, *Philosophia naturalis*, 1508; Wellcome Library, London.

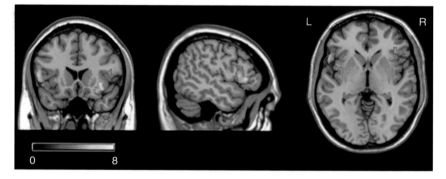

Plate 8 Example of a brain scan image acquired via functional magnetic resonance imaging (fMRI). The orange and yellow highlights indicate those parts of the brain (the left and right inferior frontal gyrus, and the right insular cortex) that showed increased activation when participants concealed their true identity. The scan was part of a study published by Chinese researchers in 2012.
Source: http://www.plosone.org/article/info%3Adoi%2F10.1371%2Fjournal.pone.0048639 (accessed May 18, 2014).

Plate 9 A trepanned skull. Excavated from a tomb in Jericho in January 1958, the skull dates from around 2200–2000 BC. The multiple holes in the skull were created through the surgical practice of trepanation, probably carried out in the hope of releasing evil spirits. Three holes are clearly visible; a fourth (the rightmost) shows signs of extensive healing, which tells us that the surgery was not fatal.
Source: Wellcome Library, London.

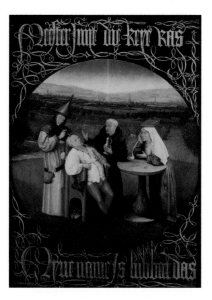

Plate 10 "The cure for folly" or "The extraction of the stone of madness" (1475–1480) by Hieronymus Bosch. On display in the Museo del Prado in Madrid, this painting depicts a form of trepanning in which "stones" are removed as a treatment for madness. Historians disagree about whether this practice really occurred.
Source: The Art Archive/Museo del Prado Madrid/Collection Dagli Orti.

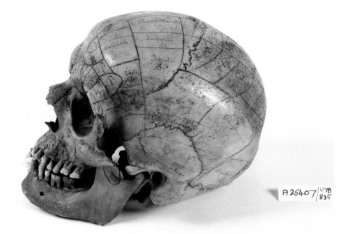

Plate 11 A skull inscribed with markings from phrenology. Thought to be of French origin, the skull shows some markings consistent with Franz Gall's phrenological teachings, and others that conform to the system developed by his disciple, Johann Spurzheim. Human skull inscribed for phrenological demonstration.
Source: Wellcome Library, London.

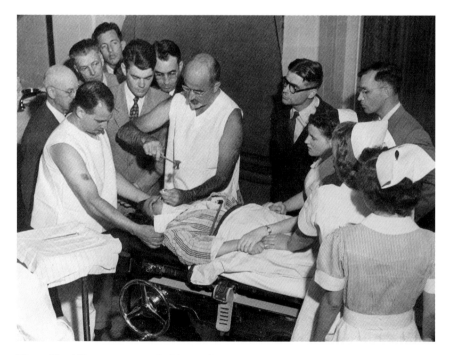

Plate 12 US neurosurgeon Dr Walter Freeman performs a lobotomy. Dated July 1949, Freeman is seen hammering a sharp instrument under the patient's upper eyelid and into their brain. This practice seems incredibly brutal today, but doctors at the time had few medical methods for treating mental illness.
Source: © Bettmann/Corbis.

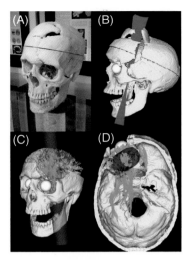

Plate 13   A reconstruction of the brain injury sustained by Phineas Gage. Nineteenth century railway worker Gage became one of the most famous cases in neuroscience after he survived a tamping iron passing right through the front of his brain. Image "A" shows his skull on display at the Warren Anatomical Museum at Harvard Medical School. "B" to "D" is a graphical reconstruction of the path the iron rod took through his brain, and the damage sustained by his connective tissues (based on an analysis published by researchers at University of California, Los Angeles). Most text books claim that Gage became an impulsive lay about after sustaining this injury, but historians are now rethinking this interpretation.
Source: Van Horn, 2012. Reproduced with permission.

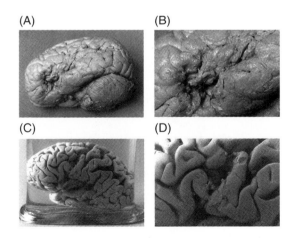

Plate 14   The brains of Paul Broca's aphasic patients Leborgne and Lelong. Photograph "A" is of Leborgne's brain; "B" shows a close-up of the lesion on his left frontal lobe. Photographs "C" and "D" show patient Lelong's brain, and a close up of the lesion on his left frontal lobe, respectively. Broca encountered patient Lelong, an 84-year-old, a few months after he treated Leborgne. These aphasic patients helped to falsify the notion that language function is distributed throughout the brain.
Source: Dronkers, Plaisant, Iba-Zizen, and Cabanis, 2007.
Photos by Bruno Delamain. Reproduced with permission from Oxford University Press.

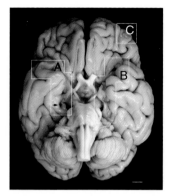

Plate 15 Photograph of amnesiac Henry Molaison's brain, as viewed from below. Boxes "A" and "B" show the lesions made inside Henry's temporal lobes during surgery for severe epilepsy in the 1950s. According to researchers at The Brain Observatory in San Diego, the black arrow shows "a mark produced by the oxidation of one of the surgical clips inserted by [surgeon] Scoville." Box "C" highlights another lesion. Henry's extreme memory loss after this surgery helped falsify the myth that memory function is spread uniformly through the cortex.
Source: Annese, Schenker-Ahmed, Bartsch, Maechler, Sheh, and Thomas, 2014. Reproduced with permission from Nature Publishing Group.

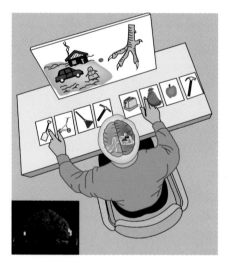

Plate 16 The interpreter phenomenon. A split-brain patient matches picture cards to the themes illustrated on a display in front of them. Because the connective tissue between the patient's two brain hemispheres has been severed, only the right-hand side of his brain sees the illustration on the left of the display, and only the left-hand side of his brain sees the image on the right-hand side. The left hemisphere shows creativity by making up reasons for the right hemisphere's choice of picture card. This runs counter to the usual "right-brain=creative, left-brain=analytical" myth. See main text for more details.
Source: Gazzaniga, 2002. Reproduced with permission from Nature Publishing Group.

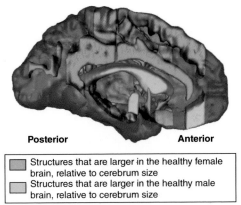

Posterior   **Anterior**

▨	Structures that are larger in the healthy female brain, relative to cerebrum size
▤	Structures that are larger in the healthy male brain, relative to cerebrum size

Nature Reviews | Neuroscience

Plate 17 An illustration of sex differences in the size of various human brain regions. This graphic is based on a study (http://cercor.oxfordjournals.org/content/11/6/490. long) that measured the size of 45 brain structures in 27 men and 21 women. It adds to the evidence showing that there are physical differences in the average brain of a man and woman. However, the functional significance of such differences is far from straightforward, and the cause of the differences is also complicated, likely reflecting a mixture of genetic and environmental factors.
Source: Cahill, 2006. Reproduced with permission from Nature Publishing Group.

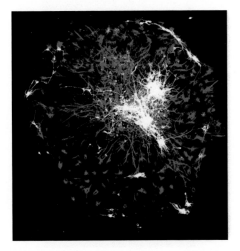

Plate 18 The growth of new brain cells after birth, including neurons. Seen through a confocal microscope, these cells were originally stem cells or "progenitor cells," which have the potential to become many different types of specialist cell. Collected from the ventricles of a mouse after birth, they were then grown in a culture dish where they differentiated into different cell types. Those dyed white became neurons; those dyed green are astrocytes; and those shown as red are oligodendrocytes. For many years mainstream neuroscience held that no new neurons are created in the adult mammalian brain. In fact, stem cells in humans and other mammals continue to develop into new neurons throughout life.
Source: University of Oxford, Eunhyuk Chang, Francis Szele laboratory/Wellcome Images.

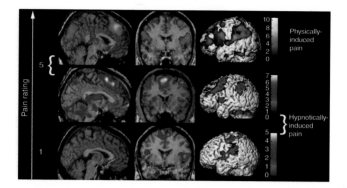

Plate 19 Brain scan images showing the overlapping neural correlates of hypnotically induced pain and physical pain. The lower two rows show scans taken from participants experiencing hypnotically induced pain. Brain areas marked blue showed increased activity during this experience. The participant in the middle row experienced a high amount of this pain; you can see their activation patterns are similar to those recorded from the participant in the top row (and marked in red), who was experiencing an equivalent amount of physical pain.
Source: Derbyshire et al., 2004. Reproduced with permission of Elsevier.

Plate 20 Visualization of a rat cortical column, produced by the Blue Brain Project. This model of a cortical column from the neocortex of the rat consists of approximately 10 000 neurons. The visualization would look even more intricate if it contained glial cells. Cortical columns are seen as a basic functional unit of the brain, although the term is today used in so many ways that its meaning has become vague and somewhat controversial. The Blue Brain Project in Switzerland states that rat brains have around 100 000 of these columns; human brains up to two million.
Source: Copyrighted to Blue Brain Project, EPFL, Lausanne, Switzerland. Reproduced with permission.

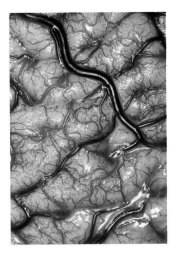

Plate 21 Close-up photograph of the surface of a living human brain. Taken as a patient underwent neurosurgery, this photograph by Robert Ludlow won the Wellcome Trust Image Awards in 2012. One of the judges, Professor Alice Roberts, said at the time: "Through the skill of the photographer, we have the privilege of seeing something that is normally hidden away inside our skulls. The arteries are bright scarlet with oxygenated blood, the veins deep purple and the 'grey matter' of the brain a flushed, delicate pink. It is quite extraordinary." Scientists and the public alike struggle to understand how the meat of the brain – shown so vividly in this photograph – can give rise to our rich mental lives.
Source: Robert Ludlow, UCL Institute of Neurology/Wellcome Images.

Plate 22 A life-size model of the brains of (from left to right) an orangutan, a human, an Asian elephant, and a Fin whale. Overall brain size isn't always synonymous with more brain power. If it were, that would make whales and elephants the geniuses of this world – their brains weigh an average of 20 pounds (9 kg) and 10 pounds (4.7 kg), respectively, compared with 3 pounds (1.3 kg) for a human.
Source: Photograph by Christian Jarrett taken at the Smithsonian's National Zoo, Washington DC.

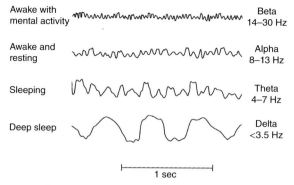

Normal adult brain waves

Awake with mental activity		Beta 14–30 Hz
Awake and resting		Alpha 8–13 Hz
Sleeping		Theta 4–7 Hz
Deep sleep		Delta <3.5 Hz

1 sec

Plate 23 Adult brainwaves recorded via electroencephalography (EEG). EEG records the brain's electricity activity from the surface of the scalp. The frequency of this activity varies depending on a person's current activities, as shown in these sample traces. EEG has superior temporal resolution compared with more modern techniques like fMRI (i.e. it can detect changes in brain activity at the level of milliseconds), but it has poor spatial resolution.
Source: © Alila Medical Media/Shutterstock.

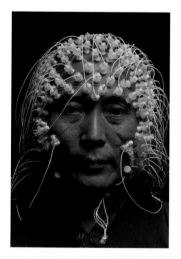

Plate 24 A meditating Buddhist has his brain activity recorded by EEG (electroencephalography). Researchers in the 1960s discovered that experienced meditators show increased brain activity in the "alpha range" (8 to 12 hertz). This prompted a neurofeedback craze, based on the idea that learning to express more alpha brain activity will bring you bliss and enlightenment. However skeptics pointed out that the simple act of closing your eyes increases alpha brain waves.
Source: Cary Wolinsky/Getty Images.

Plate 25 A man and woman sport a commercial transcranial direct current stimulation (tDCS) device each produced by US firm foc.us. Transcranial direct current stimulation involves applying weak electrical currents to the brain. Commercial manufacturers claim this is a way to enhance your brain power, but experts warn that there could be harmful side effects.
Source: © Focus Labs/European Engineers 2013.

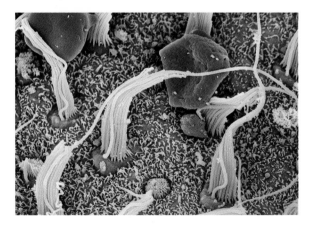

Plate 26 Cilia or "hair" cells located in the inner ear. It has become a taken-for-granted "fact" that we have 5 senses – sight, hearing, taste, touch, and smell. The reality is that we have many more senses than this, including the vestibular senses that allow us to keep our balance. The cilia cells – shown here in blue through an electron microscope – are part of the vestibular system and help us detect directional changes, such as a tilt of the head.
Source: Steve Gschmeissner/Science Photo Library.

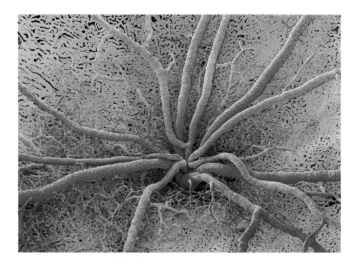

Plate 27 The blind spot on the retina. Blood vessels (red, purple) are seen here radiating out from the optic disc (yellow), as viewed through an electron microscope. The optic disc is the patch on the retina – the "blind spot" – where the optic nerve and blood vessels enter the eye. There are no light-sensitive cells on this part of the retina, which means we are effectively blind to any incoming light that falls here.
Source: Susumu Nishinaga/Science Photo Library.

Plate 28 The checkered shadow illusion. It's hard to believe but the squares marked "A" and "B" are in fact the same shade of gray. This illusion provides a fantastic demonstration of the way our perception of the world is often dramatically different from how the world actually is. See the main text on p. 247 for further explanation. Illusion developed by Edward H. Adelson at MIT.
Source: ©1995, Edward H. Adelson. Reproduced with permission.

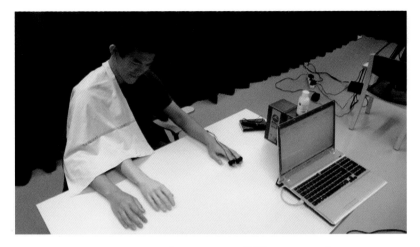

Plate 29 The third arm illusion. Science writer Ed Yong gets ready to experience the "Third Arm" illusion for himself, during a visit to the laboratory of Henrik Ehrsson, a neuroscientist at the Karolinska Institute in Stockholm. "Stroking my real arm in time with the middle (rubber) one, convinced me that the rubber one was mine," Yong said. Further explanation in the main text on p. 253.
Source: Yong, 2011. Reproduced with permission.

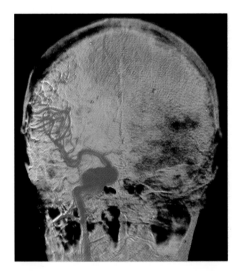

Plate 30 A brain aneurism. The photograph shows a false-color arteriograph of the head, as seen from the rear, revealing an aneurysm in the carotid artery. The aneurism appears as a red, balloon-like swelling, which is caused by the dilation of a thinned arterial wall. A ruptured aneurysm is one cause of a stroke.
Source: Alain Pol, ISM/Science Photo Library.

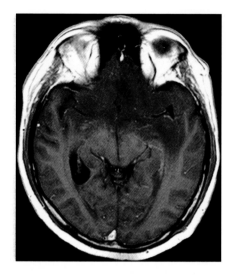

Plate 31 MRI scan of a male patient who was declared brain dead. The scan shows irreversible destruction of the white and gray matter frontal and cerebral regions of the brain of this 46-year-old male patient. In many jurisdictions around the world, the fact that the man was declared brain dead would mean his organs could be removed for donation, depending on his prior wishes, and/or his family's consent.
Source: Sovereign, ISM/Science Photo Library.

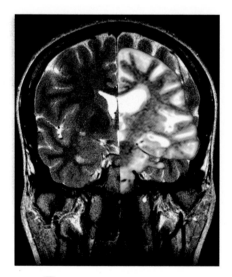

Plate 32 A composite of MRI scans, showing a healthy person's brain alongside the brain of a person with Alzheimer's disease. These MRI scans are seen from the front and in cross-section. A healthy brain is shown in brown, and superimposed is a brain with advanced Alzheimer's disease, in green. The diseased brain shows severe generalized shrinkage of brain tissue, with particularly severe loss in the temporal lobes.
Source: Medical Body Scans/Jessica Wilson/Science Photo Library.

story, the general idea of cells representing specific concepts has older origins. Gross highlights the "gnostic cells" proposed by the Polish neurophysiologist Jerzy Konorski in 1967 (single cells that respond to distinct perceptual experiences), and the cells in monkey inferior temporal cortex that he (Gross) discovered with his colleagues, which seemed to respond selectively to the sight of hands and faces. Earlier still, in 1953, the British neuroscientist Horace Barlow had described highly selective cells in the retina of the frog that he called "bug detectors."

Do They Really Exist?

The closest researchers have come to discovering a grandmother cell is through the work of Rodrigo Quian Quiroga, now based at Leicester University in the UK. Quiroga and his colleagues have used electrodes to record from individual cells in the medial temporal lobe (MTL) brain region of patients undergoing exploratory neurosurgery. This work has led to the discovery of what Quiroga calls "concept cells" that show extraordinarily specific response patterns.

In a paper published in 2005,[30] for instance, a neuron was discovered in the right anterior hippocampus (in the temporal lobe) of one patient that responded exclusively to pictures of Halle Berry, even when she was shown wearing a cat suit. Pictures of other people in a cat suit did not activate this neuron, yet the same neuron was activated by the words "Halle Berry," which suggests strongly that the cell is sensitive to the concept of Halle Berry, regardless of how that concept comes to mind. Another adjacent neuron responded to the sight of Mother Theresa, but not to Halle Berry. The researchers believe that concept cells are organized non-topographically – in other words, cells representing similar concepts aren't located near to each other – which they say is the optimal arrangement for the fast learning of new associations.

More evidence that these cells really are responsive to ideas came from a patient who confused pictures of the distinctive Sydney Opera House with pictures of the Bahai Temple in India. Consistent with his subjective confusion, the researchers identified a cell in his MTL that responded selectively to both these buildings, as if they were represented as the same concept in his brain. The same line of research has shown just how quickly neurons come to respond to specific concepts. Quiroga observed some patients with a neuron that responded to pictures of himself (i.e. Quiroga) or a colleague, even though the patients had only known Quiroga and his team for a day or two.

In other intriguing research published in 2010,[31] Quiroga's group showed that concept cells were activated not just by the presentation of celebrity pictures or names, but also by thinking of those celebrities. In fact, patients' deliberate thoughts could override incoming visual stimuli. In one case, a cell sensitive to Josh Brolin became more active when a patient focused their thoughts on that actor, even as they looked at a hybrid image that was made up of 70 percent Marilyn Monroe and only 30 percent Josh Brolin. More staggering still, in a paper published in 2009, the Quiroga lab were able to say with impressive accuracy which picture a patient was looking at simply by observing the activity levels in relevant concept cells.[32]

Is the Halle Berry neuron an example of a grandmother cell? Not according to the strictest definition of a grandmother cell – the idea that there is just one neuron that responds to just one concept, and only that concept. For a start, Quiroga's team only tested the effects of a small subset of pictures and they only recorded from a relatively small sample of neurons. This means they can't know that there aren't other stimuli that the "Halle Berry" neuron would respond to; nor can they know that there aren't other cell types that they didn't record from that would also respond to Halle Berry, and so on. It's revealing that most of the highly selective cells that Quiroga discovered were also sensitive to other related concepts, albeit more weakly. For example, a cell was found in the hippocampus of one patient that responded strongly to the picture of *Friends* actress Jennifer Aniston (thus prompting the *Daily Mail* headline I mentioned earlier). However, the same cell also responded weakly to the sight of *Friends* co-star Lisa Kudrow. Another cell was found that responded to pictures of Luke Skywalker and to Yoda – both characters, of course, from *Star Wars*.

So, is the notion of grandmother cells a complete fallacy? Some experts certainly think so. In answer to the 2014 Edge question "What Scientific Idea is Ready for Retirement?" computational neuroscientist Terrence Sejnowski at the Salk Institute proposed bidding farewell to grandmother cells.[33] Yet others continue to defend the possibility that they exist. For example, Jeffrey Bowers at the University of Bristol published a paper in 2009 "On the Biological Plausibility of Grandmother Cells: Implications for Neural Network Theories in Psychology and Neuroscience"[34] in which he said it's still possible that the grandmother cell theory is true, albeit that there is likely large-scale redundancy in the system, with many cells responding to the same concepts (this actually chimes with Lettvin's original story, in which the fictional neurosurgeon needed to excise several thousand of his patient's "mother cells").

The mainstream view held by Quiroga and others is that abstract concepts are represented not by single (grandmother) cells, nor by vast distributed ensembles of neurons as others have proposed, but by so-called "sparse networks" made up of small numbers of neurons. Because any one neuron in a sparse network can be activated by related concepts, they say this is what helps us learn associations and explains the flow of consciousness from one idea to another.

Myth
#24

Glial Cells Are Little More Than Brain Glue

The word "NEUROscience" says it all. For decades, scientists studying the cells in the brain have focused almost exclusively on neurons, of which there are billions. But there are a similar number (see box) of non-neuronal brain cells, known collectively as glia.

Traditionally, neurons have been heralded as the principal information processing units of the brain. Glia, by contrast, were long thought to be incapable of communicating, judged to be mere housekeeping cells, servants to the all-important neurons. A related function was thought to be that they helped provide structure and stability to the brain. The name glia originates from the word gliok, which means "glue" in Greek, although it can also be translated as "slime," which perhaps betrays still further the lowly regard scientists have traditionally had for these cells.

There are many different types of glia. In the central nervous system, some of the most important types include oligodendrocytes, which insulate the axons of neurons, allowing them to signal faster; microglia, which are part of the immune system and involved in synaptic growth and pruning; and astrocytes, so named because of their apparent star shape when highlighted with certain staining techniques (some say they are more bush-like than astral). In the peripheral nervous system, the most important glia cell is the Schwann cell, which insulates axons in peripheral nerves.

It is our understanding of the function of astrocyte cells in particular that has been overhauled most radically in the last decade or so. In the late 1990s, trusted neurobiology textbooks were still stating with authority that astrocytes are not capable of signaling, and that their chief function is to support neurons. Although it's true that astrocytes provide many supportive functions, for example, mopping up excess neurotransmitters and ensuring that neurons receive the blood supply and energy that they need, we now know that they are in fact capable of signaling. Astrocytes speak to each other, and they also communicate directly with neurons, they just don't do so in the same way that neurons communicate with each other.

Neuron to neuron communication occurs by means of a mix of electrical and chemical processes. I touched on this in the introduction (see p. 11) but here's a slightly more extended overview for those unfamiliar with neurophysiology. Thanks to the work of miniature pumps in the cell wall, a neuron is normally negatively charged in its interior, relative to the outside environment. This is based on the ratio of positively and negatively charged atoms (known as "ions") located either side of the cell membrane. Particularly important ions include positively charged sodium and potassium. Pumps in the cell wall eject three sodium for every two potassium that enter, which maintains the relative negativity inside the cell. It's a basic law of physics that differences in charge seek an equilibrium, so you might say this "negative resting potential" as it's known is akin to a dammed river.

As a consequence, when excitation of a neuron leads to the opening of channels in its cell membrane, this triggers a surge of positive ions into the cell, lowering its negativity. If this goes far enough then it triggers an "action potential" and a wave of current travels the length of the neuron. That usually culminates in a release of chemicals at the end region of the neuron known as the pre-synaptic terminal. These neurotransmitters travel across a tiny gap – the synapse – and bind to receiving neurons on the other side, potentially causing those neurons to initiate action potentials of their own.

Except in very rare cases, glia cells do not communicate electrically in this way, either with each other, or with neurons. Glia cells communicate with each other by changing the intercellular calcium levels of their neighbors (calcium, like sodium and potassium, is positively charged). Glia also ensheath the synapses between neurons, into which they can release neuroactive substances of their own, including glutamate and adenosine (this process is known as "gliotransmission"). And they have receptors for neurotransmitters released by neurons, meaning their activity can be influenced by chemical signals from neurons. This establishes a complex feedback loop at what are known as "tripartite synapses" (featuring a presynaptic terminal belonging to one neuron, a postsynaptic terminal belonging to another neuron, with both ensheathed by a projection from an astrocyte). In short, the glia can affect the neurons and the neurons can affect the glia.

Today it's the view of a growing number of neuroscientists that the communication between astrocytes and neurons at tripartite synapses allows those astrocytes to influence the signaling between neurons, therefore having a direct effect on information processing. Writing a prescient review in 2003,[35] Maiken Nedergaard and his colleagues explained: "Simply stated, astrocytes tell neurons what to do, besides cleaning up their mess."

The discovery of tripartite synapses also raises the possibility that neurons could influence each other via astrocytes. Remember that neurons at a tripartite synapse can signal their participating astrocyte; this in turn could lead it to affect its glial neighbors, therefore having an effect on the behavior of any neurons participating in a tripartite synapse with those affected astrocytes.

If all this sounds seriously complex, it is. Writing for the journal *Nature* in 2010,[36] Kerri Smith paraphrased the glial researcher Andrea Volterra putting it this way: "If [it's true] glia are involved in signalling, processing in the brain turns out to be an order of magnitude more complex than previously expected."

Other vital functions now attributed to glia include assisting in the creation of new synapses between neurons and selectively eliminating existing synapses – in other words they appear to play an architect's role in the formation and management of neural networks. Glia also communicate with blood vessel cells ensuring that blood flows to where it's needed most.

Furthering our understanding of glia is vital because they play a significant role in many neurological illnesses, and in the way the brain and nervous system respond to injury. Here are a few examples to give you an idea:

- When the brain or spinal cord is damaged, glial cells proliferate (known as "gliosis"), forming a kind of scar that prevents neuronal axons from repairing.
- Multiple sclerosis, one of the most common neurological illnesses, is characterized by a loss of the fatty insulation of neuronal axons that's provided by oligodendrocytes.
- The most common form of primary brain tumors, known as glioblastomas, originate from pathological glial cells.
- Epilepsy is known to affect astrocyte signaling.
- Astrocytes are involved in degrading a protein that accumulates pathologically in Alzheimer's disease.

- Defective glia are also involved in the fatal, paralyzing illness of amyotrophic lateral sclerosis (also known as motor neuron disease or Lou Gehrig's disease, after the famous US baseball player who died of it).
- Glia have also been implicated in HIV infection, depression, schizophrenia and more.

There is so much we still don't know about the way glia work and many controversies remain. Perhaps most important of all – while the functional significance of glial signaling is recognized by many, there are also expert skeptics who wonder about the techniques being used to study these cells, including the reliance on cell cultures and tissues slices, rather than studying glia at work inside living animals (known as "in vivo" studies).

One paper that particularly unnerved (excuse the pun) the burgeoning community of glia researchers was published in 2010 by Ken McCarthy and his colleagues at the University of North Carolina School of Medicine in Chapel Hill.[37] Using genetically engineered mice, they reported that obliterating calcium signaling within and between astrocytes made absolutely no difference to neuronal function in the mice hippocampus, thus casting doubt on the functional significance of glia communication, at least in that part of the brain. However, some were quick to criticize this study for its crude, sledge-hammer approach. These experts pointed to other research that used "calcium clamps" to inactivate specific astrocytes, which found that doing so *did* have an effect on neuronal functioning.[38]

These contradictions will surely only be resolved through more research on exactly how calcium signaling controls the way that glia and neurons communicate. Meanwhile, one thing's for sure – the idea of glia as mere housekeepers seems today little more than a myth. We should consider glia not so much as neuronal servants, Maiken Nedergaard and his team wrote in their review paper, "but as parents." And, slowly, there seems to be a growing chorus of experts arguing that the neglect of glia has gone on too long. For instance, writing for *Nature* in 2013, R. Douglas Fields of the US National Institutes of Health in Bethesda, Maryland, urged the Obama government's BRAIN Initiative not to forget these important cells. "That the word 'glia' was not uttered in any of the announcements of the BRAIN Initiative, nor written anywhere in the 'white papers' published in 2012 and 2013 in prominent journals outlining the ambitious plan speaks volumes about the need for the community of neuroscientists behind the initiative to expand its thinking," he wrote.[39] "In any major mapping expedition," he added, "the first priority should be to survey the uncharted regions."

Myth: Glial Cells Outnumber Neurons by Ten to One

This is a rather obscure but particularly mysterious brain myth. For decades, the most trusted textbooks have claimed with confidence that glial cells massively outnumber neurons. Take, for instance, the magisterial *Principles of Neural Science* first published in 1981 by Nobel laureate Eric Kandel, James Schwartz, and Thomas Jessell, which states: "Glial cells far outnumber neurons – there are between 10 and 50 times more glia than neurons in the central nervous system of vertebrates."

However, the latest evidence completely contradicts this claim, and suggests instead that there are a similar number of neurons and glia in the brain. The new data comes from an innovative technique developed by the lab of Suzana Herculano-Houzel, a neurophysiologist based in Rio de Janeiro (we also encountered her on p. 52). She grinds brains into a soup and uses special markers that show up the DNA of neurons to distinguish them from glia. In 2009 she and her colleagues applied this process to the brains of four men and came up with an approximate 1:1 ratio for neurons and glia.[40]

Where the idea that glia massively outnumber neurons comes from is something of a mystery. When in 2012 the neuroscience writers Daisy Yuhas and Ferris Jabr were called to task for spreading the 10:1 myth in their popular *Scientific American* Brainwaves blog, the pair turned detectives and set out to find the truth.[41] They found some older studies based on the traditional technique of counting cells in brain slices under a microscope that suggested a ratio of 0.5:1 to 2:1, but nowhere could they find mention of a 10:1 or 50:1 ratio. "After surveying the research literature, we did not find a single published study that directly supports a 10:1 glia to neuron ratio in the whole human brain," they wrote.

Ideally we need more replications of Herculano-Houzel's findings by other groups. It's also worth noting that the ratio of neurons to glia varies in different parts of the brain and between different species, so the picture is more complicated than revealed in a simple ratio. For now, however, the popular factoid that glia outnumber neurons by a multiple of ten or fifty seems to be yet another brain myth.

Myth #25 — Mirror Neurons Make Us Human (and Broken Mirror Neurons Cause Autism)

Back in the 1990s Italian neuroscientists identified cells in the brains of monkeys with an unusual response pattern. These neurons in the premotor cortex were activated when the monkeys performed a given action and, mirror-like, when they saw another individual perform that same movement. It was a fortuitous discovery. Giacomo Rizzolatti and his colleagues at the University of Palma were using electrodes to record the activity of individual cells in macaque monkey forebrains. They wanted to find out how the monkeys use visual information about objects to help guide their movements. It was only when one of the research team, Leonardo Fogassi, happened one day to reach for the monkeys' raisins, that the mirror neurons were spotted. These cells were activated by the sight of Fogassi's reaching movement and when the monkeys made that reaching movement themselves. Since then, the precise function and influence of these neurons has become perhaps the most hyped topic in neuroscience.

The Myth

In 2000, Vilayanur Ramachandran, the charismatic University of California at San Diego neuroscientist, made a bold prediction:[42] "mirror neurons will do for psychology what DNA did for biology: they will provide a unifying framework and help explain a host of mental abilities that have hitherto remained mysterious and inaccessible to experiments."

Ramachandran is at the forefront of a frenzy of excitement that has followed these cells ever since their discovery. They've come to represent in many people's eyes all that makes us human (ironic given they were actually discovered in monkeys). Above all, many see them as the neural essence of human empathy, as the very neurobiological font of human culture.

Part of Ramachandran's appeal as a scientific communicator is his infectious passion for neuroscience. Perhaps, in those early heady years after mirror neurons were discovered, he was just getting a little carried away? Not at all. For his 2011 book[43] aimed at the general public, *The Tell-Tale Brain*, Ramachandran took his claims about mirror neurons even further. In a chapter titled "The Neurons that Shaped Civilization," he claims that mirror neurons underlie empathy; allow us to imitate other people; that they accelerated the evolution of the brain; that they help to explain a neuropsychological condition called anosognosia (in which the patient denies his or her paralysis or other disability); that they help explain the origin of language; and most impressively of all, that they prompted the great leap forward in human culture that happened about 60 000 years ago, including the emergence of more sophisticated art and tool use. "We could say mirror neurons served the same role in early hominid evolution as the Internet, Wikipedia, and blogging do today," he concludes. "Once the cascade was set in motion, there was no turning back from the path to humanity." In 2006,[44] with co-author Lindsay Oberman, he made a similar claim more pithily: "Mirror neurons allowed humans to reach for the stars, instead of mere peanuts."

Ramachandran is not alone in bestowing such achievements on these brain cells. Writing for *The Times* (London) in 2009 about our interest in the lives of celebrities, the eminent philosopher A. C. Grayling traced it all back to those mirror neurons. "We have a great gift for empathy," he wrote. "This is a biologically evolved capacity, as shown by the function of 'mirror neurons.'" In the same newspaper in 2012, Eva Simpson wrote on why people were so moved when tennis champion Andy Murray broke down in tears. "Crying is like yawning," she said, "blame mirror neurons, brain cells that *make us* react in the same way as someone we're watching (emphasis added)." In a *New York Times* article in 2007, about one man's heroic actions to save another who'd fallen onto train tracks, those cells featured again: "people have 'mirror neurons,'" Cara Buckley wrote, "which *make them* feel what someone else is experiencing, be it joy or distress (emphasis added)."

Science stories about the function of mirror neurons often come with profound headlines that also support Ramachandran's claims: "Cells that read minds," was the title of a *New York Times* piece in 2006;[45] "The mind's mirror" introduced an article in the monthly magazine of the American Psychological Association in 2005.[46] But the hype is loudest in the tabloids. Try searching for "mirror neurons" on the *Daily Mail* website. To take one example, the paper ran an article in 2013 that claimed the most popular romantic films are distinguished by the fact they activate our mirror neurons. Another claimed that it's thanks to mirror neurons that hospital patients benefit from having visitors. In fact, there is no scientific research that directly backs either of these claims, both of which represent reductionism gone mad.

A brief search on Twitter also shows how far the concept of powerful empathy-giving mirror neurons has spread into popular consciousness. "'Mirror neurons' are responsible for us cringing whenever we see someone get seriously hurt," the @WoWFactz feed announced to its 398 000 followers with misleading confidence in 2013. "Mirror neurons are so powerful that we are even able to mirror or echo each other's intentions," claimed self-help author Dr Caroline Leaf in a tweet the same year.

If mirror neurons grant us the ability to empathize with others, it only follows that attention should be drawn to these cells in attempts to explain why certain people struggle to take the perspective of others – such as can happen in autism. Lo and behold the "broken mirror hypothesis." Here's the prolific neuroscience author Rita Carter in the *Daily Mail* in 2009:[47] "Autistic people often lack empathy and have been found to show less mirror-neuron activity." It's a theory to which Ramachandran subscribes. After attributing the great leap forward in human culture to these cells, he claims in his 2011 book: "the main cause of autism is a disturbed mirror neuron system." You won't be surprised to hear that questionable autism interventions have risen on the back of these claims, including synchronized dance therapy and playing with robot pets.

Mirror neurons have also been used by some researchers to explain smokers' compulsions (their mirror neurons are allegedly activated too strongly by others smoking-related actions); as part of a neurobiological explanation for homosexuality (gay people's mirror neurons are allegedly activated more by the sight of same-sex aroused genitalia); and to explain many other varieties of human behavior. According to *New Scientist*,[48] these clever cells even "control [the] erection response to porn"!

The Reality

There's no doubt that mirror neurons have fascinating properties, but many of the claims made about them are wildly overblown and speculative. Before focusing on specifics, it's worth pointing out that the very use of the term mirror neurons can be confusing. As we heard, the label was originally applied to cells in motor parts of the monkey brain that showed mirror-like sensory properties. Since then, cells with these response patterns have been found in other motor parts of the brain too, including in the parietal cortex at the back of the brain. These days experts talk of a distributed "mirror neuron system."

The term "mirror neurons" also conceals a complex mix of cell types.[49] Some motor cells only show mirror-like responses when a monkey (most of this research is with monkeys) sees a live performer in front of them; other cells are also responsive to movements seen on video. Some mirror neurons appear to be fussy – they only respond to a very specific type of action; others are less specific and respond to a far broader range of observed movements. There are even some mirror neurons that are activated by the sound of a particular movement. Others show mirror suppression – that is, their activity is reduced during action observation. Another study found evidence in monkeys of touch-sensitive neurons that respond to the sight of another animal being touched in the same location (Ramachandran calls these "Gandhi cells" because he says they dissolve the barriers between human beings).

Also, there are reports of entire brain systems having mirror-like properties. For example, the brain's so-called pain matrix, which processes our own pain, is also activated when we see another person in pain. In this case experts often talk of "mirror mechanisms," rather than mirror neurons per se, although the distinction isn't always clear.

So, not only are there different types of mirror neuron in motor parts of the brain (varying in the extent and manner of their mirror-like properties), there are networks of non-motor neurons across the brain with various degrees of mirror-like properties. To say that mirror neurons explain empathy is therefore rather vague, and not a whole lot more meaningful than saying that the brain explains empathy.

Let's zoom in on the ubiquitous idea that mirror neurons "cause" us to feel other people's emotions. It can be traced back to the original context in which mirror neurons were discovered – the motor cells in the front of the monkey brain that responded to the sight of another person performing an action. This led to the suggestion, endorsed by many experts in the field including Vittorio Gallesse and Marco Iacoboni, that mirror neurons play a *causal* role in allowing us to understand the goals behind other people's actions. By representing other people's actions in the movement-pathways of our own brain, so the reasoning goes, these cells provide us with an instant simulation of their intentions – a highly effective foundation for empathy.

It's a simple and seductive idea. What the newspaper reporters (and over-enthusiastic neuroscientists like Ramachandran) don't tell you is just how controversial it is.[50] The biggest and most obvious problem for anyone advocating the idea that mirror neurons play a central role in our ability to understand other people's actions is that we are quite clearly capable of understanding actions that we are not able to perform ourselves.

A non-player tennis fan who has never even held a racket doesn't sit baffled as Roger Federer swings his way to another victory. They understand fully what his aims are, even though they can't simulate his actions with their own racket-swinging motor cells. Similarly, we understand flying, slithering, coiling, and any number of other creaturely movements, even if we don't have the necessary flying or other cells to simulate the act. From the medical literature there are also numerous examples of comprehension surviving after damage to motor networks – people who can understand speech, though they can't produce it; others who recognize facial expressions, though their own facial movements are compromised. Perhaps most awkward of all, there's evidence that mirror neuron activity is greater when we view actions that are less familiar – such as a meaningless gesture – as compared with gestures that are imbued with cultural meaning, such as the victory sign.

Mirror neuron advocates generally accept that action understanding is possible without corresponding mirror neuron activity, but they say mirror neurons bring an extra layer of depth to understanding. In a journal debate published in 2011 in *Perspectives in Psychological Science*,[51] Marco Iacoboni insists that mirror neurons are important for action understanding, and he endorses the idea that they somehow allow "an understanding from within" whatever that means. Critics in the field believe otherwise. Gregory Hickok at the University of California Irvine thinks[52] the function of mirror neurons is not about understanding others' actions per se (something we can clearly do without mirror neurons), but about using others actions' in the process of making our own choice of how to act. Seen this way, mirror neuron activity is just as likely a consequence of action understanding as a cause.

What about the grand claims that mirror neurons played a central role in accelerating human social and cultural evolution by *making* us empathize with each other? Troublesome findings here center on the fact that mirror neurons appear to acquire their properties through experience. Research by Cecelia Heyes and others has shown that learning experiences can reverse, abolish, or create mirror-like properties in motor cells. In one pertinent study,[53] Heyes and her co-workers had participants respond to the sight of another person's index finger movement by always moving their own little finger. This training led to a change in their usual mirror activity. Twenty-four hours later, the sight of another person's index finger movement triggered more excitatory activity in the participants' own little finger muscle than in their own index finger muscle. This is the opposite to what happened pre-training and shows how easily experience shapes mirror-like activity in the brain.

The reason these findings are awkward for the bold claims about mirror neurons is that they imply experience affects mirror neuron activity as much as mirror neuron activity affects the way we process the world. In other words, it can't reasonably be claimed that mirror neurons *made us* imitate and empathize with each other, if the way we choose to behave instead dictates the way our mirror neurons work. On their role in cultural evolution, Heyes says mirror neurons are affected just as much, if not more, by cultural practices, such as dancing and music, compared with how much they likely influenced these practices. Contradicting Ramachandran and others, she wrote in 2011:[54] "mirror mechanisms are not at one end of a causal arrow between biology and culture – they owe at least as much as they lend to cultural processes."

More evidence that mirror neurons are not always positioned at the start of a causal path comes from studies showing how the activity of these cells is modulated by such factors as the monkey's angle of view, the reward value of the observed movement, and the overall goal of a seen movement, such as whether it is intended to grasp an object or place it in the mouth.[55] These findings are significant because they show how mirror neurons are not merely activated by incoming sensory information, but also by formulations developed elsewhere in the brain about the meaning of what is being observed. Of course these results don't detract from the fascination of mirror neurons, but they do show how these cells are embedded in a complex network of brain activity. They are as much influenced by our perception and understanding as the cause of it.

Finally, what about the suggestion that mirror neurons play a role in autism? It's here that the hype about mirror neurons is probably the least justified. As Morton Ann Gernsbacher put it in 2011:[56] "Perhaps no other application of mirror neuron hypothesizing has been characterized by as much speculation as that of the relation between mirror neurons and the autistic phenotype." Gernsbacher goes on to review the relevant literature, including numerous findings showing that most people with autism have no problem understanding other people's actions (contrary to the broken mirror hypothesis) and that they show normal imitation abilities and reflexes. What's more, for a review paper published in 2013,[57] Antonia Hamilton at the University of Nottingham assessed the results from 25 relevant studies that used a range of methods including fMRI, EEG, and eye-tracking to investigate mirror neuron functioning in people with autism. She concluded, "there is little evidence for a global dysfunction of the mirror system in autism," adding: "Interventions based on this theory are unlikely to be helpful."

Motor cells that respond to the sight of other people moving are intriguing, there's no doubt about that. It's likely they play a role in important social cognitions, like empathy and understanding other people's intentions. But to claim that they *make us* empathic, and to raise them up as neuroscience's holy grail, as the ultimate brain-based root of humanity, is hype. The evidence I've mentioned is admittedly somewhat selective. I've tried to counteract the hyperbole and show just how much debate and doubt surrounds exactly what these cells are and what they do. In fact, it's worth finishing this section by noting that the very existence of mirror neurons in the human brain has only been confirmed tentatively.

The first direct evidence for mirror neurons came from the recording of individual cells in the brains of epileptic patients in a paper published as recently as 2010.[58] Roy Mukamel and his colleagues identified a subset of cells at the front of the brain that responded to the sight of various facial expressions and head gestures, and to the execution of those same gestures (but not to words describing those expressions and gestures). However, bear in mind that the previous year, another human study[59] using fMRI found no evidence that cells in postulated mirror neuron areas showed signs of adaptation. That is, they didn't exhibit reduced activity to continued stimulation after executing and then viewing (or vice versa) the same hand movements, which is what you'd expect them to do if they had mirror properties. "There is no meaningful evidence for … a mirror neuron system in humans," the lead author Alfonso Caramazza at Harvard University told me at the time. His comments are a reminder of where we are at in the study of these cells. We are still trying to confirm whether they exist in humans, and if so, where they are and what exactly they do. Mirror neurons are fascinating but, for now at least, they aren't the answer to what makes us human.

Myth
#26

The Disembodied Brain

Despite folk expressions such as "I can feel it in my bones" or "I'm going to go with my gut," it's all too common these days for people to have a rather disembodied view of their mental lives. They consider the body merely a source of sensory information, sending input from the skin, eyes, ears, and other channels to the brain for processing. In response, the brain sends out commands to the body for how it wants to move. According to this neurocentric view, the brain–body connection is seen purely as a sensory-motor relationship, with moral judgments, aesthetic appreciation, decision making, and other human concerns left as entirely cerebral affairs.

There are three main corrections we should make to this brain bias. First, let's not forget that there are neurons in the body, outside of the brain and spinal cord. Indeed, neurons are found so extensively in the gut that some experts refer to them collectively as "the second brain" (likewise, others talk of "the little brain on the heart" given the extensive number of neuron-like cells there, although this is more controversial). Second, the state of the body has a profound effect on our emotions. Third, information from our bodies affects the way we think and, in turn, how we think affects our bodies. Fourth, psychological health affects our physical health, and vice versa. Let's deal with these in turn.

The Brain in the Gut

By some estimates there are 100 million neurons embedded in the wall of the human gut – that's more than you'd find in the entire brain of a cat. This "enteric nervous system," to use its formal name, allows the complicated business of digesting food to be controlled entirely onsite, without continual monitoring by the brain in our heads. Over thirty neurotransmitters are involved. In fact, according to various magazine interviews given by neurobiologist Michael Gershon, author of *The Second Brain*,[60] 95 percent of all serotonin in the body is found in the gut.[61] I couldn't find the original journal source for this claim but given Gershon's credentials it seems fair to accept that the gut produces a lot of serotonin. Serotonin, you may recall, is a neurotransmitter involved in mood, and it is serotonin levels that are targeted by many anti-depressant drugs (see p. 301).

The gut communicates with the brain via the so-called vagus nerve (actually a collection of nerves that send signals between the brain and viscera), and Gershon says that 90 percent of these fibers send information from the gut to the brain, rather than the other way around. Related to this, a team led by Lukas Van Oudenhove at the University of Leuven showed recently how infusing fatty acids directly into subjects' stomachs led them to be less affected by exposure to sad music and sad faces.[62] This finding is consistent with the idea that activity in the gut can have a direct effect on the brain, separate from any psychological effects around the cultural or personal meaning of foods.

These signals from the gut to the brain could have profound effects in everyday life. Consider a study published in 2010[63] which found that an hour after eating a meal, men's decisions in a gambling game were more conservative. This was thought to be due to the suppression of the appetite-enhancing hormone acyl-ghrelin. When the levels of this hormone are higher, we feel hungrier and are more willing to take risks to get what we want. Another study published in 2011[64] found, rather worryingly, that Israeli judges were dramatically more lenient in their parole decisions after eating, compared with at the end of a session (when they'd gone several hours without anything to eat).

There is also evidence that our mood and emotions are influenced by microbacteria that live in the gut.[65] Most of this comes from animal studies, but in the last few years research has shown tentatively that probiotic formulations that promote the growth of gut bacteria can have beneficial effects on people's mood and alter their brain function to reduce reactivity to stress. For instance, a double-blind placebo controlled study published in 2011 found that healthy participants who consumed probiotics for 30 days showed reduced psychological distress compared with controls.[66] Mouse studies suggest this could be via influences on the immune system or related to the release of short-chain fatty acids by the microbes.

Bodily Effects on Emotion

In the late nineteenth century the great American psychologist William James proposed that emotions start with bodily changes and that the feeling aspect of emotion comes afterwards, as a consequence of the body affecting the mind. He gave the example of a person running from a bear in the woods. The person runs and it is their act of running, he asserted, that leads to the feeling of fear. Although it's now known that the experience of emotion depends a lot on how situations are appraised and how bodily sensations are interpreted, James did have a valid point about the importance of bodily feedback.

Consider the relationship between facial expressions and felt emotion. We often assume that we feel an emotion and then the appropriate expression plays across our face. In fact there's evidence showing that the causal direction can run the other way too. Pulling a smiling face has been shown[67] to lead some people to feel happier and to be biased toward retrieving more positive events from memory. One pertinent study[68] involved participants holding a pen between their teeth – which forced them to imitate a smiling expression – and to watch cartoons. Those with their face in this smiling position rated the cartoons as funnier than other participants who posed with the pen held between their lips (which prevents smiling). There's even evidence that the cosmetic use of Botox can interfere with people's experience of emotions, presumably because they're unable to stretch their faces into the appropriate facial expressions, resulting in a lack of feedback from the face to the brain.[69]

Also relevant here is research conducted by Hugo Critchley and his colleagues showing how heart activity affects the way we react emotionally to pain. In a paper published in 2010,[70] the researchers first showed that brain activity in response to an electric shock was greater when participants paid attention to the shock. This initial finding was consistent with the idea that paying attention to pain enhances its effects. Relevant to our story, the researchers showed that this result was modified by the timing of the shock relative to the activity of the heart.

Specifically, the enhanced brain response to pain was entirely abolished if the shock was delivered when the heart had just ejected blood, as opposed to if the shock was delivered when the heart was midway between beats. This effect is thought to be mediated by the activity of receptors in the large arteries (baroreceptors), which tell the brainstem about higher blood pressure levels. In turn, this information is used by the brain to control the dilation of blood vessels, thus lowering blood pressure.

Somehow this "baroreceptor to brain" communication interacts with the way we respond to pain (a related study[71] showed more baroreceptor activity also reduced people's reaction to the sight of emotional facial expressions). "Our processing of salient environmental stimuli can fluctuate within each heartbeat interval," Critchley and his colleagues wrote in a review paper in 2012.[72] This is a striking example of how the activity of our bodies can influence our mental lives. Related to this, a small-scale study published in 2006[73] also found that direct stimulation of the vagus nerve (via a pacemaker-like implant in the chest) led to mood benefits for patients with treatment-resistant depression.

Consider too how even the position of our bodies can affect our experience of pain. Research published in 2011[74] by Vanessa Bohns and Scott Wilteruth found that people were able to tolerate more pain (a tight tourniquet around the arm) when they adopted a "power posture," such as a star-shaped pose, compared with a neutral or submissive posture. The researchers said they thought the effect occurred because the expansive body posture engendered a feeling of being in control.

There's also research showing that the nature of our movements – upwards versus downwards – can affect our emotions. Daniel

Casasanto at the Max Planck Institute for Psycholinguistics found that students were faster at telling positive stories from their lives when moving marbles from a lower to a higher shelf (as compared with higher to lower),[75] presumably because the upward movement resonated with the way we associate up with good things, like heaven or "being on a high," and down with negativity, as in "being down in the dumps." A later paper published in 2011[76] found that people were quicker to perform movements in response to emotional words, if the movement direction matched the emotional meaning of the word – such as an upward movement for happiness. Taken altogether, the cardiac research and the bodily movement and position studies show just how much our emotional thoughts and sensations are influenced by the body, not just by the brain.

Bodily Effects on Thoughts and Morality

Those last two studies involving marbles and upward movements come from an emerging field in psychology known as "embodied cognition," (also sometimes referred to as "grounded cognition") in which researchers are exploring the links between bodily sensations and the way we think and perceive. In one line of this research, psychologists have shown that physical sensations like warmth can affect our judgments about other people. Lawrence Williams and John Bargh found that participants who'd held a cup of hot coffee subsequently judged a stranger in more "warm terms," for example, describing him as good-natured and generous, as compared with other participants who described the stranger after holding an iced-coffee.[77]

Although some findings in this field have proven tricky to replicate, many experts think the underlying mechanism is real – that is, the physical metaphors we use in our language reflect the way we represent abstract concepts such as "goodness" in bodily terms like "warmth." Another relevant finding here, provided by Hans Ijzerman and Gun Semin, was that participants felt socially closer to an experimenter when they were tested in a warm room as opposed to a cool room.[78] The room's temperature even affected the way these participants perceived simple shapes shown on a screen. Participants in a warm room showed a bias toward focusing on how the shapes were arranged in relation to each other; those in a cooler room focused more on the form taken by the individual shapes.

Yet another line of this research highlights the way our eye movements affect our numerical thinking. In 2010, a team led by Tobias Loetscher at the University of Melbourne asked participants to produce a string of random numbers.[79] The researchers found that they could predict the relative magnitude of the next number a participant produced based on the direction of their eye movements. A glance upwards or rightwards tended to precede a larger number while a downward or leftward glance preceded smaller numbers. The finding is consistent with the idea that we think about numbers as being placed along a mental number line. "A close look at the eyes may not only reveal what is in a person's mind," the researchers concluded, "but also illustrate how abstract thoughts are grounded in basic sensory-motor processes."

Support for this interpretation came from a fun study by Anita Eerland and her colleagues published in 2011.[80] They had participants stand on a Wii balance board and make various judgments of magnitude such as the number of hits Michael Jackson had had in the Netherlands or the height of the Eiffel Tower. When the researchers used the Wii board to cause the participants to lean to the left slightly (without them knowing), the participants tended to make smaller estimates. For example, left-leaning participants estimated the Tower was 12 meters shorter, on average, than right-leaning participants. It's another demonstration of bodily move-ments interfering with the way we think about numbers on a line, and it's also a result that won the researchers an Ignobel Prize in 2012 – for research that "makes you laugh and then think."

Note, embodied cognition is not only about the body affecting our thoughts. Our thoughts can also affect our sensory perceptions. For example, one study showed that people tended to judge a book as heavier if they believed it was an important piece of work.[81] Thinking of a friend or relative has been shown to affect people's judgments about the steep-ness of a hill[82] – bringing the ally to mind led the hill to appear more easily surmountable. On the other hand, thinking of secrets can leave us feeling physically encumbered[83] (although note a paper in press at the end of 2013 failed to replicate this effect).[84] Yet another study found that participants who spent time enjoying nostalgic thoughts were able to hold their hand in a bucket of iced-water for longer.[85]

Finally, let's take a look at ways that our bodies can affect our moral judgments, and how our moral judgments can affect our bodily sensa-tions. One of my favorite examples was published in 2012[86] and involved rigging participants up to cardio equipment so that they thought they could hear their own heartbeat. They believed they were testing the equipment but really the idea was to trick some of them into thinking their heart was beating super-fast.

The participants who thought their heart was racing were more likely to offer their time for another study (taken as a sign of increased altruism) and they played more fairly in a financial game. The researchers – Jun Gu and his colleagues – said that sensing our heart is beating fast tells us that we're stressed, and in turn, that encourages us to behave more morally, to help reduce stress levels.

Another example is the so-called "Macbeth effect" – it seems that after people have transgressed they feel dirty, literally. Chen-Bo Zhong and Katie Liljenquist provided one example of how this affects people's behavior.[87] Participants who recalled one of their own past unethical misdeeds were more likely to choose an antiseptic wipe as a free gift after the study, as compared with participants who recalled an ethical behavior. A paper published early in 2014[88] failed to replicate Zhong and Liljenquist's finding, but other studies have supported the notion of a link between physical cleanliness and moral goodness. In 2011, for example, Erik Helzer and David Pizarro found that people reminded of physical cleanliness were subsequently more harsh in their moral judgments.[89] More recently, in 2012, Mario Gollwitzer and André Melzer invited some novice video game players to have a go at a violent game.[90] Afterwards these novice players were more morally distressed than experienced players (who were used to the violence) and consequently also more likely than the pros to choose a free hygiene gift, rather than a chocolate bar or tea.

Physical and Mental Health

We've seen how our bodies affect our emotions, thoughts, and morals but surely the most dramatic demonstration of the deep connections between mind and body comes from the arena of physical and mental health. Exhibit A in this regard has to be the placebo effect – wherein physiologically inactive sugar pills and other inert treatments trigger significant physical recoveries. The medic and writer Ben Goldacre calls this effect "the coolest, strangest thing in medicine." It's thought to arise when the patient *believes* a particular treatment will be effective, which initiates real bodily and neurological changes, with consequent health benefits (although strangely, a recent study[91] found the effect still occurred when patients were told the treatment was a placebo).

My favorite example comes from the treatment of Parkinson's disease – the neurological illness that renders people tremulous, rigid, and slow-moving. In one trial[92] testing the benefits of surgically implanting embryonic dopamine neurons (the illness is characterized by a loss of dopamine-producing neurons), there was a group of control patients who, unbeknown to them, received all the injections but no new neurons. Amazingly, patients in both the treatment and control conditions showed benefits over the coming year, presumably because the control group had good reason to believe they too were receiving the revolutionary new treatment.

The placebo effect has a dark side too, called the nocebo effect. Harmless technologies or medicines can have adverse effects simply because a patient believes the intervention is harmful to them. You can see this effect in action if you trick a person into thinking they've slept badly. In one study,[93] participants in a sleep lab who were told that their sleep is disturbed went on to show all the signs of insomnia as if they really were sleep deprived.

Another graphic example of the way our mental state can affect our bodies relates to the healing of skin wounds. Researchers have inflicted small puncture wounds on the skin of their participants as well as measuring their stress levels. Wounds have been shown to heal twice as slowly in stressed people[94] (this is likely the effect of immunological processes related to stress, rather than to participants' expectations). On the flip side, stress-busting psychological interventions have been shown to boost wound recovery.

It's notable too that many mental illnesses are associated with high rates of physical illness. Around a third of people diagnosed with schizophrenia are obese (this is partly because antipsychotic drugs contribute to weight gain). People with schizophrenia and depression are also at increased risk of heart attack and diabetes compared with the general population. A study from 2006 found that people with severe mental illness die, on average, 25 years younger than the mentally well,[95] although note that this was found to be largely because of indirect factors like smoking and poor access to health care.

Although a person's mental state, beliefs, and coping strategies can clearly have important influences on the body, it's important not to overemphasize these links. Most damaging is the idea that people with cancer can will themselves better if only they have the right positive mental attitude. This can create unwarranted and unfair pressure on patients to be upbeat, or possibly worse still, cause them to feel their earlier low mood or negative attitude was responsible for the onset of their cancer. When psychologist James Coyne and his colleagues tracked over a thousand cancer patients for nine years in a 2007 study,[96] they found that the patients' emotional state at the start had no bearing on their longevity. Even focusing on only the most high-spirited optimists or the most fearful pessimists, there was no relation between mental attitude and survival outcomes.

So far, most of these examples I've given have been about mental state influencing physical well-being. The relationship works the other way too. For instance, patients are particularly prone to depression after a heart attack. One in eight is estimated to suffer from post-traumatic stress disorder. According to a British study published in 2012,[97] over half of all patients who survived intensive care went on to develop psychological problems over the ensuing months, though thankfully most people do recover with time. In a policy announcement made the same year, the Mental Health Foundation summed up the inextricable link between mind and brain: "There is growing evidence to support [the fact] that mental health and physical health are very closely linked, interdependent, and even inseparable."

Myth: Consciousness Lingers in the Decapitated Head

Probably the grisliest brain myth of all relates to the idea that the owners of decapitated heads continue to blink and grimace as long as 30 seconds after they've been separated from their body. It raises the horrible possibility that beheaded people are aware, at least momentarily, of their disembodied state.

The myth likely originates in tales from the French guillotine. One story told by the medical historian Lindsey Fitzharris[98] dates from 1793 when the executioner of Charlotte Corday picked up her severed head by the hair and slapped her on both cheeks, causing her to blush with apparent ignominy.

There's also a later account from the guillotine, published in 1905,[99] in which the French doctor Gabriel Beaurieux describes his observations of the severed head of the murderer Henri Languille. After seeing the eyelids and lips spasm for several seconds, Beaurieux says he called out Languille's name, and then "[his] eyes very definitely fixed themselves on mine and the pupils focused themselves. ... I was dealing with undeniably living eyes which were looking at me." After the eyes closed, Beaurieux says he called out for a second time and once again "undeniably living eyes fixed themselves on mine with perhaps even more penetration than the first time." A third call elicited no response and the doctor estimates the entire period of awareness lasted between "twenty-five to thirty seconds."

In 1939,[100] the editors of the *Journal of the American Medical Association* challenged Beaurieux's account on several points. They said other medical witnesses estimated the period of consciousness at no more than ten seconds, and that the force of a decapitating blow, combined with the loss of oxygen and blood supply indicates "fairly conclusively that conscious processes in the brain of man cease almost simultaneously with the severance of the head from the body."

Obviously this is not a question easily addressed by modern research, especially since the welcome decline in the use of beheading as a form of punishment. Certainly if a randomized trial were ever conducted, you'd really want to be in the control condition! The most recent evidence-based insight into this myth that I could find comes from a study of decapitated rats published in 2011.[101] Clementina van Rijn and his colleagues recorded the surface electrical activity of the brains of the rats before and after they lost their heads. They observed a "fast and global" loss of activity – after four seconds, the strength of the brain wave signal was at half its initial value.

Based on this, the researchers concluded that "consciousness is likely to vanish within some seconds after decapitation." Presumably that is still long enough for a decapitated person to realize their abysmal fate, so perhaps there is some truth to this myth! To the researchers surprise they also witnessed a final surge of electrical brain activity up to 80 seconds after decapitation possibly due to "a simultaneous massive loss of membrane potentials of the neurons" representing "the ultimate border between life and death."

Notes

1   Linden, D. J. (2012). *The Accidental Mind: How Brain Evolution Has Given Us Love, Memory, Dreams, and God*. Harvard University Press.
2   Marcus, G. (2009). *Kluge: The Haphazard Evolution of the Human Mind*. Houghton Mifflin Harcourt.

3 http://empiricalplanet.blogspot.co.uk/2013/07/there-is-no-primitive-part-of-brain.html (accessed May 16, 2014).

4 http://www.huffingtonpost.com/alejandra-ruani-/overeating_b_4114504.html (accessed May 16, 2014).

5 Godin, S. (2010). *Linchpin: Are You Indispensable? How to Drive Your Career and Create a Remarkable Future.* Hachette UK.

6 Faisal, A. A., Selen, L. P., & Wolpert, D. M. (2008). Noise in the nervous system. *Nature Reviews Neuroscience*, 9(4), 292–303.

7 http://www.wired.com/science/discoveries/commentary/dissection/2008/04/dissection_0404 (accessed May 16, 2014).

8 http://www.newscientist.com/article/dn22380-our-big-brains-may-make-us-prone-to-cancer.html#.UeqZaRbPUg8 (accessed May 16, 2014).

9 Schacter, D. L. (1999). The seven sins of memory: Insights from psychology and cognitive neuroscience. *American Psychologist*, 54(3), 182.

10 Liddle, J. R., & Shackelford, T. K. (2009). The human mind isn't perfect – Who knew? A review of Gary Marcus, *Kluge: The Haphazard Construction of the Human Mind. Evolutionary Psychology*, 7(1), 110–115.

11 http://mindhacks.com/2008/06/25/review-of-kluge-by-gary-marcus/ (accessed May 16, 2014).

12 Vázquez, J. (2008). Brain evolution: The good, the bad, and the ugly. *CBE-Life Sciences Education*, 7(1), 17–19.

13 Deary, I. J., Penke, L., & Johnson, W. (2010). The neuroscience of human intelligence differences. *Nature Reviews Neuroscience*, 11(3), 201–211.

14 Deary, I. J., Penke, L., & Johnson, W. (2010). The neuroscience of human intelligence differences. *Nature Reviews Neuroscience*, 11(3), 201–211.

15 Chiang, M. C., Barysheva, M., Shattuck, D. W., Lee, A. D., Madsen, S. K., Avedissian, C., ... & Thompson, P. M. (2009). Genetics of brain fiber architecture and intellectual performance. *The Journal of Neuroscience*, 29(7), 2212–2224.

16 Jung, R. E., & Haier, R. J. (2007). The Parieto-Frontal Integration Theory (P-FIT) of intelligence: converging neuroimaging evidence. *Behavioral and Brain Sciences*, 30(02), 135–154.

17 Deary, I. J., Penke, L., & Johnson, W. (2010). The neuroscience of human intelligence differences. *Nature Reviews Neuroscience*, 11(3), 201–211.

18 Diamond, M. C., Scheibel, A. B., Murphy Jr, G. M., & Harvey, T. (1985). On the brain of a scientist: Albert Einstein. *Experimental Neurology*, 88(1), 198–204.

19 Falk, D., Lepore, F. E., & Noe, A. (2013). The cerebral cortex of Albert Einstein: A description and preliminary analysis of unpublished photographs. *Brain*, 136(4), 1304–1327; Men, W., Falk, D., Sun, T., Chen, W., Li, J., Yin, D., ... & Fan, M. (2013). The corpus callosum of Albert Einstein's brain: Another clue to his high intelligence? *Brain*, awt252.

20 Rilling, J. K., & Insel, T. R. (1999). The primate neocortex in comparative perspective using magnetic resonance imaging. *Journal of Human Evolution*, 37(2), 191–223.

21 Herculano-Houzel, S. (2009). The human brain in numbers: A linearly scaled-up primate brain. *Frontiers in Human Neuroscience*, 3.

22 Chittka, L., & Niven, J. (2009). Are bigger brains better? *Current Biology*, 19(21), R995–R1008.

23 Clayton, N. S., Dally, J. M., & Emery, N. J. (2007). Social cognition by food-caching corvids. The western scrub-jay as a natural psychologist. *Philosophical Transactions of the Royal Society B: Biological Sciences*, 362(1480), 507–522.

24 http://discovermagazine.com/2009/the-brain-2/28-what-happened-to-hominids-who-were-smarter-than-us#.UgI-HxbPUg8 (accessed May 16, 2014).

25 Cited by Hawks: http://johnhawks.net/weblog/reviews/brain/paleo/lynch-granger-big-brain-boskops-2008.html (accessed May 16, 2014).

26 http://www.dailymail.co.uk/femail/article-1081332/The-Jennifer-Aniston-brain-cell-How-single-neurons-spring-action-pictures-favourite-celebrities.html (accessed May 16, 2014).

27 http://www.nytimes.com/2005/07/05/science/05cell.html?_r=0 (accessed May 16, 2014).

28 http://www.scientificamerican.com/article.cfm?id=one-face-one-neuron (accessed May 16, 2014).

29 Gross, C. G. (2009). *A Hole in the Head: More Tales in the History of Neuroscience*. The MIT Press.

30 Quiroga, R. Q., Reddy, L., Kreiman, G., Koch, C., & Fried, I. (2005). Invariant visual representation by single neurons in the human brain. *Nature*, 435(7045), 1102–1107.

31 Cerf, M., Thiruvengadam, N., Mormann, F., Kraskov, A., Quiroga, R. Q., Koch, C., & Fried, I. (2010). On-line, voluntary control of human temporal lobe neurons. *Nature*, 467(7319), 1104–1108.

32 Quiroga, R. Q., & Panzeri, S. (2009). Extracting information from neuronal populations: Information theory and decoding approaches. *Nature Reviews Neuroscience*, 10(3), 173–185.

33 http://www.edge.org/response-detail/25325 (accessed May 16, 2014).

34 Bowers, J. S. (2009). On the biological plausibility of grandmother cells: Implications for neural network theories in psychology and neuroscience. *Psychological Review*, 116(1), 220.

35 Nedergaard, M., Ransom, B., & Goldman, S. A. (2003). New roles for astrocytes: Redefining the functional architecture of the brain. *Trends in Neurosciences*, 26(10), 523–530.

36 Smith, K. (2010). Settling the great glia debate. *Nature*, 468(7321), 160–162.

37   Agulhon, C., Fiacco, T. A., & McCarthy, K. D. (2010). Hippocampal short- and long-term plasticity are not modulated by astrocyte Ca2+ signaling. *Science*, 327(5970), 1250–1254.

38   Smith, K. (2010). Settling the great glia debate. *Nature*, 468(7321), 160–162.

39   http://www.nature.com/news/neuroscience-map-the-other-brain-1.13654? WT.ec_id=NATURE-20130905 (accessed May 16, 2014).

40   Azevedo, F. A., Carvalho, L. R., Grinberg, L. T., Farfel, J. M., Ferretti, R. E., Leite, R. E., ... & Herculano-Houzel, S. (2009). Equal numbers of neuronal and nonneuronal cells make the human brain an isometrically scaled-up primate brain. *Journal of Comparative Neurology*, 513(5), 532–541.

41   http://blogs.scientificamerican.com/brainwaves/2012/06/13/know-your-neurons-what-is-the-ratio-of-glia-to-neurons-in-the-brain/ (accessed May 16, 2014).

42   http://www.edge.org/3rd_culture/ramachandran/ramachandran_p1.html (accessed May 16, 2014).

43   Ramachandran, V. S. (2011). *The Tell-Tale Brain: Unlocking the Mystery of Human Nature*. Random House.

44   Ramachandran, V. S., & Oberman, L. M. (2006). Broken mirrors: A theory of autism. *Scientific American*, 295(5), 62–69.

45   http://www.nytimes.com/2006/01/10/science/10mirr.html?pagewanted=all (accessed May 16, 2014).

46   http://www.apa.org/monitor/oct05/mirror.aspx (accessed May 16, 2014).

47   http://www.dailymail.co.uk/health/article-1216768/Why-women-men-horror-films-scary-pain-really-mind-.html (accessed May 16, 2014).

48   http://www.newscientist.com/article/dn14147-mirror-neurons-control-erection-response-to-porn.html#.UyBDsf2-og_ (accessed May 16, 2014).

49   Kilner, J. M., & Lemon, R. N. (2013). What we know currently about mirror neurons. *Current Biology*, 23(23), R1057–R1062.

50   Gallese, V., Gernsbacher, M. A., Heyes, C., Hickok, G., & Iacoboni, M. (2011). Mirror neuron forum. *Perspectives on Psychological Science*, 6(4), 369–407.

51   Gallese, V., Gernsbacher, M. A., Heyes, C., Hickok, G., & Iacoboni, M. (2011). Mirror neuron forum. *Perspectives on Psychological Science*, 6(4), 369–407.

52   Gallese, V., Gernsbacher, M. A., Heyes, C., Hickok, G., & Iacoboni, M. (2011). Mirror neuron forum. *Perspectives on Psychological Science*, 6(4), 369–407.

53   Catmur, C., Walsh, V., & Heyes, C. (2007). Sensorimotor learning configures the human mirror system. *Current Biology*, 17(17), 1527–1531.

54   Gallese, V., Gernsbacher, M. A., Heyes, C., Hickok, G., & Iacoboni, M. (2011). Mirror neuron forum. *Perspectives on Psychological Science*, 6(4), 369–407.

55 Kilner, J. M., & Lemon, R. N. (2013). What we know currently about mirror neurons. *Current Biology*, 23(23), R1057–R1062.

56 Gallese, V., Gernsbacher, M. A., Heyes, C., Hickok, G., & Iacoboni, M. (2011). Mirror neuron forum. *Perspectives on Psychological Science*, 6(4), 369–407.

57 Hamilton, A. (2013). Reflecting on the mirror neuron system in autism: A systematic review of current theories. *Developmental Cognitive Neuroscience*, 3, 91–105.

58 Mukamel, R., Ekstrom, A. D., Kaplan, J., Iacoboni, M., & Fried, I. (2010). Single-neuron responses in humans during execution and observation of actions. *Current Biology*, 20(8), 750–756.

59 Lingnau, A., Gesierich, B., & Caramazza, A. (2009). Asymmetric fMRI adaptation reveals no evidence for mirror neurons in humans. *Proceedings of the National Academy of Sciences*, 106(24), 9925–9930.

60 Gershon, M. (1999). *The Second Brain: A Groundbreaking New Understanding of Nervous Disorders of the Stomach and Intestine*. HarperCollins.

61 For example, see http://www.scientificamerican.com/article.cfm?id=gut-second-brain and http://www.nytimes.com/2005/08/24/health/24iht-snbrain.html (both accessed May 16, 2014).

62 Van Oudenhove, L., McKie, S., Lassman, D., Uddin, B., Paine, P., Coen, S., ... & Aziz, Q. (2011). Fatty acid-induced gut-brain signaling attenuates neural and behavioral effects of sad emotion in humans. *The Journal of Clinical Investigation*, 121(8), 3094.

63 Symmonds, M., Emmanuel, J. J., Drew, M. E., Batterham, R. L., & Dolan, R. J. (2010). Metabolic state alters economic decision making under risk in humans. *PloS One*, 5(6), e11090.

64 Danziger, S., Levav, J., & Avnaim-Pesso, L. (2011). Extraneous factors in judicial decisions. *Proceedings of the National Academy of Sciences*, 108(17), 6889–6892.

65 http://www.scientificamerican.com/article.cfm?id=microbes-manipulate-your-mind (accessed May 16, 2014).

66 Messaoudi, M., Violle, N., Bisson, J. F., Desor, D., Javelot, H., & Rougeot, C. (2011). Beneficial psychological effects of a probiotic formulation (Lactobacillus helveticus R0052 and Bifidobacterium longum R0175) in healthy human volunteers. *Gut Microbes*, 2(4), 256–261.

67 Schnall, S., & Laird, J. (2003). Brief report. *Cognition & Emotion*, 17(5), 787–797.

68 Soussignan, R. (2002). Duchenne smile, emotional experience, and autonomic reactivity: A test of the facial feedback hypothesis. *Emotion*, 2(1), 52.

69 Havas, D. A., Glenberg, A. M., Gutowski, K. A., Lucarelli, M. J., & Davidson, R. J. (2010). Cosmetic use of botulinum toxin-A affects processing of emotional language. *Psychological Science*, 21(7), 895–900.

70 Gray, M. A., Minati, L., Paoletti, G., & Critchley, H. D. (2010). Baroreceptor activation attenuates attentional effects on pain-evoked potentials. *Pain*, 151(3), 853–861.

71 Gray, M. A., Beacher, F. D., Minati, L., Nagai, Y., Kemp, A. H., Harrison, N. A., & Critchley, H. D. (2012). Emotional appraisal is influenced by cardiac afferent information. *Emotion*, 12(1), 180.

72 Critchley, H. D., & Nagai, Y. (2012). How emotions are shaped by bodily states. *Emotion Review*, 4(2), 163–168.

73 Corcoran, C. D., Thomas, P., Phillips, J., & O'Keane, V. (2006). Vagus nerve stimulation in chronic treatment-resistant depression: Preliminary findings of an open-label study. *The British Journal of Psychiatry*, 189(3), 282–283.

74 Bohns, V. K., & Wiltermuth, S. S. (2012). It hurts when I do this (or you do that): Posture and pain tolerance. *Journal of Experimental Social Psychology*, 48(1), 341–345.

75 Casasanto, D., & Dijkstra, K. (2010). Motor action and emotional memory. *Cognition*, 115(1), 179–185.

76 Koch, S. C., Glawe, S., & Holt, D. V. (2011). Up and down, front and back: Movement and meaning in the vertical and sagittal axes. *Social Psychology*, 42(3), 214.

77 Williams, L. E., & Bargh, J. A. (2008). Experiencing physical warmth promotes interpersonal warmth. *Science*, 322(5901), 606–607.

78 IJzerman, H., & Semin, G. R. (2009). The Thermometer of Social Relations Mapping Social Proximity on Temperature. *Psychological Science*, 20(10), 1214–1220.

79 Loetscher, T., Bockisch, C. J., Nicholls, M. E., & Brugger, P. (2010). Eye position predicts what number you have in mind. *Current Biology*, 20(6), R264–R265.

80 Eerland, A., Guadalupe, T. M., & Zwaan, R. A. (2011). Leaning to the left makes the Eiffel Tower seem smaller: Posture-modulated estimation. *Psychological Science*, 22(12), 1511–1514.

81 Schneider, I. K., Rutjens, B. T., Jostmann, N. B., & Lakens, D. (2011). Weighty matters: Importance literally feels heavy. *Social Psychological and Personality Science*, 2(5), 474–478.

82 Schnall, S., Harber, K. D., Stefanucci, J. K., & Proffitt, D. R. (2008). Social support and the perception of geographical slant. *Journal of Experimental Social Psychology*, 44(5), 1246–1255.

83 Slepian, M. L., Masicampo, E. J., Toosi, N. R., & Ambady, N. (2012). The physical burdens of secrecy. *Journal of Experimental Psychology: General*, 141(4), 619.

84 LeBel, E. P., & Wilbur, C. J. (2013). Big secrets do not necessarily cause hills to appear steeper. *Psychonomic Bulletin & Review, November*. doi: 10.3758/s13423-013-0549-2.

85 Zhou, X., Wildschut, T., Sedikides, C., Chen, X., & Vingerhoets, A. J. (2012). Heartwarming memories: Nostalgia maintains physiological comfort. *Emotion*, 12(4), 678.

86 Gu, J., Zhong, C. B., & Page-Gould, E. (2013). Listen to your heart: When false somatic feedback shapes moral behavior. *Journal of Experimental Psychology: General*, 142(2), 307.

87 Zhong, C. B., & Liljenquist, K. (2006). Washing away your sins: Threatened morality and physical cleansing. *Science*, 313(5792), 1451–1452.

88 Earp, B. D., Everett, J. A., Madva, E. N., & Hamlin, J. K. (2014). Out, damned spot: Can the "Macbeth Effect" be replicated? *Basic and Applied Social Psychology*, 36(1), 91–98.

89 Helzer, E. G., & Pizarro, D. A. (2011). Dirty liberals! Reminders of physical cleanliness influence moral and political attitudes. *Psychological Science*, 22(4), 517–522.

90 Gollwitzer, M., & Melzer, A. (2012). Macbeth and the joystick: Evidence for moral cleansing after playing a violent video game. *Journal of Experimental Social Psychology*, 48(6), 1356–1360.

91 Kaptchuk, T. J., Friedlander, E., Kelley, J. M., Sanchez, M. N., Kokkotou, E., Singer, J. P., ... & Lembo, A. J. (2010). Placebos without deception: A randomized controlled trial in irritable bowel syndrome. *PLoS One*, 5(12), e15591.

92 McRae, C., Cherin, E., Yamazaki, T. G., Diem, G., Vo, A. H., Russell, D., ... & Freed, C. R. (2004). Effects of perceived treatment on quality of life and medical outcomes in a double-blind placebo surgery trial. *Archives of General Psychiatry*, 61(4), 412.

93 Semler, C. N., & Harvey, A. G. (2005). Misperception of sleep can adversely affect daytime functioning in insomnia. *Behaviour Research and Therapy*, 43(7), 843–856.

94 Walburn, J., Vedhara, K., Hankins, M., Rixon, L., & Weinman, J. (2009). Psychological stress and wound healing in humans: A systematic review and meta-analysis. *Journal of Psychosomatic Research*, 67(3), 253–271.

95 Svendsen, D., Singer, P., Foti, M. E., & Mauer, B. (2006). *Morbidity and Mortality in People with Serious Mental Illness*. National Association of State Mental Health Program Directors (NASMHPD) Medical Directors Council, p. 87.

96 Coyne, J. C., Pajak, T. F., Harris, J., Konski, A., Movsas, B., Ang, K., & Watkins Bruner, D. (2007). Emotional well-being does not predict survival in head and neck cancer patients. *Cancer*, 110(11), 2568–2575.

97 Wade, D. M., Howell, D. C., Weinman, J. A., Hardy, R. J., Mythen, M. G., Brewin, C. R., ... & Raine, R. A. (2012). Investigating risk factors for psychological morbidity three months after intensive care: A prospective cohort study. *Critical Care*, 16(5), R192.

98 http://thechirurgeonsapprentice.com/2012/08/13/losing-ones-head-a-frustrating-search-for-the-truth-about-decapitation/ (accessed May 16, 2014).

99 http://www.guillotine.dk/Pages/30sek.html (accessed May 16, 2014).

100   JAMA Sept 9, 1939: Queries and Minor Notes, retrieved from: http://www.scribd.com/doc/18249769/JAMA-Sept-9-1939-Queries-and-Minor-Notes-Decapitation-and-Consciousness (accessed May 16, 2014).

101   Van Rijn, C. M., Krijnen, H., Menting-Hermeling, S., & Coenen, A. M. L. (2011). Decapitation in rats: Latency to Unconsciousness and the "Wave of Death." *PloS One*, 6(1): e16514.

6 TECHNOLOGY AND FOOD MYTHS

A disproportionate amount of neuroscience press coverage is focused on revelations from brain scan studies, with frequent claims about how neuroimaging technology promises to transform everything from lie detection to marketing. Other myths have emerged about the potential harm of modern technology, especially the Internet, for our brains. Paradoxically, there are also tall tales about the potential for computer-based brain training and neurofeedback to bypass traditional forms of exercise and practice and tune our brains to perfection. This chapter takes an objective look at all this technology hype and fear mongering. It concludes by examining myths that have grown up around the notion of "brain foods" that supposedly boost our IQ or stave off dementia.

Myth # 27

Brain Scans Can Read Your Mind

The mind used to be a black box, welded shut to the outside world. Clues came from introspection, brain-damaged patients, and ingenious psychology experiments that probed the mind's probable inner workings by testing the limits of perception and memory. But then in the 1990s, functional magnetic resonance brain imaging (fMRI) came along and the lid of the box was flung wide open (see Plate 8).

Another form of brain scanning known as PET (positron emission tomography) had been around since the late 1960s but it required injection of radioactive isotopes. With the advent of fMRI, which is noninvasive, psychologists could more easily recruit participants to

Great Myths of the Brain, First Edition. Christian Jarrett.
© 2015 Christian Jarrett. Published 2015 by John Wiley & Sons, Ltd.

perform mental tasks in the scanner and then watch as activity increased in specific regions of their brains. A staggering 130000 fMRI-based research papers and counting have since been published.[1]

The technology continues to attract funding and media interest in equally generous measure. Psychologists working with these impressive new brain imaging machines have gained the scientific credence the discipline craved for so long. Now they have technical props for staring into the mind, rivaling the powerful telescopes used by astronomers for gazing out into space. And, at last, psychological research produces tangible images *showing* the brain in action (although it still measures brain activity indirectly, via changes to blood flow). The private subjective world has been turned public and objective. "Few events are as thrilling to scientists as the arrival of a novel method that enables them to see the previously invisible," wrote psychologist Mara Mather and her colleagues in a 2013 special journal issue devoted to the field.[2]

It's been a dream for newspaper and magazine editors too. Each new brain imaging study comes with a splash of colorful anatomical images. They look clever and "sciencey," but at the same time the blobs of color are intuitive. "There, look!" the pictures call out, "This is where the brain was hard at work."

The headlines have gushed with all the vigor of blood through the brain. "For the first time in history," gasped the *Financial Times* in 2007,[3] "it is becoming possible to read someone else's mind with the power of science rather than human intuition or superstition." Other times there's a tone of paranoia in the media reports. "They know what you're thinking: brain scanning makes progress," claimed *The Sunday Times* in 2009.[4] In the hands of many journalists, brain imaging machines have metamorphosed into all-seeing mind-reading devices able to extract our deepest thoughts and desires. Such paranoia is not entirely without basis. Today tech companies are appearing on the scene claiming the technology can be used for lie detection, to predict shoppers' choices, and more.

Mind-Reading Hype

The media coverage of brain scanning results often overplays the power of the technology. A review conducted by Eric Racine and his colleagues in 2005 found that 67 percent of stories contained no explanation of the limitations of the technique and just 5 percent were critical.[5] At least twice in recent years *The New York Times* has run op-ed columns making grand claims about brain scanning results. Both times, the columns have provoked the opprobrium of neuroscientists and psychologists. In 2006, headlined "This Is Your Brain On Politics," a group led by Marco Iacoboni reported that they'd used fMRI to scan the brains of swing voters while they looked at pictures and videos of political candidates.[6]

Based on overall brain activity, and the recorded activity levels in specific areas, Iacoboni and his colleagues made a number of surprisingly specific claims. For example, because the sight of Republican presidential candidate Mitt Romney triggered initial high activity in the amygdala – a region involved in emotions – the researchers said this was a sign of voter anxiety. John Edwards, meanwhile, triggered lots of insula activity in voters who didn't favor him, thus showing their emotions "can be quite powerful." Obama had his own problems – watching him triggered little overall brain activity. "Our findings suggest that Obama has yet to create an impression," wrote Iacoboni et al.

Shortly after the column was published, a group of some of the most eminent neuroimaging experts in the USA and Europe, including Chris Frith at UCL and Liz Phelps at New York University, wrote to *The New York Times*, to correct the false impression given by the column that "it is possible to directly read the minds of potential voters by looking at their brain activity while they viewed presidential candidates."[7]

The expert correspondents pointed out that it's not possible to infer specific mental states from the activity in specific brain regions. The amygdala, for example, is associated with "arousal and positive emotions," not just anxiety (more on this point later). Of course, we also now know, contrary to the signs reported in the flaky op-ed, that in little over a year Obama would be elected the first African American president of the USA.

A similar misrepresentation of brain imaging occurred on the same op-ed pages in 2011, but this time in relation to iPhones.[8] Martin Lindstrom, a self-described guru on consumer behavior, wrote that he'd conducted a brain imaging study, and that the sight and sound of people's iPhones led to activity in their insular cortex – a sign, he claimed, that people truly *love* their phones. "The subjects' brains responded to the sound of their phones as they would respond to the presence or proximity of a girlfriend, boyfriend or family member," Lindstrom pronounced.

Again, the mainstream neuroimaging community was furious and frustrated at this crude presentation of brain scanning as a trusty mind-reading tool. This time a group of well over forty international neuroimaging experts led by Russell Poldrack at the University of Texas at Austin wrote to the paper to express their concerns: "The region that he points to as being 'associated with feelings of love and compassion' (the insular cortex) is a brain region that is active in as many as one third of all brain imaging studies."[9]

Of course, it's not just *The New York Times* that falls for these spurious mind-reading claims. There's a near constant stream of stories that extrapolate too ambitiously from the results of brain scanning experiments and depict them as far-seeing mind-reading machines. "Brain Scans Could Reveal If Your Relationship Will Last" announced the LiveScience website in time for Valentine's 2012,[10] before going on to explain that using fMRI, "scientists can spot telltale regions of your brain glowing joyously when you look at a photograph of your beloved." In an article headlined "This Is Your Brain on Shopping," *Forbes* explained in 2007 that "scientists have discovered that they can correctly predict whether subjects will decide to make a purchase."[11]

Other ways the media (mis)represent brain imaging results include what Racine and his colleagues called "neuro-realism" – for example, using measures of brain activity to claim that the pain relief associated with acupuncture is "real," not imaginary; and "neuro-essentialism," whereby the imaging results are used to personify and empower the brain, as in "The brain can do x" or "How the brain stores languages." Also known as the "mereological fallacy," some critics say discussion of this kind is misleading because of course the brain can't do anything on its own. As Peter Hankins puts it on his Conscious Entities blog,[12] "Only you as a whole entity can do anything like thinking or believing."

It's reassuring to note that despite all the hype, a survey of public beliefs published in 2011[13] found that the majority of the general public aren't so gullible, at least not in the UK. Joanna Wardlaw and her colleagues obtained responses from 660 members of the British public and only 34 percent believed fMRI could be used, to some extent, to find out what they were thinking (61 percent said "not at all").

The Messy Reality

You wouldn't know it from the media stories but an ongoing problem for neuroscientists (and journalists eager for a story) is exactly how to interpret the complex dance of brain activity revealed by fMRI. The brain is always busy, whether it's engaged in an experimenter task or not, so there are endless fluctuations throughout the entire organ. Increased activity is also ambiguous – it can be a sign of increased inhibition, not just excitation. And people's brains differ in their behavior from one day to the next, from one minute to the next. A cognition-brain correlation in one situation doesn't guarantee it will exist in another. Additionally, each brain is unique – my brain doesn't behave in exactly the same way as yours. The challenge of devising carefully controlled studies and knowing how to interpret them is therefore monumental.

It's perhaps no surprise that the field has found itself in difficulties in recent years. A scandal blew up in 2009 when Ed Vul and his colleagues at the Massachusetts Institute of Technology analyzed a batch of neuro-imaging papers published in respected social neuroscience journals and reported that many contained serious statistical errors that may have led to erroneous results. Originally released online with the title "Voodoo Correlations in Social Neuroscience," their paper was quickly renamed in more tactful terms in an attempt to calm the fierce contro-versy that had started brewing before the paper was even officially published.[14]

The specific claim of Vul and his methodological whistleblowers was that many of the brain imaging studies they examined were guilty of a kind of "double-dipping" – researchers first performed an all-over analy-sis to find a brain region(s) that responds to the condition of interest (e.g. feelings of social rejection), before going on to test their hypothesis on data collected in just that brain region. The cardinal sin is that the same data were often used in both stages. Vul's team argued that by following this procedure, it would have been nearly impossible for the studies not to find a significant brain-behavior correlation. Some of the authors of these criticized papers published robust rebuttals, but the damage to the reputation of the field had been done.

Using more flawed statistics of the kind that have been deployed in a minority of poor brain imaging studies, another provocative paper published in 2009[15] (and the winner of an IgNobel Award in 2012) showed evidence of apparently meaningful brain activity in a dead Atlantic salmon! Then in 2013, a landmark review paper[16] published in the prestigious journal *Nature Reviews Neuroscience* made the case that most studies in neuroscience, including structural brain imaging (and it's likely the same is true for functional brain imaging), are woefully underpowered, involve too few subjects to have a good chance to detect real effects, and therefore risk the discovery of spurious findings.

In relation to the mind-reading claims made in newspapers – be that love for our spouse or for the latest gadget we wish to buy – two more specific points are worth outlining in more detail.

The first was alluded to in those letters from experts to *The New York Times*. It's the problem of *reverse inference*. Many times, journalists (and many scientists too), jump to conclusions about the meaning of brain imaging results based on past evidence concerning the function of specific brain areas. For example, because the amygdala has many times been shown to be active when people are anxious, it's all too tempting to interpret signs of extra amygdala activity in a new experiment as evidence of anxiety, even if the context is completely different.

But as Poldrack and his fellow correspondents explained in their letter to *The New York Times*, this is dubious logic. Activity in the amygdala is associated with lots of other flavors of emotion and mental experience besides anxiety. And extra anxiety can manifest in increased activity in lots of other brain areas besides, and not always including, the amygdala. The same argument applies to other brain regions often cited in mind-reading style newspaper reports, including the insula, the anterior cingulate, and subregions of the frontal lobes.

The second key point to bear in mind when considering mind-reading newspaper stories is that brain scanning results are often based on the *average activity* recorded from the brains of several participants. On average, a group of people may show increased activity in a particular brain region when they look at a picture of someone they really love, but not when they look at someone they don't. And yet this peak of activity might not be evident in any one person's brain. Mood, tiredness, personality, hunger, time of day, task instructions, experience and countless random factors can all interfere with the specific patterns of activity observed at any one time in a single individual. Averaging across many participants helps cancel out all this noise. Crucially, this important averaging process makes a nonsense of the way that findings are often presented in the news, as if scientists can see inside *your* brain and tell what *you are thinking*.

Protecting the Neuroimaging Baby

We've seen how the media tends to hype and oversimplify brain imaging science but it's important that we don't throw the baby out with the bath water and undervalue the contribution of this exciting field. Let's be clear, virtually all experts agree that fMRI machines are valuable tools that provide a window into the workings of the mind. When parts of the brain work harder, more blood rushes to that area to resupply it with oxygenated blood. The scanning machine can detect these changes, so when the mind is busy, we get to see what the brain is doing at the same time. A generation ago this would have seemed little short of a miracle. The technology can be used to test, complement, and refine psychological models of mental processes. It's also improved our understanding of functional brain anatomy and the dynamic interplay of brain networks.

A 2013 special issue of the journal *Perspectives on Psychological Science* was devoted to the contribution made by fMRI to psychological theory.[17] Among the essays, Denise Park and Ian McDonough[18] said the technology had raised an important challenge to traditional views of aging as a process of purely passive decline (in fact, the brain responds and adapts to lost function). Michael Rugg and Sharon Thompson-Schill pointed[19] to the way brain imaging has furthered our understanding of the distinct but overlapping ways color is represented in the brain when we see it, compared with when we remember it – important results that feed into our understanding of perception and memory more generally.

It is also true that there are exciting laboratory examples of brain scan data being decoded as a way to estimate the likely content of people's thoughts and feelings. For example, in 2011, researchers at the University of California, Berkeley, showed that they could descramble visual cortex activity recorded by fMRI from a person's brain as he or she viewed movie clips, thereby deducing what bit of film was being shown at the time the brain activity was recorded.[20] Or consider a paper from 2013, in which researchers at Carnegie Mellon University showed they could identify the emotion a person was experiencing based on the patterns of brain activity shown by that person when they'd experienced the emotion previously.[21]

These results are amazing, there's no doubt about that. But they don't yet mean a neuroscientist can put you in a brain scanner and read your thoughts straight off. As the lead researcher of the California movie study told PBS NewsHour, "We're not doing mind-reading here. We're not really peering into your brain and reconstructing pictures in your head. We're reading your brain activity and using that brain activity to reconstruct what you saw. And those are two very, very different things." It's worth reiterating – the researchers didn't have insight into the content of the movie viewers' minds. Rather, they could tell from a portion of brain activity what was being shown to the viewers at that time.

Regarding the Carnegie Mellon emotion study, this was performed with actors simulating emotions and the decoding technique had to be trained first to create the data to allow later emotions to be interpreted from brain activity. Again, this is brilliant science worth celebrating and sharing, but it's not out and out mind reading of genuine emotion. We need to strike a balance between recognizing progress in this field without overstating what's been achieved. As the Neuroskeptic blogger said on Twitter recently, "The true path of neuroscience, between neurohype and neurohumbug, is a narrow one, and you won't find easy answers on it."

"Mind-Reading" Applications

It's in the rush to extrapolate from the kind of exciting lab findings mentioned above to potential real-life applications that brain mythology often overtakes fact. Despite the caveats and caution that are needed in brain imaging, there is a growing band of entrepreneurs and chancers/ visionaries (depending on your perspective) who have already started to look for ways to use fMRI brain-scanners as mind-reading tools in the real world. Let's take a look at three of these developments in turn and see if we can separate fact from fiction.

Lie detection

Nowhere is brain imaging hype proving more controversial than in the context of the law, and the idea of the fMRI scanner as a lie-detection device. Here the mainstream media is probably more gullible than the general public. In the British public survey I mentioned earlier, 62 percent of respondents said they thought fMRI could detect lies "to some extent" – which is probably a fair assessment (although 5.6 percent said "very well," which is an exaggeration).

One of the earliest companies to move into this territory was No Lie MRI, based in California, which started offering its services commercially in 2006. The company website (www.noliemri.com) boasts that its "technology ... represents the first and only direct measure of truth verification and lie detection in human history!"

That's quite a claim and it's perhaps little surprise that many people have already been tempted to use the company to resolve private disputes, paying around $10 000 a go according to a *New Yorker* article published in 2007.[22] One of the first clients was apparently a deli owner in South Carolina who wanted proof that he hadn't lied about not setting fire to his own establishment. Jealous spouses and paranoid governments too have supposedly expressed an interest in the technology.

Still, at the time of writing, fMRI-based lie detection has not been admitted in a criminal court. An important test case took place in the summer of 2012 in Montgomery County. This was prior to the trial of

Gary Smith, who stood accused of shooting his roommate to death in 2006. Smith claimed that his friend killed himself and he turned to No Lie MRI to help prove his case. The scans suggested he was telling the truth and the judge Eric M. Johnson allowed both the prosecution (who objected) and defense to debate whether the evidence could be admitted to the trial. Intriguingly, both sides cited the same academic paper[23] (see below) to argue their side. No Lie MRI was represented in court by the psychiatrist Frank Haist; the prosecution called on the New York University psychologist Liz Phelps.

In the end the judge ruled that the evidence was inadmissible. In his published comments,[24] he revealed that the defense claimed that 25 studies had been published on fMRI lie detection, none of them finding that the technology does not work. However, the judge noted that "the tepid approval of a few scholars through 25 journal articles does not persuade this Court that such acceptance exists." The prosecution on the other hand argued that the validity of fMRI lie detection was not accepted by the mainstream neuroimaging community, and moreover, that only 9 percent of the studies cited by the defense actually used fMRI. Summing up, the judge writes that "The competing motions, expert testimonies, and submitted articles reveal a debate that is far from settled in the scientific community. This scientific method is a recent development which has not been thoroughly vetted."

The paper by Giorgio Ganis that both sides cited to support their case involved 26 participants having their brains scanned while they looked at six dates appear successively on a screen. The participants' task was to press a button to indicate whether any of the dates was their birth date. For those in a truth-telling condition, none of the dates was their birth date, so they simply indicated "no" each time. For the liars, one of the dates was their birth date, but their task was to pretend it wasn't and to answer "no" throughout. The process was repeated several times. The experimental set up was designed to mimic a real-life situation akin, for example, to a suspect looking at a selection of knives and indicating which, if any, he owned.

The result that pleased No Lie MRI and the defense was that participants in the lying condition exhibited heightened activity across the front of their brains when they lied. A simple computer algorithm could process the brain scan data and indicate with 100 percent accuracy, based on this heightened activity, which participants were liars.

But there's a twist that pleased the prosecution, who cited this study as a reason to throw out the fMRI evidence in the Montgomery trial. In a follow up, Ganis and his colleagues taught lying participants a simple cheating technique – to wiggle their toe or finger imperceptibly whenever three of the irrelevant dates appeared on-screen. Doing this completely messed up the results so that liars could no longer be distinguished from truth tellers.

The reason the cheating strategy worked is that looking out for specific dates for toe wiggling lent those dates salience, just as for the true birth dates. Experts say that the same cheating strategy could probably work simply by calling to mind a particular thought or memory when irrelevant dates appeared, without the need to move toes or fingers. Ganis and his colleagues concluded that it was important for more research on "counter-measures" like this to be conducted before brain imaging can be used as a valid lie-detection method. Incidentally, exactly the same kind of problems bedevil the standard polygraph test.

A more recent paper published in 2013[25] also showed that participants involved in a mock crime were able to scupper a lie-detection method based on brainwaves (recorded from the scalp by EEG) simply by suppressing their memories of the crime. "Our findings would suggest that the use of most brain activity guilt detection tests in legal settings could be of limited value," said co-author Jon Simons at Cambridge University. "We are not saying that all tests are flawed," he added, "just that the tests are not necessarily as good as some people claim."

It's important that the neuroscience community get its facts in order about the reliability of brain-scanning techniques in legal settings, not least because there's tentative evidence that judges and jurors are unusually persuaded by brain-based evidence. For instance, a 2011 study[26] by David McCabe and his colleagues showed that mock jurors were more persuaded by evidence from a brain scan that suggested a murder suspect was lying, as compared with similar evidence from the traditional polygraph or from technology that measures heat patterns on the face. The good news is that a simple message about the limitations of brain scanning appeared to be enough to reduce the allure of the technology.

Regardless of whether brain scan lie detection is ever allowed in court, it's worth noting that there are already signs that neuroscience evidence is becoming more common. According to an analysis in 2011, by the Royal Society, of documented US court cases in which neurological or behavioral genetics evidence have been submitted in defense, 199 and 205 took place in 2008 and 2009, respectively, compared with 101 and 105 in 2005 and 2006 – a clear sign of an upward trend.[27]

A breakthrough Italian case from 2011 gives us some further insights into the way things could be headed. On this occasion, the judge scored a first for her country by allowing the submission of brain imaging and genetic evidence, which was used by the defense to argue that a convicted female murderer had brain abnormalities, including reduced gray matter in frontal regions involved in inhibition, and in the insula, which they said was implicated in aggression (you'll recall that this is the same brain region that Martin Lindstrom in *The New York Times* linked with love). A biologist also claimed that the woman had a version of the supposed MAOA "warrior gene." If true, this would mean that her body produces lower levels of an enzyme involved in regulating neurotransmitter levels, potentially leading her to have a proclivity for aggression. However recent research has challenged the notion of a warrior gene – variants of MAOA have been linked with many behavioral and psychological outcomes, many unrelated to violence. Nonetheless, based on the afore-mentioned expert neurobiological testimony, the judge commuted the woman's sentence from 30 to 20 years.

More recently, late in 2013, a US federal jury failed to come to a unan-imous decision over whether the killer John McCluskey should receive a death sentence. This might be because the defense had presented brain imaging and other evidence to suggest that McCluskey had various neurological abnormalities, including small frontal lobes, that interfered with this level of "intent." The trial outcome led *Wired* magazine to ask:[28] "Did Brain Scans Just Save a Convicted Murderer From the Death Penalty?"

Also in 2013, a new study[29] even raised the specter of brain imaging being used to predict the likelihood of a person committing a crime *in the future*. A group led by Kent Kiehl at the Mind Research Network in New Mexico scanned the brains of 96 male prisoners shortly before they were released. In the scanner, the men completed a test of inhibitory control and impulsivity. Four years later, Kiehl's team looked to see what had become of the prisoners. Their key finding was that those prisoners who had displayed less activity in the anterior cingulate cortex (ACC), at the front of the brain, were twice as likely to have re-offended over the ensuing years.

Kiehl told the press the result had "significant ramifications for the future of how our society deals with criminal justice and offenders." However, The Neurocritic blog[30] pointed out that had the prisoners been dealt with based on their brain scans, 40 percent of those with low activity in the ACC would have been wrongly categorized as re-offenders, while 46 percent of the real re-offenders would have been released. "It's not all that impressive and completely inadmissible as evidence for decision-making purposes," said The Neurocritic.

Neuromarketing

A completely different area where the supposed mind-reading capabilities of fMRI is generating excitement is in marketing and consumer behavior. According to an article published in the *Daily Telegraph* in 2013,[31] "neuromarketing, as it's known, has completely revolutionized the worlds of advertising and marketing." But contrast this hype with the verdict of a review of neuromarketing published in the prestigious review journal *Nature Reviews Neuroscience* in 2010.[32] "It is not yet clear whether neuroimaging provides better data than other marketing methods," wrote the authors Dan Ariely and Gregory Berns.

A specific claim of neuromarketing enthusiasts is that they can use brain scanning to find out things about consumer preferences and future behavior that are beyond the reach of conventional marketing practices, such as the focus group, audience screening, taste trial or product test. The aforementioned *Daily Telegraph* article, which was based around the work of Steve Sands, chairman of the neuromarketing firm Sands Research, put it like this: "Only when he places an EEG cap on the head of his test subjects … can Sands really tell whether they like what they're seeing."

Could he not ask them? Or follow up their behavior to see if they consume the relevant products? This is the problem that neuromarketing faces – a lot of the time it simply isn't clear that it is providing information that wouldn't be available far more cheaply through conventional means. Let's consider an example cited by *The Telegraph*. Apparently, research by Sands showed that when people's brains were scanned as they watched a recent hit advertisement for Volkswagen's VW Passat, involving a young boy dressed as Darth Vader, the results (sorry, the "neuroengagement scores") went off the chart. This advert later proved to be hugely popular after it was shown at the Super Bowl and the neuromarketing company chalked this up as a major success for its techniques. What we're not told is whether traditional audience research – showing the advert to a small pilot audience – would have come to the exact same conclusion. Ariely and Berns were certainly far more conservative in their review: "it is still unknown whether neuroimaging can prospectively reveal whether an advertisement will be effective."

A further problem with this field is that many of its claims appear in newspaper articles or magazines, rather than in peer-reviewed scientific journals. One pertinent example that garnered lots of press attention was an investigation by Innerscope Research that purportedly used viewers' physiological responses to movie trailers to predict successfully which of the movies would take more earnings at the box office. The finding was reported on the Fast Company business magazine website under the headline: "How your brain can predict blockbusters."[33] Why be skeptical? First off, the research didn't measure brain activity at all! It involved "biometric belts" that measured sweat, breathing, and heart rate. Another problem from a scientific perspective is that the research is not available for scrutiny in a scholarly journal. And once again, the doubt remains – could the same finding not have emerged simply by asking people how much they enjoyed the different trailers. In their 2013 book *Brainwashed*, Sally Satel and Scott Lilienfeld call this the problem of "neuroredundancy."

I've expressed a great deal of skepticism, but it would be unfair to say that neuromarketing doesn't have promise. Although it's early days, and there's been an inordinate amount of hype, there are ways in which brain scanning techniques could complement the traditional marketing armamentarium.

For instance, let's say a new food product is a hit with consumers taking part in a conventional taste test. A potential problem for the food company and its researchers is not knowing why the new product has been such a hit. Brain scanning and other physiological measures could potentially identify what makes this product distinct – for example, higher fat content tends to be associated with extra activity in one brain area (the insula), while an enjoyable taste is usually associated with more activity in the orbitofrontal cortex. Of course there's a need to beware the risks of reverse inference discussed earlier. But picking apart these patterns of activity could perhaps give unique insight into the reasons behind the popularity of a new product. As Ariely and Berns put it, using neuromaging this way "could provide hidden information about products that would otherwise be unobtainable."

Communicating with vegetative patients

Leaving the commercial world aside, a completely different potential application of fMRI as a mind-reading tool is in healthcare, as a means of communicating with brain-damaged patients in a persistent vegetative state (PVS; that is, they show no outward signs of awareness) or a minimally conscious state (they show fleeting signs of awareness but have no reliable ability to communicate; see p. 274). Again, the media have tended to hype the story – "Scientists read the minds of the living dead" was *The Independent*'s take in 2010,[34] but at least this time there does appear to be solid justification for the excitement.

Most of the work using fMRI in this way has been conducted by Adrian Owen's lab at the Brain and Mind Institute at the University of Western Ontario. The general approach the researchers have taken is to first contrast the patterns of brain activity in healthy volunteers when they engage in two distinct mental activities – such as imagining walking around their house versus playing tennis. Next, the same instructions have been given to PVS patients, with several having shown the same contrasting patterns of brain activity as the healthy controls, as if they too followed the imagery instructions.

The most exciting evidence to date has then come from using these imagery tasks as a form of communication tool. In a study published in 2010, Owen and his colleagues appeared to have conducted a conversation with a male PVS patient (later his diagnosis was changed to minimally conscious), by having him imagine playing tennis to answer "no" to questions, and to imagine navigating his house to answer "yes."[35] Despite having no outward ability to communicate, the man appeared to manipulate his own brain activity in such a way as to answer five out of six questions correctly, such as "Is your father's name Alexander?"

It's not yet clear how many PVS patients this approach will work with, and there's still mystery regarding the nature of these patients' level of conscious experience, but the implications are enormous. The technique may offer a way to communicate with patients who might have been presumed lost forever. An obvious next step is to ask vegetative patients whether they would like to go on living (on life-support) or not, but this is an ethical mine-field. Back in 2010 Owen told me that this is something he and his colleagues plan to look at in the future, subject to the "appropriate ethical frameworks being set up." He added that "only further research will tell us what kind of consciousness these patients have."

It's also important to note that this line of research has not been immune from criticism. For instance, in 2012, two weeks after Adrian Owen's work was featured in a BBC Panorama documentary *The Mind Reader: Unlocking My Voice,* a group of physicians led by Lynne Turner-Stokes at King's College London School of Medicine wrote a critical letter to the *BMJ.*[36] The doctors challenged the claim made in the program that 20 percent of PVS patients show signs of mental activity when their brains are scanned, and they suggested that one of the two supposedly PVS patients in the documentary was in fact minimally conscious. This distinction between PVS and minimally conscious is crucial because signs of awareness in a PVS patient would suggest they'd been misdiagnosed by the usual bedside tests, whereas signs of awareness in a minimally conscious patient would be expected (see more on coma myths on p. 273).

However, Owen's group and the TV show producers wrote an angry response pointing out that the PVS patient in question, named Scott, had been consistently diagnosed as having PVS for over a decade. "The fact that these authors [led by Turner-Stokes] took Scott's fleeting movement, shown in the program, to indicate a purposeful ('minimally conscious') response shows why it is so important that the diagnosis is made in person, by an experienced neurologist, using internationally agreed criteria."

We've seen that functional brain imaging is a fantastically exciting technology that is revolutionizing psychology and cognitive neuroscience. But it's a challenging field of science, so new findings should be treated with caution. The media tend to exaggerate brain imaging results and oversimplify the implications of new findings. Entrepreneurs, pioneers, and chancers are also looking for ways to exploit the technology in real life, from neuromarketing to lie detection. This is an incredibly fast moving area and today's hype could well be tomorrow's reality.

Myth: Brain Scans Can Diagnose Psychiatric Illness

A field where the promise of brain scanning is most brazenly over-reaching itself is psychiatric diagnosis. This practice is not currently sanctioned by the American Psychiatric Association (APA) nor any other medical body and for good reason – most psychiatric disorders are officially diagnosed based on behavioral symptoms and people's subjective feelings and beliefs. The neural correlates of mental disorder are not distinct enough to distinguish between conditions or to tell a troubled brain from a healthy state. Moreover, any useful differences that do exist are only reliable at a group level, not when studying an individual.

Unfortunately, this hasn't stopped commercial brain scanning enterprises stepping into the market place. "Images of the brain give special insight that is extraordinarily valuable and which leads to more targeted treatment and better treatment success," claims the Amen Clinics, an organization that boasts of having conducted brain scans of 80 000 people across 90 countries.[37] Other copy-cat clinics include Dr SPECT scan and CereScan.

The lucrative Amen Clinics are led by the psychiatrist and TV-regular Daniel Amen and they use a form of brain scanning called single photon emission computed tomography (SPECT). According to neuro-scientist and brain imaging expert Matt Wall based at Royal Holloway, University of London, the choice of SPECT is apt[38] – "it's the cheapest of the 3D imaging techniques that can show functional activation," but Wall adds: "the spatial resolution of the images is crap, and no one uses it for clinical or research work that much anymore."

The mainstream neuroscience and psychiatry community could not be clearer in its position on brain imaging-based psychiatric diagnosis. "There are currently no brain imaging biomarkers that are currently clinically useful for any diagnostic category in psychiatry," said a consensus statement[39] published by the APA in 2012. "In my opinion, what he [Amen] is doing is the modern equivalent of phrenology," Jeffrey Lieberman (APA President in 2013) told the *The Washington Post* magazine in 2012.[40] "The claims he makes are not supported by reliable science, and one has to be skeptical about his motivation."

Myth #28 Neurofeedback Will Bring You Bliss and Enlightenment

Imagine it were possible to learn to control your brain using the latest neuroscientifically inspired technology. With just a dozen brief sessions of practice you could enjoy enhanced cognition and wave goodbye to bad moods, stress, and distraction as you became the master of your own mind. That's exactly the promise made by many neurofeedback clinics around the world that target stressed-out individuals after a quick fix.

The basis of most neurofeedback therapy is EEG (electroencephalogra-phy; devised by Hans Berger in the 1920s), which records the waves of electrical activity emitted by your brain (see Plate 23). The basic idea is that you have the frequency of these waves shown to you, via sounds or images, so that you can learn to exert some control over them.

In 2013, *The Sunday Times* published a sensationalist article about a neurofeedback clinic in London called Brainworks, which offers 12 "standard sessions" for £1320. "Those who have tried it swear it offers inner transformation," exclaimed the journalist Jini Reddy, "a pro-found lessening of anxieties, awakened states, feelings of elation and the focused, clear, calm mind more readily accessed through years of effortful practices."

This is neurofeedback therapy as a lifestyle option – a shortcut to inner peace and enlightenment. It's important to note that today neurofeedback therapy also exists as a serious, though scientifically controversial, medical intervention for psychiatric diagnoses such as ADHD – for which there is a preliminary but growing evidence base. I will return to neurofeedback services of this kind later on (see p. 197).

It's a confusing situation because many clinics offer serious medical services alongside more dubious lifestyle and spirituality options. For example, on its website, the Brainworks clinic sells treatments for ADHD but also touts neurofeedback spiritual retreats, promises permanent brain changes, boasts NASA-designed chairs, and invokes the left-brain right brain myth (see p. 55): "Smooth internal communication between our left and right brain are essential to reach our full creative potential," it says.

The London clinic is not alone in offering a confusing blend of science, hype, and New Age mysticism. A search online finds The Santa Cruz Neurofeedback Center, which offers "spiritual development through science"; The BioCybernaut Institute, which claims neurofeedback will help you expand your spiritual awareness (www.biocybernaut.com/); and The Brain Fitness Center in LA which promises to enhance your spiritual awareness (www.brainfitnesscenter.com/).

Origins of the Myth

To try to make sense of this confusing situation, let's rewind to the origins of neurofeedback therapy. The frequency of our brain waves varies according to what we're doing and, back in the 1960s, it was discovered that experienced meditators tend to exhibit a high proportion of brain waves in the "alpha range" when they're meditating (8 to 12 hertz; that is, cycles per second; see Plate 24). Meanwhile, around the same time, psychologist Joe Kamiya showed that it was possible to exert willful control over brain waves – a finding popularized in a 1968 article he published in *Psychology Today* magazine. Together these two developments opened the gates for New Age gurus to propose that controlling your brainwaves, and in particular aiming for the alpha range, could be a way for anyone to achieve Zen-like calm.

Predictably enough, companies began to spring up with names like FringeWare and Zygon Corporation, offering home EEG kits and the path to enlightenment. The idea is that these devices provide you with feedback about your brainwaves and you gradually learn with the help of rewarding pictures or sounds to achieve more waves in the alpha range – thereby reaching a state of "alpha consciousness" or "alpha thinking," without the need to spend years mastering yogic meditation techniques. Psychic fans also jumped on the bandwagon and claimed the alpha state is a way to contact spirits or enhance your extra sensory perception.

Unfortunately, many of the home EEG devices were woefully low-tech and prone to interference. The late skeptic Barry Beyerstein wrote several articles and book chapters in the 1980s and 1990s debunking this industry. This included conducting comprehensive lab tests on typical domestic EEG feedback products. "The majority of home alpha conditioners and alpha-parlor patrons have probably been 'blissing out' on a symphony of eye movements and 60-cycle wall-main interference," he wrote in *The Skeptical Inquirer* in 1985.[41] "Alpha conditioning cannot guarantee to lighten your spirits but it can easily lighten your pocketbook. Caveat emptor!" Beyerstein further showed that it was people who believed in the power of EEG feedback who generally demonstrated positive effects, regardless of what their brainwaves actually got up to.

There are many other reasons to be skeptical about using alpha feedback training to reach a state of Zen-like calm. One of the surest ways of increasing alpha waves is simply to close your eyes, with some experts suggesting that alpha waves are more related to visual processing than to mood or relaxation per se (consistent with this assertion, waves in the alpha range are more common over the visual cortex at the back of the brain).

Moreover, just because experienced meditators exhibit a high level of alpha waves doesn't mean that these waves play a causal role in their relaxed state. As such, increasing your alpha waves brings no guarantee of a relaxed state. Many other states of mind, besides relaxation, are also associated with high alpha levels, including near-death and mere drowsiness. Indeed, one study published in the 1970s showed that people were perfectly capable of broadcasting excessive amounts of alpha waves when they were stressed and anxious under threat of mild electric shock from the researchers.[42] Finally, it's notable that many animals exhibit brain waves in the alpha range, but we don't attribute to them a state of blissful mental enlightenment (although they could be relaxed).

It's not just skeptics who think the field of EEG feedback may have gotten a little carried away. One of the most up-to-date reviews of alpha feedback training, published in 2009,[43] was actually written by a group of researchers who are generally advocates for the technology. Yet David Vernon at Canterbury Christ Church University in England and his colleagues were clear – "the notion that alpha neurofeedback can enhance the mood of healthy individuals has yet to be firmly established."

Neurofeedback Mythology Today

In the second decade of the twenty-first century, the fad for alpha consciousness has calmed down, but it certainly hasn't gone away. Home EEG feedback kits are still available and more sophisticated than before. There are still many companies, gurus, and books that offer a confusing blend of neuroscientific jargon and New Age mysticism. Some take the supernatural claims further than others. Consider Anna Sayce, who describes herself as a "professional intuitive, a healer and a teacher of intuitive development." On her glossy psychicbutsane.com website (accessed in 2013) she describes the different frequency bands of brain waves and in particular how "you need to be in an alpha state ... to receive psychic information." Sayce further explains that she needs to reach this state to match the same frequency as your spirit guides. To stay in beta mode would, she says, "be like being tuned into the wrong radio station."

Away from these other-worldly claims, today EEG feedback is also touted by some as a kind of brain tuning tool that can help improve your mental performance. Companies like NeuroQuest offer feedback-based "computerized brain training programs" designed to "enhance specific cognitive skills." There is some evidence to support this idea. A 2011 study[44] led by Benedikt Zoefel, for example, found that a week of EEG alpha feedback training improved the mental rotation performance of 11 out of 14 participants compared with a control group who didn't complete the training.

However, many studies in the field, like this one, involve only small numbers of participants. They usually have an inadequate control condition (meaning we can't rule out the possibility the EEG feedback has a placebo effect, or that there is "regression to the mean" – that is, the person is recovering naturally), and the researchers are usually unable to explain the means by which the training exerts its supposed beneficial effects. Another review published by David Vernon in 2005[45] concluded "the plethora of claims regarding the use of neurofeedback training to enhance performance is matched only by the paucity of research showing a clear effect."

Another criticism is that many of these cognitive enhancement clinics employ the same kind of language favored by the mystics – they talk of balancing the brain hemispheres in the same breath as helping you achieve a balanced state of mind. "We restore natural balance for a variety of brain-based conditions," says the Brainworks clinic. How they judge the correct "brain balance" is unclear. This kind of language arguably perpetuates a confusion between the physical state of the brain and the metaphors we use to describe our emotional feelings.

From the marketing spiel issuing forth from companies that sell this kind of feedback-based brain enhancement, you'd also be forgiven for thinking there was scientific consensus on the best methods to use. However, in Vernon's 2009 review, he and his colleagues discuss how there is, as yet, no consensus on the length of time, or intensity, for which brain wave feedback needs to be conducted, to produce observable benefits.

It also turns out there is not enough evidence (not in 2009, at any rate) to demonstrate conclusively how information about brain waves should be fed back to trainees (for example, visually or using sounds); whether it is beneficial to train to decrease as well as increase alpha waves; or what the desired target frequencies should be. Perhaps most surprising to people outside of this field is the researchers' admission that it has yet to be agreed whether alpha feedback training should be conducted with the eyes open or eyes closed!

"Unfortunately," Vernon and his colleagues confess, "it is not clear at present what the most effective method to achieve [beneficial] changes would be." Consider that EEG neurofeedback technology is also developing all the time, with newer methods being even less established. One important innovation known as LORETA includes ways of recording brainwaves from deeper brain areas. This is a potentially good thing, but it adds to the sense that for many applications, the technology is still at an experimental stage of development. That's certainly the case for therapies based on feedback of fMRI functional brain imaging. Again, the prospects are exciting, especially in the area of pain management,[46] but the field is still at an experimental stage.

Similar to neurofeedback, another brain-based self-improvement concept you may come across today is "brain driving": using flashing lights and pulsing sounds to entrain the brain to the frequencies associated with alpha consciousness and enlightenment. It's true that pulsating stimuli can lead to frequency changes in the recipient's brainwaves, and to associated feelings of disorientation. But crucially, the way these are interpreted is largely down to a person's beliefs and disposition.

Today, the Monroe Institute remains a market leader in this industry, with its range of binaural "Hemi-sync" relaxation and meditation audio downloads that feed slightly different sounds to the two ears. The company claims that this variation on the entrainment technique leads to extra coherence between the hemispheres, although there's no evidence this has any special benefits (in fact, such balancing of function across the hemispheres is a hallmark of sleep and coma). Another company in the market is Brain Sync who promise their audio products will help you "activate unused brain areas, tone mental muscles and enliven every faculty."

It's highly likely that many of the subjective effects of these CDs and downloads are once again attributable to user expectations. Very few studies have tested the reliability of the methods used for producing the purported effects on brainwaves. One exception is another paper by David Vernon and his colleagues in England, this one published in 2012.[47] They used two binaural beats – one in the alpha range and one in the beta – hoping to entrain the brainwaves recorded from 22 willing volunteers. The result? There were some very modest fluctuations in the participants' brainwaves in response to the beats, but no evidence at all of the intended effects on the amount of alpha or beta frequency brain waves.

"In conclusion, presentation of interleaved one-minute binaural beats of alpha and beta failed to elicit any clear evidence of a change in the EEG," the researchers admitted. "This severely limits the potential applications of the binaural beats given that a key assumption is that they mediate behavioral change via entrainment of cortical activity." In other words, the commercial downloads are unlikely to be affecting the brain in the way they say they do, and any benefits are likely due to a placebo effect or other artifacts.

Clinical Neurotherapy

Despite the aforementioned problems and question marks over the use of EEG feedback as a relaxation and cognitive enhancement technique, the method is gradually entering the mainstream as a form of therapy for a range of neurological, psychiatric and developmental conditions, especially epilepsy and ADHD (attention deficit hyperactivity disorder). There is good evidence that neurofeedback therapy can help people with epilepsy avert the onset of seizures.[48] For ADHD, the usual aim is to increase brain waves in the beta range (12 to 30 hz), which is associated with increased concentration, and to reduce them in the theta range (4 to 7 hz), linked with inattention.

In tandem with this enthusiasm, there's been a noticeable increase in the number of neurofeedback clinics offering EEG feedback-based therapy for a range of psychiatric and developmental conditions. As I mentioned, these are often the same outlets that offer cognitive enhancement and relaxation sessions for healthy people. It's usual to find a mix of scientific language and New Age mysticism, which can be confusing for the general public. For example, the Brainworks clinic in London offers treatments for children with ADHD alongside retreats "integrating the best of Eastern traditions and Western technology."

The evidence base for clinical neurofeedback is evolving all the time. Ten years ago, the use of the technique was hard to justify. An authoritative review of the evidence published in 2001[49] by Jeffrey Lohr at the University of Arkansas and his colleagues focused on ADHD, substance abuse, anxiety disorders, and depression, with the authors highlighting the lack of properly controlled studies, the poor statistical analyses, small sample sizes, and likely risks of positive findings being attributable to placebo effects.

Where there was reliable evidence for positive effects, for example in reducing anxiety, these went hand in hand with brain wave changes in the opposite direction to those expected. The title of Lohr's review said it all – "Neurotherapy does not qualify as an empirically supported behavioral treatment for psychological disorders." The authors added that, until the evidence base improves, "behavior therapists should be cautious about the efficacy of Neurotherapy, and the AABT [Association for the Advancement of Behavioral Therapy] should be more circumspect about participation in the promotion of Neurotherapy."

However, in the intervening years, there has been an explosion of studies, many of them of better quality than before, providing more valid support for the use of EEG feedback as a therapeutic tool. Reviewing the evidence for each and every psychiatric or neurological condition is beyond the scope of this book so let's focus on ADHD, for this is the psychiatric condition for which clinical neurofeedback therapy has probably been subject to the most investigation.

An authoritative review of all relevant studies into neurofeedback for childhood ADHD was published in 2012[50] by Nicholas Lofthouse. Based on the 14 studies they found, Lofthouse and his co-authors concluded that the technique is "probably efficacious." However, they said there remains a lack of fully blind studies, in which neither the participants nor the EEG trainers, nor the raters of changes in symptoms, know which patients received the real treatment and which received the pretend "sham" treatment if there was one (i.e. in a sham control condition patients are shown fake brainwaves that aren't really linked to their own brain activity). Too few studies have such robust control conditions and yet recent research has shown that this kind of design is viable, and it is vital for ruling out placebo effects and to show for sure that the EEG feedback therapy is the active ingredient in any observed benefits. Given the lack of studies with this rigor, Lofthouse and his colleagues said the "evidence is promising but not yet conclusive."

Further issues with EEG neurofeedback treatment for ADHD are raised in the latest edition of the book *Science and Pseudoscience in Contemporary Clinical Psychology*. In a chapter dedicated to neurofeedback for ADHD, Daniel Waschbusch and James Waxmonsky at Florida International University point out that the beneficial effects tend to be smaller or nonexistent in those studies that succeed in concealing from patients and their parents whether they are receiving the real EEG feedback or not. Moreover, Waschbusch and Waxmonsky point out that many children with ADHD don't have the excess of theta waves targeted by EEG feedback, suggesting that the technique, at best, may only benefit a portion of children with the diagnosis. "Despite [the] seemingly positive results," Waschbusch and Waxmonsky warn that "there is reason for caution."

Consistent with Waschbusch and Waxmonsky's warnings, a comprehensive meta-analysis published in 2013,[51] based on nine studies involving over 1200 children, concluded that analyzing the ratio of theta and beta waves was an invalid and unreliable diagnostic tool for measuring ADHD and may only be relevant for a subgroup of children with ADHD. Remember this is the same brainwave ratio that neurofeedback therapy seeks to address.

The take-home message appears to be that neurofeedback therapy may help some children with ADHD, but it's not yet known for sure if this benefit is due to changing children's brainwaves or if it's a placebo effect. This is what the latest evidence says about one of the most researched applications of neurofeedback therapy, and it stands in contrast to the hype propagated by many over-enthusiastic practitioners in the field. In fact, as I was putting the finishing touches to this chapter, a new placebo-controlled, double-blind study of neurofeedback therapy for children with ADHD[52] was published. It failed to find any benefit of the treatment for the children's cognitive functioning, including attention and working memory. The paper also included a systematic review of previous controlled studies. "Overall, the existing literature and this study fail to support any benefit of neurofeedback on neurocognitive functioning in ADHD," the authors concluded.

Read This Before Zapping Your Brain

Neurofeedback therapy is about learning to willfully alter our own brainwaves. A completely different technological approach to brain enhancement that's generating interest today involves zapping the brain with weak electrical currents via electrodes placed on the scalp. Part of the reason for the excitement in "transcranial direct current stimulation," or tDCS, is that the first consumer device – looking like something out of *Star Trek* – received FCC approval in the summer of 2013 and is available for $249 (see Plate 25).

The manufacturers Foc.us Labs/European Engineers admit that their product offers "no medical benefits" but they say it will "increase the plasticity of your brain" and "make your synapses fire faster." These vague, sensationalist claims don't appear supported by the research literature. That said, there have been a series of positive research findings in recent years showing apparent benefits of tDCS applied to different parts of the brain. For example, positive current over the motor cortex improved performance on a motor learning task;[53] stimulation over the parietal lobes was found to improve numerical skills;[54] and in 2012[55] a study showed that stimulation over the temporal-parietal junction improved performance on a social task involving perspective taking.

However, the commercial tDCS device from Foc.us doesn't target any of these areas. Its fixed electrodes are placed over the front of the brain. Moreover, an important study published early in 2013[56] by Teresa Iuculano and Roi Cohen Kadosh at Oxford University showed that enhancement by tDCS in one domain of mental function went hand in hand with impairment in another – for instance, stimulation of the parietal cortex sped up learning but actually hampered the transfer of this new knowledge into implicit memory.

Speaking to me for an article I wrote in *The Psychologist* magazine, Cohen Kadosh also explained that tDCS alone is of little use – it needs to be combined with cognitive training. He further warned: "You need to know which brain region to target, and this is defined based on different factors including the type of training, the age of the subject, and his/her cognitive abilities."

The correct dose to use is yet another issue and potentially the most risky. Bear in mind that there is huge variation in the effects of tDCS from one person to another, and even from one stimulation to the next in the same person, likely due to factors such as fatigue and hormone levels. Even the amount of hair on your head and the amount you sweat can interact with the effect of stimulation. Doses of tDCS can also accumulate and exert long-term effects in ways not yet fully understood.

Although there are as yet no reports of serious adverse effects from properly controlled use of tDCS in lab research, misuse of the technology can risk seizures or scalp burns. Itching, fatigue and nausea are other potential side effects. The promotional spiel for the Foc.us headset advises you to "overclock your brain." This advice seems irresponsible. Cohen Kadosh told me that too much stimulation could cause damage rather than any enhancement. In a similar vein, Marom Bikson and colleagues wrote to *Nature*[57] recently, warning that "Meddling with the tDCS dose is potentially as dangerous as tampering with a drug's chemical composition." Their letter was headlined: "Transcranial devices are not playthings." Cognitive neuroscientist Nick Davis and his colleagues concur. They warned recently[58] that it's a mistake to think of brain zapping as noninvasive. "Any technique which directly affects brain tissue to generate such powerful acute and long-lasting effects should be treated with the same respect as any surgical technique," they wrote.

Myth #29

Brain Training Will Make You Smart

Our ability to think on our feet – psychologists call it "fluid intelligence" – is considered by most psychologists to be relatively fixed. Just about anyone can learn more facts (i.e. increase their "crystallized intelligence"), so they say, but our particular level of mental agility is something we are stuck with. Over the last couple of decades, however, numerous "brain training" companies have emerged, all of them challenging this conventional view. They claim that by engaging regularly in their computer-based mental exercises, you will sharpen your mind, and as a consequence enjoy wide-ranging benefits in real life.

Lumosity, one of the larger brain training companies, says on its website[59] that by completing their online exercises: "you ... can harness the power of neuroplasticity to remember more, think faster, and achieve your full potential in every aspect of life. The benefits may well be endless."

Brain training exercises and games are diverse but they frequently involve paying attention to sights and sounds on a computer, and in particular, remembering what's been presented before. The exercises are often adaptations of traditional cognitive tests used in psychology labs, embellished with shapes and colors to appear more fun and attractive. Most of the time they are designed to target "working memory" – our ability to hold in mind and use relevant information while ignoring irrelevant information.

A favorite working memory exercise is the n-back task, which involves spotting whenever the current item in a stream of letters, numbers, or symbols is identical to one shown earlier – either one, two, three, or more places previously, depending on the level of difficulty. An extra tricky version of the task involves paying attention to two streams at once, one visual, the other auditory.

A key component of many of these training games is that they get more difficult as you improve, akin to cranking up the speed on a treadmill. Indeed, writing in *Scientific American Mind* in 2012, psychologist and brain training advocate John Jonides and his colleagues likened the n-back task to "a cardiovascular routine" – that is, it boosts your overall mental fitness, unlike, say, "learning to shoot an arrow," which they said has little to no effect on fitness.

With anxious parents wanting to boost their children's chances in life, and an aging population looking to stave off the risk of dementia, perhaps it's no wonder that online brain training has become big business. In January 2013, Lumosity reported that it has 35 million international subscribers, and that its annual revenue is growing by 100 percent a year, having reached $24 million in 2012. By 2015, the entire brain fitness industry is predicted to exceed the billion dollar mark.

The Case for Brain Training

Humans generally get better at whatever they practice. The challenge for brain training companies is to show that people don't just improve on the particular games and exercises involved in the training, but that any newly acquired mental fitness also improves users' performance on completely different tasks and in real-life situations – what psychologists call "far transfer" (as opposed to near transfer, which is when gains are found for tasks similar to the brain training).

Hope that this might be possible was given a boost in 2002[60] when Torkel Klingberg and his colleagues in Sweden reported that four weeks' working memory exercises based on the commercial Cogmed program led to improvements in abstract thinking in a group of seven children with ADHD. Importantly, Klingberg's findings suggested that training working memory could lead to improvements not just on working memory tasks but also on a task (known as Raven's Progressive Matrices) thought to reflect abstract thinking and fluid intelligence.

Another influential paper was published in 2008 by Susanne Jaeggi and her colleagues at the University of Michigan and the University of Bern. They showed that working memory training in dozens of young healthy adults led to gains on measures of fluid intelligence.[61] Similar results have been replicated in other labs and are being published all the time. In a 2010 study,[62] for instance, researchers at Temple University in Philadelphia reported that working memory training led to benefits on tests of attentional control and reading comprehension.

Adding to these kinds of results, brain imaging research has also shown that working memory training can lead to changes in the way the brain responds to mental tasks.[63] The results are extremely mixed but there's some evidence that training leads initially to increases in frontal and parietal brain areas. This is as you might expect because the exercises tax those brain areas. However, there's also evidence that over time the same exercises no longer excite as much brain activity, which some have interpreted as a sign that the brain is getting more efficient at the tasks.

Based on the kind of positive results I've outlined, Cogmed, a large, Internet-based brain training company, claims that its exercises will have far-reaching benefits, helping you "to stay focused, resist distractions, plan activities, complete tasks, and follow and contribute to complex discussions." Other companies like Jungle Memory and Mindsparke, make even bolder claims, including promises that your IQ will increase and your academic grades will improve. Nintendo's brain training games are the exception. While hugely popular and designed with the help of neuroscientist Ryuta Kawashima, they have only ever marketed themselves as an entertainment product.

The Case Against

The brain training industry may be booming but every step of the way it has met with skepticism from large factions of the academic community. The first blow came from an in-depth investigation published by the British consumer watchdog *Which?* in 2009.[64] Three impartial, respected psychologists, including Chris Baird at UCL, assessed all the evidence available at that time. Their conclusion was that brain training provides no benefit, other than enhancing people's performance on the exercises involved. In particular, they concluded that the games make no difference to real-life performance, and that you'd do just as well exercising your mind by socializing, browsing the Web and being physically active.

The following year, a team of researchers led by Adrian Owen (who was then at the MRC Cognition and Brain Sciences Unit at Cambridge) conducted a huge study in collaboration with a BBC science program, involving over 11 000 participants.[65] These volunteers completed comprehensive baseline tests of their mental abilities, then they spent six weeks, for a minimum of ten minutes a day, three times a week, performing computerized training tasks in reasoning, planning and problem solving. When they were re-tested at the study end, they'd improved on the specific exercises in the training, but barely at all on any of the comprehensive baseline tests they'd taken at the study start.

The vanishingly modest transferable benefits of brain training that were observed were no greater than those found in the control group after they'd simply spent time Googling the answers to obscure general knowledge questions. Critics of the study, which was published in the prestigious journal *Nature*, pointed out that the training regimen was not intensive enough. However, Owen and his team argued that there was no evidence in their study of greater benefits among those volunteers who completed more training sessions.

Most recently, in 2013, Monica Melby-Lervåg at the University of Oslo and Charles Hume at UCL conducted a meta-analysis (a mathematical synthesis of previous data) combining all the available 23 studies into working memory training that had included a control group.[66] The results from adults and children were absolutely clear. Working memory training leads to short-term gains on working memory performance on tests that are the same as, or similar to, those used in the training (i.e. near transfer). "However," Melby-Lervåg and Hulme wrote, "there is no evidence that working memory training produces generalizable gains to the other skills that have been investigated (verbal ability, word decoding, arithmetic), even when assessments take place immediately after training."

A problem in the field, according to Melby-Lervåg and Hulme, is that so many investigations into brain training lack a robust design. In particular, they tend not to bother enrolling the control group in any kind of intervention, which means any observed benefits of the working memory training could be related simply to the fun and expectations of being in a training program, never mind the specifics of what that entails. Related to that, some of the studies that did manage to find far-reaching benefits of working memory training, actually failed to observe "near transfer" – that is, improvement on working memory tasks not used in the training. This puzzling finding completely undermines the idea that it is enhancement of working memory that underlies any observed broader gains.

Melby-Lervåg and Hulme's ultimate conclusion was stark: "there is no evidence that these programmes are suitable as methods of treatment for children with developmental cognitive disorders or as ways of effecting general improvements in adults' or children's cognitive skills or scholastic achievements."

Another paper[67] that was published the preceding year took a detailed look at all the evidence specifically related to the Cogmed program. Again, the conclusions were damning for brain training. Zach Shipstead and his colleagues at the Georgia Institute of Technology wrote: "The only unequivocal statement that can be made is that Cogmed will improve performance on tasks that resemble Cogmed training."

Even more doubts about the brain training literature were raised in 2013 by Walter Boot and his colleagues.[68] Echoing Melby-Lervåg and Hulme, they pointed out that many studies showing apparent brain training benefits fail to include an adequate control condition that inspires in participants as much expectation of benefit as is experienced by people who complete the real training. If belief and expectations are not equalized across control and treatment conditions, it's impossible to know if any observed benefits of brain training are due to the training or to a placebo effect.

Brain Training for the Elderly

Many people are attracted to the promises of brain training because they want to give themselves the edge at work, or simply because it seems a healthy way of spending their time. Yet, arguably the most important application of these programs is in the elderly, as a way to protect against the risk of dementia and mental decline. What does the literature say for this group?

Unfortunately, as with studies focused on the general population, the picture for the elderly is not as positive as one might hope. A systematic review published in 2009[69] identified 10 suitably controlled studies published between 1996 and 2008, including tests of memory training, reading and speed of processing training. The researchers, led by Kathryn Papp at the University of Connecticut, reported that they "found no evidence that structured cognitive intervention programs delay or slow progression to Alzheimer's disease in healthy elderly." Again the usual pattern was found – improvement on the specific tasks trained, but no generalization to other abilities. "The popularity of products designed to slow brain aging might have outpaced credible scientific data to show that these interventions are effective," they concluded.

A more recent review published in 2013[70] is slightly more positive. Jennifer Reijnders at Maastricht University Medical Centre and her colleagues found 35 relevant controlled studies published between 2007 and 2012. They concluded that brain training for the elderly can improve functioning across various mental faculties that are trained, including memory, attention, and processing speed. But again, they highlighted the poor quality of many studies and they cautioned that the observed benefits have yet to be shown to spill over into everyday life. "There is very little evidence for generalization effects to overall cognitive functioning and daily life situations," they concluded.

Adopting a constructive approach, another review published in 2012[71] proposed ways that the field might progress. Reflecting on the literature, Jessika Buitenweg at the University of Amsterdam and her colleagues argued that multitasking training (for increasing mental flexibility), training in decision making, training based on novelty (learning new skills), and training focused on improving decision making may have the best chance of being useful for elderly people. They called for training programs to take a multifaceted approach – training many aspects of mental function, rather than just one.

Buitenweg's team also urged researchers to pay more attention to finding out who is and isn't likely to benefit from brain training. "In the current literature elderly individuals are often measured as a group, without paying attention to the existing and evident differences between individuals," they write. "Elderly people are likely to differ more from each other than young adults do. Genetic and environmental, traumatic and advantageous influences have a lifelong effect on each person's brain and behavior ... thus exaggerating inter-individual variability as the individuals grow older."

When researchers take a systematic look at the all the findings for brain training they nearly always conclude that what psychologist Tom Stafford (author of the *Rough Guide to Brain Training*) calls the holy grail – "where you practice one thing and get better at an array of very different things" – has yet to be found. Despite this, brain training companies continue to make bold claims about the benefits of their increasingly popular programs. Although there's certainly no evidence that the brain training exercises are harmful, psychologists like Stafford remind us that physical exercise, learning new skills and socializing remain the most effective ways to train your brain.

Meanwhile, researchers in the area are turning their attention to ways to encourage the transfer of training benefits to real life. Speaking at the British Psychological Society's Annual Conference in 2013, a leading light in working memory training for children, Susan Gathercole, acknowledged that it may be the case "we've only done half the job." She added that her laboratory is now prioritizing finding ways to encourage children to apply their working memory gains in the classroom, including using virtual reality classroom settings in future research.

Myth: Brain Gym Makes Children Smarter

Brain Gym International is an "educational kinesiology" program that claims to operate in over 87 countries and to have been translated into 40 languages.[72] The program teaches teachers to engage their school pupils in physical exercises, such as crawling, bouncing balls and walking on balance beams, that it is claimed will help the children with their academic learning. Brain Gym also claims to be beneficial for children with learning difficulties.

The organization's name and its promotional literature give a very strong, misleading impression that the program of exercises and their purported benefits are based on scientific facts about brain function. In fact, the theories underlying the Brain Gym program have little to zero mainstream scientific support. One of these theories is the idea (the so-called Doman-Delacato theory) that children need to complete every stage of motor development to realize their full intellectual development. For example, the theory holds that if a child walks without crawling, he or she needs to go back and learn to crawl, thus achieving "neurological repatterning."

Another of the misguided theories guiding Brain Gym is Samuel Orton's 1937 suggestion that reading problems derive from an overly dominant right hemisphere. Although the emergence of left-hemisphere related language activity can be delayed in poor readers, there is no evidence that this plays a causal role in reading problems, nor that this pattern of development is helpfully altered through physical exercise.

Finally, Brain Gym is founded on so-called perceptual-motor training theories that claim learning difficulties are caused by faulty integration of the senses and the body. Yet studies have shown repeatedly that physical exercises aimed at increasing this integration are of no academic benefit.

On their website, Brain Gym happily admits that the strongest evidence for the effectiveness of their program comes from anecdotes. On this point, they are correct. When Keith Hyatt, an expert in special education at Western Washington University, reviewed the scientific literature for Brain Gym in a 2007 paper,[73] he identified just four studies, all of them completely undermined by poor methodology. A follow-up review was published by Lucinda Spaulding of Liberty University and her colleagues in 2010.[74] They found no new evidence, beyond Wyatt's search, and they made the case that "when teachers implement practices [like Brain Gym] that have not been validated by empirical research, they are expending valuable time that could be spent implementing practices that have been empirically validated."

Lamenting the continued popularity of scientifically unfounded programs like Brain Gym, Paul Howard-Jones at the Graduate School of Education in Bristol England wrote in 2009[75] that it is clearly not enough for criticisms and objections to be published in the academic literature. In this discussion paper entitled "Scepticism is not enough" he called on greater dialogue between neuroscience and education.

His plea is more urgent than ever. A survey of teachers in the UK and Netherlands published in 2012[76] found that the more they knew about the brain, the more likely they were to endorse educational neuromyths, including Brain Gym-type programs, presumably because their interest in the brain exposed them to marketing that's based on neurononsense (see also p. 2). Another survey of over a thousand teachers, conducted in 2013 by the British medical charity Wellcome Trust, found that 39 percent of them used Brain Gym; 76 percent also endorsed the scientifically unsupported concept of "learning styles" (the idea that we each have a preferred way of learning, such as visual or auditory). On an optimistic note, Learnus – "a policy think tank whose mission is to act as a conduit between academic research in educational neuroscience and other learning sciences and teachers in the classroom" was set up in 2012.[77] And in 2014 the Wellcome Trust announced a new £6 million fund for research into ways neuroscience can genuinely benefit education. Let's hope these initiatives are successful.

Brain Food Will Make You Even Smarter

Make no mistake, a healthy, balanced diet is good for your brain just as it is good for the rest of your body. No myth there. But the devil is in the detail and things get tricky when claims are made about specific foods or substances having specific effects on the brain.

Studies in this area are difficult to interpret because there are so many other factors besides the food in question that could be playing a role. Take as a recent example the 2012 paper[78] that linked greater consumption of blueberries and strawberries with reduced cognitive decline with age. On the one hand, this finding could be due to the berries being rich in flavonoids – chemical compounds that are believed to aid cardiovascular health and promote connectivity between brain cells. On the other hand, perhaps berry eaters also tend to be wealthier and take more exercise and it's the comfortable lifestyle and exercise that delays mental decline. "[F]or definitive evidence we have to await well designed trials as this is another observational study," said Carol Brayne, professor of Public Health Medicine, at the time. This need to wait for more evidence is true for so many other hyped brain food stories you will read in the newspapers.

Claims about food and brain power are particularly prone to exaggeration and excitement because making simple changes to our diets or popping a few dietary supplements would be such a simple way to increase or preserve our intelligence, if only the supposed food-to-brain-power links were true. The situation isn't helped by the fact that foods and supplements are not treated as medicines by regulatory bodies, even if they make medicinal claims. Over the last few decades, some of the most controversial stories have revolved around fish oil; vitamin pills; glucose and willpower; and even cheese-sandwiches and decision making.

A Fishy Tale

Probably the most hyped and contested are the claims relating to fish oil. The foci of interest are the omega-3 polyunsaturated acids found in oily fish, which can be obtained by eating salmon, mackerel, and sardines, or by taking supplements sold by companies like Equazen. These fatty acids are known to be important in brain development and they help form the membranes around our brain cells. They also have anti-oxidant properties and may have beneficial effects on gene expression. We can't make them ourselves and they are an important component of a balanced diet.

It's easy to see why there's been an intense interest in fish oil, but unfortunately, excitement about the potential benefits has tended to outpace the science. This situation reached a peak in 2006 when Durham County Council in England announced that it was running a "trial" of a fatty acid supplements provided by Equazen with over 2000 children in the area. The UK education secretary at the time also made his interest public.

The thing is, this was no scientific trial. There was no control group and no attempt at blinding (i.e. the kids knew they were taking the pills and so did the researchers, which brings powerful potential effects of expectation and bias into play). "This is – let me be quite clear – a rubbish study," said an exasperated Ben Goldacre in his Bad Science *The Guardian* column in 2006, "… designed in such a way that it cannot provide useful results: it is therefore a waste of time, resources, money, and parents' goodwill."

Lord Robert Winston, the fertility expert and science communicator, was among the celebrities who allegedly contributed to the hype and controversy at the time. He fronted an advertising campaign for Dairy Crest's milk product St Ivel Advance, which contained omega-3 fatty acid and was dubbed "clever milk" by the company. "Recent scientific studies suggest omega-3 may play an important role in enhancing learning and concentration in some children," said Lord Winston in the advertisements. But Dairy Crest was forced to pull the ads by the Advertising Standards Agency on the basis that the claims were not backed up by scientific evidence, especially given the relatively small amounts of omega-3 fatty acids in the milk.

So what does the most up-to-date evidence say about the benefits of fatty acid supplements? First, these supplements do appear to be beneficial for pregnant and nursing mothers. Based on a research overview published in 2008,[79] the World Health Organization recommends a minimum intake of 300 mg daily because of the benefits for fetal brain development. This is backed up by a more recent review of ten trials involving over 800 participants published by John Protzko and his colleagues in 2013[80] in the journal *Perspectives on Psychological Science*. The authors concluded that supplementing pregnant and nursing mothers' diets and newborns' diets with omega-3 fatty acids boosts the children's IQ in early childhood.

However, the evidence for giving fish oil supplements to young children is less convincing. A rigorous, well-conducted trial was published in 2012[81] by researchers at the University of Oxford. For 16 weeks, they gave hundreds of healthy children aged 7 to 9 a daily fish oil supplement or a placebo pill matched for taste and color.

Overall, the supplements had no benefits on the children's reading ability, behavior, or working memory ability. This didn't stop the *Daily Express* newspaper running the headline: "Fish oils do make children brainier." To be fair, there was a promising detail in the study – the supplements had a modest benefit for the subgroup of children who were poor readers. However, the researchers cautioned that there was a need for more research. And the respected NHS Choices website[82] advised that in the meantime: "there are well-established methods of improving your child's reading and behavior, such as reading with them at home and making sure they get regular exercise."

What about taking fatty acid supplements to boost brain power in old age? Again, the evidence here is rather disappointing. A systematic review published by the trusted Cochrane Collaboration in 2012[83] looked at studies where over 3000 healthy participants aged over 60 had been given fatty acid supplements or a placebo for at least six months. Up to 40 months later, the studies revealed no benefits in cognitive function for the fatty acid participants. The researchers at the London School of Hygiene and Tropical Medicine and the Tan Tock Seng Hospital in Singapore concluded: "The results of the available studies show no benefit for cognitive function with omega-3 PUFA supplementation among cognitively healthy older people."

Vitamin Pills and Power Drinks

According to data from 2006, 39 percent of US adults take vitamin supplements. This is a multibillion dollar industry and the truth about the overall health benefits or risks of taking these supplements is a vast, contentious topic in its own right. Focusing here on the brain, one of the main claims has been that vitamin pills can improve children's IQ (a UK survey in 2000[84] found that around a quarter of children take vitamin supplements). The IQ claim can be traced to 1988[85] when the researchers David Benton and Gwilym Roberts based in Wales reported promising results from an eight-month long placebo-controlled trial. The children aged 12 to 13 who took the multivitamin supplement subsequently showed increased nonverbal IQ; the control group didn't.

This sounds promising, but the picture that's emerged from further research is not so much that vitamin pills boost children's intelligence, but that a poor diet impairs it. Indeed, companies that have tried to market vitamin pills as IQ boosters have tended to find themselves on the wrong end of the law. Larkhall Natural Health (the firm that supplied the

1988 study) was fined a thousand pounds and costs in 1992 after it tried selling a brand of multivitamin pills marketed as Tandem IQ. Packaging for these pills cited Benton and Robert's 1988 study as proving conclusively that the supplements boost children's IQ. However, a local magistrate ruled that this claim was misleading as more recent evidence suggests such pills are only of benefit to malnourished children.

David Benton, co-author of the influential 1988 paper appeared to agree with this interpretation in an article for *The Psychologist* magazine published in 2008.[86] Reviewing the evidence, he said: "sadly those children most likely to benefit from supplementation may be those least likely to consume them. Those receiving the supplements may well in many instances not need them." Another issue with multivitamin research is that even when a positive benefit is found, it's unclear which component of the pills was having the effect. We're going to have to wait for more research. The 2013 review[87] of dietary and other interventions published in *Perspectives on Psychological Science* by John Protzko and colleagues concluded that there was as yet insufficient evidence to make a "firm statement" on the benefits or otherwise of multivitamins for young children's IQ.

In any case, vitamin pills are rather old hat these days. The modern way to give your gray cells a boost is to take a swig of Neuro Sonic or Brain Toniq, or one of the many other "psychoactive drinks" that have been available commercially for the last few years. These products claim to be filled with various compounds known to affect brain function, from the amino acid L-theanine to GABA and melatonin (see also box on p. 216). Although there are various studies into the effects of these compounds on their own, there is no scientific research into the effects of the drinks. Given that the specific amounts and mix of active compounds in the drinks is often not clear, there's really no way of knowing what kind of impact these drinks may or may not have.

For now, the best evidence we've probably got is from the self-experimentation performed by science writer Carl Zimmer for *Discover* magazine.[88] "As I chug through my collection of brain drinks, I wait for genius to hit me," he wrote in 2012. "I feel no surge of brilliance."

Is Glucose Really the Source of Our Willpower?

"No glucose, no willpower," wrote Roy Baumeister and his journalist co-author John Tierney in their best-selling popular psychology book *Willpower: Rediscovering Our Greatest Strength*.[89] Their claim was related to findings from research by Baumeister and others suggesting that willpower is a finite resource that can be restored by glucose drinks.

In one study,[90] participants first had their willpower depleted by performing two tasks at once – watching a video of a woman while being asked to ignore words that appeared on the screen. These same participants next drank lemonade either sweetened with sugar (a glucose drink) or with artificial sweetener (no glucose). Finally, they completed a standard lab measure of self-control called the Stroop test, which requires naming the ink that color words are written in as quickly as possible (e.g. "blue" written in red ink. Typically it's tricky to ignore the color conveyed by the word's meaning). Normally, without any intervention, you'd expect the first video task to leave people depleted, so that they struggle with the Stroop challenge. The key finding was that participants who'd had the sugary version of the lemonade showed no signs of self-control depletion in the Stroop challenge. It was as if the sugary drink had topped up their depleted levels of self-control. By contrast, participants who'd had the artificially sweetened lemonade were impaired on the Stroop challenge. This suggests it was specifically the glucose that had restored self-control levels.

"Want to Boost Your Willpower?" asked a rhetorical headline on the EverydayHealth.com website on the back of this research, "Sip Lemonade."[91] It isn't just health sites and tabloids that have embraced this idea. The American Psychological Association published a special report on willpower in 2012.[92] "Maintaining steady blood-glucose levels, such as by eating regular healthy meals and snacks, may help prevent the effects of willpower depletion," the report claimed.

It's a neat story but new research findings suggest this message is an oversimplification. Consider what Matthew Sanders and his colleagues call the "Gargle effect."[93] Like Baumeister, they drained the self-control levels of a group of students by having them complete a tiresome task (looking through a statistics book and crossing out just the Es). Next, the students completed the Stroop self-control task; half of them did so while gargling sugary lemonade, the others while gargling lemonade sweetened artificially with Splenda. The key finding here? The participants who gargled, but did not swallow, the sugary lemonade showed much higher levels of self-control.

This result undermines the idea that glucose restores self-control because the participants who gargled the sugary lemonade didn't swallow it and even if they had, there was no time for it to be metabolized. So this effect can't be about restoring low glucose levels. The rival theory proposed by Sanders's team is that glucose binds to receptors in the mouth, which activates brain regions involved in reward and self-control. A related possibility is that glucose in the mouth triggers reward-related activity in the brain, thus prompting participants to interpret the task as more rewarding, which boosts their motivation.

The key point is the new results suggest depleted willpower is about motivation and the allocation of glucose resources, not about a lack of glucose. These findings don't demonstrate that consuming glucose has no benefit for restoring willpower, but they suggest strongly that it's not the principal mechanism. This is backed up by reports in the sports science literature that gargling (without ingesting) glucose can boost running and cycling performance.[94] Self-control appears to be more about how we allocate and interpret our energy resources rather than about our need to top them up. The ability to resist temptation lies in our determination after all, not at the bottom of a lemonade bottle.

Myth: Sugar Rushes Make Kids Hyperactive

Many parents will swear to you that their children become hyperactive and naughty after guzzling sweet drinks and scoffing ice cream. In fact, research has consistently failed to demonstrate that sugar rushes cause short-term hyperactive behavior in children. This makes sense given that the levels of glucose in healthy children's (and adults') brains is mostly kept at a steady level by natural regulatory mechanisms.

Consider an authoritative meta-analysis, published in 1995, that combined the results from 23 relevant studies that looked at the immediate effects of sugar on children's behavior.[95] In all studies, children were given sugar or a placebo, and parents and researchers were prevented from knowing who'd received what. Under these controlled conditions, there was no evidence that consumption of sugar affected children's behavior. A more recent study, published in 2006, looked at the effect of chocolate and fruit consumption on the behavior of pre-schoolers.[96] The children were video-recorded before and after eating, and their antics were scored by raters who didn't know who'd eaten what or when. There was no evidence that eating chocolate or fruit affected the children's behavior. Most likely the myth of the sugar rush survives because children consume lots of sugary fare at parties when they are excited anyway.

A word of caution. This research on *short-term* sugar rushes shouldn't be interpreted as proving a *long-term* junk food diet has no negative

---

behavioral consequences. In fact, a study published in 2007 involving thousands of children found that the more processed fat and high sugar items they ate at age 4, the more hyperactive they tended to be at age 7.[97] Of course this doesn't prove the junk food was to blame – parenting style and other factors could be causally linked to both junk food intake and later hyperactivity. As we speak, researchers are busy conducting further studies to disentangle these issues.

Official! Chocolate Headlines Are Usually Overstated

In 2008, Molly Crockett and her colleagues based at UCL published a study[98] that captured the attention of the world's media. "A cheese sandwich is all you need for strong decision making," ran a headline in the *Hindustan Times*. "Official! Chocolate stops you being grumpy," exclaimed the *West Australian*. It was yet another example of the media hyping new findings about the ways food and drink can affect the brain and behavior.

Reporters get particularly excited when supposed brain benefits are linked to naughty but yummy foods like chocolate. The trouble is, in this case the research didn't even involve chocolate. Or cheese. Crockett and her team actually gave their participants a revolting drink that had the effect of temporarily depleting levels of tryptophan. An amino acid found in high protein foods, tryptophan is a precursor of the neurotransmitter serotonin, so the drink will have interfered with the function of this brain chemical.

The researchers found that participants who'd had the drink were more sensitive toward unfair offers in a financial game. Crockett and her colleagues concluded that altering serotonin function has a specific effect on people's reactions to unfairness. They added that this was in the context of *no mood changes*, which completely contradicts the *West Australian* headline.

There is no question that tryptophan levels in the brain are relevant to cognition and behavior, as this study reinforced. However, the effects are complicated and contradictory, which means it's often misleading to boil them down to a bold headline. For instance, there's research showing that tryptophan-enriched cereal improves sleep and mood in elderly people,[99] and that boosting tryptophan (either through diet or supplements) can improve memory performance.[100] But there's also research showing that *depleting* levels of tryptophan can improve decision making.[101]

One reason for the complex findings is that the effects depend on the diet and mental state of the participants tested (note the similarity here with the research on fish oil and vitamins). Often the benefits of increased tryptophan are found in people who have a deficient diet or who have mood or sleep problems.

One last point on tryptophan – there is a myth that eating turkey makes you sleepy because, being high protein, it's pumped full of this amino acid. In fact, boosting your tryptophan levels is not so straightforward as this. Because foods like turkey are richer in other amino acids besides tryptophan, they compete with it for access to the brain, and your tryptophan levels can therefore actually end up being lower than they would otherwise have been. Eating turkey probably makes people feel sleepy just because eating a large meal can have that effect (also at big holiday gatherings where turkey is regularly consumed, people often drink a lot of alcohol!). A more effective way to boost tryptophan levels is to consume carbohydrates. They raise insulin levels, which increases the uptake of nontryptophan amino acids into the muscles, which makes it easier for tryptophan to reach the brain.

You really can't go wrong if you eat a balanced, nutritious diet. Despite the hype and headlines, the evidence suggests that special dietary supplements are only likely to benefit your brain power if your diet is somehow lacking, or you have a specific medical condition that affects your metabolism.

What Are "Smart Pills"?

Over the last few years there's been a lot of hype and concern about the increasing numbers of people taking so-called "cognitive enhancing" drugs available on the Internet. This includes the stimulant Modafinil, which has been associated with increased alertness and memory performance in lab tests.

At first, the drug was researched mainly as a treatment for people with attention deficits or patients with schizophrenia, as well as a possible aid for the sleep deprived. Recent studies, however, have shown that it also has benefits for healthy, non-sleep deprived people. For instance, a study published in 2013[102] with 64 healthy alert volunteers (half given placebo) found that those taking Modafinil performed better on planning, working memory and decision making, and they enjoyed the tasks more. Effects on creativity were inconsistent.

In 2007 the psychologists Barbara Sahakian and Sharon Morein-Zamir at Cambridge University wrote to the journal *Nature* saying they were aware of many of their colleagues taking Modafinil to fight jet lag or otherwise boost their academic productivity, and they urged the neuroscience community to talk more about the ethical implications of cognitive enhancers. People who'd rather not take such drugs may feel compelled to do so merely to keep up with their colleagues. The long-term health risks are also unclear, although evidence so far suggests that Modafinil is relatively benign and not prone to being abused, at least compared with other stimulants.

Sahakian and Morein-Zamir's concerns are echoed in several pronouncements from medical and scientific bodies, including the British Medical Association. The consensus is that more needs to be done to discuss the ethics and regulation of these drugs because they are only likely to become more accessible and numerous in the years to come. As long ago as 2005, for instance, the UK Government's Foresight program published a report "Drug Futures 2025" in which it warned: "We are on the verge of a revolution in the specificity and function of the psychoactive substances available to us."

Myth #31

Google Will Make You Stupid, Mad, or Both

There's no denying that the last few decades have witnessed a revolution in our relationship with communication technology, at least in most industrialized nations. The Internet brought with it the arrival of email and the search engine, meaning instant communication and limitless information at the touch of a button. More recently, smart phones and tablets have made access to the Internet easier than ever. People are almost constantly connected, and in tandem, social media platforms like Facebook and Twitter have created new ways for us to use the Internet to conduct our relationships and share information.

Some commentators have reacted to these changes with alarm. They fear that the Internet is changing our brains for the worse. One of the first warning shots came in 2008 from Nicholas Carr in an *Atlantic* magazine article entitled "Is Google Making Us Stupid?"[103] (this later appeared in extended form as his 2010 Pulitzer Prize-shortlisted book *The Shallows: How the Internet is Changing the Way We Think, Read and Remember*).

Carr was motivated to write about the effects of the Internet from his first-hand experiences. In evocative language that clearly resonated with many people, he described how: "the Net seems to be … chipping away my capacity for concentration and contemplation. My mind now expects to take in information the way the net distributes it: in a swiftly moving stream of particles. Once I was a scuba diver in the sea of words. Now I zip along the surface like a guy on a jet ski." And this was before the advent of Twitter!

Another prominent doom merchant is Baroness Professor Susan Greenfield, a neuropharmacologist at the University of Oxford. For several years she has appeared frequently on TV and radio and in newspapers warning about the harms of too much time spent on the Internet and playing video games – an issue she calls "mind change," which she describes as being as serious as climate change. Greenfield's arguments have attracted a great deal of media attention because of her academic credentials, although she hasn't actually conducted any research into the psychological or neural effects of technology.

She outlined the basis for her concerns in a 2011 article in *The Independent* newspaper:[104] "the human brain will adapt to whatever environment impinges on it; the cyber-world of the twenty-first century is offering an unprecedented environment; therefore the brain may be adapting in unprecedented ways." Writing for the *Daily Mail*,[105] Greenfield was more specific about the nature of these brain changes: "Attention spans are shorter, personal communication skills are reduced and there's a marked reduction in the ability to think abstractly."

Elsewhere Greenfield has alluded to the idea that technological changes are also responsible for rises in rates of ADHD and autism (see p. 291). And in 2013 she published her first novel *2121*, a dystopian tale about the dehumanizing effects of the Internet set in the year of the title. Writing for the *New Statesman* Helen Lewis suggested it may be the worst science fiction book ever written.[106] "[F]or page after desolate page, nothing happens. Processions of characters simply tell the reader about how profoundly their lives have been affected by using digital technologies."

The fear mongering reached new heights in 2012,[107] with a front-page splash on *Newsweek* magazine headlined "iCrazy. Panic. Depression. Psychosis. How Connection Addiction Is Rewiring Our Brains," accompanied by a picture of a young person clasping their head and screaming. The author Tony Dokoupil shared some striking statistics – "The average teen processes an astounding 3700 texts a month, double the 2007 figure" – and he quoted selectively from a handful of experts, such as Peter Whybrow of UCLA, who described the computer as "like electronic cocaine." The article's message was clear – the Internet and social media are making us stressed, lonely, and depressed.

The Reality

These fears about the effects of the Internet and social media are part of a long-running historical trend, in which each generation frowns with worry about the latest gadgets. Writing for *Slate* in 2010,[108] neuropsychologist Vaughan Bell gave the example of the anxious Swiss scientist Conrad Gessner, who fretted publicly about the confusing effect of information overload in the modern world. Gessner didn't air his concerns this century or last, but in 1565, and the source of his fears was the still relatively young printing press. Going back further in time, we find Socrates warning against the adverse effects on memory of writing things down. More recently, the appearance of radio and then TV led to anxieties about distraction, mental imbalance and lost conversation.

Let's be realistic. The Internet, smartphones and social media are changing the way we behave. One only has to spend a short amount of time in public spaces to see people gazing fixedly at their phone screen the moment they're left alone (or even when they're not). Newspaper columnists share familiar confessions about email checking in bed: last thing at night and first thing on waking. Another recent complaint is of phantom vibrations from an iPhone in one's pocket that nobody rang. Right or wrong, many people *feel* that the ubiquity of the Internet is changing how their mind works. A survey of nearly a thousand Finns published in 2013,[109] for instance, found that almost one in five of them felt that starting to use the Internet had had an adverse effect on their memory or concentration.

But just because we've changed some of our lifestyle habits and just because we feel as though the technology is harming our memory or attention doesn't mean our brains really are being rewired in dangerous, unprecedented ways. To get to the truth, let's deal with each of the main categories of concern one at a time.

Is the Internet rewiring our brains?

"The hours and hours many people spend on the Internet, either for work or just browsing for fun, must surely be having some kind of profound effect on our brains." This is the kind of vague claim made by many techno-phones. The truth is that Yes – spending a lot of time on the

Internet will change your brain, just as doing anything changes the brain. As cognitive psychologist Tom Stafford put it in an article for the BBC Future website,[110] "Yes, the Internet is rewiring your brain. But so is watching television. And having a cup of tea. Or not having a cup of tea. Or thinking about the washing on Tuesdays. Your life, however you live it, leaves traces in the brain." The effect of this rewiring? If anything, given the nature of most browsing Internet activity, Stafford predicts that we're probably getting better at processing abstract information and communicating electronically.

Is the Internet destroying our attentional focus and atrophying our memories?

There is an important distinction to be made here. One the one hand, yes, there is evidence that the Internet is distracting. One study[111] found that students took 25 percent longer to read a passage of text when they used Instant Messenger at the same time. This is because humans are not very good at multitasking. Another piece of research[112] conducted in the offices of Microsoft found that replying to an email diverted workers from their main task, not just while they typed a response, but for many minutes afterwards. There's also evidence that the Internet could be changing the way we use our memories. A study in 2011[113] led by Betsy Sparrow involved people trying to remember trivia facts that they typed into a computer. When they were told the computer was saving their typing, they later struggled to recall the facts.

On the other hand, just because the Internet is distracting and we use computers as external memo pads doesn't mean that the Internet leaves our brains permanently addled. A hint that it might have this adverse effect came from a study published in 2009,[114] which reported that habitual media multitaskers (including those who browse the Web while trying to complete other activities) found it more difficult to ignore distracting information and switch tasks in the lab. Many techno-phobes jumped on this result, but it's important to note that the study was cross-sectional. For all we know, people with poor attentional control are more likely to become media multitaskers.

Note too, that regards using computers to store our memories, this doesn't mean our memories are atrophying. We could be using our memories for something else. Indeed, the 2011 study by Sparrow found that people were adept at remembering which computer folder they stored things in.

It's also important to emphasize the evidence suggesting that time spent on the Internet could be enhancing our brains. A 2009 study[115] led by

Gary Small at UCLA involved scanning the brains of 24 middle-aged and older participants while they read from a book and, separately, conducted Web searches. For the 12 who were Web savvy, browsing the Web led to extra activation across a raft of brain areas, as compared with reading, including frontal regions associated with decision making and complex reasoning. It was only an exploratory study and the researchers urged caution in interpreting the results, but still, it's not the kind of result you'd expect if Internet use is dulling our minds.

There's also unpublished research by Janelle Wohltmann at the University of Arizona, which found participants with an average age of 79 showed an improvement of 25 percent on tests of their working memory after they were trained to use Facebook for eight weeks; no such benefits were observed in a control group who merely kept an online diary (the results were presented at the International Neuropsychological Society (INS) Annual Meeting in Hawaii in February 2013). Meanwhile, a 2012 study by Australian researchers followed thousands of elderly men for eight years and found that those who used computers more during that time were less likely to develop dementia (of course we need to beware the possibility of the causal direction running the other way).[116] Or consider a study published in 2010 that examined mental abilities in thousands of people aged 32 to 84. At every stage of life, people who used computers more also tended to perform better on task switching and other cognitive tests.[117] These advantages may not be because of the computer use (other causal factors could be at play, such as the wealth and education of people who are more likely to use computers), but such findings certainly argue against the idea that the Internet is addling our minds.

Are Facebook and other forms of social media making us lonely?

The iDisorder *Newsweek* front-page article mentioned an influential study[118] published late in the 1990s by Robert Kraut and his colleagues at Carnegie Mellon University, who spent two years monitoring the effects of Internet use on 73 Pittsburgh families. The results appeared to support the technological doom merchants. The more time the families spent online (they mostly used email and chat rooms), the less family members talked face-to-face with one another, the more their social circles shrank, and the more lonely and depressed they became.

But what the *Newsweek* article doesn't tell you is that Kraut's team revisited these same families in 2001 and found that the apparent negative effects of Internet use had largely disappeared.[119] They also studied a new sample of participants for this paper and found that a year after logging on, most people generally reported positive effects of using the Internet, including increases in their social circle size. A detail here was that extraverts tended to benefit most from online socializing, a finding reported in some other studies too. For example, research presented by Ben Ainley at the Association for Psychological Science conference in 2009 found that students who were solitary in the physical world also tended to have fewer friends on Facebook and other networking sites.

Many other studies directly challenge the idea that Facebook is making us lonely. For a 2012 paper,[120] Fenne Deters and Matthias Mehl instructed some of their participants to increase their frequency of posting on Facebook for a week. Compared with a control group, these students actually reported reductions in feelings of loneliness, mainly because posting more frequently made them feel more connected to their friends. Similarly, for a 2007 study[121] led by Nicole Ellison at the University of Michigan, researchers surveyed hundreds of undergraduates about their Facebook use, finding that more frequent users felt more connected to their university community.

Finally, consider a paper from 2010,[122] in which undergraduates were surveyed about their shyness and Facebook use. A key result was that shy students, who used the social network site more often, reported feeling closer to friends who were on there, more satisfied with those friendships, and more socially supported in general. It was a cross-sectional study (a single snapshot in time), so it's tricky to make causal inferences. Nonetheless, the researchers concluded: "Our findings refute warnings that computer-mediated communication use might cause shy individuals to become even more socially withdrawn and isolated ... The current data clearly demonstrate that shy individuals' use of Facebook is associated with better quality friendships."

Is the Internet causing a rise in autism or ADHD?

The surge in our use of the Internet and other screen-based media has occurred hand in hand with a rise in the number of children diagnosed with autism and ADHD. This has led some academics to suggest that there is a link. In an interview with *New Scientist* magazine, for example, Susan Greenfield cited the increase in autism spectrum disorders as evidence for the idea that digital technology is changing our brains. She is also on record drawing a link between digital technology and the increase in diagnoses of ADHD. Of course there are many reasons why the prevalence of reports of autism and ADHD diagnoses may have increased, including changes to diagnostic practices and a higher profile for these conditions (see also p. 289). There is, however, no evidence that digital technology causes these conditions. So concerned was Oxford Professor of Neuropsychology Dorothy Bishop by Greenfield's unfounded claims that she wrote an open letter on her blog. "Your speculations have wandered onto my turf and it's starting to get irritating," Bishop wrote before going on to expose the flaw in Greenfield's reasoning. "A cause has to precede its effect. This test of causality [in relation to Internet use] fails in two regards. First, demographically – the rise in autism diagnoses occurred well before Internet use became widespread. Second, in individuals: autism is typically evident by 2 years of age, long before children become avid users of Twitter or Facebook."

Is the Internet addictive?

Nevermind whether the Internet is causing memory problems or autism, other commentators are seriously worried about the unprecedented amounts of time we're spending connected, leading many to conclude that Web browsing and online gaming are highly addictive. There's plenty of anecdotal evidence to back this up. In 2010, for example, a South Korean couple were charged with negligent homicide after their baby daughter died while they were visiting Internet cafes to play a game that involved tending to a virtual daughter.

Beaches and hotel lobbies today are often dotted with holidaying workers logging into their work email accounts. A 2011 study of people's daily cravings found that digital media scored higher than sex.[123] Unsurprisingly perhaps, gaming and Internet addiction clinics are springing up worldwide, but especially in technologically advanced Asian nations. And many psychiatrists now argue that Internet addiction should become a formal diagnosis (the latest edition of the profession's diagnostic bible – the DSM-5 – does not recognize Internet addiction as a formal disorder, but "Internet use gaming disorder" is listed in the appendix alongside a call for more research).

Added to this, a 2012 brain scanning study[124] published by researchers at the Chinese Academy of Sciences reported that teenage Internet addicts had reduced connectivity in frontal brain regions involved in emotions and decision making, as compared with control participants. Speaking to the BBC about the findings, Dr Henrietta Bowden-Jones, consultant psychiatrist at Imperial College London, said: "We are finally being told what clinicians suspected for some time now, that white matter abnormalities in the orbito-frontal cortex and other truly significant brain areas are present not only in addictions where substances are involved but also in behavioral ones such as Internet addiction."

Skeptics will notice that the Chinese study was unable to demonstrate that Internet addiction had caused these brain changes. Indeed, many psychologists and psychiatrists point out that the problem with Internet addiction lies not with the Internet but with the person and their social situation, and frequently you'll find that people who can't control their Internet use have other mental health problems or difficulties in their lives. The founder of Europe's first gaming addiction clinic (in the Netherlands), Keith Bakker, made this point to the BBC in 2008.[125] "[T]he more we work with these kids [who play video games excessively] the less I believe we can call this addiction," he said. "What many of these kids need is their parents and their school teachers – this is a social problem."

Probably the most strident critic of the concept of Internet or gaming addiction is neuropsychologist Vaughan Bell, a prolific blogger on the Mind Hacks website. Writing on that blog,[126] Bell points out that the Internet is a medium, not an activity, and there are many things you can be doing online. "It's important to specify specific activities," he explains, "because … the concept of a behavioral addiction logically requires one." Although acknowledging that many people with problems spend lots of time online, Bell says there is little to no evidence that the Internet is the cause of these problems and "not a single study showing that heavy Internet use causes the features of an addiction."

There's no use denying that our habits change in response to new technologies. That's been the case throughout history and it's true now with regards to computers and the Internet. Like any other activity, using these technologies will have an effect on our brains. However, we've seen from this review of the evidence that these effects are not necessarily harmful and may even be beneficial. It's likely heavy Internet users become more adept at searching for information online. Using computers in general seems to be mentally stimulating and may help stave off mental decline. And there's data showing that social use of the Internet can bring people together.

But change scares people. It always has. Even as I was writing these lines in 2013 a fresh scare story was spreading a new name for the same old Internet fears: "'Digital Dementia' on the Rise as Young People Increasingly Rely on Technology Instead of Their Brain," was the *Daily Mail* Headline.[127] "Surge in 'Digital Dementia'" said the *Daily Telegraph*.[128]

Both papers cited a report by researchers in South Korea. Co-author Byun Gi-won, a doctor at the "Balance Brain Centre in Seoul" was even quoted invoking the left-brain right-brain myth (see p. 55): "Heavy users are likely to develop the left side of their brains," he said, "leaving the right side untapped or underdeveloped."

The newspapers gave no link or reference for the Korean report and I couldn't find it after several literature searches. The term Digital Dementia appears to come from the title of a 2012 book by the German psychiatrist Manfred Spitzer. The idea that the Internet is harming our brains is yet another neuromyth that sells.

Videogames Could Even Be Beneficial

Although many articles in the popular media spread the idea that the rise of digital technology is turning us into a species of depressed zombies, there is in fact a growing literature highlighting the cognitive and social benefits of video games. Sure, action and shooting games like Call of Duty are linked with increased aggressive tendencies,[129] but they've also been shown to enhance the ability to focus on small details, to rotate visual images, and to multitask.[130] Also, cooperative games like Lemmings have been linked with increased altruism in real life,[131] and puzzle games like Tetris with improved neural efficiency and increased gray matter volume.[132]

Crucially, many of these game-playing benefits have been observed in naïve players. In other words, it's not just that people with superior mental abilities are drawn to the games. There may even be benefits for important professions. Most recently, the authors of a 2013 paper[133] found that playing sports games on the Wii console boosted the performance of post-graduate surgeons on a laparoscopic simulator.

On a more skeptical note, psychologist Daniel Simons at the University of Illinois at Urbana-Champaign co-wrote a paper in 2011[134] that pointed out the methodological limitations of much of the research in this area (including a lack of double-blind studies). Indeed many of the problems that apply to research on brain training (see p. 203) also apply to research on the potential benefits of video games.

In particular, video games studies often fail to match player expectations in the control and "treatment" conditions – for example, people playing an action game expect it to improve their multitasking more than do people playing a puzzle game in the control condition.[135]

Writing on his blog in 2013, Simons said "there's no reason to think that gaming will help your real world cognition any more than would just going for a walk."

These issues notwithstanding (it's notable that more stringent studies seem to be showing up positive results), a pair of psychologists wrote a commentary for *Nature* in 2013[136] calling for more collaboration between psychological researchers and the gaming industry to develop and bring to market games with maximal benefits. Daphne Bavelier and Richard Davidson said the challenge is to create "games as compelling as those in which many young people now indulge, but that help to cultivate positive qualities such as empathy and cooperation."

Notes

1 Passingham, R. E., Rowe, J. B., & Sakai, K. (2013). Has brain imaging discovered anything new about how the brain works? *Neuroimage, 66,* 142–150.

2 Mather, M., Cacioppo, J. T., & Kanwisher, N. (2013). Introduction to the special section: 20 years of fMRI – what has it done for understanding cognition? *Perspectives on Psychological Science,* 8(1), 41–43.

3 http://www.ft.com/cms/s/2/90820f9a-ac19-11db-a0ed-0000779e2340.html (accessed May 16, 2014).

4 http://www.thesundaytimes.co.uk/sto/news/uk_news/article166390.ece (accessed May 16, 2014).

5 Racine, E., Bar-Ilan, O., & Illes, J. (2005). fMRI in the public eye. *Nature Reviews Neuroscience,* 6(2), 159–164.

6 http://www.nytimes.com/2007/11/11/opinion/11freedman.html (accessed May 16, 2014).

7 http://www.nytimes.com/2007/11/14/opinion/lweb14brain.html (accessed May 16, 2014).

8 http://www.nytimes.com/2011/10/01/opinion/you-love-your-iphone-literally. html (accessed May 16, 2014).

9 http://www.russpoldrack.org/2011/10/nyt-letter-to-editor-uncut-version. html (accessed May 16, 2014).

10 http://www.livescience.com/18468-relationship-longevity-brain-scans.html (accessed May 16, 2014).

11 http://www.forbes.com/2007/01/05/neuroeconomics-buying-decisions-biz_ cx_ee_0105papers.html (accessed May 16, 2014).

12 http://www.consciousentities.com/?p=21 (accessed May 16, 2014).

13 Wardlaw, J. M., O'Connell, G., Shuler, K., DeWilde, J., Haley, J., Escobar, O., ... & Schafer, B. (2011). "Can it read my mind?" – what do the public and experts think of the current (mis) uses of neuroimaging? *PloS One*, 6(10), e25829.

14 Vul, E., Harris, C., Winkielman, P., & Pashler, H. (2009). Puzzlingly high correlations in fMRI studies of emotion, personality, and social cognition. *Perspectives on Psychological Science*, 4(3), 274–290.

15 Bennett, C. M., Miller, M. B., & Wolford, G. L. (2009). Neural correlates of interspecies perspective taking in the post-mortem Atlantic Salmon: An argument for multiple comparisons correction. *Neuroimage*, 47(1), S125.

16 Button, K. S., Ioannidis, J. P., Mokrysz, C., Nosek, B. A., Flint, J., Robinson, E. S., & Munafò, M. R. (2013). Power failure: Why small sample size undermines the reliability of neuroscience. *Nature Reviews Neuroscience*.

17 http://pps.sagepub.com/content/8/1.toc (accessed May 16, 2014).

18 Park, D. C., & McDonough, I. M. (2013). The dynamic aging mind revelations from functional neuroimaging research. *Perspectives on Psychological Science*, 8(1), 62–67.

19 Rugg, M. D., & Thompson-Schill, S. L. (2013). Moving forward with fMRI data. *Perspectives on Psychological Science*, 8(1), 84–87.

20 Nishimoto, S., Vu, A. T., Naselaris, T., Benjamini, Y., Yu, B., & Gallant, J. L. (2011). Reconstructing visual experiences from brain activity evoked by natural movies. *Current Biology*, 21(19), 1641–1646.

21 Kassam, K. S., Markey, A. R., Cherkassky, V. L., Loewenstein, G., & Just, M. A. (2013). Identifying emotions on the basis of neural activation. *PloS One*, 8(6), e66032.

22 http://www.newyorker.com/reporting/2007/07/02/070702fa_fact_talbot (accessed May 16, 2014).

23 Ganis, G., Rosenfeld, J. P., Meixner, J., Kievit, R. A., & Schendan, H. E. (2011). Lying in the scanner: Covert countermeasures disrupt deception detection by functional magnetic resonance imaging. *Neuroimage*, 55(1), 312–319.

24 http://www.lawneuro.org/_resources/pdf/fMRIOpinion.pdf (accessed May 16, 2014).

25 Bergström, Z. M., Anderson, M. C., Buda, M., Simons, J. S., & Richardson-Klavehn, A. (2013). Intentional retrieval suppression can conceal guilty knowledge in ERP memory detection tests. *Biological Psychology*, 94, 1–11.

26 McCabe, D. P., Castel, A. D., & Rhodes, M. G. (2011). The influence of fMRI lie detection evidence on juror decision-making. *Behavioral Sciences & the Law*, 29(4), 566–577.

27 http://royalsociety.org/policy/projects/brain-waves/responsibility-law/ (accessed May 16, 2014).

28 http://www.wired.com/wiredscience/2013/12/murder-law-brain/ (accessed May 16, 2014).

29 Aharoni, E., Vincent, G. M., Harenski, C. L., Calhoun, V. D., Sinnott-Armstrong, W., Gazzaniga, M. S., & Kiehl, K. A. (2013). Neuroprediction of future rearrest. *Proceedings of the National Academy of Sciences*, 110(15), 6223–6228.

30 http://neurocritic.blogspot.co.uk/2013/03/can-anterior-cingulate-activity-predict.html (accessed May 16, 2014).

31 http://www.telegraph.co.uk/science/science-news/9984498/Neuromarketing-can-science-predict-what-well-buy.html (accessed May 16, 2014).

32 Ariely, D., & Berns, G. S. (2010). Neuromarketing: The hope and hype of neuroimaging in business. *Nature Reviews Neuroscience*, 11(4), 284–292.

33 http://www.fastcompany.com/3006186/how-your-brain-can-predict-blockbusters (accessed May 16, 2014).

34 http://www.independent.co.uk/news/science/scientists-read-the-minds-of-the-living-dead-1888995.html (accessed May 16, 2014).

35 Monti, M. M., Vanhaudenhuyse, A., Coleman, M. R., Boly, M., Pickard, J. D., Tshibanda, L., … & Laureys, S. (2010). Willful modulation of brain activity in disorders of consciousness. *New England Journal of Medicine*, 362(7), 579–589.

36 Turner-Stokes, L., Kitzinger, J., Gill-Thwaites, H., Playford, E. D., Wade, D., Allanson, J., & Pickard, J. (2012). fMRI for vegetative and minimally conscious states. *BMJ*, 345.

37 http://www.amenclinics.com/dr-amen/about-dr-amen (accessed May 16, 2014).

38 http://neurobollocks.wordpress.com/2013/03/10/utterly-shameless-diagnostic-brain-imaging-neurobollocks/ (accessed May 16, 2014).

39 Botteron, K., Carter, C., Castellanos, F. X., Dickstein, D. P., Drevets, W., Kim, K. L., … & Zubieta, J. K. (2012). *Consensus Report of the APA Work Group on Neuroimaging Markers of Psychiatric Disorders*. APA.

40 http://articles.washingtonpost.com/2012-08-09/lifestyle/35493561_1_psychiatric-practices-psychiatrist-clinics/2 (accessed May 16, 2014).

41 Beyerstein, B. L. (1985). The myth of alpha consciousness. *Skeptical Inquirer*, 10, 42–59.

42 Della Sala, S. (1999). *Mind Myths: Exploring Popular Assumptions about the Mind and Brain*. Wiley.

43 Vernon, D., Dempster, T., Bazanova, O., Rutterford, N., Pasqualini, M., & Andersen, S. (2009). Alpha neurofeedback training for performance enhancement: Reviewing the methodology. *Journal of neurotherapy*, 13(4), 214–227.

44 Zoefel, B., Huster, R. J., & Herrmann, C. S. (2011). Neurofeedback training of the upper alpha frequency band in EEG improves cognitive performance. *Neuroimage*, 54(2), 1427–1431.

45 Vernon, D. J. (2005). Can neurofeedback training enhance performance? An evaluation of the evidence with implications for future research. *Applied Psychophysiology and Biofeedback*, 30(4), 347–364.

46 deCharms, R. C., Maeda, F., Glover, G. H., Ludlow, D., Pauly, J. M., Soneji, D., ... & Mackey, S. C. (2005). Control over brain activation and pain learned by using real-time functional MRI. *Proceedings of the National Academy of Sciences of the United States of America*, 102(51), 18626–18631.

47 Vernon, D., Peryer, G., Louch, J., & Shaw, M. (2012). Tracking EEG changes in response to alpha and beta binaural beats. *International Journal of Psychophysiology*. doi: 10.1016/j.ijpsycho.2012.10.008.

48 Tan, G., Thornby, J., Hammond, D. C., Strehl, U., Canady, B., Arnemann, K., & Kaiser, D. A. (2009). Meta-analysis of EEG biofeedback in treating epilepsy. *Clinical EEG and Neuroscience*, 40(3), 173–179.

49 Lohr, J. M., Meunier, S. A., Parker, L. M., & Kline, J. P. (2001). Neurotherapy does not qualify as an empirically supported behavioral treatment for psychological disorders. *Behavior Therapist*, 24(5), 97–104.

50 Lofthouse, N., Arnold, L. E., Hersch, S., Hurt, E., & DeBeus, R. (2012). A review of neurofeedback treatment for pediatric ADHD. *Journal of Attention Disorders*, 16(5), 351–372.

51 Arns, M., Conners, C. K., & Kraemer, H. C. (2013). A decade of EEG theta/beta ratio research in ADHD: A meta-analysis. *Journal of Attention Disorders*, 17(5), 374–383.

52 Vollebregt, M. A., Dongen-Boomsma, M., Buitelaar, J. K., & Slaats-Willemse, D. (2014). Does EEG-neurofeedback improve neurocognitive functioning in children with attention-deficit/hyperactivity disorder? A systematic review and a double-blind placebo-controlled study. *Journal of Child Psychology and Psychiatry*. 55(5), 460–472.

53 Reis, J., Schambra, H. M., Cohen, L. G., Buch, E. R., Fritsch, B., Zarahn, E., ... & Krakauer, J. W. (2009). Noninvasive cortical stimulation enhances motor skill acquisition over multiple days through an effect on consolidation. *Proceedings of the National Academy of Sciences*, 106(5), 1590–1595.

54 Cohen Kadosh, R., Soskic, S., Iuculano, T., Kanai, R., & Walsh, V. (2010). Modulating neuronal activity produces specific and long-lasting changes in numerical competence. *Current Biology*, 20(22), 2016–2020.

55 Santiesteban, I., Banissy, M. J., Catmur, C., & Bird, G. (2012). Enhancing social ability by stimulating right temporoparietal junction. *Current Biology*, 22(23), 2274–2277.

56 Iuculano, T., & Kadosh, R. C. (2013). The mental cost of cognitive enhancement. *The Journal of Neuroscience*, 33(10), 4482–4486.

57 Bikson, M., Bestmann, S., & Edwards, D. (2013). Neuroscience: Transcranial devices are not playthings. *Nature*, 501(7466), 167.

58 Davis, N. J., & van Koningsbruggen, M. G. (2013). "Non-invasive" brain stimulation is not non-invasive. *Frontiers in Systems Neuroscience*, 7.

59 http://hcp.lumosity.com/research/neuroscience (accessed May 16, 2014).

60 Klingberg, T., Forssberg, H., & Westerberg, H. (2002). Training of working memory in children with ADHD. *Journal of Clinical and Experimental Neuropsychology*, 24(6), 781–791.

61 Jaeggi, S. M., Buschkuehl, M., Jonides, J., & Perrig, W. J. (2008). Improving fluid intelligence with training on working memory. *Proceedings of the National Academy of Sciences*, 105(19), 6829–6833.

62 Chein, J. M., & Morrison, A. B. (2010). Expanding the mind's workspace: Training and transfer effects with a complex working memory span task. *Psychonomic Bulletin & Review*, 17(2), 193–199.

63 Buschkuehl, M., Jaeggi, S. M., & Jonides, J. (2012). Neuronal effects following working memory training. *Developmental Cognitive Neuroscience*, 2, S167–S179.

64 http://www.which.co.uk/technology/archive/guides/brain-training/do-brain-trainers-work/ (accessed May 16, 2014).

65 Owen, A. M., Hampshire, A., Grahn, J. A., Stenton, R., Dajani, S., Burns, A. S., … & Ballard, C. G. (2010). Putting brain training to the test. *Nature*, 465(7299), 775–778.

66 Melby-Lervåg, M., & Hulme, C. (2013). Is working memory training effective? A meta-analytic review. *Developmental Psychology*, 49(2), 270.

67 Shipstead, Z., Hicks, K. L., & Engle, R. W. (2012). Cogmed working memory training: Does the evidence support the claims? *Journal of Applied Research in Memory and Cognition*, 1(3), 185–193.

68 Boot, W. R., Simons, D. J., Stothart, C., & Stutts, C. (2013). The pervasive problem with placebos in psychology: Why active control groups are not sufficient to rule out placebo effects. *Perspectives on Psychological Science*, 8(4), 445–454.

69 Papp, K. V., Walsh, S. J., & Snyder, P. J. (2009). Immediate and delayed effects of cognitive interventions in healthy elderly: A review of current literature and future directions. *Alzheimer's & Dementia*, 5(1), 50–60.

70 Reijnders, J., van Heugten, C., & van Boxtel, M. (2013). Cognitive interventions in healthy older adults and people with mild cognitive impairment: A systematic review. *Ageing Research Reviews*, 12, 263–275.

71 Buitenweg, J. I., Murre, J. M., & Ridderinkhof, K. R. (2012). Brain training in progress: A review of trainability in healthy seniors. *Frontiers in Human Neuroscience*, 6.

72 www.braingym.org (accessed May 16, 2014).

73 Hyatt, K. J. (2007). Brain Gym® building stronger brains or wishful thinking? *Remedial and Special Education*, 28(2), 117–124.

74 Spaulding, L. S., Mostert, M. P., & Beam, A. P. (2010). Is Brain Gym® an effective educational intervention? *Exceptionality*, 18(1), 18–30.

75 Howard-Jones, P. A. (2009). Scepticism is not enough. *Cortex*, 45(4), 550–551.

76 Dekker, S., Lee, N. C., Howard-Jones, P., & Jolles, J. (2012). Neuromyths in education: Prevalence and predictors of misconceptions among teachers. *Frontiers in Psychology*, 3, 429.

77 www.learnus.co.uk (accessed May 16, 2014).

78 Devore, E. E., Kang, J. H., Breteler, M., & Grodstein, F. (2012). Dietary intakes of berries and flavonoids in relation to cognitive decline. *Annals of Neurology*, 72(1), 135–143.

79 http://www.fao.org/docrep/013/i1953e/i1953e00.pdf (accessed May 16, 2014).

80 Protzko, J., Aronson, J., & Blair, C. (2013). How to make a young child smarter: Evidence from the database of raising intelligence. *Perspectives on Psychological Science*, 8(1), 25–40.

81 Richardson, A. J., Burton, J. R., Sewell, R. P., Spreckelsen, T. F., & Montgomery, P. (2012). Docosahexaenoic acid for reading, cognition and behavior in children aged 7–9 years: A randomized, controlled trial (The DOLAB Study). *PloS One*, 7(9), e43909.

82 http://www.nhs.uk/news/2012/09September/Pages/Fish-oil-can-make-children-less-naughty.aspx (accessed May 16, 2014).

83 Sydenham, E., Dangour, A. D., & Lim, W. S. (2012). Omega 3 fatty acid for the prevention of cognitive decline and dementia. *Cochrane Database Syst Rev*, 6.

84 Gregory, J., & Lowe, S. (2000). *National Diet and Nutrition Survey: Young People Aged 4 to 18 Years*. The Stationery Office.

85 Benton, D., & Roberts, G. (1988). Effect of vitamin and mineral supplementation on intelligence of a sample of schoolchildren. *The Lancet*, 331(8578), 140–143.

86 Benton, D. (2008). A fishy tale. *The Psychologist*, 21, 850–853.

87 Protzko, J., Aronson, J., & Blair, C. (2013). How to make a young child smarter: Evidence from the database of raising intelligence. *Perspectives on Psychological Science*, 8(1), 25–40.

88 http://carlzimmer.com/articles/2012.php?subaction=showfull&id=1350426212&archive=&start_from=&ucat=15& (accessed May 16, 2014).

89 Baumeister, R. F., & Tierney, J. (2011). *Willpower: Rediscovering Our Greatest Strength*. Penguin UK.

90 Gailliot, M. T., Baumeister, R. F., DeWall, C. N., Maner, J. K., Plant, E. A., Tice, D. M., ... & Schmeichel, B. J. (2007). Self-control relies on glucose as a limited energy source: Willpower is more than a metaphor. *Journal of Personality and Social Psychology*, 92(2), 325.

91 http://www.everydayhealth.com/weight/0105/want-to-boost-your-willpower-sip-lemonade.aspx (accessed May 16, 2014).

92 http://www.apa.org/helpcenter/willpower.aspx (accessed May 16, 2014).

93 Sanders, M. A., Shirk, S. D., Burgin, C. J., & Martin, L. L. (2012). The gargle effect rinsing the mouth with glucose enhances self-control. *Psychological Science*, 23(12), 1470–1472.

94 Carter, J. M., Jeukendrup, A. E., & Jones, D. A. (2004). The effect of carbohydrate mouth rinse on 1-h cycle time trial performance. *Medicine and Science in Sports and Exercise*, 36, 2107–2111.

95 Wolraich, M. L., Wilson, D. B., & White, J. W. (1995). The effect of sugar on behavior or cognition in children: A meta-analysis. *Jama*, 274(20), 1617–1621.

96 Ingram, M., & Rapee, R. M. (2006). The effect of chocolate on the behaviour of preschool children. *Behaviour Change*, 23(01), 73–81.

97 Wiles, N. J., Northstone, K., Emmett, P., & Lewis, G. (2007). "Junk food" diet and childhood behavioural problems: Results from the ALSPAC cohort. *European Journal of Clinical Nutrition*, 63(4), 491–498.

98 Crockett, M. J., Clark, L., Tabibnia, G., Lieberman, M. D., & Robbins, T. W. (2008). Serotonin modulates behavioral reactions to unfairness. *Science*, 320(5884), 1739.

99 Bravo, R., Matito, S., Cubero, J., Paredes, S. D., Franco, L., Rivero, M., ... & Barriga, C. (2012). Tryptophan-enriched cereal intake improves nocturnal sleep, melatonin, serotonin, and total antioxidant capacity levels and mood in elderly humans. *Age*, 1–9.

100 Silber, B. Y., & Schmitt, J. A. J. (2010). Effects of tryptophan loading on human cognition, mood, and sleep. *Neuroscience & Biobehavioral Reviews*, 34(3), 387–407.

101 Talbot, P. S., Watson, D. R., Barrett, S. L., & Cooper, S. J. (2005). Rapid tryptophan depletion improves decision-making cognition in healthy humans without affecting reversal learning or set shifting. *Neuropsychopharmacology*, 31(7), 1519–1525.

102 Müller, U., Rowe, J. B., Rittman, T., Lewis, C., Robbins, T. W., & Sahakian, B. J. (2013). Effects of modafinil on non-verbal cognition, task enjoyment and creative thinking in healthy volunteers. *Neuropharmacology*, 64, 490–495.

103 http://www.theatlantic.com/magazine/archive/2008/07/is-google-making-us-stupid/306868/ (accessed May 16, 2014).

104 http://www.independent.co.uk/voices/commentators/susan-greenfield-computers-may-be-altering-our-brains-2336059.html (accessed May 16, 2014).

105 http://www.dailymail.co.uk/sciencetech/article-565207/Modern-technology-changing-way-brains-work-says-neuroscientist.html (accessed May 16, 2014).

106 http://www.newstatesman.com/2013/07/susan-greenfield-novel-2121-review (accessed May 16, 2014).

107 http://www.thedailybeast.com/newsweek/2012/07/08/is-the-Internet-making-us-crazy-what-the-new-research-says.html (accessed May 16, 2014).

108 http://www.slate.com/articles/health_and_science/science/2010/02/dont_touch_that_dial.html (accessed May 16, 2014).

109 Näsi, M., & Koivusilta, L. (2013). Internet and Everyday Life: The Perceived Implications of Internet Use on Memory and Ability to Concentrate. *Cyberpsychology, Behavior, and Social Networking*, 16(2), 88–93.

110 http://www.bbc.com/future/story/20120424-does-the-Internet-rewire-brains (accessed May 16, 2014).

111 Bowman, L. L., Levine, L. E., Waite, B. M., & Gendron, M. (2010). Can students really multitask? An experimental study of instant messaging while reading. *Computers & Education*, 54(4), 927–931.

112 Iqbal, S. T., & Horvitz, E. (2007, April). Disruption and recovery of computing tasks: Field study, analysis, and directions. In *Proceedings of the SIGCHI Conference On Human Factors In Computing Systems* (pp. 677–686). ACM.

113 Sparrow, B., Liu, J., & Wegner, D. M. (2011). Google effects on memory: Cognitive consequences of having information at our fingertips. *Science*, 333(6043), 776–778.

114 Ophir, E., Nass, C., & Wagner, A. D. (2009). Cognitive control in media multitaskers. *Proceedings of the National Academy of Sciences*, 106(37), 15583–15587.

115 Small, G. W., Moody, T. D., Siddarth, P., & Bookheimer, S. Y. (2009). Your brain on Google: Patterns of cerebral activation during Internet Searching. *American Journal of Geriatric Psych*, 17(2), 116–126.

116 Almeida, O. P., Yeap, B. B., Alfonso, H., Hankey, G. J., Flicker, L., & Norman, P. E. (2012). Older men who use computers have lower risk of dementia. *PloS One*, 7(8), e44239.

117 Tun, P. A., & Lachman, M. E. (2010). The association between computer use and cognition across adulthood: Use it so you won't lose it? *Psychology and Aging*, 25(3), 560.

118 Kraut, R., Patterson, M., Lundmark, V., Kiesler, S., Mukophadhyay, T., & Scherlis, W. (1998). Internet paradox: A social technology that reduces social involvement and psychological well-being? *American Psychologist*, 53(9), 1017.

119 Kraut, R., Kiesler, S., Boneva, B., Cummings, J., Helgeson, V., & Crawford, A. (2002). Internet paradox revisited. *Journal of Social Issues*, 58(1), 49–74.

120 große Deters, F., & Mehl, M. R. (2012). Does posting Facebook status updates increase or decrease loneliness? An online social networking experiment. *Social Psychological and Personality Science*. doi: 10.1177/1948550612469233.

121 Ellison, N. B., Steinfield, C., & Lampe, C. (2007). The benefits of Facebook "friends": Social capital and college students' use of online social network sites. *Journal of Computer-Mediated Communication*, 12(4), 1143–1168.

122 Baker, L. R., & Oswald, D. L. (2010). Shyness and online social networking services. *Journal of Social and Personal Relationships*, 27(7), 873–889.

123 Hofmann, W., Baumeister, R. F., Förster, G., & Vohs, K. D. (2012). Everyday temptations: An experience sampling study of desire, conflict, and self-control. *Journal of Personality and Social Psychology*, 102(6), 1318.

124 Lin, F., Zhou, Y., Du, Y., Qin, L., Zhao, Z., Xu, J., & Lei, H. (2012). Abnormal white matter integrity in adolescents with Internet addiction disorder: A tract-based spatial statistics study. *PloS One*, 7(1), e30253.

125 http://news.bbc.co.uk/1/hi/technology/7746471.stm (accessed May 16, 2014).

126 http://mindhacks.com/2007/08/20/why-there-is-no-such-thing-as-Internet-addiction/ (accessed May 16, 2014).

127 http://www.dailymail.co.uk/health/article-2347563/Digital-dementia-rise-young-people-increasingly-rely-technology-instead-brain.html (accessed May 16, 2014).

128 http://www.telegraph.co.uk/news/worldnews/asia/southkorea/10138403/Surge-in-digital-dementia.html (accessed May 16, 2014).

129 Engelhardt, C. R., Bartholow, B. D., Kerr, G. T., & Bushman, B. J. (2011). This is your brain on violent video games: Neural desensitization to violence predicts increased aggression following violent video game exposure. *Journal of Experimental Social Psychology*, 47(5), 1033–1036.

130 Spence, I., & Feng, J. (2010). Video games and spatial cognition. *Review of General Psychology*, 14(2), 92; Green, C. S., & Bavelier, D. (2006). Enumeration versus multiple object tracking: The case of action video game players. *Cognition*, 101(1), 217–245.

131 Greitemeyer, T., & Osswald, S. (2010). Effects of prosocial video games on prosocial behavior. *Journal of Personality and Social Psychology*, 98(2), 211.

132 Haier, R. J., Karama, S., Leyba, L., & Jung, R. E. (2009). MRI assessment of cortical thickness and functional activity changes in adolescent girls following three months of practice on a visual-spatial task. *BMC Research Notes*, 2(1), 174.

133 Giannotti, D., Patrizi, G., Di Rocco, G., Vestri, A. R., Semproni, C. P., Fiengo, L., ... & Redler, A. (2013). Play to become a surgeon: Impact of Nintendo Wii training on laparoscopic skills. *PloS One*, 8(2), e57372.

134 Boot, W. R., Blakely, D. P., & Simons, D. J. (2011). Do action video games improve perception and cognition? *Frontiers in Psychology*, 2.

135 Boot, W. R., Simons, D. J., Stothart, C., & Stutts, C. (2013). The pervasive problem with placebos in psychology: Why active control groups are not sufficient to rule out placebo effects. *Perspectives on Psychological Science*, 8(4), 445–454.

136 Bavelier, D., & Davidson, R. J. (2013). Brain training: Games to do you good. *Nature*, 494(7438), 425–426.

7 BRAIN MYTHS CONCERNING PERCEPTION AND ACTION

Our conscious experience of the world has a feel of live theater about it. It's as though we're sat somewhere behind the front of our skulls from where we enjoy an honest depiction of life outside, filtered only through the prism of our trusted five senses. This is a myth. Not only do we have many more than five senses, but the brain's representation of reality is far more like a special effects movie than live theater. What we experience is a heavily edited construction created by the brain. Patchy, delayed sensory information is stitched together to create the illusion of a seamless interface with the world. I'll begin this chapter by debunking the centuries-old fixation on humans having five senses, then move on to show the distortions in our sensory experience, not only related to the outside world but to our sense of our own bodies.

Myth #32 The Brain Receives Information from Five Separate Senses

The mistaken idea that we have precisely five senses – sight, smell, hearing, touch, and taste – is so widely accepted that it's become for most people a taken-for-granted fact. The misconception is found across nearly all cultures and it appears not just in everyday conversation, but in scientific contexts too. "The main incoming signals are dispatched by our five senses," says *The Rough Guide to The Brain*. Or consider an article published in *Scientific American* in 2012[1] about sensory cross talk (of which more later) – it begins: "Our five senses … seem to operate independently." Or what about this *New Scientist* article on "reality" published in the same year:[2] "What do we actually mean by reality?" it begins, "A straightforward answer is that it means everything that appears to our five senses." This near-universal idea of five human senses is usually traced to Aristotle's *De Anima* (*On The Soul*) in which he devotes a chapter to each sense. Testament to his influence, the magic number five seems to have stuck ever since.

The Reality

So, how many senses do we really have? Well, it's definitely more than five, but the true answer depends on how you define a sense, which is something of a philosophical question! If we assume for now that an individual sense is one distinct way of receiving information about the world and our place in it, then there are some obvious additions we can make to Aristotle's basic five.

First, there are senses that relate to the position of our bodies. Close your eyes, and then touch your right forefinger to your left elbow tip. Easy? How did you do it? Somehow you knew where the end of your finger was and you also knew the position of your left elbow. This sense is known as proprioception and it's the awareness we have of where each of our body parts is located in space. It's possible partly thanks to receptors in our muscles known as spindles, which tell the brain about the current length and stretch of the muscles.

Now imagine you are blindfolded and suspended from the ceiling by a harness. If I tilted you forwards slowly, you'd immediately have a sensation of which way your entire body's position was changing in relation to gravity. This is thanks to the fluid-filled vestibular system in your inner ear, which helps us keep balance (see Plate 26). Usefully, it also means that if you look at something while your head is upside down, you have the sense that the thing you're looking at is the right way up, and it is your head that is inverted (try this by facing away from the TV, swinging your head forwards and down, and looking at the TV through your legs). The vestibular system also gives us our experience of linear acceleration through space. Another thing: the vestibular system links up with the eyes, making it possible to cancel out our own motion. If you wiggle your head around while reading, you'll see that it makes little difference to your ability to read and stay focused on the words (by contrast, keeping your head still but wiggling the words around makes things much trickier).

There are also numerous senses providing us with information about the inner state of our bodies. The most obvious of these are hunger and thirst, inner body pain, and the need to empty the bladder or bowel (less obvious are incoming signals about blood pressure, the pH level of the cerebrospinal fluid, plus many more!).

Then we have the varieties of tactile sensation. If you again closed your eyes and I surprised you with an ice cube down your back, you'd experience a shock of cold. This sensation would be distinct from mere touch because you would have formed an awareness of the uncomfortably low temperature of the cube. In fact, alongside temperature-sensitive receptors, packed in our skin we also have receptors dedicated to mechanical pressure, pain (known as nociceptors) and itch (pruritic receptors).

The discovery of itch as a neurologically distinct tactile sense is relatively recent and remains controversial. Itch receptors in the skin sensitive to histamine have been known about for some time, but it was only in 2001 in a study[3] with cats that David Andrew and Arthur Craig of the Barrow Neurological Institute in Phoenix, Arizona reported the existence of a specialized "itch-pathway" all the way from these receptors to the spinal cord and into the brain. However, the idea of a "pure" itch pathway has been challenged recently by the discovery that some pain-inducing chemicals can also activate itch receptors, and that some itch-inducing chemicals can activate pain receptors.[4] Meanwhile, brain scanning studies suggest that areas activated by itch overlap with those activated by pain, but not entirely. While the debate continues about pain and itch, in the late 2000s, researchers complicated matters even further when they reported finding nerve fibers that were specifically responsive to pleasurable (but nonsexual) stroking of the skin.[5]

It's also possible to break the sense of taste down into specific subcategories. There are at least four primary tastes: sweet, sour, salty, and bitter, detected by receptor types located mostly along the edges of the tongue. Some scientists also argue for a fifth taste, known as "umami," which is activated by monosodium glutamate (umami is the Japanese for glutamate) and associated with a meaty sensation.

You may have noticed that I've been identifying senses largely on the basis that there is a distinct receptor for a given information source, and the receptor feeds into a specific pathway to the brain, culminating in a particular sensory experience. Following this protocol, vision is subdivided into at least four senses – lightness (detected by retinal rod cells) and then the sense of green, red, and blue (detected to varying degrees by retinal cone cells). However, it is by no means agreed that this receptor/pathway-based protocol is the correct way to classify the senses. If we turn to smell we can see how quickly the receptor approach becomes unmanageable because humans have over a thousand distinct olfactory receptors tuned to different odorous molecules!

Rather than focusing on sensory receptors, an alternative is to think about the number of discrete sensory experiences we are capable of having, but as I hinted at earlier things can start getting philosophical if we go down this road, and the number of "senses" potentially infinite. Take vision alone – who is to say how many unique visual sensations it is possible to experience or describe? Going to the other extreme, if we restrict our definition of a discrete sense to the physical categories of incoming information, we can simplify the human senses down to just three – mechanical (which takes in touch and hearing), chemical (including taste, smell and internal senses), and light.

Yet another way of approaching this issue is to think not about the category of incoming information or the perceptual experience, but about how incoming sensory information is *used*. A great example is the human capacity for echolocation, which many consider to be a distinct sense. This bat-like sensory ability depends on the traditional sense of hearing, but the perceptual experience and function is more akin to vision. Human echolocation works by a person emitting a clicking sound with the tongue and listening for how it rebounds off the immediate environment. In the USA there is a remarkable team of blind cyclists – Team Bat – led by Daniel Kisch, who use echolocation to go mountain biking (there are videos online at www.worldaccessfortheblind.org).

According to an account of echolocation by Lawrence Rosenblum and Michael Gordon,[6] the ability was first documented in practiced blind people in the nineteenth century. An early (mistaken) explanation was that the ability depended on the detection of changes in air pressure upon the skin. Confirmation that the skill in fact depends on sound apparently came from a series of studies at Cornell University in the 1940s with sighted and blind echolocators. With stockings on their feet and headphones over their ears, the blind or blindfolded participants were no longer able to stop in time before hitting a wall, thereby showing the vital role played by their hearing!

Over the years, the remarkable extent of some people's echolocation abilities have been tested, showing that it is possible to detect not only the position and size of objects with high accuracy, but also their shape and the material they're made of. A 2009 study[7] tested the palate-clicking technique used by Team Bat members and confirmed that this produces the most effective sound for echolocation. If you're interested in trying out echolocation for yourself, the research team led by Juan Antonio

Mindsight – a New Sense?

Imagine you watch a visual display closely as it depicts one picture after another. Usually the successive pictures are identical, but your task is to look out for those rare instances when there is a subtle change. Suddenly you have the *sense* that the picture has changed, but you didn't actually *see* it. This may sound like hokum, but writing in 2004,[8] the University of British Columbia psychologist Ronald Rensink proposed that this sense is real and he called it "Mindsight." From his tests, he identified a minority of participants – around 30 percent – who occasionally reported sensing a change at least a second earlier than they reported seeing it. "The results presented here point towards a new mode of perceptual processing," he wrote, "one that is likely to provide new perspectives on the way that we experience our world." However, other researchers were not so persuaded. In particular, Daniel Simons and his colleagues at the University of Illinois think it all comes down to the way that participants interpret the words "sense" and "see." Rensink's Mindsighters, they believe, are trigger-happy with sensing but conservative with seeing. Non-mindsighters are the opposite, and interpret both words similarly. Consistent with this, in a replication attempt,[9] Simons's team found that Mindsighters were far more likely to indicate they'd sensed a change even when there wasn't one.

Martinez reported that sighted people are also able to learn the ability, and that after two hours practice a day for two weeks, you should be adept enough to recognize, while blindfolded, whether an object has been placed in front of you or not.

A Sensory Cocktail

Another common misconception related to the senses is the idea that they are experienced independently. From a first-person perspective it can certainly feel to people that their senses are separate, yet the reality is that our perceptual experiences arise from a complex blending process. A great example of this is the McGurk effect (named after psychologist Harry McGurk), of which you can easily find examples on the Internet. The illusion occurs because the movement of people's lips directly affects the way we hear their speech. So, if you watch a clip of someone's lips moving as if they are saying "Ga," but the sound emitted by the video is "Ba," what you *hear* is "Da." In this case, the sensory experience reflects a blending of the sound that was expected, based on lip shape, and the sound that was actually emitted. A more mundane example of the way the senses interact is when you're at the doctors receiving an injection. Research has shown that the injection really is perceived as more painful when you look at it.

There are more examples from dining, when our sensory experience is derived from a mixture of taste and smell, which is why food loses much of its appeal when we have a blocked nose. Sound also influences our taste experience. Research by Charles Spence[10] at Oxford University's Crossmodal Research Lab has demonstrated that the sound of crispiness leads to the perception of crisps (potato chips) as fresh and crispy, and the sound made by a carbonated drink makes it taste fizzier. Likewise, working with the chef Heston Blumenthal, Spence has found that bacon and egg ice cream (!) tastes more bacony when the sound of sizzlingly bacon is played in the background, and that oysters are enjoyed more when eaten to the soundtrack of beach noises, like crashing waves. The look of food also has a big impact. People find it tricky to identify the flavor of fruit drinks dyed an inappropriate color. Another study involved diners enjoying a delicious steak in the dark. When the lights were switched back on and they saw the meat was bright blue (it had been dyed) the diners wanted to vomit!

Psychologists have exploited these cross-sensory phenomena in a cruel trick on novice oenologists published in 2001.[11] The wine specialists in training were asked to describe the aroma of what looked like a red wine, but was really a white wine that had been dyed red. Despite its true white nature, the students experienced the drink as having the aroma of a red wine. "When it comes to wine," Spence wrote about this research, "people appear to smell what they see!" They also experience what they hear. A study published in 2012[12] by Adrian North found that people experienced wine as having the properties of the music they were listening to at the same time. So, for instance, wine drunk to the tune of *Carmina Burana* by Orff, a serious and somber music composition, was described by participants as powerful and heavy.

Synesthesia

For most of us, the blending of our senses happens behind the scenes, so to speak. Ultimately, each sensory experience often feels as if it belongs to one of the classic five senses, even if in reality the percept is the manifestation of more than one sense mixed together. For people with synesthesia, things are very different. A stimulus delivered via one sense gives rise to a simultaneous, but separate, experience in another sense. For instance, people with one of the most common forms of synesthesia, "grapheme to color," experience distinct colors whenever they encounter the sight or sound of particular letters, numbers, or symbols. Another form of the condition is "lexical gustatory," in which particular names trigger concomitant tastes, as in the case of one man who reportedly made up nicknames for his friends because their real names provoked the most unpleasant tastes!

There was a time when experts were skeptical about the claims made by people with synesthesia. Now many lab tests appear to have confirmed the truth of their subjective reports. For instance, if a person with synesthesia really does experience the letter "A" alongside the color red, then you'd expect them to identify the letter "A" in a reaction time test more quickly when it was printed in red, than when it was presented in blue (which would clash with their synesthetic experience). And that's exactly what psychologists have documented in controlled tests. Similarly, people with a rarer form of the condition "hearing-motion" synesthesia, who experience beeps and whirs when they see motion, are better than normal at judging whether two streams of visual information are the same, just as you'd expect if they were able to use auditory information to help them.[13]

That's not to say controversy is today absent from this field. A long-standing theory is that the condition reflects some kind of excess cross-wiring between the senses, but a provocative new suggestion is that it's less about a mixing of the senses, and more about *concepts* triggering sensory experiences. Supporting this idea, consider a 2006 study by Julia Simner and Jamie Ward, in which they provoked people with lexical gustatory synesthesia into tip-of-the-tongue states. Having an obscure word on the tip of their tongue – such as castanets – led these synesthetes to experience that word's usual accompanying taste (such as tuna), even though they hadn't seen or heard the word. Simner and Ward said this suggests that it's the concept and not the word itself that triggers the accompanying gustatory experience.[14]

Also supporting this conceptual-based account of synesthesia are reports of new forms of the condition that involve conceptual rather than sensory triggers. In 2011,[15] for example, Danko Nikolic and his colleagues at the Max Planck Institute for Brain Research documented two synesthetes who experienced particular swimming strokes as always being a certain color. This was true whether they performed the strokes themselves, looked at them, or just thought about them. "The original name ... syn + aesthesia (Greek for union of senses) may turn out to be misleading in respect of [the condition's] true nature," Nikolic and his colleagues concluded. "The term ideaesthesia (Greek for sensing concepts) may describe the phenomenon much more accurately."

<table>
<tr><td>Myth
#33</td><td></td></tr>
</table>

The Brain Perceives the World As It Is

The brain creates the most believable virtual reality experience. As we look, listen, and touch the world it seems like we are experiencing it exactly as it is, unmediated, uncensored, raw. But it's a trick. The truth is that we catch mere glimpses of physical reality. Using this impoverished sensory information as a starting point, the brain fills in the blanks. It guesses, anticipates, embellishes. This means we don't perceive the world as it really is, but a version created by our brains that is only partly based on reality.

Not Paying Attention

Before detailing some of these specific distortions, it's important to acknowledge how much we miss in the first place simply by virtue of our limited attentional resources. Were we to process all the endlessly changing sensory information in our immediate surroundings, we would be paralyzed by data overload. For this reason the brain operates a process of selective attention. We only fully attend to information and events that fall under the beam of this spotlight.

This notion was demonstrated to dramatic effect in a modern classic of psychology research published in 1999.[16] Before I describe the study, you can experience it for yourself online in various places – for example, see tinyurl.com/2d29jw3. Christopher Chabris's and Daniel Simons's research involved participants watching a short clip of two basketball teams passing the ball. The participants were told their task was to count the number of passes made by players dressed in white, while ignoring the passes made by players in black. What Chabris and Simons were interested in was how many of the participants would notice a woman in a gorilla costume walk right through the middle of the game. Amazingly, they found that most participants were so engrossed in counting the ball passes that they were completely oblivious to the gorilla – a phenomenon the researchers dubbed "inattentional blindness."

In 2012, research at Royal Holloway, University of London in England showed that a similar principle applies to what we (don't) hear.[17] Polly Dalton and Nick Fraenkel set up and recorded a real scene involving a pair of women chatting about a party on one side of a room, and a pair of men chatting on the other side, plus there was a gorilla of sorts. Participants listened to the recording and were told to focus on one conversation or the other. Seventy percent of those who focused on the women's conversation completely failed to notice a strange man who walked through the center of the scene uttering repeatedly "I'm a gorilla." Summing up, Dalton and Fraenkel explained: "the absence of attention can leave people 'deaf' to a sustained and dynamic auditory stimulus that is clearly noticeable under normal listening conditions."

These attentional limitations could have serious real-life consequences – just think of the jobs that depend on the human ability to notice what's going on, from air-traffic controllers to radiographers. The relevance of inattentional blindness to this latter profession was illustrated in a 2013 study[18] that involved experienced radiologists and non-experts searching through lung scans looking for light, circular nodules that are a sign of lung cancer. Trafton Drew and his colleagues found that 20 out of 24 of the radiologists failed to notice the surprise presence on five of the scans of a matchbox-sized gorilla! On the plus side, the experts did better than the nonmedical participants, none of whom noticed the gorilla. As you'd expect, they also performed far better than amateurs at spotting the real nodules. Drew's team said these findings weren't an indictment of the radiologists' impressive skills, but that "the message of the present results is that even this high level of expertise does not immunize against the inherent limitations of human attention and perception."

Blindspots

Even when we are paying full attention, the basic design of our sensory equipment means we are cut off from much of reality. Think of high-pitched sounds that are beyond our detection, or infrared waves that pass before us invisible. Even for information that we can detect, there are gaps in our perception. The most obvious example is the visual blind spot (see Plate 27).

The light-sensitive rods and cones of your retina actually have their fibers on the outside – on the side nearest the world, rather than nearest your brain. They all bundle together and feed through to the optic nerve and into the brain via a hole in the retina. This means that you can't process any light that lands on that part of your retina where the hole is, leaving you with a blind spot in each eye.

Most of the time, you're blissfully unaware of this fact because your brain "fills in" the missing information. However, by following a few simple steps you can experience the blind spot for yourself. Get a piece of paper and draw an X on the left-hand side of a piece of paper and an O on the right-hand side (or use the ones printed below). Now close one eye, focus on the X and move the paper nearer and further from your face. At a certain distance you'll find that the O disappears because it has fallen slap bang on your blind spot. Rather than just seeing a blank space where the O should be, you instead see a smooth expanse of paper. This is because your brain uses the surround to predict what's in the location that corresponds to where the blind spot currently falls. This is a great example of how your brain actively constructs some of what you perceive as reality.

X   O

Another simple way to expose your sensory limitations is with the two-point discrimination test. Ask a friend to place two pencil or pin points six inches apart on your back (where sensitivity is relatively poor compared with, say, the back of your hand). Next, have your friend gradually bring the two points closer together, and your task is to say whether you can feel one or two points. Eventually, as the points get closer, there will be a stage where you are being prodded in two places, but you experience it as just one. This is because the number of brain cells given over to representing your skin is finite, and when the points are too close together you don't have the sensitivity to tell them apart. Try the test on different body parts – the closer the points can be before you feel them as one point, the higher the tactile resolution on that part of your skin.

Blackouts

The existence of the retinal blind spot means wherever you look there is a permanent gap in your view of the scene. But did you realize that in fact the whole of your vision is temporarily switched off every time you make a fast saccadic eye movement? These jerky movements are frequent – under normal circumstances, about three or four every second – and necessary, because it's only the central "foveal" part of your retina that is packed with enough light-sensitive cells to provide high acuity vision. The visual shutdown that occurs during each of these movements is known as "saccadic suppression" and it prevents the scene blurring each time you rapidly shift the direction of your gaze. It's a marvel that we're oblivious to these frequent blackouts, and the phenomenon provides yet another example of the difference between our first-person experience and reality.

Part of the reason we're oblivious to these frequent, fleeting blackouts is that our brain appears to back-date our subjective sense of how long objects have been in their current locations. Glance across the room to a table lamp, for example, and your brain factors in the temporary loss of visual input by assuming that the lamp was in its current position, not just from the moment your eyes alighted on it, but also during the blackout period. Some experts believe this process is responsible for an illusory experience known as the "stopped clock effect." This is when you glance at a second hand on an analogue clock (or the seconds counter on a digital clock) and it seems to hang for far too long, almost as if it has stopped.

Keilan Yarrow and his colleagues at UCL and Oxford University explored this stopped clock illusion in a study published in 2001.[19] They set up a numerical counter to start changing upwards from 1 as soon as a participant looked at it. The duration for which the initial number 1 was displayed varied, but the subsequent numbers were all shown for one second each. The key finding was that participants tended to overestimate how long the initial digit was displayed, as compared with the duration of the later digits. What's more, this overestimation was greater when participants made a larger, longer-lasting initial eye movement to the counter. This fits with the idea that a newly glanced upon object is back-dated by the brain, to compensate for the length of the visual blackout during the glance.

Saccadic suppression and blind spots aren't the only impediments to our ability to perceive the world as it is. An ongoing problem for all our senses is the signal transduction delay through the nervous system. Although it feels to us as though we perceive the world instantly, in fact it takes time for sensory information to work its way along our sensory pathways (about a tenth of a second for vision). Much of this is compensated for through endless anticipatory processes. The brain is constantly predicting how the world probably is now based on how it was a moment ago.

The sluggishness of our sensory pathways is a particular problem when it comes to tracking moving objects. By the time an object is perceived consciously in one location, it's already moved on to another. One part of the brain's solution is to locate a moving object ahead of its current position. In other words, we don't perceive it where it is, but where it will be, thus helping cancel out processing delays. This can be demonstrated via an illusion known as the flash-lag effect. It's easier to experience than it is to describe, so it's worth looking for some examples on the Internet (e.g. see http://youtu.be/DUBM-GG0gAk). The illusion occurs when a stationary object is flashed adjacent to a moving object. Even though both objects are in reality in alignment, the stationary object is perceived as lagging behind. This is because the moving object was perceived ahead of its actual location at the instant in time that the stationary object appeared. It's been claimed that the flash-lag effect may even be responsible for questionable off-side decisions by referees in soccer matches (such decisions are based in part on a judgment about whether a player is in front of the ball or not).[20]

Extension and Momentum

The brain's determination to compensate for its processing delays is also betrayed by a phenomenon known as "representational momentum." Stated simply, it's not only the future movement of moving objects that we second guess – we also extrapolate the future trajectory of static objects that look dynamic. This process manifests as a kind of memory distortion. Imagine I showed you a static photograph of a tennis player striking a ball. Next, I showed you another, almost identical photo, except it was taken a moment later, when the ball was ever so slightly further along its trajectory. Thanks to representational momentum, if I asked you to judge whether I'd shown you the same photo twice, you'd be highly likely to mistakenly think I had. In contrast, if the second photo was from a moment earlier than the first, when the ball was slightly nearer the start of its trajectory, you'd be far more likely to state correctly that this photo was different from the first. It's as if our memory of static scenes that imply motion evolves forwards in our minds, playing out the likely course of events.

A related phenomenon is known as "boundary extension"[21] and it occurs because of the brain's endless anticipation of what lies beyond the borders of our visual experience. Recall that it is only the center of our vision that is of high acuity. We overcome this limitation by constantly shifting our gaze about a scene. And yet despite all this movement, our visual experience does not resemble a succession of glances at the world through little spy holes. Instead vision feels fluid and seamless from one gaze shift to the next. In part, at least, this is thanks to boundary extension. Again, as with representational momentum, the process manifests as a memory distortion. Presented with a photo of a scene, and then a second zoomed outwards slightly (thus showing a larger area), most people are prone to mistaking the second photo for the first – an error they don't make if the second photo is zoomed in, rather than zoomed out.

Illusions

Illusory situations that expose the disjoint between reality and our perception of it are not only great fun by they're also used by researchers to find out more about the way the brain works. Illusions can be experienced across all our senses, and they vary according to where in the sensory pathway the brain is tricked.

Some illusions are experienced because of basic physiological processes that occur at the level of individual sensory receptors. A good example is the "waterfall illusion," which happens after you spend a few minutes staring at a waterfall (there are versions online, such as: http://t.co/D3f0Hk5Zzg). After staring a while, look to the rocks at the side of the waterfall and you should experience the strange sense that they are moving upwards, in the direction opposite to the flow of water. Also known as the "motion aftereffect," this illusion is thought to occur because of the adaptation or fatigue of your sensory receptors that are sensitive to the specific direction of motion of the waterfall. When you look at the stationary rocks, the baseline activity of these cells remains altered momentarily. Perceptual confusion arises because their suppressed signal is compared against the activity of cells that code for movement in other directions, prompting the visual system to conclude incorrectly that the rocks must be moving upwards.

Other illusions depend on "higher level" cognitive processes related to the assumptions made by the brain about the world. One of my favorites is the "checkered shadow" illusion developed by the MIT vision scientist Edward Adelson (see Plate 28). Two squares on a chess-like board appear to be completely different shades of gray when in fact they are exactly the same. Most people respond with incredulity when told the truth, which is testament to the adage that seeing is believing, even though what we see is often very different from what is real. You can destroy the illusion by covering the grid with specially prepared paper that has two cut-outs leaving the relevant squares exposed. Now you'll see that they are indeed exactly the same shade.

The checkered shadow illusion is caused by tricking the mental processes involved in "color constancy." When interpreting the light reflected off a surface, the brain makes adjustments for shadows and variations in environmental light sources. To take one example, this is what allows us to recognize grass as green, during day and night, on a sunny afternoon or under a slate gray sky. Among the color constancy strategies the brain uses is to take into account the contrast between a given target (in this case a square) and the light of its surroundings. In the checkered shadow illusion, one target square is surrounded by lighter squares, the other by darker squares. This latter square is also in shadow. Combined, these factors lead the latter square to be perceived as lighter than it really is. "As with many so-called illusions," Adelson writes on his website, "this effect really demonstrates the success rather than the failure of the visual system."

Our subjective sense of the world truly is remarkable. In the scientific jargon, it feels "veridical." That is to say, it seems to us as though reality is reproduced in our mind's eye exactly as it exists in the physical world. We're oblivious to the myriad computational processes, anticipations, and assumptions that weave together our coherent mental experience of what's going on. From a user's point of view, this is a good thing. Our perceptual experiences are subjectively compelling, and from an evolutionary perspective, they served our ancestors well in terms of survival. The downside is occasional over-confidence – when what we experience is not what is there. This can manifest in the fun of a psychologist's illusion or the tragedy of accident.

Myth: Time Slows Down When You're in an Accident

Our sense of time is particularly vulnerable to bias and frequent disconnect with reality. Pupils find that a double session of algebra on a Friday afternoon feels as though it lasts about a year. A high-adrenaline movie, on the other hand, can feel as if it's over in a flash. A popular belief in this regard is that time slows down dramatically for a person who is caught up in a terrifying accident. This would imply that their sensory processing was speeded up during the incident. Research conducted in 2008 suggests that this is no more than a myth.[22] Chess Stetson and his colleagues at California Institute of Technology placed a group of brave participants on the Nothin' But Net thrill ride in Dallas, which involves a 100 feet drop. While in midair, the participants' held a flickering digital counter and had to identify the digit on display. Earlier testing showed that on average participants were unable to identify a digit that flickered faster than once every 47 milliseconds. When they were falling through the air, they felt as though time had slowed, but crucially, their ability to identify the digit was no better than when they were safely on terra firma. In other words, their sensory processing hadn't really speeded up at all. Stetson and his co-workers concluded that fear-induced time distortion is a trick of memory that happens after the event.

Myth #34 The Brain's Representation of the Body Is Accurate and Stable

There's an old English idiom "I know x like the back of my hand" that only makes sense because it's so widely taken for granted that people know their own hand extraordinarily well. On the surface this seems reasonable. There is, after all, barely a day that goes by that we don't use and look at our hands. In fact, it's not just our hands – we live with our entire bodies all day, every day, our whole lives (horrible accidents notwithstanding). The parts we can't look at directly, we often study in the mirror. And as we discussed on p. 236, we also have proprioceptive, vestibular, and internal senses that tell the brain where our bodies are located in space and what's going on inside them. In short, it seems as though the brain knows its body well, and it's often assumed that this knowledge is both accurate and stable.

Body Knowledge

The reality is our perceptions of our bodies are frequently inaccurate and highly malleable. In a paper published in 2010,[23] the researchers Matthew Longo and Patrick Haggard at UCL even demonstrated that most people's perception of their hands is "massively distorted" – we think our fingers are shorter than they really are, and our hands wider than is true, presumably because of the way they are represented in the somatosensory cortex in the brain.

Longo and Haggard made their discovery by covering each participant's left hand, which was positioned face down, and inviting them to point out with their right hand various landmarks belonging to the hidden left, such as the positions of the different knuckles or fingertips. There was a consistent and significant mismatch between the estimated and real positions. Despite this, the participants were able to pick out the correct image of their left hand from an array of photos that included distorted versions. This suggests it is specifically our brain's representation of our hands' physical extent in space that is distorted, not our conscious memory of how the hands look.

It's not just our hands that we don't know as well as we think. For instance, there is also research suggesting that we have an inaccurate sense of the size of our own heads.[24] Ivana Bianchi at the University of Macerata and her colleagues found that the students they tested overestimated the face-on circumference of their heads by an average of 30 to 42 percent. The researchers also found supporting evidence for this overestimation from an inspection of fifteenth-century art. Heads in self-portraits tended to be larger, on average, than heads in portraits.

Our sense of our bodies is also highly malleable: tools are rapidly integrated into what psychologists call the "body schema" in the brain. Lucilla Cardinali and her colleagues showed this in a 2009 study[25] in which volunteers spent time using a 40 centimeter long (about 15.5 inches) grabbing tool. Before and after using the tool, the volunteers completed the same test – they were blindfolded and touched in the same two places on their arm and then they had to point to where they'd been touched. Crucially, the volunteers pointed to locations further apart on their arm after using the tool compared with when the same test was performed before the tool use. It's as if, after using the grabber, they now perceived their arm to be longer than it really was. For a short time after tool use, the volunteers also moved their arms more slowly, more akin to the speeds you see in people who really do have longer arms.

This idea of a rapidly modified body schema has also been supported by brain research. Consider a 1996 study[26] with monkeys trained in tool use. Before and after they'd used a rake, recordings were taken from the same individual neurons in the monkeys' parietal cortex – specifically from multisensory cells that respond to tactile and visual feedback originating from the hand. After tool use, the results showed the visual area to which the neurons responded had expanded in such a way to incorporate the length of the tool into the brain's representation of the hand.

The dynamic and sometimes unreliable way the brain represents the body can have clinical significance. People with eating disorders are often profoundly unhappy with the size, shape, and attractiveness of their bodies, possibly due to a bias in the way their brain represents their body. Certainly some research has suggested they have a negatively distorted sense of their body shape and size compared with healthy people. However, these results are inconsistent and it's clear that at least some people have an eating disorder despite an accurate perception of their physique. This shows psychological and social factors are also at play. Intriguingly, there's also evidence that some people with eating disorders may actually have an *unusually accurate* sense of the attractiveness of their bodies, and that healthy people (i.e. those without an eating disorder) have an inflated, positively biased sense of the attractiveness of their bodies.

A team of Dutch psychologists discovered this phenomenon in 2006[27] by comparing people's beliefs about the attractiveness of their own bodies with the attractiveness ratings their bodies received from a panel of strangers. Those participants with an eating disorder rated the attractiveness of their body in a way consistent with the rating they received from the strangers. Healthy people, by contrast, rated their own bodies as far more attractive than did the panel of strangers. "This points to the existence of a self-serving body-image bias in the normal controls," the researchers said. "Self-serving biases or positive illusions are prototypical for healthy people, they maintain mental health and help to protect from depression."

When a person's perception of a specific part or parts of their body is wildly inaccurate and distressing, this is usually diagnosed as body dysmorphic disorder (BDD). It can manifest as a vague feeling of extreme ugliness or it can be a more specific delusion, such as the belief that one's head is box-shaped or one's nose is freakishly large. There is no doubt BDD has a strong psychological component – people with the diagnosis often have low self-esteem and other personal problems – but there is also increasing interest in the neurobiological causes or correlates of the condition. A study published early in 2013[28] compared brain connectivity in patients with BDD and healthy controls, finding abnormalities in the patients' brains, including in the wiring between neural regions involved in processing visual detail and other regions involved in emotions.

A rare condition that used to be considered a form of BDD is amputation desire or xenomelia. This is when a person wishes desperately for one or more of their healthy limbs to be removed. One such patient who has spoken to the media about his amputation desire is Keven Wright. His yearning for the removal of his lower left leg began in childhood. In 1997, aged 37, the limb was finally amputated by a Scottish surgeon. In an interview with *The Observer* in 2000, Wright said: "'I have not regretted the operation one bit. I don't want to think of what I'd have been like without it.'"

In recent years, some experts have argued that rather than being a form of BDD, amputation desire is more accurately seen as a neurological condition. Supporting this idea, in 2009[29] Olaf Blanke and his colleagues conducted in-depth interviews with 20 patients who longed for one or more of their healthy limbs to be removed. "It [the leg] feels foreign and it does not belong to me," said one. "I should not have been born with my legs," said another. Crucially, none of the patients was delusional as such – they all recognized that the limb or limbs in question were healthy and normal-looking.

Blanke's team were also intrigued by some specific patterns in the patients' answers – for example, 75 percent wanted their left leg amputated, or their desire was stronger for removal on the left-hand side; and just over half reported odd sensations in their unwanted limb. These facts prompted Blanke and his co-workers to suggest that amputation desire is first and foremost a neurological condition related to the way the body is represented in the brain, and their favored label for the condition is "body integrity identity disorder."

This perspective was supported by a recent structural brain imaging study[30] of 13 male patients with the condition and 13 healthy controls. The patients, all of whom wanted part of one or both their legs removed (most often the left), showed abnormalities in parts of their right hemisphere involved in representing the left side of the body. This is consistent with the idea that amputation is rooted in the brain's abnormal representation of the body. However, the researchers cautioned that the causal direction could run the other way – disowning a limb could lead to brain changes.

Bodily Illusions

The malleability and fallibility of the brain's representation of the body is also exposed to dramatic effect in a series of bodily illusions devised by neuroscientists and psychologists in recent years. One of the earliest and most famous of these is the rubber hand illusion in which the participant comes to feel as though a rubber arm is a part of their body.

Described formally for the first time by Matthew Botvinick and Jonathan Cohen in a 1998 *Nature* paper,[31] the illusion requires that the participant place one of his or her real arms beneath a table and a rubber arm is positioned in its place on the table top. The inducer of the illusion then strokes with two brushes the hidden real arm and the visible fake arm, in synchrony. The participant sees the rubber arm being stroked yet feels the sensation in his or her own arm. In this situation, many people report the strange sensation that they can feel the rubber arm being stroked, as if it were a part of their body. The illusion shows how the brain's representation of the body is multimodal – that is, it incorporates input across the senses to come to a judgment about body ownership.

Remarkably, a study published in 2013[32] showed that stroking isn't even necessary for this illusion. As a researcher reached toward the fake limb, the mere expectation that it was about to be touched was enough to induce physiological arousal in some participants, consistent with the idea that they'd already begun incorporating the rubber hand into their body schema.

Another startling contemporary adaptation of the illusion published in 2011[33] showed that it is also possible to induce in people the sense of having three arms. In this version, both the participant's real arms are placed on the table top, with an additional right-handed rubber arm placed alongside their real right arm. The illusion is further facilitated by placing a sheet over the right-hand side of the participant's body all the way down to the upper forearm of the real and fake right arms, such that only the lower forearms and hands, adjacent, are visible on the table (see Plate 29).

The inducer of the illusion then strokes the real and fake right arms in synchrony. "What happens then is that a conflict arises in the brain concerning which of the right hands belongs to the participant's body," the lead author Arvid Guterstam said in a press release. "What one could expect is that only one of the hands is experienced as one's own, presumably the real arm. But what we found, surprisingly, is that the brain solves this conflict by accepting both right hands as part of the body image, and the subjects experience having an extra third arm."

This may sound wacky enough, but the illusion of having a third arm is nothing compared with the extraordinarily odd sensations induced in the lab of Henrik Ehrsson at the Karolinska Institute in Stockholm. Among the most dramatic of these is the feeling of being outside of one's own body. Ehrsson creates this illusion by having a participant sit in a chair and don a pair of goggles that show the view from a camera that's positioned directly behind the chair (so the subject sees themselves from behind). Ehrsson then prods toward the camera with a stick while in synchrony prodding the participant's chest. Remember, the participant sees the stick from the camera's perspective behind their own body, yet they feel the prodding in their own chest. The brain makes sense of this mismatch by concluding that the body is located where the stick appears to be prodding – that is, behind the participant's real body! Reporting on Ehrsson's research for *Nature*,[34] science writer Ed Yong described his own experience of the illusion: "I saw and felt my chest being prodded at the same time as I saw a picture of myself from behind. Within ten seconds, I felt as if I was being pulled out of my real body and was floating several feet behind it."

It's thought the illusion works, at least in part, by tricking neurons in the parietal cortex that incorporate visual and tactile information in the process of forming a sense of where the body is located in space. Both the rubber hand illusion and out-of-body illusion show how much influence visual input has in these judgments. Elaborations of the body illusion have even led participants to feel as if they own a mannequin body, that they've embodied a Barbie doll[35] or even swapped bodies with another person![36] People vary in how susceptible they are to these illusions. Individuals low in so-called interoceptive awareness (they are less aware of their heartbeat) are more prone to the illusions, presumably because their bodily signals are weaker and so it is easy for misleading visual information to trick them.

There are also bodily illusions that work by means other than providing misleading visual input. One of these is the "Pinocchio illusion" that depends on vibration being applied to the upper arm to trick the brain into thinking the bicep muscle is extending. While the vibration is applied, the blindfolded subject touches her nose with the fingers and keeps them there. The person feels as if her arm is extending outwards, but at the same time her fingers remain in contact with their nose. This conflicting information creates the illusion that her nose must be extraordinarily long. A similar procedure with the hand kept in contact with the top of the head can similarly give rise to the strange sense for the person that her head is tall and elongated.[37]

Most of the time the brain performs a truly remarkable job of sensing where its body is located in space. It's rare that we confuse someone else's body for our own, or vice versa. And neurological illness aside, our ability to control the movement of our bodies is an extraordinary feat of coordination. That said, it is a myth that we perceive our bodies exactly as they are, and that this sense is stable and immutable. Reviewing the literature on body perception in 2012, two key researchers in the field, Matthew Longo and Patrick Haggard at UCL, summed up the true situation: "[There is] remarkable lability of bodily awareness," they wrote. "The representation of the body can flexibly incorporate body parts and even whole bodies that are very different from one's own body, even when this incorporation conflicts dramatically with stored knowledge about the body."

Notes

1   http://www.scientificamerican.com/article/making-sense-world-sveral-senses-at-time/ (accessed May 16, 2014).

2   Westerhoff, J. (2012). Reality: What is it? *New Scientist*, 215(2884), 34–35.

3   Andrew, D., & Craig, A. D. (2001). Spinothalamic lamina I neurons selectively sensitive to histamine: A central neural pathway for itch. *Nature Neuroscience*, 4(1), 72–77.

4   Schmelz, M. (2010). Itch and pain. *Neuroscience & Biobehavioral Reviews*, 34(2), 171–176.

5   Löken, L. S., Wessberg, J., McGlone, F., & Olausson, H. (2009). Coding of pleasant touch by unmyelinated afferents in humans. *Nature Neuroscience*, 12(5), 547–548.

6   http://www.thepsychologist.org.uk/archive/archive_home.cfm?volumeID=2 5&editionID=220&ArticleID=2188 (accessed May 16, 2014).

7   Rojas, J. A. M., Hermosilla, J. A., Montero, R. S., & Espi, P. L. L. (2009). Physical analysis of several organic signals for human echolocation: Oral vacuum pulses. *Acta Acustica united with Acustica*, 95(2), 325–330.

8   Rensink, R. A. (2004). Visual sensing without seeing. *Psychological Science*, 15(1), 27–32.

9   Simons, D. J., Nevarez, G., & Boot, W. R. (2005). Visual sensing is seeing why "mindsight," in hindsight, is blind. *Psychological Science*, 16(7), 520–524.

10   Spence, C. (2010). The multisensory perception of flavour. *Psychologist*, 23(9), 720–723.

11   Morrot, G., Brochet, F., & Dubourdieu, D. (2001). The color of odors. *Brain and language*, 79(2), 309–320.

12   North, A. C. (2012). The effect of background music on the taste of wine. *British Journal of Psychology*, 103(3), 293–301.

13   Saenz, M., & Koch, C. (2008). The sound of change: Visually-induced auditory synesthesia. *Current Biology*, 18(15), R650–R651.

14   Simner, J., & Ward, J. (2006). Synaesthesia: The taste of words on the tip of the tongue. *Nature*, 444(7118), 438.

15   Nikolić, D., Jürgens, U. M., Rothen, N., Meier, B., & Mroczko, A. (2011). Swimming-style synesthesia. *Cortex*, 47(7), 874–879.

16   Simons, D. J., & Chabris, C. F. (1999). Gorillas in our midst: Sustained inattentional blindness for dynamic events. *Perception-London*, 28(9), 1059–1074.

17   Dalton, P., & Fraenkel, N. (2012). Gorillas we have missed: Sustained inattentional deafness for dynamic events. *Cognition*, 124(3), 367–372.

18 Drew, T., Võ, M. L. H., & Wolfe, J. M. (2013). The invisible gorilla strikes again: Sustained inattentional blindness in expert observers. *Psychological Science*. doi: 10.1177/0956797613479386.

19 Yarrow, K., Haggard, P., Heal, R., Brown, P., & Rothwell, J. C. (2001). Illusory perceptions of space and time preserve cross-saccadic perceptual continuity. *Nature*, 414(6861), 302–305.

20 Baldo, M. V. C., Ranvaud, R. D., & Morya, E. (2002). Flag errors in soccer games: The flash-lag effect brought to real life. *Perception-London*, 31(10), 1205–1210.

21 Seamon, J. G., Schlegel, S. E., Hiester, P. M., Landau, S. M., & Blumenthal, B. F. (2002). Misremembering pictured objects: People of all ages demonstrate the boundary extension illusion. *The American Journal of Psychology*.

22 Stetson, C., Fiesta, M. P., & Eagleman, D. M. (2007). Does time really slow down during a frightening event? *PLoS One*, 2(12), e1295.

23 Longo, M. R., & Haggard, P. (2010). An implicit body representation underlying human position sense. *Proceedings of the National Academy of Sciences*, 107(26), 11727–11732.

24 Bianchi, I., Savardi, U., & Bertamini, M. (2008). Estimation and representation of head size (people overestimate the size of their head – evidence starting from the 15th century). *British Journal of Psychology*, 99(4), 513–531.

25 Cardinali, L., Frassinetti, F., Brozzoli, C., Urquizar, C., Roy, A. C., & Farnè, A. (2009). Tool-use induces morphological updating of the body schema. *Current Biology*, 19(12), R478–R479.

26 Iriki, A., Tanaka, M., & Iwamura, Y. (1996). Coding of modified body schema during tool use by macaque postcentral neurones. *Neuroreport*, 7(14), 2325–2330.

27 Jansen, A., Smeets, T., Martijn, C., & Nederkoorn, C. (2006). I see what you see: The lack of a self-serving body-image bias in eating disorders. *British Journal of Clinical Psychology*, 45(1), 123–135.

28 Buchanan, B. G., Rossell, S. L., Maller, J. J., Toh, W. L., Brennan, S., & Castle, D. J. (2013). Brain connectivity in body dysmorphic disorder compared with controls: A diffusion tensor imaging study. *Psychological Medicine*, 1–9.

29 Blanke, O., Morgenthaler, F. D., Brugger, P., & Overney, L. S. (2009). Preliminary evidence for a fronto-parietal dysfunction in able-bodied participants with a desire for limb amputation. *Journal of Neuropsychology*, 3(2), 181–200.

30 Hilti, L. M., Hänggi, J., Vitacco, D. A., Kraemer, B., Palla, A., Luechinger, R., ... & Brugger, P. (2013). The desire for healthy limb amputation: Structural brain correlates and clinical features of xenomelia. *Brain*, 136(1), 318–329.

31 Botvinick, M., & Cohen, J. (1998). Rubber hands "feel" touch that eyes see. *Nature*, 391(6669), 756.

32 Ferri, F., Chiarelli, A. M., Merla, A., Gallese, V., & Costantini, M. (2013). The body beyond the body: Expectation of a sensory event is enough to

induce ownership over a fake hand. *Proceedings of the Royal Society B: Biological Sciences*, 280(1765).

33   Guterstam, A., Petkova, V. I., & Ehrsson, H. H. (2011). The illusion of owning a third arm. *PloS One*, 6(2), e17208.

34   Yong, E. (2011). Out of body experience: Master of illusion. *Nature*, 168–170.

35   Van der Hoort, B., Guterstam, A., & Ehrsson, H. H. (2011). Being Barbie: The size of one's own body determines the perceived size of the world. *PloS One*, 6(5), e20195.

36   Petkova, V. I., & Ehrsson, H. H. (2008). If I were you: Perceptual illusion of body swapping. *PloS One*, 3(12), e3832.

37   Longo, M. R., & Haggard, P. (2012). What is it like to have a body? *Current Directions in Psychological Science*, 21(2), 140–145.

8 MYTHS ABOUT BRAIN DISORDER AND ILLNESS

Of all the myths in this book, those that pertain to brain injury and illness have the most potential to cause harm and incite prejudice. Writers find that brain disorders make for great material and many of the public's misconceptions about brain illness and injury can be traced to unrealistic fictional depictions in film and literature. In this chapter, I'll provide you with some basic facts about brain injury, coma, dementia, amnesia, autism, and epilepsy. I'll show you how these conditions are misrepresented in fiction and I'll correct the myths that have arisen as a result. Some illness-related myths are dangerous – such as the belief that autism is caused by the MMR vaccine against measles and rubella. Others are oversimplifications, including the idea that mood disorders are caused by a simple chemical imbalance in the brain. Throughout this chapter, we'll see yet again how the truth is often more nuanced and fascinating than the mythology.

Myth #35   Brain Injury and Concussion Myths

Traumatic brain injury (TBI) incurred through accident, sports, or violence is increasingly common, especially among youths, and becoming more so. For young people in rich countries, TBI is now the leading cause of death. Data from the Centers for Disease Control and Prevention published in 2010 show that 7 million brain injuries occur in the US every year with an estimated annual financial burden of $60 billion. UK data reveal an estimated 1 million brain injuries per year, with around 500 000 people living with long-term disability associated with their brain injury.

Great Myths of the Brain, First Edition. Christian Jarrett.
© 2015 Christian Jarrett. Published 2015 by John Wiley & Sons, Ltd.

Traumatic brain injury can arise from a direct blow to the head, from penetrations of the brain (e.g. gunshot wounds), or from gravitational forces in cases where the head is thrown suddenly, causing the brain to be compressed or shaken within the skull, as might happen in a car accident. Brain injury can also arise through a stroke (see box). The effects of TBI vary hugely depending on a range of factors, including its severity, the location of the damage, whether the brain is penetrated (as opposed to a closed head injury), and the victim's health, gender, and age. The young and old tend to be more vulnerable, and there's evidence that women tend to be more adversely affected by brain injury than men.

As well as death, outcomes from TBI include coma, temporary loss of consciousness, amnesia, confusion, epilepsy, headache, vomiting, fatigue, irritability, and other mood changes. Further specific neurological and neuropsychological conditions associated with brain injury include paralysis, coordination problems (dyspraxia), an inability to attend to one side of space (known as visual neglect), problems recognizing people (prosopagnosia), and language difficulties (aphasia).

Estimates vary, but around 85 percent of TBIs are classified as mild. This assessment is usually based on administration of the Glasgow Coma Scale, which focuses on patients' responsiveness, in terms of their eye movements, reactions to pain, and verbal utterances. A CT scan may also be performed in search of signs of physical damage to the brain. It's also important to identify dangerous secondary complications that may ensue including brain swelling and blood clots.

While the majority of people recover from a mild TBI without complications, the word "mild" can be misleading because around 10 percent of these patients experience symptoms that persist for weeks or even months in a condition known as post-concussion syndrome. Children, older adults and people who've had a prior brain injury are especially likely to suffer persistent complications. Longer term, there's evidence that brain injury can also be associated with dementia, especially in cases of repeated brain insults, for example, from boxing or American football (see later sections on myths around amnesia, epilepsy, and dementia).

Myths about Symptoms and Recovery

Although most patients will recover fully from a mild TBI, experts warn that complete recovery from a serious brain injury is highly unlikely. Professor Karen Hux, an expert on TBI at the University of Nebraska-Lincoln, told me:

> People with severe brain injuries will always have some persisting deficits, although the challenges may not be readily apparent to other people. When the challenges are hidden, we often say the person, "walks and talks," because he/she will appear normal to lay people but actually has many hidden cognitive and psychosocial impairments.

A number of surveys show that a large proportion of the general public hold erroneous beliefs about traumatic brain injury, especially in terms of underestimating its seriousness and misunderstanding how symptoms manifest.

For a 2006 paper,[1] Karen Hux and her colleagues quizzed 318 people in the US and found that over 93 percent of them wrongly endorsed the idea that "after head injury, people can forget who they are and not recognize others, but be normal in every other way" (in reality, such serious deficits would always be accompanied by related impairments to mental functioning, including problems learning new information and sustaining focus); over 70 percent believed incorrectly that complete recovery from a severe brain injury is possible; and nearly 70 percent failed to realize that having one brain injury leaves a patient more vulnerable to further brain injuries (this is because of the deleterious effects of the first injury and because damaged brain cells are in a fragile state).

Around 60 percent also believed wrongly that people in a coma are usually aware of what's going on around them (see coma section for more on this); nearly half failed to realize that a loss of memory for events prior to the injury will usually go hand in hand with problems learning new material; half were unaware that a problem learning new things is more common after brain injury than problems remembering the past; around half believed wrongly that after being knocked unconscious most people wake up with no lasting effects; and approximately 40 percent believed wrongly that it is good to rest and remain inactive after a brain injury.

I asked Professor Hux for some clarification of this last point. Rest and avoidance of mental and physical stress is important and appropriate in cases of mild TBI, she explained, but it's a different story for severe injuries. There is typically an early phase of impaired consciousness where rest and inactivity are unavoidable. But after this acute recovery period, she said "people with severe brain injuries need to be active participants in rehabilitation activities to maximize their recovery – and rehab is hard work! The person will have to work and work and work to re-establish lost physical and mental skills."

It's important on this point not to fall for a related misconception – over 50 percent of Hux's participants incorrectly endorsed the statement: "How quickly a person recovers depends mainly on how hard they work at recovering." Although it is true that rehabilitation depends on dedication and effort on the part of patients, in nearly all cases the speed and extent of their recovery will also be limited by the injuries they incurred. As Hux told me: "You can't overcome a memory deficit just by trying hard; you can't force yourself to be less distractible by sheer will-power." The erroneous notion that recovery is just a case of putting in enough effort can lead to unfair stigmatization of brain injured patients. "You wouldn't blame a person with paralyzed legs for not being able to walk," says Hux. "In the same way, you should not blame the survivor of brain injury for not being able to remember (or whatever the task is) as well as they did prior to injury."

Other brain injury misconceptions were correctly identified as such by the vast majority of Hux's survey respondents, including the myth that brain damage can only happen if a person is knocked out; that whiplash cannot lead to brain injury if there is no direct blow to the head; that most people with brain damage look and act disabled; and that the recovery process is complete once a person says they feel "back to normal."

A 2010 paper[2] by Rowena Chapman and John Hudson at the University of Lincoln applied the same survey questions to 322 participants in the UK and found even greater endorsement of misconceptions regarding brain injury. Like their US counterparts, most people in the UK underestimated the seriousness of losing consciousness, misunderstood the way symptoms usually manifest, and failed to realize that brain injury patients are at increased risk for further injury.

Don't Underestimate Concussion

The term "concussion" appears to be a particular source of confusion in the field of brain injury, in part because the word is used to mean different things by different people – there are over eight concussion scales used by medics and there's no consensus on how to grade levels of severity. Many brain injury charities and online resources state that concussion is simply another way of describing mild traumatic brain injury associated with extremely brief or no loss of consciousness. It is important that concussion is treated seriously because one mild injury leaves the brain vulnerable to further injury and multiple concussions can lead to serious long-term effects.

Research published in 2010[3] provides a graphic example of the confusion that surrounds the term concussion. A team led by Carol DeMatteo at McMaster University looked at the diagnoses given to 434 TBI patients at a Canadian children's hospital. They found that children diagnosed with a mild TBI as opposed to a severe TBI (based on the Glasgow Coma Scale) were more likely to be given a diagnosis of concussion, but crucially, 23.5 percent of kids deemed to have a serious brain injury were also given the concussion label.

The group of children most likely to be described by clinicians as suffering concussion were those with a normal CT scan but some loss of consciousness. It seems clinicians were using the term to mean that a brain injury had occurred but that no structural signs of damage were present. However, there was clearly great variation in the way the term was employed. DeMatteo's team said: "This leads one to question the use of the term as being reflective of mild injury and again supports the existence of confusion about what concussion really is and how the term should best be used in the care of children."

The importance of this issue was brought home by data showing that children given the concussion label tended to be discharged earlier and sent back to school sooner. "If a child is given a diagnosis of concussion, then the family is less likely to consider it a brain injury," the researchers said. This misperception of concussion as non-serious also fits with earlier research suggesting that concussion often goes unreported by players and coaches of high-impact games like ice hockey. The correct protocol for suspected concussion is rest and avoidance of high-risk activities for a few weeks. For obvious reasons athletes and coaches often downplay symptoms so that players can continue competing. There's also evidence[4] that sports TV and commentators may exacerbate the non-serious perception of concussion by describing the condition in casual terms and describing rapid returns to play as courageous.

DeMatteo and her colleagues who conducted the children's hospital study believe a lot of the confusion would be eliminated by replacing use of the term concussion with mild TBI. "After our study, I'm of the belief that if you use the word 'brain,' that people pay attention a little bit more," De Matteo told CBC news in Canada.[5] "I still believe that a lot of people think concussion means a hit to the head and it doesn't involve the brain."

Prejudice and Support

Although mention of the word brain may encourage people to take concussion more seriously, it can also increase prejudice toward the injured. In 2011[6] Audrey McKinlay and her colleagues at the University of Canterbury and Monash University quizzed 103 members of the New Zealand general public and discovered some usual misconceptions – many people believed wrongly that concussion only occurs after a direct blow to the head and that a person with concussion should be kept awake. Their survey also showed how people's assumptions about patients are influenced by the terminology used. The participants more readily associated the words negative, kind, distractible, eager, and diligent with the term "brain injury" than the term "head injury," even though head and brain injury are often used interchangeably by experts and the public alike.

The same research group also found prejudice toward brain injury victims in a separate study that presented two versions of a character vignette. When the same car accident victim was described as having suffered a brain injury, as opposed to a head injury, as a child, participants subsequently described him as less mature, intelligent, flexible, polite, and employable.[7] McKinlay and her colleagues said this prejudice likely has an adverse effect on brain injury patients' attempts at rehabilitation. The flip side, they wrote, is that "a more positive evaluation of individuals who have experienced TBI is likely to enhance the social experience and functions for those individuals who have experienced a brain injury, which can greatly influence recovery and quality of life."

The importance of social support for brain injury recovery may explain a curious finding documented in 2011 by Janelle Jones and her colleagues:[8] patients who'd suffered a more serious brain injury reported more life satisfaction than those who'd suffered a more minor injury. The result came from a survey of 630 patients conducted in association with the Headway brain injury charity. Crucially, the greater life satisfaction of the more severely injured patients was mediated by their having developed a particularly strong sense of identity as a survivor and by their having more social support and improved relationships. "Sustaining a head injury does not always lead to a deterioration in one's quality of life," the researchers concluded,

> [D]ata from this study serves to tell a coherent story about the way in which the quality of life of those who experience acquired brain injuries can be enhanced by the personal and social "identity work" that these injuries require them to perform. ... Nietzsche, then, was correct to observe that that which does not kill us can make us stronger.

Stroke Myths

Over 795 000 people experience a stroke every year in the USA, according to the National Stroke Association, making it a major cause of brain injury and the fourth leading cause of death. Most common is an ischemic stroke, involving a blockage in a blood vessel in the brain. Around 20 percent of strokes are hemorrhagic, which is when a blood vessel ruptures, for example, because of an aneurysm (see Plate 30). The consequences of stroke vary and depend on the location and extent of any damage caused, as well as factors such as the patient's health and age. A major stroke is often preceded months or years earlier by one or more "transient ischemic attacks," the effects of which are short-lived and may even go unnoticed.

Myth: Strokes Only Affect Old People

Even as the overall prevalence of stroke is declining, the condition is becoming more common in younger people, possibly due to increased risk factors such as obesity. One in five victims is now under 55 years of age. One in ten is under 45. Many people learned of this reality when the Hollywood actress and fitness enthusiast Sharon Stone was stricken by a hemorrhagic stroke in 2001, aged 43. She has since campaigned to further raise awareness of the condition. In rare cases, stroke can also affect children and is in fact a leading cause of infant mortality in the US.

Myth: The Effects of Stroke Are Limited to Physical Disability

While the effects of stroke can be physically disabling, including paralysis, it's important for sufferers, family and professionals to recognize that the condition can also have far-reaching psychological and emotional consequences, both for the patient and those close to them. Cognitive deficits can include problems producing and comprehending language (known as aphasia) and amnesia. The Stroke Association in the UK launched a campaign in 2013 to raise awareness of the emotional aspects of the condition. Their survey of 1774 stroke survivors found that over two thirds felt depressed or anxious as a result of their stroke, and yet the majority had received no advice or help with this aspect of their condition.

Myth #36

Amnesia Myths

Amnesia is a broad term that refers to several disorders of memory. Usually the problems arise because of damage to the brain, particularly the hippocampus – a structure found in the temporal lobes on either side of the head, near the ears. One of the most famous case studies in all of neuroscience was the amnesiac Henry Molaison (see p. 45), who had large sections of both of his hippocampi removed as part of a radical neurosurgical treatment for epilepsy. Apart from brain surgery, other causes of amnesia include brain infection, asphyxiation, chronic alcoholism, and head injuries. Far rarer than these "organic" causes of amnesia, there is also a condition known as psychogenic or dissociative amnesia, in which memory loss is purportedly caused by emotional trauma or another psychological problem. Note that some scholars, such as Harrison Pope, dispute that this form of amnesia really exists. In one study, he and his colleagues reported that there were no historical references to psychogenic amnesia prior to 1800, supporting their claim that the condition is a cultural creation.

Amnesia arising from brain damage varies hugely from one patient to another depending on the location and extent of the damage. The most common presentation is for the patient to struggle to store new long-term memories, which is known as anterograde amnesia. A typical amnesiac of this kind will have intact intelligence and normal short-term memory – the kind you use for holding a phone number in mind momentarily before dialing. Usually they also often retain enough of their pre-illness autobiographical memories to have a sense of self and identity.

Most amnesiacs also have preserved memory for skills and an ability to learn new ones. A favorite test of psychologists is mirror drawing, a tricky task that involves controlling your hand based on its reflection. In common with most other amnesiacs, Henry Molaison improved with practice at mirror drawing, just as healthy people do. However, each time an amnesiac like Molaison attempts the task, they think it is the first time they've done it.

Despite any preserved functions, the inability to store new long-term memories is often crippling. If you met a person with severe amnesia of this kind today, he or she will not recognize you tomorrow. Most amnesiacs can't remember whether they've eaten or what their plans are for the day. In the words of neurologist Adam Zeman, a patient with serious anterograde amnesia is stuck in "the tyranny of the present."[9] Suzanne Corkin, who studied Molaison for 46 years, says that he never came to recognize her in all those years (although he did manage to store a few new memories after his surgery – for example, he knew the names of some characters from the popular US TV show "All in the Family," even though it premiered well after his operation).

In his book *Moonwalking With Einstein*,[10] Josh Foer provides a poetic description of what this condition must be like, based on his encounter with another profoundly impaired amnesiac known in the research literature as EP (who died in 2008). EP's memory loss was caused by the infection of his brain with herpes simplex virus in 1992, which wiped out both his hippocampi. "Without a memory, EP has fallen completely out of time," writes Foer. "He has no stream of consciousness, just droplets that immediately evaporate … [he] has achieved a kind of pathological enlightenment, a perverted vision of the Buddhist ideal of living entirely in the present."

Less often, amnesiacs experience a loss of memory for a period of time that precedes their brain damage, known as retrograde amnesia. Others suffer both anterograde and retrograde amnesia. This was true for EP. Not only could EP not store new memories, he'd also lost all his autobiographical memories back to around 1950.

The Myths

Amnesia is an incredibly popular plot device in fiction, but it's usually presented in an unrealistic way. At the movies and in literature, there is a farfetched bias toward retrograde amnesia, usually of the psychogenic kind. A classic example is the assassin Jason Bourne played by Matt Damon, who in the first part of the film franchise is pulled from the ocean with gunshot wounds and no memory of his own identity. Like many other fictional amnesiacs, Bourne has a preserved ability to lay down new long-term memories and is perfectly able to look after himself. In fact, in Bourne's case, he is more capable than most healthy people, showing supreme ingenuity, quick wittedness, and spy skills.

Examples from literature include Anne Perry's amnesiac detective William Monk and the girl in Grant Allen's Victorian novel *Recalled to Life*. Monk wakes from an accident to discover he's forgotten his life story. The girl in Allen's book suffers profound psychogenic amnesia after her father is killed. It later transpires that she was the one who killed him!

Films also have a habit of blurring the distinction between organic and psychogenic amnesia. Movie amnesiacs are often in their condition because of a blow to the head, and yet their identity-loss symptoms resemble those shown by someone with psychogenic amnesia. The prevalence of amnesia induced by head injuries is itself another bias in films. In reality, organic amnesia is more often caused by surgery, infection, or stroke.

There's evidence that these portrayals are skewing the public's perception of amnesia. Daniel Simons and Christopher Chabris published a survey of memory understanding in 2011[11] based on the answers of 1500 people in the US. They found that 69.6 percent agreed with the statement that "people suffering from amnesia typically cannot recall their own name or identity." An even higher figure of 81.4 percent agreement was obtained in a follow-up that Simons and Chabris published in 2012[12] based on responses from people enrolled with the Amazon Mechanical Turk survey website.

Similar to the movie world's fixation with amnesia as a cause of identity loss, there are also many fictional amnesiacs whose condition profoundly alters their personality and morals. There are hints of this in the Bourne films, as Damon's amnesiac hero appears shocked to learn of his past violent misdeeds. The idea is also taken to the extreme in *Overboard* (1987) in which Goldie Hawn's character Joanna, a selfish, spoiled socialite, hits her head on a yacht and transforms into a doting mother.

In her witty analysis of amnesia at the movies (published in the *British Medical Journal*)[13] neuropsychologist Sallie Baxendale highlighted another ridiculous myth perpetuated by many films – the idea that a second knock on the head can have a curative effect such as happens to Tarzan in the film *Tarzan the Tiger* (1922). Things get even more mixed up in *Singing in the Dark* (1956) when a bang on the head helps a character overcome psychogenic amnesia caused by the trauma of the Holocaust.

Yet another myth propagated in film is the idea of nightly amnesia, in which the patient has normal memory abilities during the day but then has their mind wiped clean at night. This is what happens in *50 First Dates* (2004) when Adam Sandler's character has to woo his amnesiac girlfriend Lucy (played by Drew Barrymore) anew each day. "Some viewers might envy Ms Barrymore's ability to forget her romantic encounters with Mr Sandler," observes Baxendale drily, "but her affliction seems to be the result of a head injury rather than the unconscious suppression of traumatic memories." The notion of nightly amnesia is also the main plot device in the best-selling 2011 novel *Before I Go To Sleep*, by S. J. Watson. Currently being adapted for film, the story involves the lead character attempting to reconstruct her life each day using a journal.

In a curious example of life imitating art, a 2010 study[14] documented the real-life case of a car accident victim "FL" who claimed that her memory function was intact during the day but was wiped clean each night. However, brain scans showed the woman wasn't brain damaged. And when the researchers tricked her into thinking she was being tested on material from earlier in the day, but which had in fact been shown to her the day before, she performed at normal levels. The researchers led by Christine Smith at the University of California concluded that the woman had a form of psychogenic amnesia influenced by the film *50 First Dates*. Other experts aren't so sure. In 2011, in the *Skeptical Inquirer*,[15] a group led by Harald Merckelbach published a scathing response to Smith's paper. Merckelbach and his colleagues, Scott Lilienfeld and Thomas Merten, criticized the lack of background information about the patient, the failure to test whether she was deliberately feigning her apparent deficits, and the journal's unwillingness to publish critical commentaries alongside controversial case reports. "If FL only believes that she suffers from a memory impairment, and her memory actually functions largely within the normal range, her condition would more accurately be described as pseudo-amnesia, not amnesia," wrote Merckelbach and his colleagues.

We've seen where movies give a distorted impression of amnesia, but let's also give credit where it's due. Baxendale highlighted three films for their accurate portrayals of the condition. *Se Quien Eres* (2000) features a realistic portrayal of Korsakoff's (see below), while the animation *Finding Nemo* (2003) stars a blue tropical fish with amnesia, whose serious daily difficulties provide an accurate reflection of what life is like for most amnesiacs. But it is for the 2000 film *Memento*, starring Guy Pearce as amnesiac Leonard, that Baxendale reserves special praise. Leonard is left brain damaged and amnesic by a man who attacks him and his wife, leaving her dead. Unable to store new information to memory, Leonard hunts the killer by making notes and tattooing clues on his own body. "The fragmented, almost mosaic quality to the sequence of scenes in the film ... cleverly reflects the 'perpetual present' nature of the syndrome," writes Baxendale.

When Truth Is Stranger than Fiction

There's no doubt that most writers of fiction present amnesia in a misleading way. After all, the typical amnesiac struggling to remember anything new is rarely seen in film or literature. And yet it's worth also bearing in mind the views of neuroscientist Sebastian Dieguez and neurologist Jean-Marie Annoni. In their 2013 book chapter[16] they argue that we should be cautious about being too dismissive of fictional portrayals when truth can often be far stranger than fiction.

The Swiss researchers highlight a series of astonishing real-life tales including the ten French soldiers who were discovered after the Great War with no knowledge of their own identities. These amnesiacs were dubbed the "living dead" by the press at the time, and arguments ensued about who they really were. One man named Anthelme Mangin was claimed by over 300 families as being their long-lost son or husband! It seems likely these soldiers were suffering, at least partly, from psychogenic amnesia. The typical patient with this condition is in what psychologists call a "dissociative fugue" state, in which they experience a loss of identity and varying degrees of memory loss for the trauma that caused their state, and sometimes much of their life beforehand. Unlike organic amnesiacs, patients with psychogenic amnesia usually retain the ability to form new long-term memories.

In relation to the idea of amnesia causing complete changes in personality, you can't get much more drastic than the real-life case of Chris Birch, a Welsh rugby player who suffered almost total retrograde amnesia in 2005 after the brain injury he suffered from a stroke that was triggered by rolling down a slope. According to a report on the BBC, not only did Birch forget most of his former life, he also awoke from his injury as a gay man whereas he'd previously been straight. He also reportedly changed careers from banking to hairdressing.

When it comes to recovery stories, it's also worth considering two real-life cases of sudden memory retrieval documented by Federica Lucchelli and her colleagues in 1995.[17] One amnesiac suddenly remembered his forgotten life story while lying on an operating table waiting for surgery to implant a pacemaker; apparently he was transported back in time to an operation he'd had 25 years previously. The second patient recovered his lost autobiographical memories in a flash on a tennis court – all thanks to a mistake that reminded him of a similar error years ago. These aren't quite the same thing as a curative second knock to the head, but if true (and it's not clear how thoroughly they've been verified) they are certainly bizarre instances of sudden recovery.

Dieguez and Annoni argue "the view that literary amnesia is clinically inaccurate or far-fetched is at best too simplistic, and at worst misguided." They make the point that studying fictional depictions of amnesia is scientifically informative because it reveals how people think about memory and identity. In turn, these fictional depictions may actually end up influencing how memory disorder manifests, especially in cases of psychogenic amnesia. Indeed, as we heard earlier, this may be exactly what happened to the patient studied by Christine Smith and her colleagues, who believed her memory was wiped clean each night. "Whether and how entirely new types of amnesia can be invented and spread through society, perhaps under the influence of fictional and artistic depictions is an interesting question," Dieguez and Annoni conclude.

Other Forms of Amnesia

In 2011, the news was filled with amusing but shocking headlines like this from ABC: "Mind-Blowing Sex Causes Amnesia in 54-Year-Old Woman." It sounded like a bad joke but was actually based on a genuine case study reported in the *Journal of Emergency Medicine*.[18] The authors of the paper, Kevin Maloy and Jonathan Davis, described how the woman arrived at hospital complaining that she was unable to recall anything from the 24 hour period preceding the moment that she climaxed during recent sex with her husband. Her symptoms soon faded and the researchers diagnosed transient global amnesia (TGA). This is a rare form of temporary amnesia usually caused by disrupted blood flow to areas of the brain involved in memory function. Other forms of strenuous activity, a minor knock to the head, or even immersion in cold water, can all trigger TGA. The good news is that the symptoms usually pass quickly and the experience tends not to return.

Another form of amnesia arises from Korsakoff's syndrome, a condition most often suffered by alcoholics who don't have enough vitamin B1 in their diet. Some medics call it "alcohol amnesic syndrome." Korsakoff's can lead to both anterograde and retrograde amnesia. Another key feature of the condition is "confabulation" – patients will make up stories to fill in the blanks in their memory.

Finally, it's worth noting a form of amnesia that we all experience, which is our inability to remember the first few years of our lives. For most people, their earliest memories are from when they were aged three- to four-years old. You could travel the world with an infant and it's almost guaranteed that when they get older they won't remember a single boat trip, plane ride, or sunset. Psychologists have struggled to explain this "infantile amnesia," especially since three-year-olds are perfectly capable of remembering events from a year earlier. This observation suggests the memories were in long-term storage but for some reason are gradually lost as the child develops. Perhaps that's why the boundaries of infantile amnesia shift with age, so that younger children report earlier first memories than older children, and children of all ages report earlier first memories than adults.

A groundbreaking study published online in 2013[19] suggested that this forgetting process usually kicks in around age 7. The researchers at Emory University recorded mothers talking to their three-year-olds about past events such as zoo visits or first day at pre-school. The researchers then caught up with the same families again, when the children were aged 5, 6, 7, 8, or 9 years, and recorded the mothers attempting to discuss the exact same topics with their children.

At ages 5 to 7, the children remembered over 60 percent of the events they'd chatted about at age 3, but their recall was immature in the sense of containing few evaluative comments and few mentions of time and place. By ages 8 and 9, the children recalled fewer than 40 percent of the events they'd discussed at age 3 – a sign that infantile amnesia had really taken hold – although those memories they did recall were more adult-like in their content. One possibility is that the immature form of recall seen at ages 5 to 7 could actually contribute to the forgetting of autobiographical memories – a process known as "retrieval-induced forgetting." Interestingly, mothers who used a more elaborative style when chatting to their children at age 3 – for example, they said things like "tell me more" – tended to have children who recalled more earlier memories later on.

This last observation complements prior research suggesting that cultural factors are also relevant to the process of infantile amnesia. For example, a study[20] by researchers at the University of Otago found that the age of the earliest first memories claimed by participants differed between New Zealand European, New Zealand Maori, and Asian samples. Maori participants have a culture that places high value on the past and it is they who claimed to have the earliest first memories of all. No effort was made by the researchers to verify the veracity of these first memories so this needs to be checked in future. However, alongside the Emory University study showing the influence of mothers' conversational style, it certainly seems plausible that a greater cultural emphasis on the value of the past could lead to a delay in the onset of infantile amnesia, or at least a weakening of its effects.

More Memory Myths

Myth: Traumatic Memories Are Usually Repressed

Although victims of trauma may strive not to recall or discuss their painful memories, the idea that such memories are routinely repressed by the brain is untrue. A worrying study from 2007[21] found that abuse memories "recovered" in therapy were less likely to be corroborated than forgotten abuse memories remembered outside of therapy or never-forgotten abuse memories. This substantiates the fear some experts have that abuse memories apparently recovered in therapy are often the result of suggestion. In 2014, the American Psychological Association website states that: "there is a consensus among memory researchers and clinicians that most people who were sexually abused as children remember all or part of what happened to them although they may not fully understand or disclose it."

Myth: Memory Works Like a Video Recorder

Simons's and Chabris's 2011 survey[22] found that 52.7 percent of the public agreed with the statement "human memory works like a video camera, accurately recording the events we see and hear so that we can review and inspect them later" (their 2012 survey[23] found that only 46.9 percent of people agreed with the myth so there may be some progress here, unless this was merely something to do with this later sample being recruited online). The truth is, unlike a recording, memory is an active, creative, reconstructive process. For this reason it is also extremely vulnerable to suggestion and misinformation.

Myth: There Is Such a Thing as Photographic Memory

World memory champions who can memorize and recall strings of tens of thousands of digits are often described colloquially as having a photographic memory. In fact, their performance depends on hours of practice and the use of mnemonic strategies that turn meaningless information into highly memorable images. A related concept is eidetic memory – the claim that some people are able to retain in memory a photograph-like after-image of a scene. Apparently more common in children than adults, there is research showing that eidetic imagery is associated with more accurate recall.[24] However, there is no evidence that these people have perfect recall. A 1985 study,[25] typical of the field, tested 11 German child "Eidetikers" and found that none of them could name all the letters that had featured in a scene they'd studied.

Myth: Flashbulb Memories Are Highly Accurate

Memories for highly emotive events, such as 9/11 or the day Michael Jackson died, are often referred to as flashbulb memories because of their unusual persistence and vividness. Despite these qualities, at least one study suggests such memories are no more accurate than normal. Researchers at Duke University showed this[26] when they asked students on September 12, 2001 about their memories of the attacks and a recent everyday memory. Weeks or months later, the students were tested again on their memories for the attacks (a flashbulb memory) and the earlier everyday memory. The results showed the students were more confident in their memories from 9/11 but in fact just as much forgetting had occurred for these memories as for the everyday memory.

Myth #37

Coma Myths

Coma and Vegetative State

Coma is a medical term used to describe a "disorder of consciousness" in which a person is still alive but lacks any wakefulness or awareness. Causes of this tragic state include severe brain injury, stroke, infection, heart failure, and drug poisoning. To see a loved one apparently trapped in limbo between life and death is unbearably distressing for family and friends. Like other medical conditions involving the brain, coma is often misunderstood and subject to mythical distortion in popular fiction. Unfortunately, these distortions can interfere with the desperately difficult ethical decisions that doctors and families are forced to make about how to treat and care for a person in a coma.

Coma Facts

Coma occurs when the reticular system in the brain stem is damaged. As a result, patients' brains no longer show any signs of a sleep/wake cycle, their eyes are usually closed, and they are utterly unresponsive and unaware. Coma is frequently confused with the persistent vegetative state (PVS), in which the brain is severely damaged but the reticular system is intact. In PVS, the patient is unaware and almost entirely unresponsive, but his or her brain shows evidence of a sleep/wake cycle. Coma is also often confused with a "locked-in state," in which a profoundly paralyzed patient is fully conscious and mentally intact.

Most coma patients who go on to make a significant recovery wake up within a few days of their original injury or infection. If they survive but don't awaken, they will often progress to a vegetative state. Whereas the eyes are nearly always shut in coma, a vegetative patient's eyes are open when they are awake and closed when they sleep. The periods of "wakefulness" can be confusing for family and friends because it can seem as if the person must also be aware. When awake, vegetative patients also often move their face, eyes, and limbs involuntarily, which can also raise hopes. Sometimes they may also make groaning sounds, respond to noises, and even momentarily track moving targets with their eyes. Crucially, if they are diagnosed as being in a vegetative state, then these responses are considered purely reflex and not signs of any genuine awareness.

Of course, it is impossible to know truly the contents and state of another person's mind and so the issue of diagnosing disorders of consciousness is fraught with difficulty and dependent on careful testing. If it is believed that a vegetative patient has some rudiments of awareness – for example, they appear to respond to very simple commands – then this is classified as a minimally conscious state – a term that was introduced in 2002. Diagnostic errors are said to be high in this field, with some studies suggesting that up to half of minimally conscious patients are misdiagnosed as being in a vegetative state. In reality, the boundaries among coma, vegetative state, and minimally conscious state are rarely clear cut.

Differences between the disorders of consciousness can appear in brain scans, and recordings of the brain's electrical activity (using EEG). Coma patients show drastically reduced metabolic activity in the brain, resembling the activity levels you see in a person under general anesthesia. This loss of metabolic activity is also significant, but less extreme, in the vegetative and minimally conscious states. Patients in a minimally conscious state also show more extensive activity in higher brain areas when they are spoken to, as compared with patients in a vegetative state. Minimally conscious patients and some vegetative patients also show spikes of activity in an EEG scan when their name is spoken.

Recently, brain imaging has been used to communicate with patients previously diagnosed as being in a vegetative state (see also p. 189). In one groundbreaking study[27] a patient's brain was scanned while at the same time she was asked to imagine playing tennis or walking around her home. These two forms of visualization led to different patterns of brain activity in the patient, just as is seen in healthy participants. This provides a strong indication that the patient, previously assumed to be without awareness, had heeded the task instructions. In a later study,[28] another vegetative patient appeared able to use these contrasting forms of imagery to answer yes or no to a series of questions.

These results are exciting and are interpreted by some as suggesting that vegetative patients have previously hidden levels of awareness. Those of a more skeptical persuasion argue it is more likely that the vegetative patients had simply been misdiagnosed and had in fact recovered to a minimally conscious state. Issues of diagnosis aside, there is also uncertainty over whether these apparent feats of communication mean the patients are consciously aware in the same sense as you or me.

Coma Myths

In the film *Kill Bill Volume 1*, Uma Thurman's character "The Bride" is left in a four-year coma after being shot in the head. Typical of Hollywood, when the audience sees Thurman's comatose character lying in a hospital bed, she looks groomed, healthy, and there are few signs of the extensive medical equipment and procedures that would likely be required to keep her alive, such as feeding tubes or a tracheotomy (an incision in the neck that aids breathing). Most farfetched is the way the vengeful bride suddenly awakens from her coma to almost normal functioning, save for some initial weakness in her legs.

In their 2006 paper,[29] Eelco Wijdicks and Coen Wijdicks analyzed 30 movies, including *Kill Bill*, released between 1970 and 2004, and found that this kind of unrealistic depiction of coma was virtually ubiquitous (one rare exception praised for its coma portrayal was the 1998 film *Dream Life of Angels*). Across the 30 films, all comatose patients, bar one, were shown to be healthy looking, muscular, and tanned. Personally, I think the award for most healthy looking coma patient of all time must go to the tanned and luxuriantly eye-browed Peter Gallagher, in the 1995 movie *While You Were Sleeping*. In the Wijdicks's analysis, all long-term coma patients were shown apparently asleep with their eyes closed – in other words, there were no realistic portrayals of patients in a persistent vegetative state. Missing were the groaning noises, grimaces, and contorted hands and limbs (known as "contractures") that are frequently experienced by these patients in reality. Also there were rarely signs of the medical equipment and complications involved in coma care. "Not showing the muscle atrophy, decubital ulcers, bladder and bowel incontinence, and gastronomy [feeding tubes] may be a conscious decision to maximize entertainment," said Wijdicks and Wijdicks, "but is a disservice to the viewer." Finally, as in *Kill Bill* and *While You Were Sleeping*, many comatose characters woke and got up suddenly as if simply rising from a deep sleep.

Worryingly, when the father and son team of Wijdicks and Wijdicks showed these coma clips to 72 film viewers, they found they were unable to spot inaccuracies in one third of the clips. Moreover, over a third of the viewers said they'd use the cinematic portrayals to guide their ethical decisions relating to a coma patient in real life.

Depictions of coma are also unrealistic on TV. For a 2005 paper,[30] David Casarett and his colleagues analyzed nine US soap operas shown between 1995 and 2005 and found scenes involving 64 coma patients. The shows they analyzed included *General Hospital, Passions*, and *The Bold and the Beautiful*. Casarett's main concern was with the unrealistic levels of recovery depicted in the soap operas. For instance, of 16 coma characters who'd suffered a traumatic brain injury, only one died, whereas real-life data show that around 67 percent of such patients usually die from their injuries. When patients were portrayed awaking from coma, 86 percent had no initial residual disabilities, and in the end, every one recovered fully. Yet in reality, the researchers pointed out that patients awaking from a non-traumatic coma (i.e. from infection or drug poisoning) recover fully only 10 percent of the time.

As a general rule, the longer a patient is in a coma, vegetative or minimally conscious state, the slimmer his or her chances of recovery. For coma arising from non-traumatic causes, if the patient has yet to recover after three months, then his or her chances of ever regaining awareness are thought to be very slim. The former Prime Minister of Israel, Ariel Sharon, who died in 2014 after eight years in a coma, is illustrative of the more typical (and unhappy) prognosis for long-term coma patients. Prognosis after traumatic-induced coma is more hopeful but still nowhere near the levels seen in TV dramas – after 12 months without recovery the odds of waking are thought to be miniscule. Overall, a majority of vegetative patients die within five years, although some have been known to survive for decades. Many families try to assist the chances of recovery by playing music to their comatose relative, or exposing them to evocative smells or pictures. Sadly, these kinds of interventions seem to be ineffective.

"In the interests of public health," Casarett and his colleagues concluded, "soap operas and other forms of mass media should seek to balance stories of improbable survival and recovery with compelling and compassionate stories of characters who die with comfort and dignity."

Ethical Dilemmas

The public's beliefs about coma recovery and their understanding of a coma or vegetative patient's levels of awareness are important because of the difficult decisions that often have to be made about a patient's treatment. Patients in coma or a vegetative or a minimally conscious state usually depend on sustained medical care for survival. The usual protocol is to continue life-sustaining treatment indefinitely if it is understood that that is what the patient would have wanted. Inevitably there are times when the patient's own wishes are unclear, and family members can end up disagreeing about whether to continue treatment or withdraw it. (In 2005 the world watched as the family of Terri Schiavo, a Florida woman who suffered severe brain damage following a cardiac arrest, faced this very situation.) This is where relatives' religious beliefs, their understanding of a coma patient's levels of awareness and suffering, and their beliefs about recovery chances – potentially skewed by fictional portrayals – can influence decision making.

Revealing insights into the way some people think about patients in a vegetative state come from a study published in 2011 by Kurt Gray and colleagues.[31] In an initial experiment, 202 participants in New England read about a fictional man called David who had a car accident. Participants were further told either that he had died, or was left in a permanent vegetative state and would never wake up. Then they answered questions about his mental life – for example, whether he knew right from wrong and whether he had a personality. Those who read that David was in a vegetative state actually attributed to him less mental life than participants told that he had died. "These results suggest that patients in a permanent vegetative state are uniformly perceived to have mental functioning less than that of the dead," the researchers said.

Of course, the results of surveys like this are likely to vary in different cultures around the world. There's evidence, for instance, that doctors in Japan are more likely to advocate relentless attempts to sustain a coma or vegetative patient's life compared with doctors in the US or UK. Orthodox Jews and highly conservative Christians also tend to advocate sustaining life in all circumstances, even if it's believed the patient would prefer being allowed to die.

In a follow-up experiment, Gray's team had participants read a vignette about their own involvement in a car crash. The participants said they believed it would be worse for them and their families if they were to end up in a permanent vegetative state than to die in the crash. Gray's team also discovered an irony – highly religious participants were especially given toward attributing more mental life to a dead person than to a vegetative patient, and yet, as I mentioned already, it is ultra-religious people who are usually the most ardent campaigners for sustaining vegetative patients on life support.

Brain Death

A related issue that's relevant here is the concept of brain death. This is when a neurologist judges a person to be dead based on the condition of their brain in accordance with the Uniform Determination of Death Act (UDDA) drafted in 1981. Accepted by all 50 US States, this Act determines that a person is dead if either their cardiovascular functioning has ceased or their brain has irreversibly stopped functioning (see Plate 31). There is some international variation in the agreed criteria, but at a minimum, brain death is only diagnosed in the absence of any brain stem function and when the patient's condition is unequivocally irreversible. The issue of brain death has proven highly controversial in the past, largely because in many jurisdictions organ donation is permitted to ensue after a patient is declared brain dead. There was a furor in 1980 when the BBC broadcast a documentary "Transplants: Are the Donors Really Dead" in which some US experts claimed the UK criteria for brain death were too lax.

Note, brain death is not the same as vegetative state or coma. By definition a person in a vegetative state cannot be brain dead because functioning in their brain stem is spared and he or she shows associated periods of sleep and wakefulness. Brain-dead patients are also not in a coma. They do lack all awareness and wakefulness, as if in a coma, but their situation is irreversible and their lack of brain functioning is total – they are dead. Conversely, coma patients are not brain dead because some have preserved brain stem function, and as mentioned, many will awaken or progress to the vegetative state.

The media and general public are prone to confuse coma and vegetative states and brain death. In January 2014, for example, the *Daily Telegraph* in the UK reported[32] on a high-profile US case, with the subheading "Texas law forbids death of woman in vegetative state in order to preserve life of child." In fact the pregnant woman had been declared brain dead, so she was not in a vegetative state (her family ultimately won the right for her artificial ventilators to be switched off). A related misunderstanding is to refer to brain death as only a half-way house toward "real death" or final death. For example, consider this from *The New York Times* in 2005:[33] "That evening Mrs. Cregan was declared brain-dead. The family had her respirator disconnected the next morning, and she died almost immediately." Surveys show that the general public and also a surprising number of medical professionals do not realize that US law and current medical consensus states that brain death is death. This is despite the fact that many elements within mainstream Judaism, Islam, and Christianity accept the notion of brain death as death.

It is easy to understand why there is so much confusion. Many people implicitly associate life with breathing and heart function, and to see a person breathing (albeit with artificial support) and to be told they are in fact dead can be difficult to comprehend. The ability after brain death to carry a fetus, for wounds to heal, and for sexual maturation to occur also adds to many people's incomprehension at the notion that brain dead means dead. But for those more persuaded by the idea of death as irrevocably linked, not with brain function, but with the end of heart and lung activity, consider this unpleasant thought experiment (borrowed from an article by Samuel LiPuma and Joseph DeMarco[34]). If a decapitated person's body could be maintained on life support – with beating heart and circulating, oxygenated blood – would that person still be "alive" without their brain? And consider the converse – the classic "brain in a vat." Would a conscious, thinking brain, sustained this way, though it had no breath and no beating heart, be considered dead? Surely not. Such unpalatable thought experiments demonstrate how brain death can actually be a more compelling marker of end of life than any perspective that focuses solely on bodily function.

Epilepsy Myths

Epilepsy is a relatively common neurological condition (50 million people are affected worldwide) associated with recurring aberrant electrical activity in the brain. Most often the cause is unknown, but can include brain injury, stroke, a brain tumor, or an inherited vulnerability. Depending on the type of epilepsy, the excessive electrical activity can spread across large parts of the brain or remain relatively localized. For the patient, each cerebral paroxysm or "electrical storm" manifests as a form of seizure, the precise nature of which will depend on the location and spread of the electrical activity. These seizures, which often involve a loss of consciousness, can be frightening and unpredictable for the patient and onlookers alike, so perhaps it's no wonder that through history the condition has attracted a great deal of folklore, superstition, and misinformation.

Today the majority (around 70 percent) of patients with epilepsy are able to control their seizures with medication or more radical treatments like neurosurgery (see p. 33), and many lead healthy and successful lives. Despite this, many myths and misunderstandings about epilepsy continue to thrive, as reflected in lay beliefs and in representations of the condition in newspapers, film, song, and on the Internet. In 2006,[35] a revealing analysis of US newspaper coverage of 11 neurological conditions found that epilepsy was the most likely to be subject to stigmatizing language.

Basic Myths and Facts

Beginning in ancient times, epilepsy was considered a form of possession by evil spirits or even gods – hence the Ancient Greeks referred to it as "the Sacred Disease." This myth would last for millennia, despite the fact that, first Hippocrates and then Galen, argued that it was a physical ailment.

Even as the medical interpretation of epilepsy came to dominate in the seventeenth century, it continued to be associated with mental illness and flaws of personality. As late as 1892,[36] a Dr Joseph Price wrote in a medical journal that its "origin outside of physical causes" could be traced to debauchery, chocolate, coffee, and amorous love songs. In the same era, some physicians castrated their epileptic patients, believing excess masturbation to be the cause. Even as interest in the neurological underpinnings of the condition intensified, its true basis remained elusive. Through the Victorian and Edwardian eras, the mistaken, favored neurological theory was that epilepsy is a vascular condition, caused by abnormalities in the flow of blood in the brain.

The 1930s were a key decade for modern understandings of the illness. The development by Hans Berger of electroencephalography (which measures the surface electrical activity of the brain) gave rise to the correct realization that the biological basis of epilepsy is the spread of uncontrolled electrical activity through the brain's neurons. Remarkably, however, it wasn't until the 1960s that the World Health Organization (WHO) made the first official classification of epilepsy as a neurological illness, as opposed to a mental illness.

Despite the WHO ruling, which is reflected in all modern diagnostic criteria, today many people still mistakenly think of epilepsy as a form of mental illness, especially in developing countries. For instance, a 2009 survey of 164 people in Cameroon found that 62.8 percent thought epilepsy was "a form of insanity."[37] Another survey, published in 2007, of 16 044 people living in various parts of Jordan found that 9 percent believed people with epilepsy are insane.[38] And a survey in Greece, published in 2006, reported that 15 percent believed the condition is a form of insanity.[39] Many of these kinds of surveys also reveal evidence of extreme stigma toward epilepsy – including people not wanting to employ someone with epilepsy, nor wanting their children to marry an epileptic person. A British survey published in 2004[40] of over 1600 people found that epilepsy was ranked second highest among the health conditions that the respondents would be most concerned about, in terms of a work colleague having the diagnosis (depression was top).

Although epilepsy is today categorized as a neurological illness, it is true that people with the condition are at increased risk for a range of mental health problems compared with the general population, including depression, suicide, and psychosis. At the same time, it's important to recognize that many people with epilepsy are free of any mental health problems, especially if seizures are brought under control. Where psychiatric problems do arise, the reasons are varied and may be indirect. For instance, depression may result from the stigma of the illness or the restrictions it imposes on a person's life (in other words, people's prejudices toward epilepsy can become self-fulfilling as patients suffer the price of the stigma). Where psychosis co-occurs with epilepsy there are many possible reasons. For example, it can be related to the epileptic activity in the brain, or it can be a serious side effect of anti-convulsant medication, or there can be some other underlying cause.

A related myth concerns the links between epilepsy and learning difficulties, with many wrongly assuming that the two necessarily go hand in hand. It is true that epilepsy is more prevalent in people with learning difficulties (and those with autism) than in the general population, and epilepsy does often arise after a brain injury. There is also some evidence that serious seizures can have a cumulative harmful effect on the brain. However, the cognitive functioning and intelligence of many people with epilepsy is unaffected by their condition (apart from the acute effects experienced during a seizure).

A myth that's largely defunct in Western cultures but still prevalent in some developing countries is that epilepsy is contagious. A 1989 study[41] found that most Nigerians, including some medical students, considered epilepsy to be catching. For this reason, most people would usually flee a person seen having a seizure in a public place. The Cameroon survey I mentioned earlier found that 23 percent of respondents believed epilepsy is contagious. Other myths that persist in some traditional cultures are the idea that epilepsy is a punishment for moral transgressions, and paradoxically, that some people with epilepsy have divine powers (usually this is attributed to people with temporal lobe epilepsy, which can be associated with the patient having dream-like, religious experiences; see also p. 81).

Another form of mythology around epilepsy is the attribution of the illness to historical figures who never had it. For a review published in 2005,[42] neurologist John Hughes surveyed the evidence pertaining to 43 prominent people from the past who at one time or other have been described as epileptic. In each case, Hughes concludes on the basis of the available evidence that none of them really did suffer from epilepsy. Examples range from Aristotle (for whom Hughes found no evidence suggestive of epilepsy), to Isaac Newton (he was at times completely absorbed by work and he suffered from emotional problems, but he was not epileptic), to Charles Dickens (his seizures were caused by renal colic), to the actor Richard Burton (his seizures were caused by alcohol withdrawal). Notable figures who really did or do have epilepsy include Fyodor Dostoyevsky, the pop star Prince (who has talked publicly about his childhood epilepsy), the rock singer Neil Young (whose nickname was Shakey), and the contemporary British hurdler Dai Greene.

Portrayals of Epilepsy in Popular Culture

An important reason why misunderstandings about epilepsy continue to thrive is because of the way the condition is represented in literature, film, TV, and popular music. Analyzing the fates of epilepsy patients in modern literature Peter Wolf[43] found recurring themes including patients as victims (e.g. in Patricia Cornwell's *From Potter's Field*); as scapegoats (e.g. Agatha Christie's *The Murder on the Links*); and as divine children (e.g. P. D. James's *The Children of Men*). "There is a clear notion, among several authors," concluded Wolf, that people with epilepsy suffer twice, "as possible victims of … the seizures … and the aggression of other people." He added: "At the same time, the fates of people with epilepsy, especially children … are presented by some authors with unusual respect." For good or bad, in literary fiction, it seems people with epilepsy can't avoid being defined by their condition.

What about epilepsy at the cinema? For a review published in 2003,[44] Sallie Baxendale at the National Hospital for Neurology and Neurosurgery in London examined the way people with epilepsy were depicted in 62 movies released between 1929 and 2003 and spanning nine genres. Common themes were epilepsy as a character's fatal flaw (e.g. in the 2001 film *T'ien Hsia de Yi*, the Chinese Emperor Zhou, the last of his dynasty, has epilepsy); epileptic patients as murderous baddies (e.g. Tim Roth as the killer James Wayland in 1997's *Deceiver*); links between epilepsy and spirituality (e.g. 1991's *Vampire Trailer Park*, which features a detective's assistant who, during her seizures, makes contact with her dead grandmother); and, particularly in science-fiction films, epilepsy as a form of mind control (e.g. the 1974 film *The Terminal Man*, starring George Segal as an epileptic computer programmer who has his brain connected to a computer). Baxendale noted how this last theme "of possession by an external force has a fascinating parallel with ancient ideas of demonic possession."

Baxendale has also analyzed references to epilepsy and seizures in modern popular music.[45] Again, she found evidence in song lyrics linking the condition with madness (e.g. in *Howl of the Profound Past*, the group Meressin sing "Full uncontrolling of myself / Seizure of strangers from within / Violence of the mind in the ways of sufferings") and low intelligence (e.g. in *Lets Get Retarded*, the Black Eyed Peas sing: Ya'll test this drill, Just and bang your spine / Bob your head like epilepsy, up inside your club or in your Bentley). In certain cultures, especially hip hop, Baxendale also found evidence that the language of epilepsy had been appropriated for new uses, for example, in conveying "sexual ecstasy and dance abandon."

Unsurprisingly, epileptic fits are also a common occurrence in popular medical TV dramas including *ER*, *House MD*, *Private Practice*, and *Grey's Anatomy*. A team led by Andrew Moeller at Dalhousie University analyzed all the episodes of these dramas broadcast between 2004 and 2009, finding 65 depictions of epilepsy.[46] Unfortunately, when first aid was delivered in the programs, usually by a health professional, it was done so in an inappropriate manner 57.1 percent of the time – for instance, attempts were made to stop the patient's seizure-induced movements, the patient was held down, or something was inserted in his or her mouth, ostensibly to prevent choking.

All these are condemned practices according to modern expert guidelines, such as those issued by the Epilepsy Foundation of America. If you do witness a person having a tonic-clonic seizure (see box for seizure terminology), the correct thing to do is to time the seizure; clear the area around the person of dangerous objects or furniture; put something soft underneath his or her head; turn the person gently on his or her side; and be reassuring when he or she returns to consciousness, including offering to call a friend or taxi. It's only necessary to call an ambulance if the seizure lasts more than five minutes, you know it's their first seizure, they injure themselves, or you can clearly see there's some other reason for urgent medical attention.

Unfortunately, there's evidence that misleading TV portrayals of epilepsy have influenced the viewing public, which could have serious real-life implications for the way people respond to the sight of a person having a seizure. With her colleague Annette O'Toole, Baxendale[47] published the results of a public survey in 2007 with the revealing title: "Epilepsy Myths: Alive and Foaming in the 21st Century." Responses from 4605 Brits showed that two thirds would call an ambulance immediately if they saw a person having an epileptic fit; one in three said they'd try to put something in the person's mouth; and nearly 14 percent believed that a person usually or always foams at the mouth when they have a seizure (in reality this is rare).

Sadly, prejudice and misinformation about epilepsy is also making its way onto social media. Kate McNeil and her colleagues at Dalhousie University identified over 10 000 tweets[48] recorded over a 7-day period in 2011 that mentioned either the word "seizure" or "seizures." Forty-one percent of these were metaphorical or jokey references to seizures derogatory in tone, such as "my Blackberry just had a seizure" or "what do you do when someone's having a seizure in the bathtub? Throw in the laundry." Recent decades have seen "significant strides in eliminating offensive terms for other medical conditions," the researchers said, "but there is a definite lag in this regard for seizures and epilepsy."

On a more positive note, in 2013 an analysis of YouTube videos depicting seizures or seizure-related information found that the vast majority (85%) were positive or sympathetic in nature, either providing personal accounts of living with epilepsy, or educational information, or depictions of the condition.[49] This compared with 9 percent rated as neutral and 6 percent derogatory. The researchers led by Victoria Wong at Oregon Health and Science University said this more positive picture was likely due to the fact that YouTube allows users to generate their own content. Concluding their paper, the researchers struck an optimistic tone – "the present popularity of Internet media, such as video content, will play a large role in influencing the public perception of epilepsy, as prior forms of media including books, movies, and television have done before." Campaigners are also becoming more creative in their efforts to educate the public about epilepsy. In 2014, for instance, the London-based photographer Matt Thompson published a photographic ebook featuring his former partner, Helen Stephens, who has epilepsy. Accompanied by extracts from Helen's personal diary, the book shows the emotional toll that the condition can take: www.mattthompson. co.uk/helen-s-story.

Types of Epileptic Seizure

When uncontrolled electrical activity is localized to a specific part of the brain, this is known as a *focal* or *partial seizure*. The accompanying symptoms vary and depend on the source of the epileptic activity and where it spreads. It may or may not be associated with a loss of awareness. Other symptoms can include, but are not limited to: involuntary movements, feeling sick, flashbacks, and unusual sensory experiences. Telling sensations predictive of an imminent seizure are known as an *aura*. When epileptic activity is located across both brain hemispheres, this is known as a *generalized seizure*, which is usually associated with a loss of consciousness. The most common form of generalized seizure (and the kind that most people picture when they imagine a seizure) is a *tonic-clonic seizure*. The tonic phase is when all the muscles of the body go stiff causing the person having the seizure to fall to the floor. The clonic phase occurs as the muscles tighten and relax in spasms. Another type of generalized seizure is the *absence seizure*, in which consciousness is lost for just a few seconds. People nearby might not even realize what has happened. In a *myoclonic seizure*, the whole body or, more often, a particular limb, jerks involuntarily (many people without epilepsy experience these movements upon falling asleep). There are also *atonic seizures* in which the whole body goes limp, usually for just a few moments. Another category to be aware of is the *reflex epilepsies* when a person's seizures are triggered by a particular cue or cues in the environment. Flashing lights would be one example, although triggers can also be internal – such as a particular thought or memory. Contrary to popular belief, photosensitive epilepsy is rather rare, affecting only 3 in 100 people with epilepsy. Lastly, there are *psychogenic non-epileptic seizures*. These often have the appearance of a tonic-clonic seizure, except there's no accompanying abnormal electrical activity in the brain. The patient is usually not acting: the seizure is involuntary and loss of consciousness may also occur. The cause is usually thought to be emotional distress or psychological trauma of some kind.

Myth #39 Autism Myths

First described by US psychiatrist Leo Kanner in 1943, autism (now formally called autism spectrum disorder) is a neurodevelopmental condition characterized by a triad of behavioral traits: social difficulties, communication problems, and repetitive, rigid behaviors and interests. The first reliable behavioral signs of the condition usually appear in the third year of life. Autism is incredibly heterogeneous and is now widely seen as a spectrum that overlaps with variation seen in the "normal" population.

At one extreme you might find an individual unable to speak and whose social skills and narrow interests severely impact their ability to live an independent life. At the other are those people previously diagnosed with Asperger's syndrome (Asperger's as a separate diagnosis was dropped from US psychiatry's latest diagnostic manual published in 2013), who may appear socially awkward, enjoy routine, and have intense interests, but who are perfectly capable of independent living, and may well excel in their chosen profession. Around one in a hundred people are now thought to have a diagnosis of an autistic spectrum disorder.

Myth: Everyone with Autism Has a Rare Gift

Before the 1980s most people hadn't heard of autism. Then along came the Oscar-winning film *Rain Man*. Suddenly the profile of autism was elevated enormously – a good thing – but at the same time, the film presented a distorted version of the condition. The character "Raymond Babbitt" played by Dustin Hoffman in *Rain Man* appears to have a severe form of autism together with extraordinary powers of recall and calculation. In psychiatric jargon, he is an autistic savant. In one particularly memorable scene Babbitt deduces in an instant the precise number of tooth picks – 246 – that a waitress drops on the ground.

High-profile real-life individuals with autism, including the animal welfare scholar Temple Grandin, math genius Daniel Tammet, and the city-scape artist Stephen Wiltshire, have further encouraged the mistaken belief among many people that giftedness is a key component of autism. Estimates vary, but according to the National Autistic Society (NAS) in the UK, the reality is that around 0.05 percent of people with autism have a truly outstanding savant ability. More common is the presence of relatively good performance on certain tasks (so-called "splinter skills"), such as rote memory or absolute pitch, against a background of low general IQ.

The real-life individual who provided the inspiration for *Rain Man* was in fact a non-autistic savant[50] named Kim Peek, who died in 2009 aged 58. Peek had brain abnormalities including a malformed cerebellum and a missing corpus callosum – the bundle of fibers that connect the two brain hemispheres. He was impaired, including having difficulty with abstract and conceptual thinking, and even buttoning his own clothes. But Peek – his friends nicknamed him "Kim-puter" – also had astonishing mental abilities, including calendar calculating (the ability to name the day of the week of any given date), and an encyclopedic memory. It's estimated he'd read and memorized over 12 000 books in his lifetime.

Rain Man was hugely successful and has inspired countless more fictional autistic savants. In recent years, Kiefer Sutherland has starred in the Fox series *Touch* as the father of 11-year-old Jake who is mute and "emotionally challenged," but also obsessed by numbers and able to see "the hidden patterns that connect every life on the planet." In their 2012[51] analysis of autism at the movies, Rory Conn and Dinesh Bhugra identified other examples, including the mathematical genius in *Mercury Rising* (1998); the eponymous Molly (1999) who counts millions of street lights in an instant and has supersonic hearing; and the girl Sally in *House of Cards* (1993) who can construct impossibly intricate buildings out of cards and has superhuman reflexes.

Reflecting on Hollywood's obsession with super-gifted autistic people, Shannon Rosa (co-founder of the Thinking Person's Guide to Autism blog) told the io9 website:[52] "People can't handle the fact that some people are just different without having something fabulously acceptable as balance, because otherwise we'd just have to accept autistic people on their own terms, and that's hard and challenging and takes patience and work."

Myth: Autism Is Caused by the MMR Vaccine

The film *House of Cards* commits another common error – confusing diagnostic categories. Sally develops her problems (mutism and emotional detachment) and super abilities after her father dies, thereby implying that her autism is a kind of traumatic or grief-related disorder. In reality autism is not caused in this way. Neither is it caused by "refrigerator mothers" – the ill-judged psychoanalytic theory proposed in the 1950s that autism is a reaction to a cold, unaffectionate mother.

Autism is a condition associated with atypical development of the brain including, but not limited to, excess white matter connections. The nature and significance of these brain differences is not yet understood – virtually every brain area has been implicated in autism at one time or another.

The causes of the atypical brain development in autism are complex and reflect a mix of genetic and environmental factors. The condition is more prevalent in boys than girls, by a factor of four to one, which has implicated genes on the male Y chromosome. Twin studies have also shown that each element of the autistic triad (social impairments, communications difficulties, and repetitive behaviors) is linked with different genes.

It is in the search for environmental risk factors that dangerous myths have taken root. Most harmful have been the persistent claims by the disgraced British pediatrician Andrew Wakefield and others that autism is caused by the triple MMR (measles, mumps, rubella) vaccine. The fears escalated with publication by Wakefield and his co-authors of a small study in the Lancet medical journal in 1998. Based on their investigations of 11 boys and 1 girl with gastrointestinal complaints – nine diagnosed as autistic – the authors implied that MMR may play a causal role in autism.

The 1998 paper generated huge media interest but is now known to be not only scientifically limited but also fraudulent.[53] It was fully retracted by the Lancet in 2010. Several studies[54] involving thousands of children have since failed to identify any link between the MMR vaccine and risk of autism. A statement by the American Academy of Pediatrics published in

2009 said: "While it is likely that there are many environmental factors that influence the development of autism, vaccines are not the cause of autism."

Ongoing work by investigative journalist Brian Deer has also exposed Wakefield's conflicts of interest – prior to 1998 he'd filed patents for single-shot vaccines and was in the pay of solicitors acting for parents who wished to sue the manufacturers of MMR. In 2010, after a lengthy inquiry by the General Medical Council in the UK, Wakefield was found guilty of numerous charges of dishonesty and failing to fulfill professional duties, and was struck off the doctors' register.

The cost of Wakefield's fraudulent science and campaigning has been great: vaccination rates plummeted in the UK, USA, and elsewhere, putting many children at risk of measles outbreaks. These problems continue to this day. In Wales in 2013, a measles epidemic related to reduced vaccination rates affected over a thousand children, prompting health officials to say they were "hugely concerned." Recent years have also seen claims from sections of the media and parent groups, about a causal link between thiomersal-containing vaccines and autism. Thiomersal is a mercury-based preservative that stops vaccines from becoming infected with microbes. The scientific consensus, backed by the Institute of Medicine, the World Health Organization, and others, is that thiomersal-containing vaccines do not cause autism.

Myth: There Is an Autism Epidemic

"Are we facing an autism epidemic?" asked the *Daily Mail* in 2003, before linking the rise in diagnoses with the MMR vaccine. "Autism epidemic being ignored," claimed the *Daily Telegraph* in 2007. It is true the prevalence of autism has sky-rocketed over the last few decades. A UK study published in 1966 put the figure at around 4.5 cases per 10 000, whereas the current prevalence is estimated at around one in a hundred. The latest US data published in 2014 put the prevalence at 1 in 68 (up from 1 in 150 in 2002).

However, a large part of the increase is thought to be due to increased awareness of the condition and a gradual broadening of the diagnostic criteria over time, taking in ever larger numbers of people who might previously have been considered merely unusual or to fit some other diagnosis, rather than autistic. For example, when "infantile autism" was first introduced formally into psychiatry's diagnostic manual in 1980, it required that the child have a language impairment. This changed in 1994 with the introduction of the separate diagnosis of "Asperger's syndrome" – a mild form of autism associated with high functioning and normal or near-normal language development. In 2013, the situation changed again, as the Asperger's diagnosis was swallowed up by the new diagnosis of Autistic Spectrum Disorder, which accommodates people with autism of various degrees of severity.

The way the diagnosis of autism has changed over time is illustrated by a clever study published by Dorothy Bishop and her colleagues in 2008.[55] The researchers contacted young adult participants who'd taken part as children in research Bishop had conducted years ago into "specific language impairment." This is a developmental diagnosis made when language delays exist in the absence of other problems, including autism. Bishop's team assessed their former participants – now young adults – using modern autism diagnostic tests. They also found out more about their former participants' behavior as children by interviewing their parents. The revealing result was that many of the former participants (21% or 66% depending on use of one or two modern autism tests) now reached the criteria for an autism diagnosis. They fulfilled these autism criteria largely because of behaviors and symptoms they'd in fact displayed since childhood. This shows how today's criteria attribute an autism diagnosis to more people today, compared with 10 or 20 years ago.

Raised awareness is also thought to explain the occurrence of autism clusters – such as the area in West Hollywood, California that has rates of the condition at four times normal levels. According to a report in *Nature*, it can't be the water because the district shares a supply with neighboring regions with normal autism levels.[56] At least one expert, sociologist Peter Bearman, thinks it has to do with an intensification of autism awareness in a particular neighborhood. In turn this attracts autism specialists to the area and other families who are affected by the condition.

"The jury is still out," Professor Uta Frith – one of the world's leading authorities on autism – told me. "But to me it looks like the increase in autism numbers can be explained by broadening of criteria, increased awareness, earlier diagnosis, etc. It remains to be seen if there is a real increase in incidence."

If something else is going on to explain the rise in autism – and certainly there are experts who think so – the other causes remain largely a mystery (air pollution is one possible environmental risk factor according to a small study published in 2013). Large-scale investigations are underway that may shed light on the question, including the Study to Explore Early Development, funded by the CDC and the Early Autism Risk Longitudinal Investigation (earlistudy.org), funded by the NIH and "dedicated to studying families that already have a child with an autism spectrum disorder ... [where the mother is] pregnant or ... might become pregnant in the future." These studies aim to pick apart the interaction between genetic risks and environmental factors that combine to give rise to autism.

Unfortunately, as we've heard, the mystery and for some people, fear, around the fast rise in autism has led to myths like the MMR scare story. Another example is Professor Susan Greenfield's suggestion that the rise in autism may be related to the ubiquity of screen technologies. "I point to the increase in autism and I point to Internet use. That's all," she told *The Observer*.[57] As I mentioned in Chapter 6, so dismayed was she by Greenfield's speculations, Dorothy Bishop was moved to write publicly to Greenfield. "You may not realize just how much illogical garbage and ill-formed speculation parents are exposed to," she wrote, before pointing out the fundamental flaws in Greenfield's hypothesis – the rise in autism predates the spread of the Internet, and signs of autism appear before children start using the Internet.

Myth: People with Autism Are Asocial and Uncaring

Fictional depictions of autism propagate a further hurtful myth, the idea that people with the condition are asocial and lack empathy. It is true that people on the autism spectrum often avoid eye contact and score lower on empathizing questionnaires that include items like "I prefer animals to humans." There is evidence[58] too that they are less prone to contagious yawns (although a recent study challenged this idea)[59] and display less automatic facial mimicry when watching other people's emotions.[60]

However, psychologists distinguish between two aspects of empathy – the cognitive component, which is the mental skill of standing in another person's shoes; and the feeling or emotional component, which is about whether you are moved by another person's pain or happiness. Research suggests that children with autism struggle with the cognitive component but are normal on the feeling component. Children with psychopathic tendencies show the opposite pattern – they can work out what you're thinking and feeling but they don't show any concern for your needs or pain. Related to the mistaken idea that autistic people lack empathy is the "broken mirror" theory, which proposes that autism is caused by a malfunction of the mirror neuron system. A recent review[61] found virtually no evidence supporting this theory – the one exception being that autism is associated with less susceptibility to emotional contagion, including contagious yawning (see also p. 159).

Nicole Nicholsen a writer diagnosed with Asperger's, is among many on the autism spectrum who have aired their frustration at the low empathy myth. Writing on her Woman with Asperger's blog[62] she called the myth "particularly damaging" and went on to describe her own intense feelings. "I ache when I find my stressed-out fiancé at the end of a day," she said. "I ache when my coworkers experience deaths in their families or other difficulties in their lives. I ache when I hear the pain inside the work of some of the poets in my community."

It is a mistake to assume that people with autism are asocial, simply because they find face-to-face meetings difficult or stressful. Autistic people vary just like everyone else – some are more introverted, some more outgoing. The rise in social media and virtual communities has allowed many autistic folk to express their social instincts without the need to meet face-to-face or to follow the rules of social etiquette imposed by neurotypicals. "I think the virtual world is levelling the playing field – a lot of people use text rather than the speech function, so this may be allowing people with autism and Asperger's to slow down the flow of information," Simon Bignall, a psychologist who studies online communities, told me.[63] "It makes communication a bit like a flow of text messages: you have to be succinct, to the point and unambiguous, which suits people with a condition like autism."

Myth: Autism Is Only about Disability

Paradoxically, although many people associate autism with extraordinary giftedness, elements of the media, fiction writers, and even researchers also have a tendency to discuss autism purely in terms of disability and disorder. It is true that 10 percent of autistics are mute and 44 percent of adults with autism continue to live with their parents (according to a NAS survey in the UK). But to focus on rare gifts and extreme disability is to neglect the less sensational advantages to the condition: the benefits of an eye for detail and of having an obsessive fascination and persistence for a particular topic or challenge. Some companies, including Specialisterne in Denmark, are wising up to these advantages with deliberate policies to employ people with autism to work on software testing and programming.

The psychiatrist Laurent Mottron at the University of Montreal has written about the bias toward autism disability that exists in research.[64] He points out, for example, how different studies have identified the cortex as being thinner or thicker in the people with autism, and yet the difference is framed as a deficit either way. Actions speak louder than words and for over ten years Mottron has employed a researcher with autism named Michelle Dawson. Together they've written more than 13 journal papers and published several book chapters. Mottron describes how Dawson has a superior memory for data and the detail of past experiments, whereas his own strengths lie with generating ideas and new models. "Combining the two types of brains in the same research group is amazingly productive," he says.

Greater recognition of the advantages to autism has given rise to an "autism pride" movement and the concept of neurodiversity, whereby autism is seen as a distinct form of being rather than a disorder to be cured. The movement is celebrated on autism pride day every year on 18 June. Theirs is an important message, especially in celebrating the strengths of autism and in drawing attention to ways the world operates that may be insensitive to the perspective and needs of autistics. Just think how offensive newspapers headlines about miracle autism cures and autism screening must be for people who are proud to be autistic. But it's also important to remember the condition can be extremely difficult for many people and for their families. So it's a case of striking a balance and respecting differences. "To avoid talk of autism deficits may ultimately be a disservice" Professor Frith told me.

Myth: There Is a Miracle Cure

Just as there are dangerous myths concerning supposed causes of autism, so too there are unhelpful claims about fictitious "miracle cures" – everything from special diets and vitamins to injections of the hormone secretin; from homeopathy and intensive behavioral therapy (certainly beneficial for many, but not a cure) to swimming with dolphins. In their analysis of the way autism is represented in the print media from 1996 to 2005, talk of such cures was one of the key themes identified by Sandra Jones and Valerie Harwood at the University of Wollongong.[65] Unfortunately, many people with autism and their parents are driven by frustration and lack of support to experiment with therapies and interventions that lack a scientific evidence base. In a survey published by the autism research charity Autistica in 2013, a third of adults with autism said they'd resorted to interventions that they knew had no scientific foundation.

There aren't any miracle cures for autism but there are effective techniques for helping children with autism to communicate more effectively, including TEACCH, which uses environmental modifications to help nonverbal children learn, and visually presented information to give children a reassuring sense of what's going to happen next. There are also ways that people can learn to communicate better with autistic children, including using simple sentences and visual aids.[66] Speaking at the Royal Society in 2011, Professor Francesca Happé of the Institute of Psychiatry provided some perspective. "Expert enlightened education with understanding really works," she said, "these are miracles happening every day in our special schools and units around the country."

Myth #40 Dementia Myths

It's 1901 and a doctor asks his 51-year-old female patient her last name. "Auguste," she replies. But that's her first name. Later at lunch he asks her what she's eating. "Spinach," she says, though it's actually cauliflower and pork. Asked to write her name, she gets only as far as "Mrs." – the doctor has to remind her of the rest. "I have lost myself," she tells him.[67]

The patient was Auguste Deter, the first person ever diagnosed with Alzheimer's disease, and her doctor was Alois Alzheimer, the German researcher after whom the disease is named. When Auguste died, Alzheimer was able to examine her brain and he found it was ravaged with plaques and tangles of protein – pathological hallmarks that are still used to diagnose the disease at autopsy today (until recently, autopsy was the only way to confirm diagnosis of the disease but a scan that can detect the plaques was developed in 2012). The pathological process destroys neurons, especially in the hippocampus – a part of the brain that's important for memory – and the cortex. Eventually, the brain weight of a person with Alzheimer's may be reduced by 40 to 50 percent of its healthy size (see Plate 32).

Apart from some rare genetic forms of Alzheimer's, the cause of the disease is not known. The most popular theories focus on amyloid beta – the protein fragments that form in clumps or "plaques" between neurons. However, it's a confusing picture because while all people with Alzheimer's have these plaques, many people have the plaques without Alzheimer's.

Unfortunately, several drugs that target amyloid beta have so far proven unsuccessful, so the search for an effective treatment goes on. Promising avenues of research are focusing on the short chain subtype of amyloid beta called "oligomers," which it's thought might be primarily responsible for the destructive effects of Alzheimer's. Also, in 2013,[68] a team led by Stuart Lipton at the Sanford-Burnham Medical Research Institute, in La Jolla, California, published new results that suggested amyloid beta harms neurons by ramping up the sensitivity of receptors for the neurotransmitter glutamate. Further insights into amyloid beta's effects will hopefully lead to new advances.

Myth: Alzheimer's Is the Same Thing as Dementia

Alzheimer's is a neurodegenerative disease and the leading cause of dementia, with approximately 36 million people currently living with the condition worldwide. A common misconception is that Alzheimer's and dementia are one and the same thing. In fact, dementia is a rather vague term that describes a widespread, progressive loss of mental function. In the case of Alzheimer's, the loss of mental ability is usually gradual but relentless. The first signs are simple forgetfulness, but in later stages the patient will be severely impaired, confused, will struggle to recognize loved ones, and may experience hallucinations.

The next most common cause of dementia after Alzheimer's is vascular dementia, which accounts for around 20 percent of dementia cases around the world. Vascular dementia arises from a loss of adequate blood supply to the brain due to a narrowing of blood vessels.

Other forms of dementia include frontotemporal dementia, which is associated with loss of inhibition and changes to personality; semantic dementia, which particularly affects the temporal lobes and is associated with a loss of the meaning of words and knowledge about the world; dementia with Lewy bodies (clumps of protein); chronic alcoholism; and repeated brain injuries. The old-fashioned term "senile dementia" or "senility" simply refers to dementia in old age, with likely causes being Alzheimer's or vascular dementia.

Dementia has been recognized since at least Ancient Egyptian times and was associated with old age by the Ancient Greeks. Some say that the specific term dementia was coined by Philippe Pinel, the eighteenth century pioneering French psychiatrist, although others claim the word has much older origins. Notable sufferers of dementia of the Alzheimer type include US president Ronald Reagan, UK Prime Minister Harold Wilson, novelist Iris Murdoch (whose experience of Alzheimer's disease was described in memoir by her widower John Bayley, and made into a 2001 feature film), and in recent years the novelist Terry Pratchett, who has a rare form of Alzheimer's known as posterior cortical atrophy, which afflicts the rear of the brain.

Myth: Dementia Only Affects Old People

Another myth is that dementia only affects older people. It is true that the prevalence of dementia increases markedly with older age, but it can afflict younger people too. In the UK, the Alzheimer's Society states that the prevalence in people aged 40 to 64 is 1 in 1400; this rises dramatically to 1 in 100 among those aged 65 to 69; 1 in 25 in those aged 70 to 79; and 1 in 6 among the over eighties. There is a form of Alzheimer's disease known as "early onset" Alzheimer's that can strike people in their thirties, forties and fifties (this is the form of the disease that Auguste Deter had). In many cases the reason for the early onset is unknown, but some families have specific genes that predispose them to the illness. In 2012 researchers analyzed Deter's DNA preserved in microscope slides and found that she had one of these dominant genes for early onset Alzheimer's.[69]

A related contentious issue is the idea that dementia is an inevitable part of aging. Most experts and Alzheimer's charities claim this is false. Mental slowing and poorer memory are part of growing older, but these changes are not the same thing as dementia or Alzheimer's, they say. Supporting this, many people live into their eighties, nineties and beyond without any signs of dementia. Researchers at Northwestern University, USA are even studying[70] a group of volunteers in their eighties who they've dubbed "Super Agers" because their brains have remained so youthful and their mental performance so sharp, all of which challenges the idea of dementia as an inevitable part of aging.

There is a minority of experts who dissent from this mainstream view. We've seen that the prevalence of dementia increases dramatically with greater age and some think this is because the disease process of Alzheimer's is related to aging. For instance, George Bartzokis, a psychiatry researcher at the University of California, Los Angeles, believes that Alzheimer's is linked to the brain's increasing inability with age to maintain repair of the fatty insulation around neurons. If true, this would mean Alzheimer's would eventually afflict every brain that grew old enough that it's capacity for repair was significantly diminished.

Myth: People with Dementia Are Like Zombies

An unfortunate metaphor that has emerged in discussion of dementia of the Alzheimer type is the idea of the disease as a form of living death. In her 2011 paper,[71] Susan Behuniak of Le Moyne College, New York, points to books with titles like "*Alzheimer's Disease: Coping With a Living Death,*" "*The*

Living Dead: Alzheimer's in America," and *"A Curious Kind of Widow: Loving a Man With Advanced Alzheimer's."* It's a similar picture in the titles of papers about Alzheimer's used in nursing journals, such as "Caring for the 'Living Dead'" from *Nursing Spectrum* in 2004.

The temptation to refer to patients in this way is in a sense understandable – it can seem as if the person with advanced-stage Alzheimer's is lost even while his or her body lives on. Journalist Lauren Kessler (cited by Behuniak) recalls her own stigmatizing view of Alzheimer's when she started working as a resident assistant at an Alzheimer's care facility: "'When you lose your mind, you lose your self,' I would have said. 'Alzheimer's makes people into zombies,' I would have said. 'The walking dead. Give me anything, but spare me this disease I would have said.'" Fueling the zombie parallels are the constant media headlines about the rising threat of the disease as the population ages, provoking in people a growing fear of developing the illness. Just as characters in zombie films dread turning into one of the monsters, older people today fret about "senior moments" and the thought that they too might turn into another Alzheimer's victim.

But it's vital that we challenge this zombie narrative, says Behuniak. Referring to people with Alzheimer's in this way is "destructive," she says, "and supports the oppression of human beings by encouraging fear and disgust." Fear of Alzheimer's is understandable, but we should also strive to remain compassionate and to believe in the value of their lives. As Behuniak points out, this ties in with a very important difference between zombies and patients with Alzheimer's. The movie monsters are emotionless automatons, whereas people with Alzheimer's need people's support; moreover, they express emotion and provoke it in others. They are not brain dead (see p. 278). "Resistance to the zombie trope may be strengthened by emphasis on a kind of dependence that is built on sympathy and respect," says Behuniak.

From a statistical point of view, data published in 2013 also challenge the usual scare-mongering headlines about the inevitable rise in Alzheimer's disease. A team led by Carol Brayne tested a group of seniors in three English regions between 2008 and 2011 and found lower rates of dementia as compared with similarly aged seniors tested in those same regions between 1984 and 1994.[72] Coincidentally, a Danish study published the same year[73] found superior rates of cognition in a group of 95-year-olds tested in 2010 compared with a group of 93-year-olds tested a decade earlier. It's possible that better diet, better management of cardiovascular health and better education are helping to reduce rates of age-related dementia (including of the Alzheimer's type), although some experts remain skeptical until more data is in.

There Is Light in the Darkness

John Zeisel, President of the "I'm Still Here" Foundation and co-founder of ARTZ: Artists for Alzheimer's is a prominent champion of the idea that a life with Alzheimer's is still a "life worth living." Zeisel's message is all about recognizing and enjoying the spared capabilities and identities of people with Alzheimer's. For instance, people with Alzheimer's often derive great pleasure and comfort from the arts because their aesthetic tastes (and often their abilities too) are preserved. There are even reported cases[74] of people with frontotemporal dementia displaying new artistic talents in the early stages of their illness.

Consider a study published in 2008[75] by Andrea Halpern in which participants were asked to place three sets of eight art postcards in order of preference. Tested again two weeks later, 16 older people with probable Alzheimer's showed as much consistency in their preferences as did healthy control participants. "In judging artworks," Halpern concluded, "people with and without dementia really do know what they like."

There are other islands of preserved function in Alzheimer's, especially in the early stages, including aspects of implicit learning that can be exploited by specially tailored training programs to help patients adapt to their impairments. The appropriate rehabilitative approach is slow, repetitive, and paced over time so that learning resembles the way you learn to swim or ride a bike. A study published in 2004,[76] for example, found that patients with mild Alzheimer's improved by an average of 170 percent on tests of faces and names after a three-month training program. The training also had a beneficial effect on their sense of time and place.

"We all hope that we, and the people we love, will not develop Alzheimer's disease – and with good reason," wrote Zeisel in 2011.[77] "The truth, however, is that it is possible to have a decent life with Alzheimer's disease, even though most people don't believe it … In fact, a great many people in the first 10 years of this condition live their lives to the fullest – renewing and deepening relationships with those they love and who love them."

Dementia at the Movies

Hollywood does a fairly good job of conveying the memory and other impairments associated with dementia (usually of the Alzheimer's type), according to a 2007 analysis[78] of 24 films by Kurt Segers, a neurologist at Brugmann University Hospital in Brussels.

From *Where's Poppa* (1970) to *The Notebook* (2004), Segers finds a bias toward movie Alzheimer patients being female and well-educated – perhaps to maximize the drama involved in their deterioration. In showing the difficulties of dementia, an omission is the experience of visual hallucinations, while a favored plot device is characters going wandering. It's true that real-life patients with dementia do often get lost in this way, but Segers thinks there's another motive: "it gives the screenwriter the occasion to change rapidly and unexpectedly the story's location, to create tension and to introduce new characters and conflicts."

Where movie portrayals especially lack authenticity, Segers says, is in the strange absence of physicians, with only 58 percent of the films depicting the process by which dementia is diagnosed. "There is a remarkable therapeutic and even diagnostic nihilism" writes Segers, "often the patient and his family do not seem to find it important to consult a doctor, and even [when they do] ... therapeutic interventions and further follow-up of the patient are rarely mentioned."

Segers draws specific attention to how rarely films depict dementia patients being treated with psychotropic drugs (only 3 of 25 patients are seen to be treated this way). In real life, such drugs are frequently prescribed, especially in the latter stages of Alzheimer's. This is a controversial issue with campaigners arguing that use of drugs is often unnecessary, a "chemical cosh," or a substitute for care and kindness.

Overall, the lack of cinema's focus on the medical side of dementia reflects the fact that Alzheimer's remains one of the last medical taboos, Segers says. He adds that this mirrors the situation in real life, with surveys suggesting that only a minority of doctors reveal an Alzheimer's diagnosis to their patients.

A more up-to-date analysis of dementia portrayals in movies was published in 2014.[79] A team of psychologists led by Debby Gerritsen identified 23 relevant films broadcast between 2000 and 2012. These researchers noted that modern films tend to present "romantic portraits" of dementia. For example, patients' agitation is rarely portrayed, and in films like *The Notebook* (2004) severely impaired patients are depicted enjoying moments of full lucidity, often after encounters with a close relative – a kind of "love miracle" (to borrow a phrase from literary scholar Aagje Swinnen[80]).

The Chemical Imbalance Myth of Mental Illness

Misunderstanding and misuse of brain science are also found in the way that the media, general public and even many medical professionals think about mental illness. It's a tragic fact that the lives of many millions of people around the world are blighted by depression and anxiety. Wouldn't things be straightforward if their suffering were caused by a simple chemical imbalance in the brain, one that could be tweaked back to normality simply by popping a few pills? For many years that is precisely what many pharmaceutical companies and some psychiatrists would have had you believe. I had first-hand experience of this myth myself in 2014, at a class for parents expecting twins. In her warning about the perils of post-natal depression, the instructor told us with misplaced confidence that the condition was simply a "chemical imbalance" – a physical problem akin to sprained ankle.

Rewind ten years, and according to an advertisement broadcast on behalf of the drug company Pfizer, their widely taken anti-anxiety and antidepressant medicine Zoloft (sertraline hydrochloride) "works to correct the chemical imbalance in the brain." Similar arguments have been put forward by other pharmaceutical companies for their own medicines. "[R]esearch suggests that depression is caused by an imbalance of certain chemicals in the brain, most notably serotonin," said a press statement that was still available on the Forest Pharmaceuticals website when I checked in June 2013. It continued: "LEXAPRO [trade name for their antidepressant escitalopram] is thought to work by helping to restore the brain's chemical balance."

This seductively simple idea that depression and anxiety are caused by a chemical imbalance has been accepted by many people diagnosed with mental disorders, numerous newspaper reporters, many psychiatrists and mental health campaigners. There are members of this last group who believe that the identification of a supposed biological cause is de-stigmatizing and validating because they think it shows the suffering associated with mood disorders has a real physical basis and is not "all in the mind."

Consider the statements made in 2013 by the British actress and TV presenter Denise Welch when she spoke to the *Daily Mirror* about her decades-long experience of depression and how she'd been inspired to volunteer as a mental health campaigner. "Depression is not about being sad," she told the newspaper.[81] "It's a chemical imbalance in the brain."

"Don't tell me to cheer up," wrote the journalist and broadcaster Steve Oliver in a similar vein the same year.[82] "More needs to be done to raise awareness of the fact that depression is a chemical imbalance in the brain," he said, before describing his own experiences of the illness. The imbalance myth even made it into the high profile court case in 2013 between Michael Jackson's mother and AEG, the concert promoter behind his ill-fated final tour. The company's CEO denied mention of "chemicals" in an email he'd sent back in 2009 had been related to drug taking by the star. Rather he said he'd been inquiring about a possible "chemical imbalance" in Jackson's brain that could have been affecting him psychologically. So ubiquitous is the chemical imbalance myth, the CEO assumed reasonably that jurors would know what he was getting at.

The origins of the imbalance myth can be traced to the 1950s and early 1960s when psychiatric researchers realized, partly by accident, that drugs that interfere with some of the neurotransmitters in the brain, including norepinephrine, dopamine, and serotonin, can sometimes change people's mood. For instance, Iproniazid, which increases levels of these brain chemicals, was given to people with tuberculosis and it was noticed that some of them became happier. By contrast, in some people, an unwelcome side effect of the blood pressure drug Raudixin, which lowers levels of serotonin, was found to be low mood.

These and other observations led researchers including Joseph Schildkraut and Seymour Kety to propose a formal theory linking people's emotional states with levels of the so-called "monoamine" neurotransmitters: first norepinephrine and later serotonin. These pioneers were cautious not to attribute an exclusive causal role to brain chemistry. "[A]ny comprehensive formulation of the physiology of affective state will have to include many other concomitant biochemical, physiological and psychological factors," they wrote in 1967.[83] Despite their caution, the chemical imbalance myth took hold. "In the world of American pop culture, the current view of mental illness is that someone is walking down the street, everything is going fine, life is good, the sun is shining, and then, all of a sudden, out of the blue, there is a chemical shortage," wrote Jonathan Leo, one of the myth's staunchest critics.[84]

The Reality

Recognition of the important role played by brain chemistry in mood proved incredibly helpful to the biological study of depression and anxiety, and of course it gave rise to huge amounts of research into drugs that targeted the function of serotonin and other neurotransmitters. There's little doubt that brain chemistry is an important aspect of depression and anxiety. However, there is no clear evidence that these mental disorders are *caused* by a chemical imbalance in the straightforward way implied by the myth.

In truth no one knows what the "correct" levels for different neurotransmitters should be. And in reality, levels of these brain chemicals are just one factor in a complex cycle of interacting influences that includes genetic vulnerability, stressful events, habits of thought, and social circumstances. "The legend of the 'chemical imbalance' should be consigned to the dust-bin of ill-informed and malicious caricatures," wrote the psychiatrist and editor of the *Psychiatric Times*, Ronald Pies, in 2011.[85]

For many years it is levels of the neurotransmitter serotonin that people have had in mind when they advocate the idea of a chemical imbalance ("he wanted to preserve his good spirits, his serotonin-rich mood," Jonathan Franzen writes of a character in his 2001 novel, *The Corrections*). However, various studies have struggled to show consistently that serotonin function is lower in people who are depressed or anxious – this includes postmortem tests[86] and measures of chemical levels in the cerebrospinal fluid of patients and healthy people.[87] A 2007 study[88] based on blood samples even found that serotonin turnover was doubled in patients with major depression compared with controls, and that drug treatment lowered this turnover. There is also a lack of consistent evidence showing that L-tryptophan, which boosts serotonin levels, helps boost depressed people's mood;[89] and artificially reducing people's levels of serotonin doesn't have a reliably depressing effect[90] (it affects some people but not others).

Ignoring these findings, proponents of the chemical imbalance myth point to the effectiveness of a specific class of modern antidepressants as proof of their case. These drugs, known as "selective serotonin reuptake inhibitors (SSRIs)," boost serotonin by slowing the speed with which the chemical is cleaned up between neurons. If drugs that boost serotonin levels relieve depression, so the argument goes, then surely depression is caused by too little serotonin in the brain. However, this is specious logic. As Jeffrey Lacasse and Jonathan Leo explained by analogy in a 2005 paper,[91] just because aspirin treats headache effectively doesn't mean that headaches are caused by a lack of aspirin. Also, there's evidence that the drug Stablon (tianeptine) is an effective antidepressant for many people. Stablon is a "selective serotonin reuptake enhancer" – that is, it does the opposite of SSRIs, by reducing the amount of serotonin available between neurons!

Doubts have also been raised in recent years about just how much of the effect of SSRIs is down to their chemical effect in the brain. In 2008,[92] a team led by psychologist Irving Kirsch at Hull University in the UK obtained access to all antidepressant drug trials submitted by drug companies to the US Food and Drug Administration (FDA) – both those that had been published and those that the companies had held back.

Analyzing all the data together in a meta-analysis, Kirsch and his colleagues found that both the drugs and placebo pills had a large effect for most depressed people. But crucially, for all except the most seriously depressed, the difference in the size of the effect for the pills versus placebo was insignificant in clinical terms. In other words, the data suggested the main reason antidepressant drugs work for most people is not because they target a chemical imbalance, but because of a powerful placebo effect. "Given these data, there seems little evidence to support the prescription of antidepressant medication to any but the most severely depressed patients," Kirsch and his colleagues wrote. Admittedly, another team of experts led by Erick Turner also analyzed FDA data on antidepressants and came to a different conclusion.[93] They agreed with Kirsch and colleagues that many journal articles overestimate the effect of antidepressants, and that placebo effects are large, but unlike Kirsch's group, they maintained that most antidepressants are more effective than placebo. Either way, both sets of results surely undermine those who would point to SSRI effectiveness as proof of the chemical imbalance hypothesis. If depression were *purely* a serotonin imbalance, you'd expect the effectiveness of antidepressants that "correct" this imbalance to be more clear cut.

Similar problems have arisen when attempting to pin depression and anxiety on the levels of other brain chemicals besides serotonin. In 2011, researchers at the Max Planck Institute of Psychiatry in Munich focused on corticotropin-releasing hormone, which is released when we're stressed. Past research had suggested that an excess of this hormone could contribute to depression and anxiety. To test this, Jan Deussing and his colleagues genetically engineered mice so that some of their neurons no longer had receptors for this hormone to bind to – an intervention past research suggested would reduce anxiety.

A calming effect was indeed found when the researchers targeted neurons that usually produce an excitatory neurotransmitter known as glutamate, but the exact opposite effect was observed when they targeted receptors on neurons that produce dopamine, another brain chemical. In other words, interfering with the action of the corticotropin-releasing hormone in the mouse brain doesn't have a straightforward effect – the consequences vary depending on the neuron type in question.[94] It's yet another result that shows it's unrealistic to describe mood disorders in terms of the levels of one specific brain chemical.

Rather than focus on a supposed chemical imbalance, a more fruitful line of modern research is pursuing the idea that the important action of antidepressants (beyond the placebo effect) is to increase levels of neurogenesis (the growth of new neurons; see p. 75) in the hippocampus. Research with mice has shown that their brains produce fewer new neurons when they're stressed. But if they're given Prozac (an SSRI), their levels of neurogenesis return to normal and their behavior improves in a way that suggests they're not so stressed anymore, including increased exploration and eating. Crucially, this behavioral recovery has been shown to stall if the growth of new neurons is blocked. In other words, the rehabilitative effect of Prozac in mice appears to depend on neurogenesis. The same research with humans isn't possible, but a post-mortem study published in 2012[95] found that patients who'd had major depression and taken SSRIs had more signs of neurogenesis in their hippocampus as compared with untreated patients.

An advantage of the neurogenesis line of work is that it helps explain why antidepressants typically take a few weeks to make a difference. If their beneficial action were all down to restoring serotonin levels then they should make a difference immediately because they have a very quick effect on levels of that neurotransmitter. However, neurogenesis takes time, so if this process is crucial to the drugs' beneficial effect, it makes sense that treated patients take time to show improvement.

Overturning the Myth

The idea that mood disorders are caused by chemical levels in the brain going awry is proving increasingly popular, at least in the US. An analysis of public perceptions of mental illness in the USA published in 2010[96] by Bernice Pescosolido and her colleagues found that 80 percent of hundreds of respondents endorsed the chemical imbalance cause for mental illness in 2006, compared with 67 percent of respondents in 1996. Another US survey published in 2007[97] of 262 participants found that 54.2 percent agreed that "depression is primarily caused by an imbalance of chemicals in the brain." A significant minority of these participants further believed (wrongly) that psychiatrists can measure levels of a patient's brain chemicals and tweak them with drugs to arrive at the correct level.

Part of the reason for the dominance of the myth in the USA is likely the impact of direct-to-consumer advertising by pharmaceutical companies – a practice that is prohibited in all other nations except for New Zealand.

Consistent with this hypothesis, there's some evidence that the myth is endorsed less strongly in other countries. For instance, a survey of university students in South Africa published in 2010[98] found that only 16 percent thought a chemical imbalance was the most likely cause of depression (the second most popular reason after stressful events). That said, a survey published in 2013[99] of hundreds of Australian adults found that over 80 percent endorsed the chemical imbalance explanation of depression, and a survey of thousands of Canadians published in 2011[100] found that over 90 percent endorsed the myth.

Another reason for the strength of the myth is likely the fact that it is endorsed by some mental health charities in the hope of reducing stigma. For instance, the National Alliance on Mental Illness (NAMI) in the USA has for some time championed biological explanations. "Scientists believe that if there is a chemical imbalance in these neurotransmitters [norepinephrine, serotonin and dopamine], then clinical states of depression result," the NAMI said in a depression factsheet available on its website in 2013.[101]

Unfortunately, there is now a large evidence base suggesting that biological accounts of mental illness are actually increasing stigma rather than reducing it, and that they dent patients' hopes for recovery. For instance, Pescosolido's 2010 survey mentioned earlier found that increased endorsement of biological explanations for mental illness had gone hand in hand with increased community rejection of patients, with no reduction in stigma. Similarly, a meta-analysis published in 2012 by Georg Schomerus and his colleagues looked at collective results from 16 studies of lay people's perception of mental illness.[102] They found an increased awareness of biological explanations over time, but a possible worsening of attitudes toward people with mental illness in the same period. Part of the explanation of this may be that biological accounts make mental illnesses seem harder to treat and less amenable to psychotherapy.

The reticence of the psychiatric profession in challenging the myth may also have played a part in its survival and increasing popularity. "Individual psychiatrists and their professional organizations ... have made very few efforts to correct these erroneous claims [about the chemical imbalance]," wrote Jonathan Leo and Jeffrey Lacasse in 2008.[103] A clue as to why psychiatrists may have been reluctant to correct the myth comes from a blog post written by psychiatrist Ronald Pies in 2011:[104] "some doctors believe that they will help the patient feel less blameworthy by telling them, 'You have a chemical imbalance causing your problem,'" he wrote. "It's easy to think you are doing the patient a favor by providing this kind of 'explanation'."

Meanwhile the mainstream media continues to spread the chemical imbalance myth. In that 2008 paper by Leo and Lacasse, they tracked down numerous examples, including a 2006 *The New York Times* article about Joseph Schildkraut (the biological psychiatry pioneer who linked mood disorders with neurotransmitters). The reporter attributed to Schildkraut a "ground breaking paper" that "suggested ... chemical imbalances in the brain must account for mood swings ... a hypothesis that proved to be correct [emphasis added]." For each of the examples they found, Leo and Lacasse contacted the relevant reporters and asked them to supply scientific citations to support their endorsement of the myth. Not one journalist provided any references or sources that explicitly endorsed the idea of a chemical imbalance. "In some cases, we forwarded our dialogue with the reporters to their respective editors," added Leo and Lacasse. "To date not one of them has responded."

The Pleasure Chemical and Cuddle Hormone

"Beer Makes Brain Release Pleasure Chemical Dopamine," announced a headline in the *Huffington Post* in 2013.[105] The article was about a brain imaging study that found small sips of alcohol-free beer were sufficient to increase dopamine activity – an effect described by the journalist as "a pleasurable response in the brain." Similar news articles appear almost weekly. People's favorite music evokes the same feelings as good food or drugs, claimed *The Guardian* in 2011, because it releases "the brain's reward chemical dopamine."[106]

In reality, most neuroscientists today agree that to describe the neurotransmitter as a "reward chemical" is a huge distortion and oversimplification. Dopamine is involved in many functions, including the control of movement, and it's found in many different brain pathways, only some of which are related to reward. Dopamine is released not just when we score a high from food, sex, or money, but also when we fail to get a reward we were expecting.[107] And there's research[108] that found increased dopamine activity in so-called "reward pathways" when distressed bereaved people looked at pictures of a lost relative. This dopamine activity went hand in hand with participants' reports of sadness and yearning, certainly not pleasure in the usual sense of the word.

A more accurate characterization of dopamine is to say that it is important for motivation and finding salience in the world. Indeed, schizophrenia is associated with excess dopamine activity and one theory[109] proposes that many of the illness's problematic symptoms, such as paranoia, are related to reading too much importance and meaning into largely random situations.

Another brain chemical that's acquired its own mythology is oxytocin, produced by the hypothalamus, and nicknamed variously as the "cuddle hormone," "love molecule," or "moral molecule." It's released in extra doses when we hug (hence one of its nicknames) and have sex; and giving people more of the hormone via a nasal spray has been linked with a range of positive emotions from trust[110] and empathy[111] to generosity.[112] No wonder it's been subject to such hype – the io9 website even ran a feature:[113] "10 Reasons Why Oxytocin Is The Most Amazing Molecule In The World." Some excitable scientists are already speculating that the hormone could form the basis of a treatment for a range of psychological problems from shyness to personality disorder.

The trouble is, as with dopamine, the truth about oxytocin is far more nuanced than the media's "hug hormone" epithet would suggest. One paper showed that extra oxytocin can increase feelings of envy.[114] Another found that the effects varied from person to person – people with a healthy attachment to their mother felt even more positively toward her when given extra oxytocin; by contrast, giving oxytocin to people with an anxious style of attachment led them to view their mothers less positively.[115] Still further research has shown the hormone can increase trust toward people we know well, but reduce it toward outsiders.[116] And here's one more – a 2014 study found that oxytocin can increase an aggressive person's inclination to be violent toward their partner.[117] It's clear there's a lot more we've yet to learn about the cuddle hormone. As usual the true picture is more complicated, but ultimately more fascinating, than the media myths would have us believe.

Notes

1 Hux, K., Schram, C. D., & Goeken, T. (2006). Misconceptions about brain injury: A survey replication study. *Brain Injury*, 20(5), 547–553.

2 Chapman, R. C., & Hudson, J. M. (2010). Beliefs about brain injury in Britain. *Brain Injury*, 24(6), 797–801.

3 DeMatteo, C. A., Hanna, S. E., Mahoney, W. J., Hollenberg, R. D., Scott, L. A., Law, M. C., ... & Xu, L. (2010). My child doesn't have a brain injury, he only has a concussion. *Pediatrics*, 125(2), 327–334.

4   McLellan, T. L., & McKinlay, A. (2011). Does the way concussion is por-trayed affect public awareness of appropriate concussion management: the case of rugby league. *British Journal of Sports Medicine*, 45(12), 993–996.

5   http://www.cbc.ca/news/health/story/2010/01/18/concussion-children-brain-injury.html (accessed May 16, 2014).

6   McKinlay, A., Bishop, A., & McLellan, T. (2011). Public knowledge of "con-cussion" and the different terminology used to communicate about mild traumatic brain injury (MTBI). *Brain Injury*, 25(7–8), 761–766.

7   McLellan, T., Bishop, A., & McKinlay, A. (2010). Community attitudes toward individuals with traumatic brain injury. *Journal of the International Neuropsychological Society*, 16(4), 705.

8   Jones, J. M., Haslam, S. A., Jetten, J., Williams, W. H., Morris, R., & Saroyan, S. (2011). That which doesn't kill us can make us stronger (and more satisfied with life): The contribution of personal and social changes to well-being after acquired brain injury. *Psychology and Health*, 26(3), 353–369.

9   www.thersa.org/fellowship/journal/archive/summer-2009/features/cultural-creatures (accessed May 16, 2014).

10 Foer, J. (2011). *Moonwalking with Einstein: The Art and Science of Remembering Everything*. Penguin.

11 Simons, D. J., & Chabris, C. F. (2011). What people believe about how memory works: A representative survey of the US population. *PloS One*, 6(8), e22757.

12 Simons, D. J., & Chabris, C. F. (2012). Common (mis) beliefs about memory: A replication and comparison of telephone and mechanical Turk survey methods. *PloS One*, 7(12), e51876.

13 Baxendale, S. (2004). Memories aren't made of this: Amnesia at the movies. *BMJ*, 329(7480), 1480.

14 Smith, C. N., Frascino, J. C., Kripke, D. L., McHugh, P. R., Treisman, G. J., & Squire, L. R. (2010). Losing memories overnight: A unique form of human amnesia. *Neuropsychologia*, 48(10), 2833–2840.

15 Merckelbach, H., Merten, T., & Lilienfeld, S. O. (2011). A skeptical look at a remarkable case report of 'overnight' amnesia: Extraordinary symptoms, weak evidence, and a breakdown in peer review. *Skeptical Inquirer*, 35(3), 35–39.

16 Dieguez, S., & Annoni, J. M. (2013). Stranger than fiction: Literary and clinical amnesia. In J. Bogousslavsky, & S. Dieguez (eds), *Literary Medicine: Brain Disease and Doctors in Novels, Theater, and Film*. Karger, pp. 147–226.

17 Lucchelli, F., Muggia, S., & Spinnler, H. (1995). The "Petites Madeleines" phenomenon in two amnesic patients: Sudden recovery of forgotten memo-ries. *Brain*, 118(1), 167–181.

18 Maloy, K., & Davis, J. E. (2011). "Forgettable" sex: A case of transient global amnesia presenting to the emergency department. *The Journal of Emergency Medicine*, 41(3), 257–260.

19 Bauer, P. J., & Larkina, M. (2013). The onset of childhood amnesia in childhood: A prospective investigation of the course and determinants of forgetting of early-life events. *Memory* (Nov. 18, Epub), 1–18.

20 MacDonald, S., Uesiliana, K., & Hayne, H. (2000). Cross-cultural and gender differences in childhood amnesia. *Memory*, 8(6), 365–376.

21 Geraerts, E., Schooler, J. W., Merckelbach, H., Jelicic, M., Hauer, B. J., & Ambadar, Z. (2007). The reality of recovered memories corroborating continuous and discontinuous memories of childhood sexual abuse. *Psychological Science*, 18(7), 564–568.

22 Simons, D. J., & Chabris, C. F. (2011). What people believe about how memory works: A representative survey of the US population. *PloS One*, 6(8), e22757.

23 Simons, D. J., & Chabris, C. F. (2012). Common (mis)beliefs about memory: A replication and comparison of telephone and mechanical Turk survey methods. *PloS One*, 7(12), e51876.

24 Furst, C. J., Fuld, K., & Pancoe, M. (1974). Recall accuracy of eidetikers. *Journal of Experimental Psychology*, 102(6), 1133.

25 Richardson, A., & Francesco, J. D. (1985). Stability, accuracy and eye movements in eidetic imagery. *Australian Journal of Psychology*, 37(1), 51–64.

26 Talarico, J. M., & Rubin, D. C. (2003). Confidence, not consistency, characterizes flashbulb memories. *Psychological Science*, 14(5), 455–461.

27 Owen, A. M., Coleman, M. R., Boly, M., Davis, M. H., Laureys, S., & Pickard, J. D. (2006). Detecting awareness in the vegetative state. *Science*, 313(5792), 1402.

28 Monti, M. M., Vanhaudenhuyse, A., Coleman, M. R., Boly, M., Pickard, J. D., Tshibanda, L., … & Laureys, S. (2010). Willful modulation of brain activity in disorders of consciousness. *New England Journal of Medicine*, 362(7), 579–589.

29 Wijdicks, E. F., & Wijdicks, C. A. (2006). The portrayal of coma in contemporary motion pictures. *Neurology*, 66(9), 1300–1303.

30 Casarett, D., Fishman, J. M., MacMoran, H. J., Pickard, A., & Asch, D. A. (2005). Epidemiology and prognosis of coma in daytime television dramas. *BMJ*, 331(7531), 1537.

31 Gray, K., Anne Knickman, T., & Wegner, D. M. (2011). More dead than dead: Perceptions of persons in the persistent vegetative state. *Cognition*, 121(2), 275–280.

32 http://www.telegraph.co.uk/news/worldnews/northamerica/usa/10559511/Brain-dead-pregnant-woman-kept-alive-against-family-wishes-to-deliver-child.html (accessed May 16, 2014).

33 http://www.nytimes.com/2005/04/24/fashion/sundaystyles/24plastic.html (accessed May 16, 2014).

34 LiPuma, S. H., & DeMarco, J. P. (2013). Reviving brain death: A functionalist view. *Journal of Bioethical Inquiry*, 10(3), 383–392.

35   Caspermeyer, J. J., Sylvester, E. J., Drazkowski, J. F., Watson, G. L., & Sirven, J. I. (2006). Evaluation of stigmatizing language and medical errors in neurology coverage by US newspapers. *Mayo Clinic Proceedings*, 81(3), 300–306.

36   Price, J. (1892). The surgical treatment of epilepsy. *The Journal of Nervous and Mental Disease*, 17(6), 396–407.

37   Njamnshi, A. K., Yepnjio, F. N., Bissek, A. C. Z. K., Tabah, E. N., Ongolo-Zogo, P., Dema, F., ... & Muna, W. F. (2009). A survey of public knowledge, attitudes, and practices with respect to epilepsy in Badissa Village, Centre Region of Cameroon. *Epilepsy & Behavior*, 16(2), 254–259.

38   Daoud, A., Al-Safi, S., Otoom, S., Wahba, L., & Alkofahi, A. (2007). Public knowledge and attitudes towards epilepsy in Jordan. *Seizure*, 16(6), 521–526.

39   Nicholaos, D., Joseph, K., Meropi, T., & Charilaos, K. (2006). A survey of public awareness, understanding, and attitudes toward epilepsy in Greece. *Epilepsia*, 47(12), 2154–2164.

40   Jacoby, A., Gorry, J., Gamble, C., & Baker, G. A. (2004). Public knowledge, private grief: A study of public attitudes to epilepsy in the United Kingdom and implications for stigma. *Epilepsia*, 45(11), 1405–1415.

41   Awaritefe, A. (1989). Epilepsy: The myth of a contagious disease. *Culture, Medicine and Psychiatry*, 13(4), 449–456.

42   Hughes, J. R. (2005). Did all those famous people really have epilepsy? *Epilepsy & Behavior*, 6(2), 115–139.

43   Wolf, P. (2000). Epilepsy in contemporary fiction: Fates of patients. *The Canadian Journal of Neurological Sciences*, 27(2), 166–172.

44   Baxendale, S. (2003). Epilepsy at the movies: Possession to presidential assassination. *The Lancet Neurology*, 2(12), 764–770.

45   Baxendale, S. (2008). The representation of epilepsy in popular music. *Epilepsy & Behavior*, 12(1), 165–169.

46   Moeller, A. D., Moeller, J. J., Rahey, S. R., & Sadler, R. M. (2011). Depiction of seizure first aid management in medical television dramas. *The Canadian Journal of Neurological Sciences*, 38(5), 723–727.

47   Baxendale, S., & O'Toole, A. (2007). Epilepsy myths: Alive and foaming in the 21st century. *Epilepsy & Behavior*, 11(2), 192–196.

48   McNeil, K., Brna, P. M., & Gordon, K. E. (2012). Epilepsy in the Twitter era: A need to re-tweet the way we think about seizures. *Epilepsy & Behavior*, 23(2), 127–130.

49   Wong, V. S., Stevenson, M., & Selwa, L. (2013). The presentation of seizures and epilepsy in YouTube videos. *Epilepsy & Behavior*, 247–250.

50   Treffert, D. A., & Christensen, D. D. (2005). Inside the mind of a savant. *Scientific American*, 293(6), 108–113.

51   Conn, R., & Bhugra, D. (2012). The portrayal of autism in Hollywood films. *International Journal of Culture and Mental Health*, 5(1), 54–62.

52   http://io9.com/5879242/why-do-we-want-autistic-kids-to-have-superpowers (accessed May 16, 2014).

53 Godlee, F., Smith, J., & Marcovitch, H. (2011). Wakefield's article linking MMR vaccine and autism was fraudulent. *BMJ*, 342.

54 For example, Baird, G., Pickles, A., Simonoff, E., Charman, T., Sullivan, P., Chandler, S., ... & Brown, D. (2008). Measles vaccination and antibody response in autism spectrum disorders. *Archives of Disease in Childhood*, 93(10), 832–837.

55 Bishop, D. V., Whitehouse, A. J., Watt, H. J., & Line, E. A. (2008). Autism and diagnostic substitution: Evidence from a study of adults with a history of developmental language disorder. *Developmental Medicine & Child Neurology*, 50(5), 341–345.

56 Weintraub, K. (2011). Autism counts. *Nature*, 479(7371), 22–24.

57 http://www.guardian.co.uk/society/2011/aug/06/research-autism-internet-susan-greenfield (accessed May 16, 2014).

58 Senju, A., Maeda, M., Kikuchi, Y., Hasegawa, T., Tojo, Y., & Osanai, H. (2007). Absence of contagious yawning in children with autism spectrum disorder. *Biology Letters*, 3(6), 706–708.

59 Usui, S., Senju, A., Kikuchi, Y., Akechi, H., Tojo, Y., Osanai, H., & Hasegawa, T. (2013). Presence of contagious yawning in children with autism spectrum disorder. *Autism Research and Treatment*, 2013.

60 McIntosh, D. N., Reichmann-Decker, A., Winkielman, P., & Wilbarger, J. L. (2006). When the social mirror breaks: Deficits in automatic, but not voluntary, mimicry of emotional facial expressions in autism. *Developmental Science*, 9(3), 295–302.

61 Hamilton, A. (2013). Reflecting on the mirror neuron system in autism: a systematic review of current theories. *Developmental Cognitive Neuroscience*, 3, 91–105.

62 http://womanwithaspergers.wordpress.com/2010/05/09/a-few-words-about-empathy/ (accessed May 16, 2014).

63 http://www.thepsychologist.org.uk/archive/archive_home.cfm?volumeID=22&editionID=176&ArticleID=1517 (accessed May 16, 2014).

64 Mottron, L. (2011). Changing perceptions: The power of autism. *Nature*, 479(7371), 33–35.

65 Jones, S. C., & Harwood, V. (2009). Representations of autism in Australian print media. *Disability & Society*, 24(1), 5–18.

66 This paragraph is based with permission on a conference report by Judith Jarrett (then Spies) published in *The Psychologist* magazine: http://www.thepsychologist.org.uk/archive/archive_home.cfm?volumeID=20&editionID=144&ArticleID=1139 (accessed May 16, 2014).

67 This is based on Alzheimer's original notes, taken from: Maurer, K., Volk, S., & Gerbaldo, H. (1997). Auguste D and Alzheimer's disease. *The Lancet*, 349(9064), 1546–1549.

68 Talantova, M., Sanz-Blasco, S., Zhang, X., Xia, P., Akhtar, M. W., Okamoto, S. I., ... & Lipton, S. A. (2013). Aβ induces astrocytic glutamate release, extrasynaptic NMDA receptor activation, and synaptic loss. Proceedings of the National Academy of Sciences. doi: 10.1073/pnas.1306832110

69   Müller, U., Winter, P., & Graeber, M. B. (2013). A presenilin 1 mutation in the first case of Alzheimer's disease. *The Lancet Neurology*, 12(2), 129–130.

70   Harrison, T. M., Weintraub, S., Mesulam, M. M., & Rogalski, E. (2012). Superior memory and higher cortical volumes in unusually successful cognitive aging. *Journal of the International Neuropsychological Society*, 18(6), 1081.

71   Behuniak, S. M. (2011). The living dead? The construction of people with Alzheimer's disease as zombies. *Ageing and Society*, 31(01), 70–92.

72   Matthews, F. E., Arthur, A., Barnes, L. E., Bond, J., Jagger, C., Robinson, L., & Brayne, C. (2013). A two-decade comparison of prevalence of dementia in individuals aged 65 years and older from three geographical areas of England: Results of the Cognitive Function and Ageing Study I and II. *The Lancet*, 382(9902), 1405–1412.

73   Christensen, K., Thinggaard, M., Oksuzyan, A., Steenstrup, T., Andersen-Ranberg, K., Jeune, B., ... & Vaupel, J. W. (2013). Physical and cognitive functioning of people older than 90 years: A comparison of two Danish cohorts born 10 years apart. *The Lancet*, 382(9903), 1507–1513.

74   Miller, B. L., Cummings, J., Mishkin, F., Boone, K., Prince, F., Ponton, M., & Cotman, C. (1998). Emergence of artistic talent in frontotemporal dementia. *Neurology*, 51(4), 978–982.

75   Halpern, A. R., Ly, J., Elkin-Frankston, S., & O'Connor, M. G. (2008). "I know what I like": Stability of aesthetic preference in Alzheimer's patients. *Brain and Cognition*, 66(1), 65–72.

76   Loewenstein, D. A., Acevedo, A., Czaja, S. J., & Duara, R. (2004). Cognitive rehabilitation of mildly impaired Alzheimer disease patients on cholinesterase inhibitors. *American Journal of Geriatric Psych*, 12(4), 395–402.

77   http://www.huffingtonpost.com/john-zeisel-phd/alzheimers- diagnosis-care_b_856662.html (accessed May 16, 2014).

78   Segers, K. (2007). Degenerative dementias and their medical care in the movies. *Alzheimer Disease & Associated Disorders*, 21(1), 55–59.

79   Gerritsen, D. L., Kuin, Y., & Nijboer, J. (2014). Dementia in the movies: The clinical picture. *Aging & Mental Health*, 18 (3), 276–280.

80   Swinnen, A. (2013). Dementia in documentary film: Mum by Adelheid Roosen. *The Gerontologist*, 53(1), 113–122.

81   http://www.mirror.co.uk/3am/celebrity-news/denise-welch-depression-battle-tried-1940575 (accessed May 16, 2014).

82   http://www.thisisnottingham.co.uk/Steve-Oliver-depression-don-t-tell-cheer/story-19260268-detail/story.html#axzz2W07HloDB (accessed May 16, 2014).

83   Schildkraut, J. J., & Kety, S. S. (1967). Biogenic amines and emotion. *Science*, 156(771), 21–37.

84   Leo, J. (2002). The chemical theory of mental illness. *Telos*, 2002(122), 169–177.

85   http://www.psychiatrictimes.com/couch-crisis/psychiatry's-new-brain-mind-and-legend-"chemical-imbalance" (accessed May 16, 2014).

86   Cheetham, S. C., Crompton, M. R., Katona, C. L., & Horton, R. W. (1990). Brain 5-HT1 binding sites in depressed suicides. *Psychopharmacology*, 102(4), 544–548.

87   Asberg, M., Thoren, P., Traskman, L., Bertilsson, L., & Ringberger, V. (1976). "Serotonin depression" – a biochemical subgroup within the affective disorders? *Science*, 191(4226), 478–480.

88   Barton, D. A., Esler, M. D., Dawood, T., Lambert, E. A., Haikerwal, D., Brenchley, C., ... & Lambert, G. W. (2008). Elevated brain serotonin turnover in patients with depression: Effect of genotype and therapy. *Archives of General Psychiatry*, 65(1), 38–46.

89   Shaw, K., Turner, J., & Del Mar, C. (2002). Tryptophan and 5-hydroxytryptophan for depression. *Cochrane Database Syst Rev*, 1.

90   Delgado, P. L., Price, L. H., Miller, H. L., Salomon, R. M., Aghajanian, G. K., Heninger, G. R., & Charney, D. S. (1994). Serotonin and the neurobiology of depression: Effects of tryptophan depletion in drug-free depressed patients. *Archives of General Psychiatry*, 51(11), 865.

91   Lacasse, J. R., & Leo, J. (2005). Serotonin and depression: A disconnect between the advertisements and the scientific literature. *PLoS Medicine*, 2(12), e392.

92   Kirsch, I., Deacon, B. J., Huedo-Medina, T. B., Scoboria, A., Moore, T. J., & Johnson, B. T. (2008). Initial severity and antidepressant benefits: A meta-analysis of data submitted to the Food and Drug Administration. *PLoS Medicine*, 5(2), e45.

93   Turner, E. H., & Rosenthal, R. (2008). Efficacy of antidepressants. *BMJ*, 336(7643), 516–517.

94   Refojo, D., Schweizer, M., Kuehne, C., Ehrenberg, S., Thoeringer, C., Vogl, A. M., ... & Deussing, J. M. (2011). Glutamatergic and dopaminergic neurons mediate anxiogenic and anxiolytic effects of CRHR1. *Science*, 333(6051), 1903–1907.

95   Boldrini, M., Hen, R., Underwood, M. D., Rosoklija, G. B., Dwork, A. J., Mann, J. J., & Arango, V. (2012). Hippocampal angiogenesis and progenitor cell proliferation are increased with antidepressant use in major depression. *Biological Psychiatry*, 72(7), 562–571.

96   Pescosolido, B. A., Martin, J. K., Long, J. S., Medina, T. R., Phelan, J. C., & Link, B. G. (2010). "A disease like any other"? A decade of change in public reactions to schizophrenia, depression, and alcohol dependence. *American Journal of Psychiatry*, 167(11), 1321–1330.

97   France, C. M., Lysaker, P. H., & Robinson, R. P. (2007). The "chemical imbalance" explanation for depression: Origins, lay endorsement, and clinical implications. *Professional Psychology: Research and Practice*, 38(4), 411.

98 Samouilhan, T., & Seabi, J. (2010). University students' beliefs about the causes and treatments of mental illness. *South African Journal of Psychology*, 40(1), 74–89.

99 Pilkington, P. D., Reavley, N. J., & Jorm, A. F. (2013). The Australian public's beliefs about the causes of depression: Associated factors and changes over 16 years. *Journal of Affective Disorders*, 150(2), 356–362.

100 Cook, T. M., & Wang, J. (2011). Causation beliefs and stigma against depression: Results from a population-based study. *Journal of Affective Disorders*, 133(1), 86–92.

101 Accessed in July 2013 via http://www.nami.org/Template.cfm?Section=Depression&Template=/ContentManagement/ContentDisplay.cfm&ContentID=88956 (accessed May 16, 2014).

102 Schomerus, G., Schwahn, C., Holzinger, A., Corrigan, P. W., Grabe, H. J., Carta, M. G., & Angermeyer, M. C. (2012). Evolution of public attitudes about mental illness: A systematic review and meta-analysis. *Acta Psychiatrica Scandinavica*, 125(6), 440–452.

103 Leo, J., & Lacasse, J. R. (2008). The media and the chemical imbalance theory of depression. *Society*, 45(1), 35–45.

104 http://psychcentral.com/blog/archives/2011/08/04/doctor-is-my-mood-disorder-due-to-a-chemical-imbalance/ (accessed May 16, 2014).

105 http://www.huffingtonpost.com/2013/04/16/beer-brain-pleasure-chemical-dopamine_n_3086508.html (accessed May 16, 2014).

106 http://www.guardian.co.uk/science/2011/jan/09/why-we-love-music-research (accessed May 16, 2014).

107 http://www.guardian.co.uk/science/2013/feb/03/dopamine-the-unsexy-truth (accessed May 16, 2014).

108 O'Connor, M. F., Wellisch, D. K., Stanton, A. L., Eisenberger, N. I., Irwin, M. R., & Lieberman, M. D. (2008). Craving love? Enduring grief activates brain's reward center. *Neuroimage*, 42(2), 969–972.

109 Jarrett, C. (2007). The chemical brain. *Psychologist*, 20(8), 480–482.

110 Kosfeld, M., Heinrichs, M., Zak, P. J., Fischbacher, U., & Fehr, E. (2005). Oxytocin increases trust in humans. *Nature*, 435(7042), 673–676.

111 Hurlemann, R., Patin, A., Onur, O. A., Cohen, M. X., Baumgartner, T., Metzler, S., … & Kendrick, K. M. (2010). Oxytocin enhances amygdala-dependent, socially reinforced learning and emotional empathy in humans. *The Journal of Neuroscience*, 30(14), 4999–5007.

112 Zak, P. J., Stanton, A. A., & Ahmadi, S. (2007). Oxytocin increases generosity in humans. *PLoS One*, 2(11), e1128.

113 http://io9.com/5925206/10-reasons-why-oxytocin-is-the-most-amazing-molecule-in-the-world (accessed May 16, 2014).

114 Shamay-Tsoory, S. G., Fischer, M., Dvash, J., Harari, H., Perach-Bloom, N., & Levkovitz, Y. (2009). Intranasal administration of oxytocin increases envy and schadenfreude (gloating). *Biological Psychiatry*, 66(9), 864–870.

115 Bartz, J. A., Zaki, J., Ochsner, K. N., Bolger, N., Kolevzon, A., Ludwig, N., & Lydon, J. E. (2010). Effects of oxytocin on recollections of maternal care and closeness. *Proceedings of the National Academy of Sciences*, 107(50), 21371–21375.

116 Declerck, C. H., Boone, C., & Kiyonari, T. (2010). Oxytocin and cooperation under conditions of uncertainty: The modulating role of incentives and social information. *Hormones and Behavior*, 57(3), 368–374.

117 DeWall, C. N., Gillath, O., Pressman, S. D., Black, L. L., Bartz, J. A., Moskovitz, J., & Stetler, D. A. (2014). When the love hormone leads to violence: Oxytocin increases intimate partner violence inclinations among high trait aggressive people. *Social Psychological and Personality Science*. doi: 10.1177/1948550613516876.

AFTERWORD

With all the hype and mythology that swirls around the brain, the risk is that people will become disillusioned with neuroscience for failing to provide the revolution in human understanding that many have heralded. In 2013, there were signs of a backlash. The year saw publication of articles with revealing headlines: "Neuroscience Under Attack" (Alissa Quart in *The New York Times* Sunday Review[1]); "Pop Neuroscience Is Bunk"[2] (Sally Satel and Scott Lilienfeld in *Salon*, although note the title was not chosen by the authors), and "Beyond the Brain"[3] (David Brooks in *The New York Times*), to name but a few.

There seems to be a rising mood of skepticism, weariness with the clichéd media coverage of new results, and a growing recognition that neuroscience complements psychology, it can't possibly replace it. But let's remember too that neuroscience is in its infancy. We are unearthing new findings at an astonishing rate, many of which are already helping people with devastating brain disorders. This includes the dawn of computer-brain interfaces allowing paralyzed people to interact with the world, and the exciting potential of stem-cell technologies for repairing damaged brains. Neuroimaging is also informing and constraining our psychological theories of how the mind works (see p. 183).

Let's celebrate our progress and acknowledge the great work of our talented neuroscientists. Often their most important results don't make for catchy headlines. Yet many are conducting research that holds out the promise of a better tomorrow – a world with less suffering from neurological illness, and a greater understanding of human intelligence and emotion.

The search for the truth is a never-ending journey and the accounts in this book certainly aren't the final destination. Hopefully, what I've done is help you face in the right direction as you continue your discovery of the wonder that is the science of the human brain.

Notes

1 http://www.nytimes.com/2012/11/25/opinion/sunday/neuroscience-under-attack.html?hp&_r=1& (accessed May 16, 2014).
2 http://www.salon.com/2013/06/08/pop_neuroscience_is_bunk/ (accessed May 16, 2014).
3 http://www.nytimes.com/2013/06/18/opinion/brooks-beyond-the-brain.html (accessed May 16, 2014).

INDEX

Great Myths of the Brain, First Edition. Christian Jarrett.
© 2015 Christian Jarrett. Published 2015 by John Wiley & Sons, Ltd.